Wissenschaftliche Untersuchungen
zum Neuen Testament · 2. Reihe

Herausgeber / Editor
Jörg Frey (München)

Mitherausgeber / Associate Editors
Friedrich Avemarie (Marburg)
Markus Bockmuehl (Oxford)
Hans-Josef Klauck (Chicago, IL)

265

Simon S. Lee

Jesus' Transfiguration and the Believers' Transformation

A Study of the Transfiguration and Its Development
in Early Christian Writings

Mohr Siebeck

SIMON S. LEE, born 1968; 2000 M. Div at Gordon-Conwell Theological Seminary; study of New Testament and Early Christianity at Harvard Divinity School; 2002 M.T.S. degree, 2008 Th.D degree; since 2008 assistant professor of New Testament and Early Christianity at Andover Newton Theological School, Newton Centre, MA.

ISBN 978-3-16-150003-9

ISSN 0340-9570 (Wissenschaftliche Untersuchungen zum Neuen Testament, 2. Reihe)

The Deutsche Nationalbibliothek lists this publication in the Deutsche Nationalbibliographie; detailed bibliographic data is available in the Internet at *http://dnb.d-nb.de*.

The book was printed by Laupp & Göbel in Nehren on non-aging paper and bound by Buchbinderei Nädele in Nehren.

Printed in Germany.

To HyunJeong and Isaiah

Preface

This monograph is a revision of my doctoral dissertation submitted to the Divinity School of Harvard University, Cambridge, Mass., in May of 2008. I first want to thank Prof. François Bovon, my book advisor, for helping me from the beginning of the project to its end with his knowledge of the New Testament and the Apocrypha. He also supported me with his wisdom when I went through difficult times. I am also indebted to Prof. Karen L. King who challenged me to read some texts differently from the way I was used to reading them and sharpened my ideas by raising different options of readings. Prof. Laura S. Nasrallah also helped me rearrange the contents of the chapters for clarification and encouraged me to pay attention to the texts' historical situations.

Many members of the Harvard Divinity School community have contributed to this project in different ways. I want to thank my colleagues in the book seminar, especially those who offered formal responses to chapter drafts: Catherine Playoust, Katherine Baine, Brent Landau, Glenn Snyder, and Margot Stevenson. My thanks to Sean Freyne, John Townsend, Elisabeth Schüssler-Fiorenza, Youn-Rack Chung and Paul Hanson for their advice. This work would not have been possible without the help of the librarians at the Andover-Harvard Theological Library, to name a few, Cliff Wunderlich, Renata Kalnins, Gloria Korsman, Laura Whitney, Steven Beardsley, and Donna Maquire.

I am grateful to many of my friends, both in Korea and in the US, for their love. I especially want to thank my friend Anna Watson for reading and editing my drafts and Milton Kornfeld for improving my writing style. I also want to thank my friends at Harvard Divinity School, Sin-kyue Lee, Sijin Oh, Eunyoung Lim, Jeongseob Oh, CheolKyu Kim, Seongchan Auh, Junghyun Choi and Sooho Park.

I want to thank Prof. Jörg Frey for his prompt acceptance of my book for publication in the *WUNT* series II, and Dr. Henning Ziebritzki and the editorial team at Mohr Siebeck for their kind assistance throughout the editing process. I also would like to express my gratitude to the IT department of Andover Newton Theological School for their help with IT support.

Lastly, I must confess that I could not finish this project without my family's loving support. I thank my father, Kil-soo Lee, and my mother, Young-ae Lee, for releasing me from my familial duty as their eldest son so that I could pursue my academic dream in the US. They showed me the best example of unyielding faith, spirit and wisdom. I am so grateful to Hyunjeong Shim, my wife, and Isaiah Lee-Shim, my son, for enduring

Preface

with me throughout the entire process; they rejoiced when I was successful and encouraged me when I felt low. I dedicate this book to Hyunjeong and Isaiah.

February 2009   Simon Seunghyun Lee

Table of Contents

Chapter 1

Introduction

1.1 Topic / Thesis

In this study, I examine Jesus' Transfiguration story found in the narrative account of Mark, tracing the development of its multiple readings through the first two centuries of the Christian era. I pay special attention to texts in which Peter is described as being the main witness to the event – the Synoptic Gospels, 2 Peter, *Apocalypse of Peter*, and *Acts of Peter*. I also analyze 2 Corinthians 3, in which Paul explains the transformation of the believers. In comparing Paul's account with that of Mark, I show that there are some common patterns or ideas behind their accounts and that both inherited certain views from early Christian traditions.[1]

The Transfiguration story is especially interesting for the study of early Christianity, since this story reveals Jesus' glory, or his luminosity; his glorious appearance is one of the most popular themes in early Christian writings. In these writings, those who witness Jesus' glorious appearance often gain credentials for their apostolic authority or for a truth claim for the genuineness of their messages (cf. 1 Cor 15:2–11). As we examine differing interpretations of these traditions, the Transfiguration story becomes a window through which we can take a peek at how different groups of people interacted with one another. I believe that although there was great diversity among different groups of believers in early Christianity, early Christians shared some common traditions and engaged in dialogue rather than existing in isolation, sometimes seeking harmony, other times marginalizing those with different opinions. In this process, early Christians interpreted common traditions similarly or differently in order to define themselves and their destiny. Interpretations were also influenced by particular cultural expectations, since early believers had to come to terms with surrounding cultures.

In this book, I contribute to the study of early Christianity by (1) helping bridge the gap between the study of the New Testament and the study of the apocrypha, (2) explaining how various Christian readers understood the Transfiguration story in ways that were particular to their own historical contexts, (3) fleshing out common ideas or patterns of thought as well

---

[1] I use the term "Christian" anachronistically for the sake of convenience. I am aware of the debate regarding its use in the discussion of early Christianity.

as differences in various interpretations of the Transfiguration, and (4) locating the Transfiguration in the general phenomenon of metamorphosis with epiphany.

There is a distressing scholarly gap between the study of the New Testament and the study of the Apocrypha. Scholars from each discipline study their own texts in great detail, but they have not effectively compared the two corpora of texts with one another, nor have they explored how such a comparison might shed light on the history of early Christianity. Heeding François Bovon's call for the need to bridge the gap between the two corpora, it is my ambition to compare both groups of texts by focusing on the theme of the Transfiguration.

The Transfiguration, in which Jesus appears in a glorious form with Elijah and Moses, is a fascinating and complicated story. Modern scholarship on this topic, however, seems to have focused exclusively on possible backgrounds or sources for the Transfiguration or on literary dependencies among various documents containing the story. I am more interested in considering these sources as parts of the dynamic process of the complicated development of the Transfiguration, and exploring the Transfiguration story's multifaceted development in various narrative accounts.

In addition, I emphasize socio-historical aspects of the texts by showing how the development of the Transfiguration story reflects ancient readers' needs in their historical context. In this process, I believe that both specific historical events and multiple Jewish as well as Hellenistic ideas contributed to the various interpretations of the Transfiguration.[2] In view of this, the textual instances of the Transfiguration may offer us some indirect information about the emergence of various Christian groups which came about in conjunction with the ideological trends of the times – both Jewish and Hellenistic. The various tellings of the Transfiguration story indicate how these early Christians modified the trends in ways that were distinctive to their self-identity and that met their communal needs. As modern readers of the Transfiguration, we scholars must explore the developments of the Transfiguration, moving from one text to another as well as from one generation to another, in order to better grasp how and when this story may have functioned to resolve different historical issues of early Christian groups.

---

[2] Following scholarly consensus, I do not draw a sharp distinction between Judaism and Hellenism in this time period, although I recognize that both had their own distinctive local features and particulars.

1.2 Theological, Historical, and Methodological Concerns

As interpretative questions and methods stand in reciprocal relationship with one another, both influencing and being influenced, choices of interpretative methods are made in response to the questions a reader brings to the texts under examination as well as to the current scholarship in the field. I have several major concerns: What are the common traditions relevant to the Transfiguration in Mark and the believers' transformation in Paul? How do the synoptic authors understand the Transfiguration, and in what kind of contexts do they locate it and with what sorts of implications? How do various later Christian readers in the second century understand the Transfiguration in ways that are similar to or different from interpretations of the first readers? What did metamorphosis (transfiguration / transformation) mean to people in antiquity? How is Jesus' transfiguration different from or similar to both the general Hellenistic concept of metamorphosis and the theophanic instances in the Hebrew Bible? Since all these issues are socio-historical, literary, and theological, I employ methods which are a synthesis of historical, social, theological and literary criticism.

First, instead of simply pointing out possible sources and antecedents of the Transfiguration and showing literary dependencies among various Christian texts, I speak about the various functions of the Transfiguration in Christian texts of the first two centuries, especially in texts where Peter is claimed to be the main eyewitness to the event. I explore the dynamic interpretive movement of the Transfiguration story as we move forward and backward, from one text to another and from one generation to another. I base my work to some degree on James Robinson and Helmut Koester's insight that behind the texts there are developmental processes in the history of ideas as well as a historic reality of the movement of their transmission.[3] I am also indebted to François Bovon's emphasis on the history of interpretation in the Synoptic Gospels and apocryphal texts.

Second, as this project explores the development of the story, I am careful to keep in mind that there were real people who venerated their founder Jesus, a Jew who experienced a tragic death on the cross, as one in unique relationship with God. These people had to live a real life with their belief system, being inextricably caught up in the course of their culture. From various sociological implications of the Transfiguration, they may have struggled to find solutions for their crises. In view of this, a sociological

---

[3] James M. Robinson and Helmut Koester, *Trajectories through Early Christianities* (Philadelphia: Fortress Press, 1971).

approach helps us better grasp how the Transfiguration story helped those Christians cope with their social reality.[4]

Third, my analysis of the development of the Transfiguration story also draws upon "tradition criticism," which often supplements form criticism, and is sometimes called "the history of the transmission of traditions." Since I am examining how the Transfiguration is understood in the Synoptic gospels as well as how later canonical and apocryphal texts interpret it similarly or differently, my project is about the history of the transmission of the Transfiguration during the first two centuries. For many scholars, "tradition criticism" is considered to be a part of historical criticism.

Fourth, I make use of various insights of historical criticism. One of the main purposes of historical criticism is to achieve an understanding of texts in their historical and cultural contexts. In order to situate texts in their own contexts, I pay attention both to the historical situations described in the texts and to those of their authors and first recipients. In order to understand the Transfiguration in various texts in light of the general phenomenon of metamorphosis in antiquity and of theophanic events in Judaism, I take advantage of the insights of the "history of religions" approach. According to this view, a reading of ancient texts such as the New Testament and the Christian apocrypha must be guided by the language, world view, imagery, and symbols of their own time period. Therefore, I posit that it is the Jewish as well as the Hellenistic concepts of metamorphosis and epiphany that both constrain and allow meaningful implications of the Transfiguration for its ancient readers. I analyze parallels in the contemporary literature and in the religious environment of my texts for comparison.

Fifth, in contrast to the method of historical criticism, literary criticism focuses on the written texts, dealing with vocabulary, grammar, style, and rhetorical figures. What is important for my purpose is redaction criticism, the study of editorial activity. Redaction criticism aids in my understanding of the kind of theological expressions the biblical and apocryphal authors employ in writing about the tradition of the Transfiguration, and how they change or modify the story. I also base my analysis upon diachronic and synchronic readings of the story.[5] The diachronic reading demonstrates how later authors' new perspectives on Jesus alter the story that they received from their traditions. The synchronic reading shows how the Transfiguration story in each account is related to the rest of its entire literary context. This shows how the ancient writers develop or modify various

---

[4] E.g. Gerd Theissen, Social Reality and the Early Christians: Theology, Ethics, and the World of the New Testament, trans. Margaret Kohl (Minneapolis: Fortress, 1992).

[5] On these methods, see Graham N. Stanton, A Gospel for a New People: Studies in Matthew (Louisville, KY: Westminster/John Knox Press, 1993), especially part 1.

ideas found in the Transfiguration story in order to make the story fit into its new narrative contexts.

And finally, I explore the theological implications of the Transfiguration in its various interpretations. Here, I draw upon the recognition that these texts are not mere literary products of certain people at certain time periods, but are products of the theological understandings of religious groups of people. These people lived religiously devoted lives and anticipated their future destiny according to the theological orientations that they found in the texts.

1.3 Chapter Divisions

In chapter one, I begin with the Gospel of Mark, as it contains the earliest narrative account of the Transfiguration story. The Markan author had the Transfiguration story available orally; this story probably had Jesus' divine Sonship as its central message. In his redactional activity, Mark chose to situate the story in the context of Jesus' teaching at Caesarea-Philippi (Mk 8:27–9:13), claiming that Jesus is not only a human or human messiah from below, but also a divine being from above. Jesus not only transcends the division between the *heavenly* and the *earthly*, but also merges the two different realms in his life and ministry.

By placing the Transfiguration in a chiastic structure, Mark also wants to show the correspondence between Jesus' teaching (8:31–38) and the Transfiguration (9:2–9). In Mark's version of the story, Jesus' revelation of his divine identity through the Transfiguration, which God confirms from a cloud, reinforces his previous teaching about his destiny and identity as well as about the destiny and identity of his followers. Furthermore, the Transfiguration event assures his followers that they will experience a similar transformation to Jesus' after having followed him along the same path of suffering and death. According to my literary analysis of the Markan Transfiguration, this story may have functioned to answer various questions raised by members of the Markan community regarding the identity of Jesus (Christology), their own identity (ecclesiology), the possibility of their transformation (anthropology), and what will happen at the end of the history (eschatology). In addition, my analysis reveals this community's strong conviction that Jesus' tragic death on the cross is a crucial part of God's salvation program as well as being divinely planned, and that their own suffering, perhaps in the milieu of destruction of the Second Temple, is also a necessary part of discipleship.

In chapter two, I look into the precursor to the Markan version of the Transfiguration by analyzing 2 Corinthians 3 and comparing it with Mark. I find this comparison interesting and fruitful, since the Moses transforma-

tion story functions as a basic storyline for both Paul and Mark. In 2 Corinthians 3, Paul is not only aware of the Mosaic transformation story
along with its rich Jewish interpretive traditions, but also takes advantage
of them in the defense of his apostleship. In this process, Paul promotes his
ministry in the New Covenant beyond Moses' ministry in the Old Covenant. I do argue, however, that before the Mosaic transformation tradition
reaches the hand of Paul, early Christian thinkers reinterpreted it for their
Christological claim that Jesus goes beyond Moses as God's Son who carries God's glory. The first chapters of Hebrews are another independent
witness to this claim.

My comparison of Mark and Paul demonstrates that both share many
similar ideas which are also attested to in the Mosaic transformation tradition: (1) the term μεταμορφόομαι, (2) the motif of the glory in the face and
(3) the transformative as well as legitimizing functions of the glory. These
common themes clearly indicate that both Mark and Paul have taken advantage of the Mosaic transformation tradition for their description of Jesus' Transfiguration and the believers' transformation, respectively. Paul
and Mark also share ideas not found in the Mosaic transformation traditions: (1) the paradoxical nature of glorification, (2) glorification in connection with the idea of the Suffering Servant and (3) the apocalyptic implication of glorification – standing before the Son of Man (Mk 8:38) or
before the judgment seat of Christ (2 Cor 5:10). Since Paul's and Mark's
transformation accounts are so deeply rooted in these ideas of the Suffering Son of Man[6] and the Mosaic transformation story, it is reasonable to
conclude that behind their accounts there lies an early Jesus tradition in
which Jesus is glorified through his experience of suffering and death and
goes beyond Moses as God's Son and as the carrier of the divine glory.

In chapter three, I analyze the Transfiguration accounts of Matthew and
Luke in comparison with the Markan Transfiguration, as the Markan story
was first read by Matthew and Luke at the end of the first century CE.
Both Matthew and Luke keep the basic storyline of the Markan Transfiguration intact: (1) Jesus' transfiguration in front of the three disciples, (2)
Peter's proposal to build three tents, and (3) God's confirmation of Jesus'
Sonship. Matthew adds a new motif, however: that of Jesus' brilliant face,
and Luke introduces the term "glory" as well as "Jesus' exodus in Jerusalem." Both Matthew and Luke rehabilitate the disciples, especially Peter,
by omitting Peter's misunderstanding of Jesus' mission or by emphasizing
Peter's correct understanding of Jesus' identity as God's Son.

---

[6] It is true that Paul tends to transform "the Son of Man" into "the Son" (cf. 1 Thes
1:10) and therefore, the phrase "the Son of Man" does not appear in the Pauline corpora.
However, the idea of the Son of Man as the eschatological judge is still present in his
writings.

In addition, in its immediate context of the Transfiguration, Matthew adds Jesus' establishment of his church on the rock, Peter. Matthew sees at the Transfiguration a new Sinai event between God and His people, now the church. For Matthew, the story functions as a foundational legend for his community and legitimates that community's recent separation from mainline Judaism. For Luke, the Transfiguration functions to resolve the tension raised by Herod's perplexity about Jesus' identity. By removing most of Mark 6–8, Luke makes chapter nine a single scene about Jesus' identity. Furthermore, by introducing a new theme of Jesus' exodus at the Transfiguration, Luke makes the story a prelude to Jesus' Travel account (cf. Lk 9:51), which will culminate at his resurrection and ascension in Jerusalem. Jesus' fulfillment of the exodus in Jerusalem is not the end of his story, but rather begins the exodus of the disciples. In his description of the story of the disciples, Luke attempts to reconcile the ministry of the Twelve with that of the Hellenists by making the visions of Stephen and Paul comparable to the three disciples' experience of the Transfiguration.

Next, I explore the understanding of the Transfiguration in the second century CE by analyzing 2 Peter, the *Apocalypse of Peter* and the *Acts of Peter*.[7] In chapter four, I examine 2 Peter and the *Apocalypse of Peter*, since they are often looked at together by scholars due to their great similarity in vocabulary, themes, and use of Peter as a pseudonym. 2 Peter shows that in the second century CE, the Transfiguration continued to be related to Christian anthropology ("partakers of the divine nature" in 1:4) and to Christology (Jesus' receiving honor, glory, and majesty from God the Father in 1:17). More importantly, however, the Transfiguration story functioned for some believers as evidence of Jesus' second coming at the Parousia (3:8–10). The connection between the Parousia and the Transfiguration had already been made by Mark when he used the concept of the Son of Man, the eschatological Judge. This connection is found in more detail in the *Apocalypse of Peter*, a second century apocryphal writing. In the *Apocalypse of Peter*, Jesus answers Peter's request for evidence of the certainty of the Parousia by revealing what will happen in paradise at the end of the time. Although the context is clearly reminiscent of the Transfiguration in the Synoptic version, it is not Jesus' transfigured body, but the glorified bodies of Moses and Elijah that signify the believers' transfigured bodies at the Parousia. In these two Petrine writings, Peter appears as the very guarantor of the Transfiguration story or of its legitimate version. This shows how church traditions are transformed into apostolic traditions and in turn, apostles become legitimate guarantors of traditions.

---

[7] Although they are all ascribed to Peter, it is hardly the case that Peter himself wrote them. In this regard, they can be categorized as Pseudepigrapha.

In chapter five, I examine Peter's sermon on the Transfiguration and its reenactment in the form of polymorphy in the *Acts of Peter* (2CE). Even after the Transfiguration story was utilized and preserved in the canonical writings, it continued to be transmitted with various interpretations in multiple forms in later Christian apocryphal texts,[8] though not without experiencing its own "transformation" according to its new theological as well as historical contexts.[9] In Peter's sermon, the Transfiguration is interpreted in light of the Christian idea of incarnation and Greco-Roman mythology about polymorphism. While the incarnation reveals Jesus' human form, the Transfiguration demonstrates his glorious divine form. It is especially interesting that in the *Acts of Peter*, Jesus' Transfiguration is reenacted in the form of polymorphy in the experience of its community: Jesus appears in multiple human forms, as an old man, a young man and a boy. This polymorphy represents Jesus' on-going care for his people in multiple ways depending upon their particular needs. Similarly to the *Apocalypse of Peter* and 2 Peter, the *Acts of Peter* betrays the apologetic tendency of not mentioning Peter's failure in understanding Jesus' teaching of suffering and death. Instead, the Peter in the *Acts of Peter* emphasizes Jesus' role as the Suffering Servant and follows him on the path of martyrdom, where he experiences crucifixion with his head downwards.

---

[8] I have in mind such texts as the *Apocalypse of Peter, Acts of Peter, Acts of John, Acts of Thomas, Shepherd of Hermas, Apocryphon of John, Gospel of Philip, Pistis Sopia, Treatise on the Resurrection*, and the *Acts of Philip*.

[9] The Transfiguration in this apocryphal literature often denotes Christ's divine unity among his polymorphic appearances and also offers a theological foundation for the disciples' own transformation – resurrection or polymorphy on earth.

Chapter 2

The Transfiguration Narrative in Mark (9:2–10)

2.1 Introduction

The Transfiguration is such a fascinating story that it has not stopped inspiring later Christian readers in multiple ways. But at the same time, because it is a polyvalent story with multiple traditions and implications, its readers will immediately notice how complicated the story is. Before it was utilized by the Markan author, the Transfiguration story probably enjoyed its own independent life orally. Also, Paul's description of the believers' transformation in 2 Cor 3 is an interesting parallel to the Markan Transfiguration story of Jesus, since they describe similar transformation phenomena by drawing upon the Mosaic transformation tradition and the Hellenistic transformation (metamorphosis) stories. The Markan story has been read by Matthew and Luke, and the author of 2 Peter had access to the story in a synoptic form, especially the Matthean version.[1] Even after it was preserved in scriptural writings, the Transfiguration story did not stop being interpreted in different ways in later apocryphal texts, such as the *Apocalypse of Peter*, *Acts of Peter*, *Acts of John*, *Acts of Thomas*, *Shepherd of Hermas*, *Apocryphon of John*, *Gospel of Philip*, *Pistis Sophia*, *Treaty on the Resurrection*, and the *Acts of Philip*.

The Transfiguration story in Mark manifests that its author is familiar with the Jewish traditions about messianic ideas and the Mosaic transformation story in Exod 34 and the Hellenistic metamorphosis stories by gods. The author is sophisticated enough to incorporate them into his own Christological presentation of Jesus in the Transfiguration story. Scholars who have worked on the Transfiguration have suggested several different sources from which it may have come and ways of understanding it: (1) as a misplaced resurrection narrative,[2] (2) as a story of a Hellenistic divine

---

[1] For more on this, see Jerome H. Neyrey, "The Apologetic Use of the Transfiguration in 2nd Peter 1:16–21," *CBQ* 42 (1980): 504–19.

[2] Hans D. Betz, "Jesus as Divine Man," in *Jesus and the Historian*, ed. F.T. Trotter (Philadelphia: Westminster Press, 1968), 114–33; Rudolf Bultmann, *History of the Synoptic Tradition* (New York: Harper and Row, 1976), 259ff; C.E. Carlston, "Transfiguration and Resurrection," *JBL* 80 (1961): 233–40; and J.M. Robinson, "On the Gattung of Mark (and John)," *Perspective* 11 (1970): 99–129.

man,[3] (3) as an apocalyptic revelation,[4] (4) as part of the Sinai/Mosaic tradition,[5] (5) as a story related to the binding of Isaac,[6] (6) having to do with the Feast of Booths,[7] (7) as part of the enthronement pattern,[8] and (8) part of Epiphany/Christophany.[9] It is my conviction that, although each of these traditions contributed to Mark's Christological inquiry in a certain way, one single tradition cannot fully exhaust the implications of the Markan Transfiguration story. Its readers should be sensitive to different aspects of each tradition and, at the same time, should pay due attention to how Mark synthesizes them in his presentation of Jesus in the new narrative framework.

As the hermeneutical keys for the story, I especially find useful three main options from the list above, (1) the Mosaic transformation story with its ideology, (2) metamorphosis resulting in epiphany and (3) Jewish messianic ideas of the Son of God and the Son of Man. I propose that at the Transfiguration, within its immediate context of the Caesarea-Philippi incident (Mk 8:27–9:13), Mark is presenting a "two-level Christology"[10] on the axis of space – *one from above* and *the other from below*. The Markan Jesus appears to be a paradoxical combination of the heavenly Son / the Son of Man and the earthly suffering messiah. This combination is para-

---

[3] Betz, "Jesus as Divine Man," 143–33; Barry Blackburn, *Theios Aner and the Markan Miracle Traditions, WUNT* (Tübingen: Mohr, 1991); Adela Yarbro Collins, "Rulers, Divine Men, and Walking on the Water," in *Religious Propaganda and Missionary Competition in the New Testament World*, ed. L. Bormann, K. del Tredici, and A. Standhartinger (Leiden/New York: Brill, 1994), 207–27; C. R. Holladay, *Theios Aner in Hellenistc Judaism* (Missoula: Scholars Press, 1977); J. D. Kingsbury, "The 'Divine Man' as the Key to Mark's Christology – The End of an Era?" *Interpretation* 35 (1981): 243–57; and W. L. Knox, "The 'Divine Hero' Christology in the New Testament," *HTR* (1948): 229–49.

[4] H.C. Kee, "The Transfiguration in Mark: Epiphany or Apocalyptic Vision?" in *Understanding the Sacred Texts*, ed. J. Reumann (Valley Forge, Pa: Judson Press, 1972), 135–52; and E. Loymeyer, *Das Evangelium des Markus* (Gottingen: Vandenhoeck & Ruprecht, 1967), 178–81.

[5] J.A Ziesler, "The Transfiguration Story and the Markan Soteriology," *ExpTimes* 81 (1969–70): 263–68.

[6] D. Flusser, *Jesus*, trans. R. Walls (New York: Herder & Herder: 1969); and A.R.C. Leaney, *The Christ of the Synoptic Gospels* (Auckland: Pelorous Press, 1966).

[7] Harald Riesenfeld, *Jésus transfiguré, l'arriére-plan récit évangélique de la transfiguration de Notre-Seigneur* (Kobenhavn: E. Munksgaard, 1947); and W.R. Roehrs, "God's Tabernacles among Men: A Study of the Transfiguration," *CTM* 35 (1964): 18–25.

[8] Riesenfeld, *Jésus transfiguré.*

[9] John P. Heil, *The Transfiguration of Jesus* (Roma: Editrice Pontificio Instituto Biblico, 2000); and John A. McGuckin, *The Transfiguration of Christ in Scripture and Tradition* (New York: Edwin Mellen Press, 1986).

[10] I am borrowing this term from François Bovon, *Luke*, vol. 1 (Minneapolis: Fortress Press, 2002), 372.

doxical, especially because the heavenly Son should subject himself to a human fate of suffering and death. Furthermore, the Markan "two-level Christology" is explained on the axis of time through Jesus' transcending the temporal division of "present and future": Jesus in the present is the Son of Man who will come back as the eschatological judge in the future.

For Mark, Jesus may not simply be an eschatological human messiah as the agent of God's will found in Israelite traditions (*from below*), but also a divine Son of God who disguises his true divine identity in human form in order to accomplish his divine mission (*from above*).[11] In this scheme, the motif of secrecy has an important literary function for Mark, similar to the Homeric accounts of gods and to the stories of angels.[12] Jesus, having appeared on earth as a human being, reveals his true identity at the Transfiguration (epiphany) by changing his form from human to divine (metamorphosis).[13] Jesus' belonging to the divine realm as God's Son is further strengthened by the contrast between the heavenly three (Jesus, Moses and Elijah) and the earthly three (Peter, James and John). By placing the Transfiguration in the Caesarea-Philippi context, Mark further identifies a Jew named Jesus who suffers, dies, and rises from the dead *on earth*, with the *heavenly* Son of Man. In this presentation, the Markan Jesus can transcend the division of heaven-earth on the *spatial* axis.[14] At the Parousia, this Jesus, who lives a tragic life at some point in human history, will come back as the eschatological Son of Man with "his Father's Glory", accompanied by angels (Mk 8:38).[15] In this scheme, the ministry and life of the Markan Jesus is laid out through overcoming the division of present-future on a *temporal* axis.[16]

This Markan *Christological* and *eschatological* understanding of Jesus in the Caesarea-Philippi Transfiguration episode has further *apologetic /*

---

[11] Docetism has not yet evolved at this stage of Christian theology, and therefore, we may not read Docetism into the story. Also, as will be shown later, it was common in antiquity for gods to appear on earth in human disguises for intervention in human affairs – this, in turn, implies that the human domain is closely bonded with that of the divine.

[12] Joel Marcus, *Mark*, vol. 1 (New York: Doubleday, 2000), 525–27; and William Wrede, *The Messianic Secret*, trans. J.C.G. Greig (Cambridge, England: J. Clarke, 1971).

[13] Mark does not describe the descent of Jesus nor does he narrate the birth story of Jesus, as do Matthew and Luke. However, in the beginning of Mark, only supernatural beings such as God and demons recognize Jesus as a divine being, indicating his belonging to the heavenly realm (cf. 1:11; 1:23–24; 1:34; 5:7).

[14] The term Son of Man may not have been a fixed messianic title in that time period, but the term in Mark is definitive rather then generic.

[15] The word play on heaven and earth may indicate that Jesus needs to descend and ascend in order to travel through these spatial categories, although Mark does not explicitly flesh out those concepts of descent and ascent.

[16] These *temporal* and *spatial* axes will play a great role in the narrative description of Jesus' descent and ascent in the *Ascension of Isaiah*.

polemical, *validating*, *ecclesiological*, and *ontological* implications for his followers. In addition, the issue of *spiritual enlightenment* in terms of understanding Jesus properly is also at issue. Just as Jesus experiences glorious metamorphosis (transfiguration) on his way to suffering and death, so also do his followers experience similar transfiguration, after having followed him in the same path of suffering and death.[17] This may indicate how the Markan community comes to terms with their founder's tragic death on the cross as well as their own suffering in the milieu of the destruction of the second Temple.

I will begin this chapter by first analyzing (1) the content and genre of the Transfiguration (9:2–11) and then, (2) explore its implication in the immediate context of the Caesarea-Philippi Transfiguration cycle (8:27–9:13). In this process, I hope to differentiate what the Transfiguration means on its own from what Mark intends the story to mean in its new literary context. Having analyzed the Transfiguration in its immediate context, (3) I will conclude by exploring the historical situation of the Markan community. I will examine what kind of socio-political exigency leads them to understand the Transfiguration in a way that is particular to the Gospel of Mark. I will place the Markan version of the Transfiguration on the map of its trajectories, pointing both at what comes prior to Mark and what comes next.

2.2 The Transfiguration as the Divine Credentials for Jesus' Sonship and His Ministry: *Exegetical Analysis of Mark 9:1–10*

In the Transfiguration story, the revelation of the heavenly identity of Jesus as God's Son functions as the main message. A mountain is used as the meeting place for heavenly and earthly beings, not least because it is considered to be halfway between earth and heaven. The appearance of Moses and Elijah from heaven makes Jesus important in the salvation history of Israel as their long-awaited messiah. However, their accompanying the transfigured Jesus indicates that he belongs to the heavenly realm, especially by creating a sharp contrast between the heavenly three (Moses, Elijah and Jesus) and the earthly three (Peter, James and John). Jesus' transfigured glorious body with the white clothes reinforces Jesus' belonging to the heavenly realm; and God's own divine testimony to Jesus' Sonship reaches the climax of the story. In this part of the discussion, I will ex-

---

[17] This is the exact message that Paul conveys in 2 Cor 3 and 4. Although Paul and Mark describe the transformation differently, their message is the same: true discipleship through following Jesus' path of suffering and death and its final vindication through glorious transformation.

amine how each of these contributes to the Markan understanding of Jesus and his Sonship at the Transfiguration, especially by accounting for the Jewish ideas of the messiah, the Mosaic transformation tradition and the Hellenistic metamorphosis phenomenon.

2.2.1 Literary Structure (Mk 9:1–10)[18]

Jesus' prediction of the manifestation of the coming *Kingdom of God* to *some* (v.1)

A. Jesus' *going up* to a high mountain with three disciples (v.2a)

    a. Jesus' Transfiguration and his radiant garments (vv.2b–3)   *– divine: "visible"*
       Appearance of Elijah and Moses (v.4):

    b. Peter's proposal (vv.5–6a)   *– human*
       Three disciples' response – being terrified (v.6b)

    c. God's presence in cloud (v.7a)   *– divine: "audible"*
       God's own testimony to Jesus' divine Sonship (v.7b)

    d. Jesus is found alone   *– human*
       With his disciples (v.8)

A′. Jesus' *going down* from a mountain with three disciples (v.9a)

Jesus' ordering of *secrecy* until the *resurrection of the Son of Man* (v.9b)

    – disciples' wondering what Jesus' saying meant (v.10)

In this literary structure, we see that the Transfiguration story is framed by a kingship motif (9:1) and a resurrection motif (9:9–10) with similar implications of *limitedness*: "some" and "secrecy." Mark 9:1 is a redactional hinge between the prophecy of the Parousia (8:38) and the Transfiguration story.[19] Jesus here predicts that *some* of the disciples who listened to his previous teachings in ch. 8 will witness the Kingdom of God coming in power, not Jesus' enthronement. In its literary context, readers will not miss that the three disciples in the Transfiguration story are those *some* who will have that experience.[20] Then, we can easily conjecture that the

---

[18] My literary analysis is partially dependent upon Bovon's literary analysis of the Transfiguration in Luke (Bovon, *Luke,* vol.1, 371).

[19] E. Nardonni, "A Redactional Interpretation of Mark 9:1," *CBQ* 43 (1981): 365–84; and Joel Marcus, *The Mystery of the Kingdom of God* (Atlanta: Scholars Press, 1986), 52. Also, A.D.A. Moses, *Matthew's Transfiguration Story and Jewish-Christian Controversy* (JSNTSup 122; Sheffield: Sheffield Academic Press, 1996).

[20] Ulrich Luz argues in his analysis of the Matthean version of the story that this prediction of the Kingdom of God reveals the evangelists' expectation of the imminent End Times. See Ulrich Luz, *Matthew*, ed. Helmut Koester, trans. James E. Crouch, 3 vols., vol. 2, *Hermeneia* (Minneapolis: Fortress Press, 2001), 387. He misses not only the narrative implication of the term *some*, but also the temporal hinge of "six days later" which connects both Jesus' prediction of the Kingdom of God and the Transfiguration. Most commentators agree that "after six days" expresses an interval of time which connects both what comes earlier (Kingdom of God) and what follows (Transfiguration). See Heil, 151; M. A. Tolbert, *Sowing the Gospel: Mark's World in Literary-Rhetorical Perspectives* (Minneapolis: Fortress, 1989), 205; Morna Dorothy Hooker, *A Commentary on the Gospel according to St. Mark* (London: A & C Black, 1991), 214–15; and Robert H.

Transfiguration story has much to do with the ideas of the eschatological Kingdom of God in power and the Son of Man. Although the question of how they are related to one another should be explained through exegetical analysis of the text, it is clear in Mark's scheme that at the Transfiguration, Jesus is not enthroned nor exalted as the Son of Man, the eschatological judge at the Parousia, but his hidden cosmic rulership is temporarily revealed on a small scale ("to some"). These converging lines with "secrecy motif until the resurrection" and "the Kingdom of God to some" may point to a Markan view that it is only after his resurrection that Jesus' exalted status as the true cosmic – not simply Israelite – ruler of the world will become manifest to the public on a universal scale.[21]

The Transfiguration begins with Jesus' initiation to go up on a high mountain with *some* of his disciples (A) and ends with his coming down from the mountain with them (A$'$). Jesus is transfigured and Elijah and Moses appear and talk with him (a). There is a strong contrast between the heavenly three (the transfigured Jesus, Elijah and Moses) and the earthly three (Peter, James and John). This scene manifests, in a *visible* way, Jesus' *divine* identity in terms of his belonging to the heavenly realm. This point is reinforced by Jesus' transfigured appearance, his radiant garments and the three disciples' human response to them with fear. Human fear is a literary topos in epiphany. This *visible divine* phenomenon is followed by the improper *human* responses of Peter and other disciples (b). While Peter suggests building up three booths, Mark clearly says that Peter does not understand true implication of what is happening here. Although Jesus continues God's salvation program in Israelite history, he should not be ranked with Moses and Elijah. Furthermore, Jesus should not stay there on the mountain, but he has to go down the mountain again to accomplish his earthly mission. God appears in the cloud and speaks out – this is the second *divine* manifestation in an *audible* form (c). God, through His voice, responds not only to Peter's incorrect proposal, but also reveals what Jesus' Transfiguration means from His perspective, "This is My beloved Son." God's voice functions as the divine interpretation of the manifestation of Jesus' identity as His Son and his belonging to the heavenly realm.[22] However, God stresses the importance of Jesus' earthly mission, which he already taught in 8:31, by adding to it His divine credentials: "Listen to him!"

Gundry, *Mark: A Commentary on His Apology for the Cross* (Grand Rapids, Mich.: Eerdmans, 1993), 457. Bovon, in his commentary on Luke, says that according to Luke, the end time is not any more in the imminent future; for Luke, the Kingdom of God is always present in Jesus and *some* refers to the believers who listened to Jesus' previous teaching, especially the Twelve (*Luke*, 368).

[21] Joel Marcus, *The Way of the Lord*, 89.

[22] Bovon, *Luke*, vol.1, 371.

Then, it follows that Jesus is found alone with his disciples in human form. This corresponds to Jesus' Transfiguration in a way that he should now conceal his divine identity again in order to continue to fulfill his earthly ministry in obedience to God's will. Peter was wrong to suggest building three booths, as he did not understand the paradox that Jesus' Sonship and messiahship cannot be fully understood without grasping his earthly destiny of suffering and death (8:31–33). In this structure, Jesus is both a humble human messiah who is destined to experience a tragic death, and a glorious Son of God. Both identities are mysteriously converged into the *historical* Jesus and thus he transcends the division of heaven and earth.

In conclusion, within the Transfiguration there is a stark contrast between Jesus' appearance in a human mode and that of Jesus in a divine mode, and also between the human response of the three disciples to the Transfiguration and God's divine response. Jesus' transfiguration functions as the visible aspect of the epiphany, while God's voice as its audible attestation. Jesus' belonging to the heavenly realm is portrayed through his glorious transformation, heavenly clothes and angelic companions. This idea is strengthened by God's own testimony to Jesus' Sonship.

2.2.2 The Manifestation of the Kingdom of God to Some

In Mk 9:1, Jesus predicts that "some who are standing here will not taste death until they see the Kingdom of God coming with power." It is clear that "some" in this story refers to the three disciples Peter, James, and John. In Mark, these three constitute an inner core of the already special group of the twelve for Jesus' ministry. In Galatians 2:9, Paul even calls them the "three pillars of the Church." According to David Wenham and A.D.A. Moses, the prestigious position of these three apostles in the Jerusalem Church had something to do with their experience of the Transfiguration and with their special status as witnesses to Jesus' majesty and glory.[23] I find their argument convincing, as in antiquity there is an explicit link between the divine revelation and the special status of the recipient.

In Mk 5:37, Jesus only allows these three to witness his miracle of resurrecting a daughter of a synagogue officer. The theme of resurrection is also important for the Transfiguration, as it is only after his resurrection that the glorious Jesus will become permanently manifest to the public. In 13:3–37, the so-called Olivet discourse, Jesus delivers an apocalyptic message to the three, this time, with Andrew. The Olivet discourse contains

---

[23] After James the apostle's martyrdom, James the brother of Jesus quickly takes over his position in the Jerusalem Church. See David Wenham and A.D.A. Moses, "'There are Some Standing Here...': Did They Become the 'Reputed Pillars' of the Jerusalem church? Some Reflections on Mark 9:1, Galatians 2:9 and the Transfiguration," *Novum Testamentum* 36 (1994), 146–63.

Jesus' prediction of the coming Son of Man at the Parousia and his judgment. Mark here explains in a much clearer way what Jesus taught in 8:38. Also in 14:33, it is these three who witness Jesus' prayer and struggle at the Gethsemane scene.[24] An interesting comparison has been noticed between the Transfiguration and the Gethsemane scene: (1) the theme of suffering and death, (2) as God's will, (3) the presence of three apostles, and (4) Peter's being rebuked for not getting at what is happening in both stories.[25] It is likely that there is, in Mark's mind, a connection between the events in Gethsemane and at the Transfiguration.

The emphatic adverbial phrase "privately, alone" (κατ' ἰδίαν μόνους) not only highlights the mysterious character of the following episode of the Transfiguration, but also underlines the prerogative of the three in their eyewitness experience. That Jesus takes along Peter, James, and John prepares the readers of Mark for a new and further private revelation regarding Jesus' previous teaching in 8:27–9:1. That these three are among "some of those standing here" (9:1) alerts the readers to the possibility that they will experience something special; and this private event of the Transfiguration will be related to the eschatological "coming Kingdom of God in power" (9:1; cf. 8:38). However, the Kingdom of God will not become manifest on a full scale now, but only in a limited way – "to some."

There has been a scholarly debate regarding the nature of the Kingdom of God in Mark as well as Jesus' kingship. Although Peter's confession of Jesus as Christ, the kingly Messiah of Israel, is not rejected by Mark (8:29), the kingship of the Markan Jesus goes beyond that of a local Jewish messianic king. This is one of the reasons Mark places the Transfiguration as a sequel to Peter's confession of him as a messiah. The Markan Transfiguration does not represent the enthronement of Jesus as a king, but the revelation of his cosmic kingship. When I later analyze the concepts of the Son of Man, the preexistent heavenly messiah (cf. 4 Ezra 13), and the Son of God, I will further demonstrate this aspect of Jesus' cosmic rulership. The heavenly hierarchy of Father-Son-angels in Mk 13:32 and the recognition of Jesus' *divine* Sonship by God and demons make Jesus one of their kind in the heavenly realm.

2.2.3 Elijah with Moses on a Mountain

It is interesting to note that at the Transfiguration, Mark mentions Elijah first, then Moses, who is the single most important figure of the Judaism of the day. It is no accident that Elijah is first named by Mark, probably

---

[24] Also cf. Mark 10:35–45; 13:3; 16:7.

[25] T. A. Burkill, *Mysterious Revelation: An Examination of the Philosophy of St. Mark's Gospel* (Ithaca, N.Y.: Cornell University, 1963); and A. Kenny, "The Transfiguration and the Agony in the Garden," *CBQ* XIX (1957): 444–52.

through his redactional activity of changing the original order of Moses and Elijah (cf. Mk 9:5, and the Transfiguration stories in Mt and Lk).[26] Why do they appear in the Transfiguration account? Do Moses and Elijah stand for the Law and the Prophets, telling the readers that Jesus has come to accomplish what the Law and the Prophets prophesized? While Moses is considered to be the representative of the law throughout Mark (1:44; 7:10; 10:3–4; 12:19, 26), Elijah does not stand for the Prophets, but instead, John the Baptist does. The prophecy of the Prophet-like-Moses on the basis of Deut 18:15 is claimed to be popular in the Second Temple Judaism, as is attested in Qumran Florilegium.[27] Peter's sermons in Acts 3 and 7 show that the idea of Jesus as this eschatological prophet seems to be old and the Transfiguration story is clearly reminiscent of this idea, as is especially found in God's witness, "This is My beloved Son; *listen to him!*" (9:7). This way of understanding Jesus as the Prophet-like-Moses is, however, what Mark tries to overcome by placing Elijah prior to Moses. Mark further changes the function of the expression "listen to him" from the fulfillment of the Deuteronomistic prophecy to God's divine command for the readers to *obey* Jesus regarding his previous teaching in 8:31–38. In any case, the appearance of Elijah and Moses at the Transfiguration should have something to do with what both commonly represent or where both appear at the same time in the Jewish traditions.

In Jewish traditions, Elijah has an apocalyptic role as the harbinger of the Lord.[28] For example, Mal 4:4–5 reads:

"Remember the law of *Moses* My servant, even the statues and ordinances which I command him in Horeb for all Israel. Behold, I am going to send you *Elijah* the prophet before the coming of the great and terrible *Day of the Lord*" (*Italics are mine*).

It is very important for our purpose that, in this text, both Moses and Elijah are remembered together through the concept of the law in Horeb; and their appearance warns readers to remember Moses' law in order to avoid the terrible judgment on the Day of the Lord. Furthermore, Elijah's coming is expected to be eschatologically important, since he becomes the forerunner of the Lord on His Day. At the Transfiguration, Mark seems to claim that it is Jesus who is the Lord for whom this prophecy has been

---

[26] The Transfiguration story is based upon the Mosaic transformation story in its major storyline. As I will discuss further in chapter two, there were debates regarding Jesus and Moses in early Christianity. So, it is natural and logical that Moses appeared in the primitive Transfiguration story and then Elijah was added. Mark in his story puts Elijah in front of Moses in order to make the story respond to people's misunderstanding of him as Elijah.

[27] Kee, "The Transfiguration in Mark: Epiphany or Apocalyptic Vision?" Also, for the comprehensive study of Moses in the Jewish traditions and John, refer to Wayne A. Meeks, *The Prophet King* (Leiden: Brill, 1967).

[28] Kee, 146; and J. Jeremias in *TDNT* 2.928–41.

made. Mark makes this point clear by identifying Elijah with John the Baptist. In the context of Mark, it is John the Baptist who fulfills the return of Elijah as the forerunner of the Lord (Mk 9:13; 1:2–9). But in what way does John the Baptist fulfill the return of Elijah? In Mk 1:2–4, Mark presents John the Baptist as the one who prepares for the way of the Lord and thereby, claims Jesus to be the Lord (cf. Isa 40:3). The appearance of Elijah and the identification of the returning Elijah with John the Baptist in the Caesarea-Philippi context further claim that Jesus' journey up to Jerusalem in the way of suffering and death is *the Way of the Lord*.[29]

Moses, on the other hand, is remembered as the representative of the law throughout Mark (1:44; 7:10; 10:3, 4; 12:19, 26), but Jesus' own teaching often overcomes the Mosaic law, e.g. regarding the Sabbath law (2:27–28). In the context of the Transfiguration, it is not the Mosaic law, but Jesus' teaching regarding the disciples' suffering and death for his sake as well as the Gospel's (8:35) that determines the disciples' fate at the Parousia. In any case, the rhetorical effect of these two figures makes the point that in Jesus all the expectations related to the law of Moses and Elijah's return as the harbinger of the Lord are to be fulfilled.[30]

In the Jewish traditions of the day, Moses and Elijah along with Enoch are claimed not to taste death, so that they become heavenly citizens with angels.[31] In Jewish apocalyptic traditions, the righteous are believed to be in angelic status as immortal beings and often receive white clothes as a symbol for their belonging to heaven (cf. Dan 12:1–5). Considering that Mark 9:1 is connecting the Transfiguration of Jesus to his prediction of "the coming of the Son of Man in his Father's glory with his *angels*" (8:38), on a limited scale, Moses and Elijah can also represent for the Markan readers the angelic beings who accompany Jesus the Son of Man. It will be interesting to examine whether later Christian writings describe them as angelic beings or their bodies as resurrected glorious bodies (e.g. the *Apocalypse of Peter*).[32]

In the Hebrew Bible, these two are especially claimed to have experienced God's Theophany on a mountain, either Horeb, or Zion, or Sinai. In response to their common desire to see God, their wish was only partially granted: Elijah only heard God's voice and Moses saw only the back part of God (cf.1Kg 19:9–13). Does Mark want to say that their desire to see God is now satisfied at the Transfiguration of Jesus, as Irenaeus of

---

[29] For more on this, see Marcus, 31–32.

[30] Adela Y. Collins, 401.

[31] B. C. Chilton, *God in Strength: Jesus' Announcement of the Kingdom* (Freistadt: Plöchl, 1979), 269.

[32] In chapter four, I will show how the *Apocalypse of Peter* interprets the glorious bodies of Moses and Elijah as the future resurrected bodies of the believers.

Lyons argues?[33] Sacred mountains and mountain symbolism are common features in Israelite religious traditions from earliest times up to the end of the Second Temple period. Sinai and Zion are especially sacred, not least because it was there that God bound His people to Himself in covenantal relationship. These covenantal promises will be fulfilled in the eschatological future.[34] More than sixty times, the accounts of the giving of the law are located in the mountain (הר) in Pentateuch. In these instances, the term הר is juxtaposed with סיני or חורב (Dt 33:2; Ex 3:1; 33:6). Although Sinai and Horeb are never directly equated with each other, Ex 3:12 weaves together the accounts of the burning bush on Horeb and the giving of the law on Sinai, resulting in the equatiing of the two. Mount Sinai is remembered in Israelite traditions through two significant theological features: first, God encounters His people on Sinai in the form of Theophany, and second, that Theophany is a part of the covenant making ceremony (Ex 19:9; 19:18; 34:5; 3:12).[35] It is interesting that in Deuteronomic history, Mosaic covenant is remembered in the mountain Horeb, not Sinai (1 Ki 8:9; 2 Chr 5:10). The mountain Horeb appears in the account of Elijah and his experience of Theophany (1 Ki 19:8). Before God sends Elijah into a great journey of divine mission, He feeds Elijah for forty days and forty nights. Does the author of Deuteronomic history present Elijah here as "the prophet like Moses"? R.A. Carlson answers affirmatively.[36]

Considering that many aspects of the Sinai and Zion theology of the Hebrew Bible can be generally described in cosmic terms, the concept of the cosmic mountain may have played a certain role in Israelite mountain theology.[37] The cosmic mountain includes the idea of the mountain as the *axis mundi* with its roots in the underworld and its peak in the heavens; it is the place where heaven, earth, and the underworld are linked together. Likewise, in our story of the Transfiguration, it is on the mountain that both the heavenly beings and the earthly beings meet with one another.[38]

---

[33] Irenaeus of Lyons, *Adversus Haereses,* 4.20, 8. See Andreas Andreopoulos, *Metamorphosis: the Transfiguration in Byzantine Theology and Iconography* (Crestwood, New York: St Vladimir's Seminary Press, 2005).

[34] Terence L. Donaldson, *Jesus on the Mountain* (JSNT Supp. 8; Sheffield: JSOT Press, 1985), 41–49.

[35] Ibid., 32–33.

[36] R.A. Carlson, "Elie à l'Horeb," *VT* 19 (1969): 416–39; and Donaldson, *Jesus on the Mountain*, 45.

[37] Donaldson, *Jesus on the Mountain*, 26.

[38] It has been suggested that the mountain in our context is Mt. Hermon, as the Transfiguration happens in the Caesarea-Philippi near Galilee (cf. Mk 8:27 and 9:30). The areas around Dan Banias were cultic centers from Bronze age times up to the Late Roman period. According to Nickelsburg, it is in this territory that the *Book of Watchers*, the *Testament of Levi* and Mt 16 relate sacred revelations to Enoch, Levi and Peter. See George E. W. Nickelsburg, "Enoch, Levi, and Peter: Recipients of Revelation in Upper

Various Jewish apocalyptic texts also show that the mountain is the place where eschatological and messianic events occur, where special divine knowledge is communicated with human mediators, and where things hidden are revealed in end times.[39] For example, in Dan 2:35 and 44, the stone in Daniel's vision becomes a great mountain, symbolizing the final establishment of the world-wide kingdom of God; and in Dan 7, the Son of Man appears with the Ancient of Days in order to receive dominion and power. Also in 4 Ezra 13, the Son of Man stands on the mountain of stone cut out without human hands. It is very likely that Jesus' going up on a high mountain with three disciples prepares the Markan readers for an upcoming special event with eschatological importance.

Before Jesus' Transfiguration on a high mountain, he healed and fed multitudes of people (Mk 8:1–9). We find its parallel in the banquet of Israel during their covenant making with God in Exodus at Mt Sinai. If the Transfiguration stands in parallel to the Sinai event,[40] then, can we imagine that the Markan Jesus is bounding his people to God through a certain kind of covenant making ceremony in the Caesarea-Philippi Transfiguration context? Do Jesus' prediction of his suffering and death and his ordering the disciples to follow him in the same path in Mk 8:31–38 give us any supporting hint for this idea of covenant making ceremony for the Markan community? Although it is only later in Mk 14:21–25 that he proceeds to make a covenant of blood with his disciples, it is clear that in 8:31–38, Mark intends to present Jesus' teaching of his suffering and death as a crucial part of the blood covenant between God and his community. For the disciples' attitude toward his teaching determines their fate on the judgment day (8:37–38), just as the Israelites' fate was determined by their obedience to the Mosaic covenant. In another version of the Transfiguration story, Matthew adds a claim that Jesus will build his church on the rock, Peter. Matthew clearly sees here a covenant-like foundational story where Jesus binds his people, the church, to God through his ministry and death.

Galilee," *JBL* 100 (1981): 575–600. Also, 'Excursus: Sacred Geography in 1 Enoch 6–16' in George E. W. Nickelsburg, *1 Enoch: A Commentary on the Book of 1 Enoch* (Minneapolis: Fortress, 2001). See also, C.H.T. Fletcher-Louis, "The Revelation of the Sacral Son of Man. The Genre, History of Religions Context and the Meaning of the Transfiguration," in *Auferstehung – Resurrection*, ed. F. Avemarie and H. Lichtenberger (Tübingen: Mohr Siebeck, 2001), 261–71.

[39] Donaldson, *Jesus on the Mountain*, 76–80.

[40] I will consider it proven that the Transfiguration is drawing upon the theophanic stories in Exodus 24 and 34, since most scholars agree upon that.

2.2.4 Jesus' Transfiguration

In our current text of the Transfiguration, Jesus climbs up with his three disciples on a high mountain. Those readers who are familiar with the kind of apocalyptic and eschatological concept of mountains, as I described above, will expect that something special will happen on the mountain. For their satisfaction, Jesus is transfigured with radiant garments and Elijah appears with Moses, talking with him. The appearance of Elijah and Moses colors the event of the Transfiguration in an apocalyptic way. It alerts to the readers that something important in terms of the end times or the messianic age is happening. In this episode, there exists a strong contrast between the three heavenly beings (Jesus, Moses, and Elijah) and the other three earthly beings (Peter, James, and John).[41] This contrast between divine and human is further intensified by Peter's improper human response to the Transfiguration and God's correct interpretation of it (v. 7). In this line of thought, the Transfiguration is related to a heavenly realm which human beings may not have an access to or may not correctly understand without God's revelation.[42]

As I have already argued above, the presence of Moses and Elijah together with "listen to him" in Mk 9:7 evokes the promise of Moses to the people in Deut 18:15 – the Prophet-like-Moses and the promise of Malachi regarding the day of the Lord. Deut 18:15 is interpreted eschatologically in Second Temple Judaism and the expectation of an eschatological prophet is reflected in the Dead Sea Scrolls (4Q175.5–8; CD 6:11).[43] Mal 5:4–5 presents that Elijah will come back as the forerunner of the Lord at the end times. In Mk 1:2–3, John the Baptist takes the role of forerunner and Jesus is claimed to be the Lord. It is beyond doubt that the Markan Transfiguration story is clearly dependent upon these Jewish apocalyptic ideas. The transfigured Jesus, however, transcends the Prophet-like-Moses or even the Messiah of the Hebrew Bible through the concept of divine Sonship, "This is My beloved Son" (9:7). Jesus' Sonship in Mark is more than merely a functional one, since the Son has divine origin (12:35–37; 1:11) and stands in the middle of the Father and the angels in the heavenly hierarchy

---

[41] According to Bovon, there is a symmetry between the three figures above and the three disciples below. This symmetry underscores human participation in the glory of God (Bovon, 377). In my opinion, this human participation in the glory of God will be further strengthened if we understand Moses and Elijah as the glorified righteous ones. This idea is often found in Jewish apocalyptic thoughts.

[42] Matthew in his account of the Transfiguration emphasizes this aspect by calling the event "a vision."

[43] John J. Collins, *Scepter and the Star* (New York: Doubleday, 1995), 112–14 and 16–17; and Joel Marcus, *The Way of the Lord* (Louisville, Kentucky: John Knox Press, 1992), 81–82; and Adela Yarbro Collins, "Mark and His Readers: The Son of God among Jews," *HTR* 92 (1999), 401.

(13:32). Furthermore, Jesus' being the Lord puts him on the side of God rather than that of Moses and Elijah.

Jesus' belonging to the *heavenly* realm is further supported by the white shining clothes, which "no one *on earth* could bleach" (9:3). The motif of white, shining clothing recalls the depiction of heavenly beings in Jewish and early Christian texts.[44] In Mk 16:5, three women encounter a man in white clothes at the empty tomb who clearly represents an angelic being. The Ancient of Days in Dan 7:9 and the angel in Mt 28:3 have clothing as white as snow. Also in Rev 15:6 and 19:14, angels are clothed in clean and pure white linen. In Jewish mysticism, the one who ascends into heaven has to be transformed into an angelic nature and this transformation includes receiving a glorious garment.[45] In view of this, both Elijah and Moses can be understood to have acquired heavenly citizenship like angels. If this is how Mark and his readers understood Elijah and Moses, then can the glorified bodies of Moses and Elijah represent what the righteous (suffering) ones are expected to receive after their resurrection (cf. Dan 12)? [46]

It is striking that Mark mentions only the change of Jesus' clothes during his transfiguration (metamorphosis), but his transfiguration account does not provide much information about what the transfigured feature of Jesus itself looks like. However, the Transfiguration should not be interpreted as only his clothes whitened, but it is supplemented by the bright heavenly clothes. Considering that both Matthew and Luke contain a reference to the alteration of the face of Jesus on the basis of the Mosaic glory on the face, Mark seems to have removed it from his tradition in order to overcome Mosaic typology in his theological understanding of Jesus. Or, if it is not found in Mark's tradition, both Matthew and Luke are filling out Mark's gap, probably by drawing upon orally transmitted knowledge about the Transfiguration.[47]

Already in mid-19th century, David Friedrich Strauss noted similarity between the Transfiguration and the stories of Moses in the Sinai tradi-

---

[44] A. Collins, "Mark and His Readers," 400. Even in the Greco-Roman texts, gods are claimed to put on white garments with bright light.

[45] Jarl E. Fossum, *The Image of the Invisible God* (Göttingen: Vandenhoeck and Ruprecht, 1995), 83–84.

[46] I think this is very likely. First, as I previously mentioned, the Transfiguration is related to Jesus' prediction that some will experience the Kingdom of God in power (Mk 9:1). And, Mk 9:1 rhetorically functions to support Jesus' prediction of the Son of Man's coming at the Parousia (8:38). Jesus claims that at the Parousia, he will come as the Son of Man in his Father's glory with the *holy angels*. Then, Moses and Elijah may represent these angels who inhabit heaven as its citizens. Second, later Christian writings such as *Apocalypse of Peter* and *Treaty on the Resurrection* consider the bodies of Moses and Elijah as what the resurrected believers will acquire in heaven.

[47] For the oral transmission of the Transfiguration, see Bovon, 370.

tion.[48] The primary parallels are found in two different passages of Ex 24:1–18 and Ex 34:29–35, both containing Moses' theophanic experience. In the Judaism of Mark's time, the two theophanic occurrences are often merged into one. For example, Pseudo-Philo places the event of Ex 34:29–35 immediately after that of Ex 24:15–18 (*Bib. Ant.* 11:15–12:1).[49] J. Jeremias further articulates similar aspects of parallels as follows:

Mark		Exodus	
9:2a	six days	24:16	six days
9:2a	three disciples	24:1, 9	Aaron, Nadab, and Abihu
9:2b	ascent of mountain	24:9, 12–13	ascent of Sinai
9:2b–3	Jesus' transfiguration	34:29	Moses' glory on the face
9:7b	God' presence in the clouds	24:15–16, 18	God's presence in the clouds
9:7b	God's voice from the clouds	24:16	God's voice from the clouds

In addition to these parallels, J. Marcus adds one more motif, astonishment: just as the Israelites are astonished when they see Moses' glorious face (Ex 34:29–35), so also is the crowd astonished at seeing Jesus, after he descends the mountain (Mk 9:15).[50] It is beyond doubt that the Mosaic typology with his glorious transformation is crucial for the narrative framework of the Transfiguration. However, Mark tries to surpass the Mosaic typology by describing Jesus as someone far superior to him as God's Son and by attributing the glory to Jesus as something permanent, though hidden, against that of Moses which he temporarily receives after his encountering with God.

It is indisputable that Jesus' transfiguration takes advantage of both Jewish apocalypticism and the tradition of Moses' glorious transformation in the Sinai traditions. However, some differences between them should not be missed. First, in the Jewish apocalypticism, a human being ascends into heaven and as a result acquires a new garment, which is a sign of heavenly citizenship. However, Jesus in our text does not ascend into heaven, but instead, Moses and Elijah (and God in the clouds) descend to meet Jesus on the mountain, which is halfway between heaven and earth. Furthermore, Jesus' radiant garments do not tell us that he is currently acquiring a heavenly citizenship at the very moment of his transfiguration. But instead, it reveals his divine identity by manifesting what he has been hiding. In this sense, the genre of the Transfiguration better fits into epiphany than enthronement or apotheosis.

---

[48] Even before Strauss, the interpretation of the Transfiguration in the light of the Mosaic glory tradition in Exodus has a long history in Christian Interpretation. For more on this, see Dale C. Allison, *The New Moses. A Matthean Typology* (Minneapolis: Fortress, 1993).

[49] Marcus, *The Way of the Lord*, 81–82; and E. Schweizer, *The Good News According to Mark* (Atlanta: John Knox Press, 1970), 82.

[50] Marcus, 82–83.

Second, in relation to the Sinai tradition, while Moses' face shone after his meeting with God (Exod 34), Jesus' face is not mentioned here at all. Rather, his whole appearance is transfigured in the beginning of the event before God's appearance, not after hearing God's voice, as is the case of Moses. Furthermore, in Exod 24 and 34, it is God who reveals His Glory on the mountain and with whom Moses was talking; and Moses' glory is a reflection of God's glory, not something inherently belonging to him. But at the Transfiguration, it is not God but Jesus with whom Moses is talking; and although Jesus' glory is relational to God his Father (Mk 8:38), it is not God's glory but Jesus' transfigured glorious appearance that stands at the center of the epiphany event. The glorious description of God's appearance, which is the most crucial element of the Theophany, is never mentioned at the Transfiguration. God only reveals His voice from the cloud.

If we can call the genre of the Transfiguration Theophany, the Theophany is here totally focused upon the transfigured glorious Jesus. God is hiding Himself in a cloud until He gets a chance to speak. Does this imply that Jesus is taking over some prerogative of God in the Hebrew Bible by becoming a visual content of Theophany? Or, does Mark understand the transfigured Jesus as the visible manifestation of the invisible God, which finds its parallel in Paul's understanding of Christ as God's image and glory (2 Cor 4:6)? And thereby, does Jesus stand in unique relationship with God, transcending Moses as God's divine Son? I think all their answers are affirmative in Mark's understanding of Jesus. Already in Mk 2:10, the Markan Jesus makes a claim for a prerogative of forgiving sins on earth, which is only attributed to God in the Hebrew Bible. This claim of Jesus is considered a blasphemy from the perspective of Jewish scribes in the first century (2:6–7). In Mk 1:2–3, Mark identifies Jesus with the Lord, which is God's unique title in LXX. Jesus' election of the twelve apostles as representatives for Israel is similar to God's election of the twelve tribes in the Hebrew Bible. Jesus' walking on the sea (Mk 6) finds its parallel in Job 9:8, where God alone can control the waves of sea. Also, the three disciples' responding with fear to the transfigured Jesus is the most typical literary topos in the epiphany of gods (cf. Mk 4:41; 5:15, 33; 9:32; 10:32). All of them put Jesus on the same divine side of reality as God.

2.2.5 The Genre of the Transfiguration and the Secrecy Motif

I would like to compare the Transfiguration with the ideas of epiphany and metamorphosis in antiquity for two main reasons. First, the Sinai and apocalyptic traditions cannot fully exhaust the meaning possibility of Jesus' transfiguration, despite their common aspects. Second, Mark understands

Jesus to belong to the heavenly realm as God's Son who is higher than the angels in the heavenly hierarchy. The idea that a deity has a divine form and appears in visibly perceptible forms to human beings is found in Greek religion. In the Homeric epics, gods walk on earth in their own or other forms and intervene in human affairs. They also continually take and change forms.[51] For Homer, these appearances are mostly for the heroes of his epics, and those forms are often familiar ones to the humans who see them.[52] The Homeric *Hymn to Demeter* tells how Demeter, a queen among the goddesses, disguised herself in the form of an old woman and is again *transformed* to the divine state of being in order to reveal her identity to her human employer.[53] Ancient novels and legends also tell of the presence of gods, spirits and heroes appearing on earth in bodily forms.[54]

In the Hellenistic Roman world, the phenomenon of metamorphosis developed into a literary genre, as is shown in Ovid, Apuleius, and Ps.-Lucian. Proteus is well-known for his ability to take different forms. Sometimes, magicians are said to invoke spiritual beings to appear in visible form and to receive their divine strength.[55] The idea that gods have their own forms and can temporarily take human forms for communication with human beings, though challenged or sublimated in philosophy,[56] is current throughout antiquity.

In this kind of anthropomorphic presentation of gods in antiquity, the term metamorphosis (a noun from the verb form μεταμορφόω) comes to mean "to remodel" or "to change into another form," predominantly in its passive or middle form.[57] The simplest meaning of the term *epiphany* may be a manifestation of a deity in his/her glorious form. Epiphany can occur either through direct revelation of deity, presumably descending from heaven, or through metamorphosis from human form into divine form. Since gods can take multiple forms through metamorphosis, they can be called

---

[51] E.g., Aphrodite (Hom. Hymn. Ven., 81ff), Demeter (Hom. Hymn. Cer. 275ff), Dionysus (Hom. Hymn. Bacch., 2ff), and Athene (The Odyssey).

[52] J. Behm, "μορφή," in *TDNT*, ed. G. Kittel (1967), vol.4, 747.

[53] I borrowed this example from Adela Yarbro Collins, "Mark and His Readers: The Son of God among Greeks and Romans," in *HTR* 93 (2000), 91.

[54] Cf. Ovid *Metamorphoses*, VIII, 626ff (visit of Jupiter and Mercury to Philemon and Baucis); and Cic. Nat., II.12.6.

[55] E.g., Preis. Zaub., XIII, 581ff; IV, 3219ff; and IV, 1174ff.

[56] Robin Lane Fox, *Pagans and Christians* (New York: Alfred A. Knopf, Inc., 1987), 110; and B. C. Dietrich, "Divine Epiphanies in Homer," *Numen* 30 (2004), 69. See also Walter Burkert, *Greek Religion*, trans. John Raffan (Cambridge: Harvard University Press, 1985).

[57] Behm, 755.

polymorphous. For example, in *The Odyssey*, Athena the goddess appears in different forms to help her favorite hero, Odysseus:[58]

And Athena drew near him *in the form of young man*, a herdsman of sheep, one most delicate, as are the sons of princes. In a double fold about her shoulders she wore a well-wrought cloak, and beneath her *shining feet* she had sandals, and in her hand a spear. (XIII.221–25; *Italics are mine*)

Shortly after, she again metamorphoses from man to woman in front of Odysseus:

And the goddess, flashing-eyed Athena, smiled, and stroked him with her hand, and changed herself to *the form of a woman*, comely and tall and skilled in glorious handiwork. (XIII.287–90).

In response to these polymorphous appearances of Athena, Odysseus expresses his frustration that he can never know whether he is in the presence of the divine:

It is hard, goddess, for a mortal man to know you when he meets you, however wise he is, for you take *whatever shape* you want. (XIII.312–14)

I would like to mention two things from these examples in regard to Jesus' transfiguration in Mark. First, while the divine can disguise themselves in human forms, their divinity cannot be fully covered by those human forms – their divine power shines through human confinements. For example, when Athena draws near to Odysseus in the form of a young man, her feet still shine brightly. Likewise, in the Markan narratives, while his human disciples cannot grasp who he really is, Jesus' divine power and identity cannot be missed by the demonic powers: "Whenever the unclean spirits saw him, they would fall down before him and shout, 'You are the Son of God!'" (Mk 3:11).

Second, divine metamorphosis in the case of epiphany is described through an idea of dazzling brightness. The radiant light emanating from the divine body is the most common topos of epiphanic metamorphosis (cf. *Homeric Hymn* to Demeter, 275–80). The shining garments are another way of expressing the radiant light of the divine body, since the ancients found it difficult to describe the glorious divine body.

What does the glorious body of the divine look like? Answering this question, Jean-Pierre Vernant argues, "the powers that act upon the inside scene in order to move and animate it, find on its outside extensions that

---

[58] I am borrowing this example and the following one from Candida R. Moss, "The Transfiguration: An Exercise in Markan Accommodation," *Biblical Interpretation* 12 (2004): 69–89.

permit them to enlarge their field of action and to reinforce their effects."[59] When the gods create Pandora, they create her body and ornaments in the same way that will make this body "operative." This provisioning of Pandora's clothing is integrated into her anatomy to compose the bodily physiognomy of a creature. All the precious accoutrements of the heroes and gods, such as the lion's skin on Heracles' shoulders, Ajax's bow, Peleus' javelin in Achilles' hand, and the thunderbolt brandished by Zeus, are also efficacious symbols of divine powers.[60] Likewise, Mark's description of the transfigured Jesus' "dazzling white" garments as "no fuller *on earth* can bleach them" (Mk 9:3) may demonstrate for ancient readers Jesus' divine identity and his glorious divine body. The Markan Gentile readers will consider without difficulty the transfigured Jesus as a divine being or god walking on the earth in a modest disguise.

There may arise questions about Mark and his readers: How familiar are they with these Greco-Roman notions of epiphany and metamorphosis? Are the Jewish Christian readers of the group also able to understand Jesus in this way? After Martin Hengel, there seems to be a scholarly consensus that the whole Mediterranean world was thoroughly Hellenized in Mark's time, though with different degrees and local particulars. It is certain that these ideas were also available to Mark and his readers as parts of their cultural norms. Even in the Hebrew scripture, although Israelites are proscribed from producing images as related to the worship of Yahweh and from making any attempt at a sensual objectification of the divine form, God and angels often appear among Israelites in human forms.[61] The interpretation of the Song of the Sea in the Mekilta de-Rabbi Ishmael is an example of how some Jews in the Tannaitic period (and earlier) understood God's appearance on earth in the forms of warrior, elder, and the Ancient of Days as the expression of His divine favor for Israel.[62]

---

[59] See Jean-Pierre Vernant, *Mortals and Immortals: Collected Essays*, ed. Froma I. Zeitlin (Princeton, N.J.: Princeton University Press, 1991), especially section V of the chapter entitled, "Mortals and Immortals."

[60] Ibid.

[61] Although they often have to be understood in a metaphorical sense, God is described as a Warrior in the Sinai tradition and the Ancient of Old Days in Daniel 7, and there are many references to God as a being who has a face, ears, eyes, nose, mouth, lips, tongue, arms, back, etc. Also in Ezekiel 1:26, God's glory appears as "someone like human being." Metaphor has no meaning, unless it has a conceptual correspondence in real life situation.

[62] Mekilta de-Rabbi Ishmael is the earliest Midrash on Exodus which was compiled in the Tannaitic period, the time of rabbis who produced the Mishna, from about the first to the third CE. See Daniel Boyarin, *Intertextuality and the Reading of Midrash* (Bloomington & Indianapolis: Indiana University Press, 1990), viii; and Menahem Kahana, "The Editions of the *Mekilta de-Rabbi Ishmael* on Exodus in the Light of Geniza Fragments," *Tarbiz* 45 (1986): 515–20.

Already in Second Temple Judaism, Hellenistic Jewish writers have captured these Greco-Roman metamorphosis ideas.[63] For example, Tobit (3–2 BCE) describes how the angel Raphael was sent to earth to heal those who prayed.[64] Tobit 3.16–17 considers Raphael's commission as a heavenly event which God initiates as a response to human prayers. Raphael's commission results in his appearance in human form to Tobias and others, yet he remains undetected as a heavenly being until he reveals himself and departs (Tobit 12.15). Tobit describes the moment of Raphael's ascension as when the mediator's identity is revealed (Tobit 12.20). Tobit 12.19 states that people saw Raphael eating and drinking, not for his physical need but because he wanted to conceal his identity – the motif of secrecy! In Tobit, the human form functions to keep the secret of the heavenly mediator who is sent by God to earth. Another interesting point in Tobit is that Raphael is identified as "the Angel of the Lord" (Tobit 12.22). This confirms the fact that the Angel of the Lord in Pentateuch developed from a being indistinguishable from God to one distinguishable with his own distinct name and identity.

Another parallel we should consider is that of the angel Israel in the *Prayer of Joseph* (1CE). This prayer describes the angel Israel as the angel who manifested himself in Jacob.[65] The angel Israel descended and lived among humans and was called Jacob. He forgot his heavenly identity, but Uriel came forth and told him who he was. He is "the Angel of God," "the first born," and "the power that stands before the face of the Father." What is important in the *Prayer of Joseph* is that a preexistent heavenly mediator descended and lived as a human being.[66] It is interesting to note that already in the Hebrew Bible, the angel of the Lord descended from

---

[63] Martin Hengel already challenged the dichotomy made by the history of religions school between Aramaic-speaking Palestinian Judaism and Greek speaking Hellenistic Judaism in the Diaspora. He documented in detail how even the Jews in Palestine experienced enormous amount of Hellenization in his monograph, *Judaism and Hellenism: Studies in Their Encounter in Palestine during the Early Hellenistic Period*, 2 vols. (Philadelphia: Fortress, 1974).

[64] Concerning more discussion of Tobit, see Jonathan Knight, *Disciples of the Beloved One* (Sheffield: Sheffield Press, 1996), 146–48; and Charles A. Gieschen, *Angelomorphic Christology* (New York: Brill, 1998), 135–36.

[65] [*Prayer of Joseph* 1–9] "I, Jacob, who is speaking to you, am also Israel, an angel of God and a ruling spirit. Abraham and Isaac were created before any work. But I, Jacob whom men call Jacob, but whose name is Israel, am he whom God called Israel, which means a man seeing God, because I am the firstborn of every living thing to whom God gives life. And when I was coming up from Syrian Mesopotamia, Uriel, the angel of God, came forth and said that I had descended to earth and I had tabernacled among men and that I had been called by the name of Jacob..."

[66] The *Prayer of Joseph* was preserved by Origen in his *Commentary on John* (2.31) in the context of his presentation of John the Baptist as the incarnate angel.

heaven and dwelled among Israelites in order to guide them throughout the journey in wilderness (Exod 23:20–23). This text is exactly where Mark is appropriating the Sinai tradition of Moses for his description of the Transfiguration. It is striking that God commands Moses and Israel to "obey his [the angel of the Lord's] voice" (ἀκοῇ ἀκούσητε τῆς φωνῆς). God asserts that He put His name in the angel of the Lord (Exod 23:21). In this text, God's name is also hidden and kept in secrecy.

I mentioned above how the glistening garments of angels help Mark's portrayal of the transfigured Jesus as one of the kind belonging to the heavenly realm. The angelic parallels further help us understand the Transfiguration story in two ways. First, as Simon Gathercole argues, the unique expression of "I have come + purpose" appears many times in Mark in order to sum up the entirety of Jesus' mission from God.[67] According to Gathercole, the expression is exclusively found in Jewish descriptions of the angelic missions (twenty four times) and speaks of the divine origin of the angels. He further argues on the basis of its exclusive use in the angelic missions that just as the angels are commissioned by God from heaven, so is Jesus.

Second, the motif of secrecy in Mark has an affinity with the notion of a deity or an angel disguising him/herself as a human being. In this line of thought, when Jesus appears again in a human form after God's own testimony (Mk 9:8), Mark tells us that his mission has not been accomplished yet and therefore, his identity should be kept hidden until the resurrection, which signals the end of his earthly mission (Mk 9:9–10). Just as Raphael's true identity is to be revealed at the moment of his coming to heaven in Tobit, so also is Jesus' identity to be revealed after the accomplishment of his earthly mission at the resurrection. The major difference between the Markan Jesus and Tobit along with other angelic parallels is: Jesus' glorious identity can only be revealed through his accomplishing the paradoxical mission of suffering and death.

The secrecy motif is also a part of Mark's own literary resolution for the tension between his literary structure in narrative and his personal post-Easter theological perspective regarding a historical event in the past.[68] In other words, although Mark and his community now understand the risen Jesus as the exalted Son of God, the full truth about him cannot be revealed prematurely before the Markan narrative reaches its climax of the crucifixion and resurrection. In the Markan narrative, however, Jesus is

---

[67] Simon Gathercole, *The Preexistent Son: Recovering the Christologies of Matthew, Mark, and Luke* (Grand Rapids, Mich.: W.B. Eerdmans, 2006), 107–18. For Bovon's understanding of it as a technical term for Messiah and others' critic of his position, see Gathercole, 107 and 118.

[68] On the secrecy motif and relevant bibliography, see Marcus, *Mark,* 526–27. cf. William Wrede, *The Messianic Secret,* trans. J.C.G. Greig (Cambridge: J. Clarke, 1971).

such a powerful figure that the secrecy about his identity cannot help being breached by God (1:11; 9:7), demons (1:24; 3:11; 5:7), and a Gentile centurion (15:39). Also for the Markan community in the post-Easter period, it is impossible for the separation between Jesus "then" and Jesus "now" to remain neatly in place. It is unavoidable for them that Jesus "then" in the narrative keeps reflecting Jesus "now."[69]

2.2.6 God's Voice and the Son of God

Responding to Jesus' transfiguration, Peter proposes erecting three tents for the transfigured Jesus, Moses and Elijah. Whether these tents are for eschatological dwelling places for God or places for communication with heavenly beings,[70] Mark states that Peter's offer is improper: "For he did not know what to answer" (Mk 9:6). According to Mark, while Peter correctly recognizes the eschatological importance of the event by proposing three tents for the heavenly three, his proposal is improper for two major reasons. First, Jesus should not be honored by being ranked with Moses and Elijah – Peter is still far from recognizing Jesus' true status. In Mark's scheme, although Moses and Elijah constitute heavenly citizens as angelic beings, there is still a divine hierarchy between the Father, the Son, and angels (cf. 12:35–37). Second, Jesus should not stay on the mountain in a glorious status, but go down to accomplish his mission of suffering and death.

Peter's response creates a dramatic tension, that is not resolved until the voice of Godis heard. Immediately after Peter's wrong proposal, God Himself appears hidden in a cloud and witnesses Jesus' Sonship, "This is My beloved Son, listen to him!" (9:7). God elevates Jesus far beyond both Moses and Elijah by confirming the divine filial relationship (cf. Heb 1:4–5; 3:3).[71] There is a sharp contrast between Peter's response to the transfigured Jesus and God's own interpretation of the transfiguration. The readers have seen in Mark a human Jesus in hostility, homelessness, and suffering, while observing his miraculous power as well as the demons' submission to him. Here at the Transfiguration, God offers a special revelation of the truth about Jesus and his identity from His divine perspective. In this way, Mark portrays Jesus as the paradoxical combination of the heavenly Son with glory and the earthly human in misery. At the Transfiguration, the Christological debates regarding Jesus' identity during his Galilean ministry are finally resolved by God, and Jesus prepares his way

---

[69] Marcus, 527.

[70] Ulrich Luz, 398.

[71] According to Howard Kee, Peter's suggestion is again to bypass the suffering and death, seeking a shortcut to the Kingdom of God. Kee, "The Transfiguration in Mark: Epiphany or Apocalyptic Vision?," 147–48. I agree with Kee.

to Jerusalem in order to accomplish the divinely planned program of suffering and death (δεῖ in Mk 8:31).

The designation of Jesus as the Son of God has long been discussed in historical-critical research.[72] It is beyond question that in the Jewish traditions, the title Son of God has a connotation of kingship. Israelite kings are understood to rule the nation as the representative of God, as is shown in Ps 2:7, "You are My Son; today I have begotten you."[73] Ps 2:7 goes beyond the oracle of 2 Sam 7:14, where the king is legally adopted by God as His royal executive. The kingship in Ps 2:7 presents the Israelite king as the bearer of the personal presence of God Himself, especially through the

---

[72] Wilhelm Bousset took the position that the oldest community of Jesus' followers in Palestine described him as the "Servant of God" in a messianic interpretation of the servant songs in Second Isaiah (Wilhelm Bousset, *Kyrios Christos: Geschichte des Christusglaubens von den Anfängen des Christentums bis Irenaeus* [Göttingen: Vandenhoeck & Ruprecht, 1935]). He furthered the view that the "Servant of God" was in tension with the Son of God, which originated on Greek ground, in the Greek language, not Palestine. Bousset's argument cannot stand due to three reasons. First, his argument is based upon an old dichotomy between Aramaic speaking Palestine Judaism and Greek speaking Judaism of Diaspora, which Martin Hengel overcomes. Second, already in the Hebrew Bible, the Son of God is found to be closely related to God's calling of the Jewish kingly messiah as His Son, let alone angels and Israelites. Third, in Second Temple Judaism, the Isaianic Suffering Servant is related to the heavenly Son of Man, as is attested in Enoch, 4 Ezra, and the Wisdom of Solomon, and is further colored with qualities of the kingly Messiah. Against Bousset, Ferdinand Hahn argued that the motif of divine Sonship in its distinctive form practically belongs to the royal Messianism within the sphere of Palestinian late Judaism (Ferdinand Hahn, *The Titles of Jesus in Christology*, trans. Harold Knight and George Ogg [Cambridge: James Clarke & Co., 2002], 284). According to Hahn, this title experiences a transformation in the Hellenistic Jewish Christianity and refers to the exalted Jesus whom God adopts and installs in his heavenly office. In the Hellenistic Gentile Christianity, the divine Sonship, which was thought of as primarily *functional*, becomes a *physical* divine Sonship, and later, the ideas of pre-existence and incarnation are developed to reinforce this kind of physical familial sense of divine Sonship for the title Son of God. Although I am still oscillating over whether Hahn's strict division between Hellenistic Jewish and Hellenistic Gentile Christianity can explain the location of the Markan Christology in the complex development of early Christian Christology, Mark seems to attest to Jesus' Sonship not as functional, but as physical/familial, which Hahn ascribes to Hellenistic Gentile Christianity. Although Hahn's division between Palestinian late Judaism, Hellenistic Jewish Christianity, and Hellenistic Gentile Christianity sounds too schematic, his insight regarding the evolution of the idea of the Son of God from functional to physical correctly explains the trajectory of the title Son of God.

[73] For the use of Ps 2:7 and Gen 22 in the Transfiguration story, see William Richard Stegner, "The Use of Scripture in Two Narratives of Early Jewish Christianity (Matthew 4.1–11; Mark 9:2–8)," in *Early Christian Interpretation of the Scripture of Israel*, ed. Craig A. Evans and James A. Sanders (Sheffield: Sheffield Academic Press, 1997), 121–40.

endowment of the Spirit.[74] The kingship in Ps 2:7 is claimed to be influenced by the Egyptian conception of the king's descent from God.[75] The phrase, "today I have begotten you," however, provides the title Son of God with a high interpretation that transcends the boundaries of juridical adoption by implying a divine lineage to God as His Son in a physical and filial sense (cf. Mk 12:35–37).[76] This explains the main reason for its relative unpopularity as a messianic title in Judaism, except in the Qumran community.[77]

H. Kee argues that the Son of God is a synonym for Christ, the kingly Messiah.[78] This claim may be true for the Jewish traditions, but as Bousset, Hahn, Zeller and many others have already claimed, the original Jewish idea of the Son of God experiences transformation in its wider Hellenistic context, especially Greek gods and the Roman imperial cult.[79] According to A. Collins, those familiar with Greek polytheistic traditions are likely to associate the Jewish term Son of God with terms like "son of Zeus" and "son of Apollo."[80] Greek poets, such as Hesiod and Homer, honor Zeus as the father of both gods and human beings. The Olympian gods are members of a family dynasty and sons/daughters of Zeus. Also, "divine men," such as heroes, warriors, and wise men, are considered to physically descend from individual gods and are claimed to perform miracles and to exhibit supernatural knowledge due to their divine nature.[81] After their miraculous death, they join the society of gods in heaven as immortal beings. For example, Dionysus is the son of Zeus by a mortal mother and is considered to be a god from birth. Heracles is also a son of Zeus by a human

---

[74] H. J. Kraus, *Die Königsherrschaft Gotes im Alten Testament* (Tübingen: J. C. B. Mohr, 1951), 69.

[75] H Klein, "Zur Auslegung von Psalm 2: Ein Beitrag zum Thema: Gewalt und Gewaltlosigkeit," *TBei* 10 (1979): 63–71; and O. Keel, *The Symbolism of the Biblical World: Ancient Near Eastern Iconography and the Book of Psalms* (New York: Seabury Press, 1978), 248. I will further discuss this point later, when I examine the concept of the divine men.

[76] Marcus, *Way of the Lord*, 71.

[77] For Jewish avoidance of the title Son of God, see Hans-Jörg. Steichele, *Der Leidende Sohn Gottes.* (Münchener Universitäts-Schriften; Regensburg: Pustet, 1980), 139–47.

[78] Kee, "The Transfiguration in Mark: Epiphany or Apocalyptic Vision?," 140.

[79] See Dieter Zeller, "New Testament Christology in its Hellenistic Reception," *NewTestStud* 46 (2001): 312–33.

[80] Collins, "Mark and His Readers: The Son of God among Greeks and Romans," 86.

[81] Betz, "Jesus as Divine Man," 46–69. And see also Dieter Zeller, "The ΘΕΙΑ ΦΥΣΙΣ of Hippocrates and of Other Divine Men," in *Early Christianity and Classical Culture*, ed. John T. Fitzgerald (Leiden; Boston: Brill, 2003), 46–69.

mother; and after his tragic death and apotheosis, he is received into the circle of the Olympian gods.[82]

In the context of the Greek ruler cult and the Roman imperial cult, it is significant to notice that kings and imperial rulers are often portrayed as descendents from gods and therefore called "son of god" or "son of Zeus." At the oracle of Ammon in the Libyan desert, Alexander the Great is called "son of Ammon," "son of Zeus" in Greek. The Ptolemies, the successors of Alexander in Egypt, claim the same title. After the official deification of Caesar in 42 BCE, Octavian begins to call himself officially *divi filius*, that is, "son of a god." Augustus' official name in Greek documents also includes the expression, "son of god."[83] In the context of the imperial cult, the term "son of god" has the implication of the true ruler of the known world with physical/filial relationship with a god. Since the Markan readers lived with these Greek and Roman ideas in their everyday lives, the title "Son of God" was likely to deliver the divine filial connotation to the transfigured Jesus as well as the cosmic ruler-ship of the world (cf. Mk 15:39).

The title Son of God has important ramifications for Mark's understanding of Jesus. Mark begins his Gospel narrative by calling it "the gospel of Jesus Christ, the Son of God" (1:1)[84] and then, in Jesus' baptism, God witnesses to Jesus' Sonship, "you are My beloved Son, in you I am well-pleased" (1:11). Ironically, it is not disciples but demons who first recognize Jesus as the Son of God (1:34; 3:11). It is not until the Transfiguration that God reveals Jesus' divine Sonship to human beings, three disciples, but they still do not get it (9:6). It is a Gentile centurion who is the first human being to recognize Jesus as the Son of God (15:39). Whether his acclamation of Jesus as the Son of God is genuine or not, in the Markan narrative it plays the significant role of expressing Markan gentile readers' understanding of Jesus that way.

It is also noteworthy in Mk 15 that Mark makes a shift from peopl mockingly calling Jesus the Jewish kingly messiah to the centurion's confession of him as the Son of God. In 15: 2, 9, and 12, Pilate calls Jesus the King of the Jews, and in response to Pilate, the Jews in the Markan narrative request to crucify him (15:15). And then, Roman soldiers mockingly shout, "Hail, King of the Jews!" (15:18) and the inscription of the charge at the scene of Jesus' death on the cross reads, "The King of the Jews" (15:26). Even those who are crucified with Jesus insult him, saying, "Let

---

[82] Hesiod, *Theogony*, 940–44, 950–55; and *Homeric Hymns* 1, 26.

[83] I am borrowing these examples from Collins, "Mark and His Readers," 94–95.

[84] There is a textual issue regarding this passage. For this, refer to Bruce M. Metzger, *A Textual Commentary on the Greek New Testament*, 2nd ed. (Stuttgart: Deutsche Bibelgesellschaft; United Bible Societies, 1994), 62.

this Christ, the King of Israel, now come down from the cross, so that we may see and believe" (15:32). By the centurion's confession, "[t]ruly, this man was the Son of God" (15:39), Mark asserts that all these claims of understanding Jesus as the kingly messiah of Israel are simply wrong.

I would like to mention two more things regarding Mark's understanding of the title Son of God or Jesus as God's Son in terms of his belonging to the heavenly realm. First, as is already implied in Ps 2:7, the title Son of God in Mark transcends the concept of Israelite king as an adopted juridical figure. This becomes clear that it is not human beings but God and demons who acknowledge Jesus as the Son of God. In the Markan portrayal of the demons' confession, the Son of God is claimed to belong to a heavenly realm rather than to an earthly realm. Even though Mark does not fully discard the Jewish conception of the Son of God as the king of Israel, Mark's portrayal of Jesus' messiahship is a more heavenly and cosmic type than the traditional human royal or warrior type. In Mark, it is not with human powers or kings, but with demonic powers that Jesus engages in battles.

The heavenly origin of the Sonship is further clarified in Mk 12:35–36 and Mk 14:62. In the former passage, Jesus argues against the scribes, asking, "[w]hy does David call the Christ his Lord?" In this passage, the Markan Jesus claims that he is David's Lord, not his descendant. In the latter passage, Jesus equates the Son of God with the exalted Son of Man who is a cosmic judge in the Danielic tradition – this equation is already found in our current text of the Caesarea-Philippi Transfiguration context. Furthermore, as we have already seen above, when the Gentile centurion confesses that Jesus is the Son of God, he considers Jesus not as an Israelite king, but as the true ruler of the known world.[85] The idea of the Son of God as an Israelite king has no implications to the Gentile centurion. It is, I think, Mark's intention to put the Son of God in the mouth of the Gentile centurion, so that he may emphasize the cosmic kingship of Jesus over the known-world, including the Roman empire.

Second, in his use of the title Son of God or the expression God's Son, Mark develops a physical and familial relationship between God and Jesus as Father and Son, especially through the expression "My *beloved* Son" (9:7). This is already shown in God's confession in Jesus' baptism. The term "beloved," which is an allusion to Gen 22:2, 12 and 16, accompanies an affectionate aspect rather than a legal aspect.[86] The concept of legal adoption is inadequate to describe God's confession in Jesus' baptism,

---

[85] For more on the Son of God in Gentile culture, see Adela Collins, "Mark and His Readers: the Son of God among Greeks and Romans," 85–100.

[86] Bovon, 129.

"You are My *beloved* Son, in you I am well-pleased" (1:11).[87] Instead, Jesus' Sonship is revealed by means of a metaphor of one of the closest human relationships, father and son.[88] Jesus, as the Son of God, shares in God's glory and God's effective opposition to the cosmic powers. Jesus participates in God's power and the same glorious reality as the Father (cf. 8:38). In this sense, Jesus' Sonship in Mark is more ontological than functional, or of the same kind as that of Israel or the king in the Hebrew Bible.[89] This "Christian" notion of Jesus as God's Son in a filial sense is further clarified in the parable of vineyard (Mk 12:1–11).[90] In this story, while the prophets of the Israelite traditions, including Moses, are called "servants," Jesus is designated by God "a beloved Son" (12:6). Jesus becomes superior to all the heroes of the Israelite traditions and is expected to experience death by his own people, just as Abraham's beloved son Isaac was about to experience death. Mark makes a clear distinction between the angels, the Son and the Father, and elevates Jesus farther than the angels in the heavenly hierarchy (8:38; 13:32).

Finally, the phrase, "listen to him" (v.7b), which follows God's confession of "This is My beloved Son," is an allusion to Deut 18:15 which prophesizes Prophet-like-Moses in an eschatological sense. It is likely that Jesus in the early "Christian" traditions has been claimed to be like Moses or the fulfillment of the Prophet-like-Moses, being the same kind as Moses (cf. Peter's sermons in Acts 3 and 7). In Mark, however, Moses and Elijah are subordinated to Jesus, as they are not called God's Son, and Peter's proposal of building tents for them is rejected by God. Mark turns Jesus into a being different from Moses or a being much more superior to him. This tendency prevails throughout the rest of the New Testament. For example, in 2 Cor 3:1–18, Paul compares Jesus and Moses in terms of the glory and subordinates Moses' temporal glory to Jesus' permanent glory. The author of Hebrews theologically argues that Jesus is the Son of God, while Moses is merely His servant (Heb 3:1–19), similarly to Mark's parable of the vineyard on a narrative level. This unknown author exalts Jesus above the angels, arguing "to which angels did He [God] ever say, 'You are My son, Today I have begotten You'?" (Heb 1:4–5). In this theological scheme, Mark has the expression "listen to him" acquire a new rhetorical function: God draws readers' attention to Jesus' previous teaching in 8:31–38 of the suffering and death for him and his disciples. In this sense, John

---

[87] Marcus, 71.

[88] See also, Bovon, 129–30.

[89] See also, Gathercole, 274–76.

[90] This Sonship equates Jesus with the cosmic judge, the Son of Man in 8:38; "the Son of Man...comes in the glory of *his Father.*" Who else in Mark can call God his Father, except Jesus?

P. Heil is right to call the Transfiguration "the pivotal mandatory epiphany."[91]

2.3 The Transfiguration in Its Immediate Context (Mark 8:22–9:13)

In this part of the discussion, I would like to expand what I observed above in its immediate context of the Caesarea-Philippi Transfiguration cycle (8:22–9:13). At the Transfiguration, Jesus is claimed to transcend the *spatial* boundary between heaven and earth. Jesus' transfigured appearance and God's testimony assert that Jesus, a mere human being on earth, is the heavenly Son of God. In the immediately preceding context of Mk 8:31–38, this Jesus, who is *presently* a mere suffering human being, is guaranteed to reappear as the judge of the world in the *future* Parousia. In his grandiose portrayal of Jesus, by identifying him with the heavenly Son of Man and the Son of God, Mark makes him overcome the temporal and spatial limits to which all human beings are subjected.

This Son of Man concept indicates the Markan understanding of Jesus' vindication by God after his suffering and death. It also shows how Mark is involved in an apologetic defense of Jesus' tragic death. The Son of Man also guarantees his disciples' vindication, as long as they show their loyalty to him by following him in the way of the Suffering Servant. Their vindication results from their submission to a form of discipleship – the path of suffering and death. As a result, I argue that the Markan Christological claim in the Caesarea-Philippi Transfiguration episode connotes for its readers multiple implications: *eschatological, anthropological, ecclesiological, apologetic* and *vindicating*. If we take into consideration that Mark wraps these episodes with two miracles of healing the blind and thereby puts a sharp contrast between the restored sight of the blind and the disciples' spiritual blindness (8:22–26; 10:46–52), we may add to this list another Markan emphasis on the *spiritual* power of recognizing the truth of Jesus' identity. It is interesting that later Christian writings develop some of these implications in a much more expanded way so that they make the story speak to their communities in particular ways.

2.3.1 Literary Analysis of the Caesarea-Philippi-Transfiguration Cycle

My analysis of literary structure of the Caesarea-Philippi Transfiguration context is as follows:

A – Question 1 by Jesus: "who do people say that I am?" (8:27–28)

---

[91] Heil, *The Transfiguration of Jesus.*

Answer 1: "John the Baptist, Elijah, and one of the prophets"
– Question 2 by Jesus: "who do you say that I am?" (8:29)
Answer 2: "the Christ"

(*Silence Motif* (8:30))

B – Jesus' Teaching 1: "the Son of Man's suffering, death and resurrection" (8:31)
    (Peter's inappropriate response and Jesus' rebuking him (8:32–33))
– Jesus' Teaching 2: "the disciples should follow Jesus' example" (8:34–37)

    C – Jesus' prediction: the Son of Man's coming at the Parousia for
        vindication/judgment (8:38)
    C' – Jesus' prediction: the proleptic manifestation of the Kingdom of God in
        power to *some* (9:1)

B'– Divine manifestation 1: "Jesus' transfiguration" – *visible* (9:2–4)
    (Peter's inappropriate response (9:5–6))
– Divine manifestation 2: "God's interpretation/command" – *audible* (9:7)
    Jesus' human appearance with his disciples (9:8)

(*Silence Motif* (9:9–10))

A' – Question 1 by the disciples: "Why should Elijah come first?" (9:11)
    Jesus' answer 1: "to restore all things" (9:12a)
– Question 2 by Jesus: "Why should the Son of Man suffer and die?" (9:12b)
    Jesus' answer 2: "Elijah came and suffered" (9:13)

In this literary structure, we can see that the Caesarea-Philippi Transfiguration episode begins with Jesus' two questions, followed by disciples' answers (A) and also ends with two questions with answers (A').[92] And the silence motif connects both A and B, and A' and B'. In the middle of both B and B', Peter's inappropriate responses stand and connect what comes prior and what follows by raising tension which should be resolved by Jesus and God, accordingly. All these literary features manifest literary correspondence between Jesus' teaching (B) and the Transfiguration (B'). Agreeing with Heil, I already argued that God's command "listen to him" (9:7) draws the readers' attention to Jesus' two-fold teaching.

How does the Transfiguration reinforce Jesus' previous teaching? While the B part consists of Jesus' two-fold teaching, the B' part has two-fold divine manifestation with two-fold human response. Jesus' two-fold teaching in B is followed by his prediction of the Son of Man's coming with glory at the Parousia (C) and similarly, the two-fold divine manifestation at the

---

[92] Considering that all the answers of people regarding Jesus' identity are prophetic figures, the appearance of Moses and Elijah at the Transfiguration tells the readers that Jesus is not one of the prophetic figures, but a much superior being to them, "God's Son" (9:5).

Transfiguration is preceded by Jesus' prediction of the proleptic manifestation of the Kingdom of God to *some* (*C'*). In above discussion, I already
argued that the Transfiguration is fulfilling Jesus' prediction of manifestation of the Kingdom of God to some on a limited scale (*C'*) and thereby,
further supports the credulity of Jesus' previous prediction of the Parousia
with its cosmic manifestation on a full scale (*C*). The Son of Man's coming
at the Parousia (*C*) heightens the importance of Jesus' two-fold teaching by
showing the listeners' eternal fate, either vindication or judgment. If my
literary analysis is correct, then the Caesarea-Philippi Transfiguration episode contains a kind of chiastic structure.

In support of my claim that there exists a close literary correspondence
between Jesus' two-fold teaching (*B*) and the Transfiguration (*B'*), Ulrich
Luz, in his analysis of the Matthean version of the Transfiguration, maintains that the Transfiguration story is a narrative reprise of Jesus' previous
teachings, but does not present in detail how the former recaptures the latter in the overall structure of the Caesarea-Philippi Transfiguration episode.[93] John P. Heil, having analyzed epiphanic stories in the Jewish traditions, calls the literary genre of the Transfiguration "pivotal mandatory
epiphany." Heil argues that the Transfiguration narrative puts the dis-
ciples/readers in a final dramatic tension as to whether they will listen to
Jesus' teaching in 8:31–38. While Heil's point is insightfully correct, he
puts too much emphasis on the phrase "listen to him" (9:7), neglecting the
visual aspect of the transfigured Jesus as well as God's calling him His
Son. As we have already seen in the above analysis of the Transfiguration,
both Jesus' divine manifestation of his Sonship and God's witness to it
should receive as much emphasis as or even more than the phrase "listen to
him." As a result, Heil does not spend much space on analyzing the metamorphosis as the manifestation of the divinity and the concept of the Son
of God.

In regard to the issue of genre, I propose that the epiphany with metamorphosis phenomenon best fits into that of our Transfiguration story. It
should, however, be recognized that the story is a result of multiple literary
genres and concepts, such as the Mosaic transformation ideology, angelol-
ogy, divine man, and apocalyptic tradition. As a result, one single category
of literary genre may not fully exhaust the implication of the Transfiguration story. On the other hand, the story can best be grasped only in the
combination of these various literary genres and concepts, while acknowledging their contribution to the sophisticated message of the story with
their own distinctive features.

As we can see from my literary analysis, there clearly exists an issue of
Christology in that cycle; the whole context is wrapped up by two Christo-

---

[93] Luz, 394.

logical questions both in the beginning (8:27–28) and at the end (9:11–13). In this context, all four questions can be summarized into one for its readers: what does it mean to say that Jesus is Christ (cf. Mk 1:27; 4:41; 8:27; 12:10)? As is shown in Peter being rebuked, there is a wide gap between asserting that Jesus is the Christ and the awareness of what his messiahship involves.

In the *B* part, Mark answers the question through Jesus' teaching that his messiahship can only be understood through the path of suffering and death. Without understanding the destiny of the Messiah in this paradoxical path, Peter's confession of Jesus as the Messiah is only partially correct.[94] In the Transfiguration story (*B'*), God orders the disciples as well as the readers to "listen to" Jesus' previous teaching in the *B* part, revealing that Jesus' messianic identity can only be fully understood within his destiny of suffering and death. Although Jesus accomplished what had been predicted by the Hebrew scriptures regarding God's messianic agent in the salvation history, he is more of a divine origin from the heavenly realm. Jesus' divine origin becomes manifest by his transfiguration, the angelic attendants and God's own testimony. By reappearing in a human form at the Transfiguration, Jesus reconfirms God's message that he has an unfinished mission, which he already taught in the *B* part.

Overall, we cannot miss Mark's emphasis that the readers should not misunderstand Jesus as Moses, or Elijah, or one of the prophets.[95] In Mark's mind, the coming of Elijah,[96] which is the first (πρῶτον in 9:11, 13) in a series of divinely determined events of the salvation program (δεῖ in 8:31), which has been already laid down in the scriptures (καθὼς γέγραπται in 9:12–13), refers to John the Baptist. In three occurrences, Mark links closely the fate of Jesus and that of John the Baptist (2:18–20; 6:14–29; 9:12). It is also clear that Mark further wishes to extend this progression of suffering and death from John the Baptist to Jesus to the church in the form of true discipleship. Mark makes an ecclesiological application of his Christological understanding of Jesus' life to the lives of the believers.

2.3.2 Jesus as the Suffering Servant and the Son of Man

In the Caesarea-Philippi Transfiguration episode, Mark uses other key messianic concepts of the Son of Man and the Suffering Servant in addition to the Son of God and Prophet-like-Moses. Since Jesus' teaching in

---

[94] See also Kingsbury, "The 'Divine Man' as the Key to Mark's Christology – The End of an Era?," 255–56.

[95] Kingsbury, 254.

[96] In 1 Kgs 19:2, Elijah is expected to have suffering and martyrdom. In general, the prophets are expected to suffer due to hardness of the listeners in the Hebrew Bible.

Caesarea-Philippi is based upon these two terms of the Son of Man and the Suffering Servant, I would like to explain how they are interpreted in Jewish traditions as well as in the particular way that Mark applies them to his narrative discourse, both similarly and differently.

In the Markan narrative story, the Son of Man, who is uniquely a *heavenly* messiah in Jewish traditions, has both heavenly and earthly aspects, which are situated in and unfolded through the drama of salvation history. Mark specifically uses the term Son of Man in his description of both Jesus' earthly ministry (2:10, 28) and his eschatological role as the cosmic heavenly judge (8:30–38). From the beginning of his ministry, Jesus is claimed to be the Son of Man *on earth*. It is important to note that Mark insists on putting the term Son of Man in the mouth of Jesus – none ascribes the expression to Jesus except for himself, and that this concept especially appears when he predicts his suffering and death (8:31; 9:9–12, 31; 10:33–34, 45). In this way, Mark correlates the concept of the Son of Man, who is also God's Son (8:38), to the concept of the Suffering Servant in Second Isaiah.[97] In the Caesarea-Philippi-Transfiguration cycle, all these messianic concepts are intertwined through the idea of Jesus' divine Sonship and collapsed into one historical figure, Jesus.

The term Son of Man seems to have multiple implications in the Jewish traditions.[98] First, in the Psalms, the expression "son of man" (בןאדם in Hebrews) appears 14 times, mostly designating man or human being in contrast to God. For example, Ps 8:5 reads, "What is *man* that you thought of him? And the *son of man* that you cared for him?" While this is based upon an idea that the first Adam before the fall was like a king in his status, it comes to be interpreted Christologically by early Christians, as is shown in Hebrews 2:6. Second, in Ezekiel, God addresses the prophet Ezekiel as "son of man" about 93 times, expressing either the prophet's mere human status before God, or his high status as prophet distinct from the rest of the people.[99] Third, the term "Son of Man" appears with a theologically charged aura, especially in apocalyptic literature during the latter part of Second Temple Judaism. At the root of this apocalyptic understanding of the Son of Man as the heavenly judge is the occurrence of the Son of Man (בר אנש in Aramaic) in Dan 7:13. It is out of question that this term Son of

---

[97] There arises a question: is this combination of the Suffering Servant and the Son of man a Markan creation? Or is there ongoing Jewish tradition about that combination? I will demonstrate in the following discussion of the Son of Man that the latter is more likely.

[98] Bovon shared with me his recent observation that while the expression "Son of Man" appears without articles in LXX, it does so with articles in Mark and its parallels. This tells me that in the New Testament, the Son of Man becomes a technical term, exclusively referring to Jesus.

[99] George E. W. Nickelsburg, "Son of Man," in *Anchor Bible Dictionary*, VI:137.

Man with its Danielic context has influenced so many Jewish and Christian texts in terms of their messianic expectations and that its Markan occurrences have something to do with this third understanding of it.

Daniel is considered to have been written around persecution of the Jews by Antiochus IV Epiphanes (2 BCE). In Daniel 7–12, two different stories are told on two levels: *on earth*, the holy ones of God are persecuted by an evil worldly king and the temple is being desecrated; *in heaven*, the Ancient of Days and the Son of Man, His eschatological agent, defeat the beasts in the court scene, the fourth beast of which stands for Antiochus IV Epiphanes. In Dan 7:13–14, the Son of Man appears and is presented to the Ancient of Days in order to receive dominion, glory and kingship. This heavenly figure the Son of Man is a distinct figure with his own identity rather than a symbolic metaphor for God's people, although he stands in solidarity with the suffering people of God and functions as their heavenly patron. What is important for our text is: (1) the Son of Man is not an earthly messianic figure, but a heavenly eschatological figure; (2) the Son of Man is provided with royal qualities and prerogatives, which often refer to the Jewish kingly messiah in the Hebrew Bible; (3) the Son of Man stands in solidarity with God's people, (4) who are currently experiencing suffering and persecution – *suffering servants*!; and (5) the context is about the desecration of God's temple in Jerusalem by evil rulers.

The idea of the Son of Man is very prevalent in later apocalyptic writings and appears vested with the character of the Suffering Servant and the kingly Messiah. For example, in Wisdom of Solomon 1–6, written around the turn of the era, although the term Son of Man does not appear in this text, it is significant to notice that the story of the righteous one is drawing upon the vindication of the Suffering Servant in Second Isaiah. The righteous one is called "Son of God." Also the occurrence of the judgment scene parallels to that in 1 Enoch 62–63 and 46, which is similar to Dan 7. In this text, both concepts of the kingly Messiah and the Suffering Servant are combined into one person, but it is not the Davidic kingly messiah, but the vindicated Suffering Servant with royal features who becomes an eschatological judge.[100]

In 4 Ezra (1 CE), the two visions in chs. 11–12 and 13 parallel the scene in Dan 7 and present a coming of "someone like the figure of a man" who is also called "the Anointed One," The phrase "the Anointed One" may refer to the Davidic kingly messiah. This figure gathers God's people and is called by God "My Son" (13:32, 37, and 52). It is interesting that this figure, like the man in 4 Ezra, is also a heavenly pre-existent figure similar to the Son of Man in Daniel and has been kept for ages (4 Ezra 1:26, 52); and he exhibits qualities of the kingly Messiah. The same idea of the tran-

---

[100] Nickelsburg, 140.

scendent figure with kingly connotation, "My Anointed One," is also attested in 2 Baruch (1 CE). These three texts with Daniel show that in Second Temple Judaism, there exists an exegetical tradition of combining such Jewish traditions as the Son of Man, the Son of God, and the Suffering Servant, into one *heavenly* agent of God. [101] Since it is already in Second Isaiah that the Suffering Servant, "my chosen one with whom I am pleased," is declared by God to become the eschatological judge who will bring forth justice, which belongs to the task of the kingly Messiah, we can safely say that the combination of the three ideas in apocalyptic writings is a further development of the Isaianic idea (cf. Isa 42:1–4).

Although it is hard to date the text of the Parables of Enoch (1 Enoch 37–71) – scholars date it from 2 BCE to 1 CE,[102] here we can see another striking example of the combination of those three messianic traditions into one heavenly preexistent figure. 1 Enoch portrays this heavenly figure on the basis of languages found in Dan 7 (the Son of Man), Is 11 and Ps 2 (the Son of God, the Davidic King), and Is 42, 49 and 52–53 (the Suffering Servant). This transcendent figure is also called in 1 Enoch "the Righteous One," "the Chosen One," "the Anointed One," and "this/that Son of Man." He appears as an eschatological heavenly judge of his enemies, "the kings and the mighty," and is claimed to be preexistent. In this sense, this tradition may also be influenced by the Jewish speculation about the Wisdom tradition (cf. Prov 8; Sir 24; Bar 3:9–4:4; 1 Enoch 42).[103]

At the judgment scene of 1 Enoch, however, we see a deviation or development from Daniel, since it is not the Ancient of Days, who takes a role of judge in Dan 7, but the Son of Man who stands as an eschatological judge. The Son of Man is both vindicating his people and condemning their persecutors (cf. 1 Enoch 47). It is also noteworthy that in the last chapter (ch. 71) of the present form of the text, the Lord of the spirits greets Enoch and identifies him as the Son of Man. In the previous chapters of 1 Enoch, the Son of Man has been a distinct figure from Enoch and there has been no hint at his earthly existence. The Son of Man has been kept in secret by God and has been the object of Enoch's revelation.

While scholars like John Collins and G. Nickelsburg correctly consider this identification of Enoch with the Son of Man as a later addition, this idea shows a striking parallel to Jesus in the Caesarea-Philippi Transfigu-

---

[101] Ibid.

[102] E. Isaac, "1 Enoch," in *The Old Testament Pseudepigrapha*, ed. James H. Charlesworth (New York; London; Toronto; Sydney; Auckland: Doubleday, 1983), 5–89. George Nickelsburg in *1 Enoch: A Commentary on the Book of 1 Enoch* (Minneapolis, MN: Fortress, 2001) dates "the book of parables" to the late 1 BCE.

[103] Nickelsburg, 139.

ration context.[104] In our current text of Mark 8:27–9:13, Jesus, a Jew on earth, is claimed to be the Son of Man, eschatological heavenly judge; furthermore, he is called God's Son and is expected to take the role of the Suffering Servant in his fate of death and vindication. Mark finds it appealing to adopt the Danielic Son of Man for his description of Jesus, not least because there is a parallel in the Danielic context and his own, especially desecration or destruction of the Temple in Jerusalem and the context of suffering. All of these Jewish messianic ideas help Mark understand Jesus' earthly and heavenly ministry as God's suffering Son and the eschatological judge. Mark puts in Jesus' teaching what these ideas tell about his ministry, and the Transfiguration confirms both *visually* and *audibly* this Markan understanding of Jesus' fulfilling these roles.

It is, however, interesting to note a Markan deviation or development from this line of Jewish thought that at the judgment scene, the Markan Jesus as the Son of Man will not condemn kings and powers, but will decide the fate of the believers depending upon their attitude toward the earthly Jesus and his words (Mk 8:38).[105] It is striking that Mark does not mention the Son of Man's judgment of the Roman rulers for the destruction of the Temple. Why is he silent about it? Does Mark see it as a part of God's plan, in which the Roman rulers play a certain role? Mark's answer to the question may be affirmative (cf. 13:1–2; 15:38).

Ferdinand Hahn has already maintained that in Mark there are three types of sayings regarding the Son of Man: about the *earthly* activity of the Son of Man, about the suffering of the Son of Man, and about the *heavenly* activity of the Son of Man, which belongs to the Danielic tradition.[106] It is interesting that Mark does not try to prove that Jesus is the Danielic Son of Man, but instead, presupposes it. Even in the other synoptic gospels, the term Son of Man is never explicated in any way, but is always assumed that Jesus' hearers will understand perfectly what he means when he speaks of "the Son of Man."[107] In Mark, Jesus treats the Son of Man as a known quantity and does not hesitate to refer this term to himself (2:10; 8:31–38; 14:62). The heavenly Son of Man with its Danielic echo is clearly found in 8:38, 13:26, and 14:62. The Son of Man in Mark is an exalted heavenly Judge as well as a cosmic ruler, but he has to go through humiliation in the unfolding drama of God's saving act of His people. In Mark

---

[104] This later addition might be a Jewish counterargument against the Christian claim for Jesus as the Son of Man. See John Collins, "The Heavenly Representative: the 'Son of Man' in the Similitude of Enoch," in *Ideal Figures in Ancient Judaism*, ed. John J. Collins and George E. W. Nickelsburg (Chico, Calif.: Scholars Press, 1980).

[105] According to Kee, the Danielic apocalyptic Son of Man cannot be separated from the assurance for the righteous sufferers (Kee, 149).

[106] Ferdinand Hahn, 41.

[107] Marcus, The Way of the Lord, 528.

16:19, Mark argues that Jesus' prophecy of the Son of Man sitting at the right hand of God (14:62), which is a Christian conflation of Ps 110:1 and Dan 7:13, is accomplished in the exalted Jesus right after his resurrection and ascension.

Having equated Jesus with the exalted Son of Man, which probably represents a post-Easter understanding of the risen Jesus by the Jerusalem church, Mark further extends this term in a retrospective way to the earthly Jesus even before his resurrection. In Mk 2:10, Jesus as the Son of Man claims that he has *authority* to forgive sins on earth – in Daniel, the Son of Man is claimed to receive *authority* from the Ancient of Days at the eschatological judgment scene. In 2:28, Jesus as the Son of Man is also the Lord of the Sabbath. In our current text of the Caesarea-Philippi Transfiguration context, Jesus claims that he, as the Son of Man, should suffer, die, and resurrect, taking the role of the Suffering Servant.

Regarding Mark's appropriation of the Suffering Servant tradition, it is interesting to note that it is in three major predictions of his suffering, death and resurrection that the Markan Jesus exclusively calls himself the Son of Man (Mk 8:31; 9:9–12, 31; 10:33–34, 45). In 8:38, the Son of Man who walks in the path of the Suffering Servant is further designated as the Son of God: he will come in his "Father's Glory!" As I have already shown above, just as the three key Jewish messianic ideas are often merged into one figure in Jewish apocalyptic traditions, so also do they appear in a combined way into a historical Jew, Jesus, in our current text of Mark. Mark sees Jesus accomplish these messianic roles in the different phases of his life in the salvation history.

2.3.3 Jesus' Return as the Son of Man in His Father's Glory

In the Hebrew Bible, the term glory (כבוד) in relation to God implies what makes God impressive to man as the force of His self-manifestation.[108] In LXX, the term glory (δόξα) means "divine honor," "divine splendor," "divine power," and "visible divine radiance," and refers to God's divine nature or essence or mode of being either in its invisible or its perceptible form.[109] For example, in Ez 1:26 and 28, God's glory appears in human form, sitting on the throne. In our text, the term "glory," while it represents the divine mode of being similar to the Hebrew Bible, is also a relational term, since it functions as a window onto the father-son relationship. In Mk 8:38, Mark claims that the Son of Man will return at the Parousia with his "Father's glory." When Jesus makes these promises, he is claiming his participation in the same glory as God's and thereby, in the divine mode of

---

[108] G. Kittel, "δόξα," in *TDNT*
[109] Ibid., 244.

being. In the following Transfiguration story, Jesus' transfigured appearance with glory visually demonstrates his sharing with God's divine mode and God's voice audibly witnesses Jesus' divine Sonship.[110] This idea of Jesus' participation in God's divine mode of being has been explained by Mark in many ways: Jesus is called the Lord (1:2–3), shares the same prerogative of forgiving sins as God, belongs to the heavenly hierarchy with angels and is recognized by demonic powers. In the Caesarea-Philippi context, however, Mark nails a point to the wall that the glory should be revealed not through magnificent manifestation of miracles or power, but through his suffering and death.

In the Jewish traditions, glory has often been given to humans, so that they become the heavenly citizens along with angels. Similar to biblical heroes and the righteous martyrs who are expected to participate in the glory, Jesus' faithful followers are also guaranteed to share in this glory, when he collects his people at the Parousia (cf. 13:27). In this line of thought, Jesus' glory stands as the paradigm of glory that he will bestow upon all his faithful followers. Moses and Elijah can be understood as scriptural examples which have already experienced this glory.[111] The idea of Jesus' glory as the paradigm of glory in Mark is almost identical to Paul's understanding of Christ as God's glory and the image after which believers are being transformed "from glory to glory" (2 Cor 3:18).

2.4 Conclusion

In conclusion, first, in our current text of the Transfiguration, the concepts of Israelite eschatological Messiahs – Son of God and Prophet-like-Moses – are claimed to be fulfilled in Jesus, but at the same time, Jesus transcends those earthly exalted leaders through the notion of the divine Sonship. While at first sight the appearance of Moses and Elijah makes Jesus a fulfillment of Jewish messianic hope, their angelic status and Jesus' transfigured appearance with white clothes quickly reinforce his heavenly belonging. This point is further strengthened by the sharp contrast between the heavenly three and the earthly three, and reaches its climax in God's own testimony to Jesus' Sonship. In this way, Mark can claim that Jesus has a heavenly origin and constitutes the heavenly council with God and the angels (cf. 13:32). In the Markan scheme, Jesus is not only a human or human messiah from below, but also a divine being from above. He not only transcends the division between the *heavenly* and the *earthly*, but also merges the two different realms in his life and ministry.

---

[110] See also Bovon, 375.

[111] See also McGuckin, *The Transfiguration of Christ in Scripture and Tradition*.

Second, it is now indisputable that the Mosaic transformation story in Exodus provides the narrative framework for the Transfiguration story and that Jewish apocalypticism colors the story with various apocalyptic ideas. However, the idea of Jesus' transfiguration can be further explained by the metamorphosis phenomenon with a result of epiphany. This idea finds its parallels in the stories of Hellenistic gods and angels. In this line of thought, Jesus is described as the divine being who disguises his true identity in a human form until he accomplishes his mission in the paradoxical way of suffering and death. In the Markan scheme, it is only after resurrection that there comes a full revelation of his true identity to the public which has been kept hidden in his human form (9:8–9; cf. 13:27).

Third, having placed the Transfiguration in its immediate context of Caesarea-Philippi, I have shown how the Son or the Son of God has been intertwined with the Son of Man and the Suffering Servant of Isaiah. As is often the case in the Jewish apocalyptic writings, these three concepts are intermingled and collapsed into one historical figure – in this case Jesus – so that they contribute to Mark's description of Jesus' life and ministry with their own distinctive features. According to Mark, Jesus' earthly life is what Isaiah prophesized in terms of the destiny of the Suffering Servant and his heavenly life will become manifested through his role as the eschatological judge, the Son of Man. The concepts of the Son of Man and the Suffering Servant help Mark portray Jesus as someone who overcomes the temporal division of present-future, since Jesus *now* on earth is the very heavenly Son of Man who will come at the Parousia in the *future*. In Jesus, both present and future events coexist, only waiting for their accomplishments according to the divinely planned program. In this way, the two-level Christology at the Transfiguration, which overcomes the spatial division of heaven and earth ("from below" and "from above"), comes to transcend the temporal division of *present* and *future* as well. As a result, Mark situates Jesus at the juncture where the two axes of time and space are eschatologically colliding through the merger of the three important Christological ideas of the Son of Man, the Suffering Servant, and the Son of God into the *historical* Jesus.

Fourth, I also want to emphasize that the literary correspondence between Jesus' teaching at Caesarea-Philippi and the Transfiguration is reinforced through the concept of the Father-Son relationship and their sharing in the same glory. In his teaching, Jesus has promised to come with his Father's glory at the Parousia and the Transfiguration confirms the promise in a way that his transfigured appearance manifests the glory and God the Father testifies back to their filial relationship. In this sense, the Transfiguration is the visual confirmation of his divine Sonship and the validity of his promise of future coming as the Son of Man in glory.

The story further *validates* Jesus' teaching regarding the divine necessity of both his and his disciples' suffering and death, especially through the rhetorical power of God's own command, "listen to him" (9:7). In this process, Mark defends the necessity of Jesus' Crucifixion by putting it in God's salvation plan, something both necessary and predicted ahead of time by Jesus himself as well as by the scriptures (cf. 8:31–33; 9:30–31; 10:32–34) – *apologetic* function.[112] The Markan Jesus also clarifies for the readers what his followers should do in order to be his genuine disciples; they should follow their hero Jesus in the same path of humiliation – *ecclesiological* function! Moreover, Jesus guarantees that his disciples, if they faithfully follow the path of suffering and death, will also experience similar vindication to that of the Son of Man. The vindication will include their glorious transfiguration and sharing in the same glory as Jesus and the Father – *ontological* function![113] Though at the Transfiguration, they see this promise fulfilled on a limited scale, at the Parousia, they will see all of this happening on a cosmological scale – *eschatological* function![114]

Fifth, regarding the function of the Transfiguration for the Markan community, Jesus' teaching of his suffering and death as an expression of the genuine discipleship may tell us about the historical situation of the Markan community around the milieu of the destruction of the Temple in Jerusalem (cf. 13:1–2).[115] The frequent use of the Danielic Son of Man may further hint at this historical milieu. Facing the subsequent persecutions, they have to not only defend Jesus' tragic death on the cross, but also explain their own experience of suffering. Mark not only ascribes Jesus' Crucifixion to what God had preplanned as a necessary part of the salvation program, but also links Jesus' fate with that of his followers (8:34–38; 9:42–48; 10:17–31, 38–39) by putting them in the mouth of Jesus in the form of prophecy. In this way, Mark apologetically defends the importance of Jesus' death on the cross and at the same time, deliberately prepares his readers for their own martyrdom.

---

[112] See also Gundry's discussion of Mk 8:32–38 in Gundry, *Mark: a Commentary on His Apology for the Cross*.

[113] It is a popular concept in Jewish apocalyptic thought that the righteous will be in glorious status like angels (cf. Dan 12:1–5). It is, therefore, very likely that the Markan text can convey this idea to its readers. This idea is clearly seen in Mt 19:28. Also according to Hebrews 12:22–23, the glorified righteous sufferers will constitute the heavenly citizens along with the angels.

[114] It will be interesting to note in the following chapters that later Christian writings tend to emphasize one or two aspects of them in their own appropriations of the Transfiguration story, in spite of whether they are drawing upon the synoptic version or an oral version.

[115] Marcus, *Mark*, 28–37.

Finally, regarding the development of the Transfiguration story, in the following chapter, I would like to examine Paul's account of the believers' transformation in 2 Cor 3. Since Paul is a generation earlier than Mark, it is hard to prove contacts between Paul and Mark. However, there seem to exist some common elements between them: the use of the Mosaic transformation story in Ex 34, the occurrence of the rare Greek term μεταμορφόομαι, Jesus' glory as the paradigmatic glory, and glorification through suffering. Since in antiquity, it is expected that the followers of a hero will share his destiny, and gods or goddesses can transform their loved ones into a glorious status, the comparison between the two accounts of Paul and Mark, one for the believers' transformation and the other for Christ's, respectively, can still be interesting to students of the New Testament. In spite of the fact that there is no literary dependence between them, they can still tell us how early believers developed two different yet similar accounts out of the same Mosaic story in light of the Jesus event and the Hellenistic metamorphosis phenomenon, and in two distinctive forms: one in a narrative form and the other in a theological discourse form.

Chapter 3

Paul and the Transfiguration:
Analysis of the Believers' Transformation in 2 Cor 3 and Its Comparison with the Markan Transfiguration Story

3.1 Introduction

In this chapter, I examine 2 Cor 3 to explore how and why Paul interprets the believers' transformation in the New Covenant on the basis of Jewish traditions about the transformation/glorification of Moses. I will demonstrate that Paul, in the face of his opponents' claim that he must submit a recommendation letter to the Corinthian church (2 Cor 3:1; 4:2), argues that the transformed Corinthians are Christ's recommendation letter for his own apostleship (3:3). In this argument, Paul clearly draws upon the Exodus story of Moses' glorious transformation along with its later Jewish interpretive traditions and compares them with the believers' general transformation. According to Paul, the believers' transformation results from their encountering the glorious Lord when listening to the gospel message.

It is interesting to note that the Mosaic transformation story in the Exodus context functions as the main framework for 2 Cor 3 and for the Markan Transfiguration story. This observation begs a comparison of Paul to Mark, in order to explore to what extent they share a common story line based on Moses' experience at Sinai. Furthermore, their comparison may shed light on how early Christians interpreted the Moses' story through their new lens of the Jesus event. Also, observation of the common themes may help us understand how Mark and Paul interpret the Moses' transformation story similarly or differently in their contexts. This will reveal their exegetical commonalities as well as distinct differences.

For this purpose, after having discussed in brief the identity of Paul's opponents, I will first examine the Jewish traditions regarding the Mosaic transformation. Because I hypothesize that on the basis of the Mosaic transformation story there may be common plots or themes behind both Paul and Mark, I will try to explore what kinds of Jewish exegetical traditions regarding Moses' glorious transformation are available in the Second Temple Judaism.

Second, I will offer an exegetical analysis of 2 Cor 3 in order to see how Paul takes advantage of those traditions in the new context of the Corinthian correspondence, especially regarding a debate about his ministry as well as his apostleship. I conclude that Paul puts Moses' experience of God's theophanic glory parallel to both his own experience of encountering the risen Christ and to the believers' general experience of the Lord's glory in the New Covenant. In doing so, Paul claims that the transformed Corinthians are his recommendation letter from Christ and that they function as his ministerial credentials.

Finally, I will compare the transformation accounts of both Paul and Mark and demonstrate that Moses' transformation experience in the Exodus story functions as a common major storyline for both. However, I further suggest that before the Mosaic transformation reaches the hands of Mark and Paul, early Christian thinkers reinterpreted it for their Christological claim in a way that Jesus as God's Son with His glory goes beyond Moses. Interestingly, both Paul and Mark commonly manifest some ideas which do not appear in Moses' transformation traditions, including the Suffering Servant and the glorious Son of Man. This leads me to speculate that they share a Jesus tradition where his glory is interpreted in light of the Suffering Son of Man. I suggest that these two ideas – (1) the comparison between Moses and Jesus through the glory and (2) the interpretation of Jesus' glory in light of the Suffering Son of Man, lie behind the two accounts of Paul and Mark, the believers' transformation and Jesus' Transfiguration, respectively.

3.2 The Identity of Paul's Opponents in 2 Corinthians 3

As for the identity of Paul's opponents, which is closely bound up with the issue of literary integrity, numerous books and articles have addressed this issue.[1] In 1973, J. J. Gunther isolated about thirteen identifications of

---

[1] For a comprehensive discussion of the integrity of 2 Corinthians and a relevant bibliography, see Victor P. Furnish, *2 Corinthians, The Anchor Bible* (Garden City, NY: Doubleday & Company, Inc., 1984), 30–48; Linda L. Belleville, *Reflections of Glory* (JSNTSup 52; Sheffield: JSOT Press, 1991); Victor P. Furnish, *2 Corinthians, The Anchor Bible* (Garden City, NY: Doubleday & Company, Inc., 1984); and Murray Harris, *The Second Epistle to the Corinthians, The New International Greek Testament Commentary* (Grand Rapids, Michigan: William B. Eerdmans Publishing Co., 2005). There has been immense scholarly debate about the literary integrity of 2 Corinthians as well as about the identity of Paul's opponents in general, and about Paul's hermeneutical approaches in 2 Cor 3 in particular. As for the first general issue of literary integrity, 2 Cor has been claimed to be a combination of several separate Pauline letters: (1) of six letters by J. Weiss (Johannes Weiss, *Earliest Christianity. A History of the Period A.D. 30–150*, trans. Frederick C. Grant, 2 vols. [New York: Harper, 1959]), (2) of five letters by G. Bornkamm, being followed by many with some minor adjustments (Günther Bornkamm, *Die Vorgeschichte des sogenannten Zweiten Korintherbriefe* [Heidelberg: Carl Winter,

Paul's opponents that various Pauline scholars had proposed.[2] M. Harris adds six more,[3] and Furnish notes that most proposals can be listed under one or another of three broad headings: some kind of (1) Judaizers, (2) Gnostics,[4] and (3) Christian propagandists from a Hellenistic-Jewish background.[5] The large quantity of books and articles makes us wonder how these scholars can draw so much from such limited evidence now available to us in 2 Corinthians. Accordingly, in this chapter, I will analyze 2 Cor 3 on its own terms as Paul's own perspective, without imposing any theory of opponents on the text.

Within the immediate context of 2 Cor 3, Paul accuses his opponents of peddling the Word of God (2:17), of falsifying that Word by craftiness (4:2) and of boasting "in outward appearance and not in the heart" (5:12). Also, according to Paul, his opponents repudiate him for not submitting a recommendation letter about his apostolic credentials (3:1–3; 4:2; 5:11ff; 6:4) and claim that Paul's message is unclear and veiled (4:3). These descriptions in the first letter of 2 Corinthians correspond well with the profile of the opponents in the second letter (10:7, 10–12; 11:18; 12:11), so we may conclude with some caution that Paul is referring to the same opponents in both letters of 2 Cor.[6]

From the perspective of the opponents, Paul is "out of mind" (5:13) and his suffering as well as his physical weakness only speak against his apostleship (4:7–12; 5:4–10; 7:4–10). It is very likely that these opponents are itinerant preachers from outside, who themselves carry a recommendation letter, possibly from the Jerusalem church.[7] It is also possible that Paul

---

1965]; Helmut Koester, *History and Literature of Early Christianity*, 2 vols. [Philadelphia: Fortress, 1982]), (3) of three letters by Margaret Thrall (Margaret E. Thrall, *The Second Epistle to the Corinthians*, 2 vols., *A Critical and Exegetical Commentary* [Edinburgh: T&T Clark, 1994]), and (4) of two letters by V. Furnish (chs. 1–9 and 10–13), with whom I side. Regardless of which composition theory one agrees with, there seems to be a scholarly consensus on both the Pauline authenticity of 2 Corinthians and the literary unity of 2 Cor 2:14 – 7:4, to which the current text of 2 Cor 3 belongs. Thus, my analysis of 2 Cor 3 will not be much influenced by those partition theories. Also, although 2 Corinthians is a composite letter, all the parts should be considered to be critical sources for the Corinthian correspondence between Paul and the Corinthian church. In addition, all those letters must have been composed within a very short amount of time and are certainly relevant to one another.

[2] J. J. Gunther, *St. Paul's Opponents and Their Background: A Study of Apocalyptic and Jewish Sectarian Teachings* (*NovTSup* 35; Leiden: Brill, 1973).

[3] Harris, *The Second Epistle to the Corinthians*.

[4] I use the term Gnostics as an umbrella term, while acknowledging the danger of its scholarly use without defining it. As for the difficulties of the scholarly use of the term Gnostics, see King, *What is Gnosticism?*

[5] Furnish, *2 Corinthians*, 49.

[6] Ibid., 51.

[7] Belleville, *Reflections of Glory*, 212.

compares his ministry with that of Moses, as his opponents somehow see a strong continuity between their ministry and that of Moses.[8] However, since the text does not provide enough information about the nature of their ministry, we cannot reach a definitive conclusion about how the opponents base their ministry on Moses. In the current text of 2 Cor 3, Paul begins to counterattack them by challenging the concept of recommendation letters. He presents his own ministry of the New Covenant as superior to that of Moses of the Old Covenant, since his Gospel enables the believers to experience transformation, while Moses' Law leaves its readers "in veil" (2 Cor 3:15). In this process, Paul reinterprets for his own sake Jewish biblical as well as post-biblical traditions about Moses' transformation by making use of the Jewish exegetical skills of his day, not without innovating them with his own Christological edge.

3.3 Moses' Propaganda and Jewish Exegetical Traditions on His Transformation

In 2 Cor 3, Paul is not creating a midrashic commentary on Exod 34, nor is his hermeneutics controlled solely by the literary or theological features intrinsic to the scriptural narrative story of Moses.[9] Instead, Paul not only

---

[8] It is important to note that, unlike in Galatians, Paul in 2 Corinthians does not discuss any Jewish rituals such as circumcision. This indicates that Paul's opponents may not be Judaizers.

[9] Scholars have made Herculean attempts at categorizing Paul's use of scripture in 2 Cor 3 according to one or more hermeneutical principles. The most popular label on Paul's hermeneutical methodology in 2 Cor 3 is "Christian Midrash." The origin of this term goes back to the debate between J. Goettsberger ("Die Hülle des Moses nach Exod 34 und 2 Kor 3," *Biblische Zeitschrift* 24 (1924)) and Hans Windisch (*Der Zweite Korintherbrief*, 9 ed. [Göttingen: Vandenhoeck und Ruprecht, 1970]) in 1924, regarding the relationship between 2 Cor 3 and Exod 34. While Goettsberger tries to demonstrate continuity between them, Windisch concludes that Paul's reading of Exod 34 is a freely composed Midrash on Exod 34, motivated by the polemical situation between Paul and the Corinthian church and controlled by his own Christian presuppositions (See Scott J. Hafemann, *Paul, Moses, and the History of Israel* [Tübingen: Mohr, 1995]). Windisch's position has been the most popular among exegetes of 2 Cor 3 and has been followed by numerous scholars with some minor changes, including H. Lietzmann, C. J. A. Hickling, J. D. G. Dunn and A. T. Hanson (For bibliographical information on this position, see Belleville, *Reflections*, 172–73; and Sigurd Grindheim, "The Law Kills but the Gospel Gives Life," *JSNT* 84 (2001): 97–115). It is, however, necessary to make a distinction between Midrash as a literary classification – commentary on scripture – and Midrash as a type of exegesis (Belleville, 172). It is wrong to call 2 Cor 3 "Christian Midrash" in a literary sense as, strictly speaking, Paul is not producing a commentary on Exodus stories, but is reinterpreting them to make his own case in a polemical situation. On the other hand, it is clear that Paul in 2 Cor 3 takes advantage of various midrashic techniques in

appropriates the scriptural story, but also takes advantage of its various interpretive traditions which have already existed in multiple forms in Second Temple Judaism. As I will show later in my exegetical analysis of 2 Cor 3, Paul reinterprets these traditions along with the scriptural narrative through his new lens of the Christ event.

It is now indisputable that Moses was a towering figure in the Hebrew Bible as well as in various forms of Judaism in the Second Temple period. Moses' popularity in 1 CE is well attested in Philo, Josephus and the New Testament.[10] According to John Gager, Moses as lawgiver even captures the attention of the pagan world to the almost complete exclusion of other Jewish figures.[11] In the Jewish social and intellectual climate of the time, Jewish propaganda regarding Moses especially lies in the Sinai event along with his reception of the Law and experience of glorious transformation. It is, therefore, crucial for our purposes to examine Jewish interpretive traditions about Moses' glorious transformation by the time of Paul, especially because Paul draws upon those traditions in his comparison between Moses' encounter with God's glory at Sinai and the believers' experience of

---

his use of the Exodus stories. As for Paul's midrashic techniques, James Dunn and many others have discussed the Pesher-like contemporization in 2 Cor 3:17, "[n]ow the Lord is the Spirit" (James D. G. Dunn, "2 Corinthians 3.17 – 'the Lord Is the Spirit'," *JTS* 21 (1970); also C. K. Stockhausen, *Moses' Veil and the Glory of the New Covenant: The Exegetical Substructure of 2 Cor 3.1–4.6, Anbib* 116 [Rome: Pontifical Biblical Institute, 1989]). Also other scholars have pointed out that in 2 Cor 3:7–11, Paul is concerned with demonstrating the superiority of the New Covenant over the Old or of his own ministry over Moses' by utilizing a principle of *a minori ad maius*, which is similar to Rabbinic *kal wahomer* (e.g., Bernd Kuschnerus, "You Yourselves are Our Letter," in *Metaphor, Canon and Community*, ed. Ralph Bisschops and James Francis [New York: Peter Lang, 1999]; and J. Lambrecht, "Structure and Line of Thought in 2 Cor 2.14–4.6," *Biblica* 64 (1983)). Joseph Fitzmyer contends that it is through free association of ideas by catchwords that Paul moves from the topic of the recommendation letter to a veil on Moses' face, then to the theology of God's glory on the face of Christ (Joseph A. Fitzmyer, "Glory Reflected on the Face of Christ (2 Cor 3.7–4.6) and a Palestine Jewish Motif," *Theological Studies* 42 (1981)). Cf. Siegfried Schulz, "Die Decke des Moses: Untersuchungen zu einer vorpaulinischen Überlieferung in 2 Cor 3:7–18," ZNW 49 (1958): 1–30. This method is similar to the rabbinic logic of *gezera shava* or "inference by analogy." Linda Belleville tries to draw exegetes' attention to the haggadic character of 2 Cor 3:12–18. She argues that there is a discernible pattern of "opening statement," "text" and "commentary," and that this kind of haggadic expansion is especially characteristic of the Targumim (Belleville, "Tradition of Creation?," 169). However, I am not convinced that we can put the whole argument in 2 Cor 3:12–18 into a single pattern, without straining the meaning possibilities of the text.

[10] For more on this topic, refer to E. Auerbach, *Moses* (Detroit: Wayne, 1975); J. Bright, *A History of Israel* (London: SCM Press, 1980); G. W. Coats, *Moses: Heroic Man, Man of God* (Sheffield: JSOT Press, 1988); and Meeks, *The Prophet King*.

[11] John Gager, *Moses in Greco-Roman Paganism* (Nashiville: Abingdon Press, 1972).

the Glory – Paul at the Damascus road and the Corinthians through the Spirit's powerful manifestation of the Gospel of Christ.[12]

First of all, in Jewish literature, Moses is remembered as God's unique representative on earth, especially because of his experience of God's Theophanic appearances in the Exodus stories. Moses' encounter with God for the second tablets of the Torah in Exod 34 never stops being reinterpreted by later Jewish interpreters in various forms with multiple implications. It inspires those Jewish writers to emphasize Moses' uniqueness as a mediator between God and Israel and to elevate him as "God's beloved one" (Sir 45.1), "God's chosen one" (*Liv. Proph.* 2.14–15), "God's son" and "one like the Son of Man" of Dan 7 (Ezek. Trag. 96–100). It is at this event that Moses becomes the prophet *par excellence* (Sir 46.1) and is crowned king of Israel (Ezek. Trag. 96–100). Moses' ascent on Mount Sinai is characterized as "heavenly ascent" (Sir 45.5; *Bib. Ant.* 12.1) and Mount Sinai becomes celebrated as the single most important place for God's residence and special revelation.[13]

Second, it is, however, more important for our purposes that Moses is claimed to experience glorious transformation in this event at Sinai. Interpreting the glory on the face of Moses in Exod 34, Philo in *Mos.* 1.158–59 describes Moses' ascent at Sinai as a kind of mystical transformation. According to Philo, Moses enjoys God's presence "in the darkness where God was" and is initiated into the office as king (1.158–59), high priest (2.67–71, 74, 75–76) and hierophant (*Gig. 53–54*).[14] *Mos* 2.70 reads, "he [Moses] descended with a *countenance* far more beautiful than when he ascended...the *dazzling brightness* that flashed from him like the rays of the *sun*." For Philo, Moses' transformation is somewhat similar to an apotheosis of divine men.[15] In *Quaest. in Exod*, Moses is "changed (μετεμορφώθη) from an earthly man into the divine so that such men become kin to God and truly divine" (2.46–47; 2:29). While Philo elevates Moses virtually to a second god, he still restricts Moses to the realm of human beings, thus making him remain within the sphere of divine men.[16] A similar claim for Moses' divinization through the glorious transformation at Sinai is also attested to in Sir 45:2 and in Josephus (*Ant* 3.320).

---

[12] I should also remind readers that in the Markan Transfiguration story, Moses' transformation provides Mark with a narrative framework for Jesus' Transfiguration.

[13] I am borrowing these references from A.D.A. Moses, *Matthew's Transfiguration Story and Jewish-Christian Controversy*, 61–78.

[14] Moses, *Matthew's Transfiguration*, 52.

[15] Meeks, 123; and J. Jeremias, "Moses," in *TDNT* (1967), 850. Although the concept of the divine men has been debated a lot, I think that in that time period, there exists at least a certain pattern of divine men, if not a concrete definition of it. For more on this debate, refer to ch.1.

[16] Meeks, 102.

Third, for Philo, it is because of Moses' function as God's spokesperson that he is allowed to experience the glorious transformation – he does not hesitate to link the splendor of Moses' face with his office as lawgiver (*Mos.* 2.271). Similarly, Josephus claims that Moses is ranked "higher than his own [human] nature" due to his intimate relationship to this "Law of God" (*Ant.* 3.320). The glory on the face of Moses is the very glory of God and the glory accompanies God's offering of the Law in order to confirm the very divine origin of the Law. Furthermore, the glory legitimizes Moses' authority as God's mediatory agent of the lawgiver between Him and His people. In this sense, all the theophanic appearances of God in the Exodus stories may function to give Moses divine credentials for his mediatorial role as God's representative on earth.[17] It is in obedience to Moses and his command that the judgment of God and the demonstration of Israel's loyalty to God become manifest.

Fourth, in some Jewish writings, there seems to exist a parallel between Adam and Moses,[18] which is of special significance for our purposes in that it may illustrate a conceptual background for Paul's Adam Christology (2 Cor 3 and 4; 1 Cor 15; Rom 3–5; Phil 2–3). According to Sirach, Adam "was glorified (ἐδοξάσθη) above every living thing in creation" (49:16) and was given "knowledge" as well as "the law of life" (17:11). Sirach further claims that God established with Adam an eternal covenant and revealed to him His Glory and voice (17:12–13). In this line of thought, the first creation is God's first enactment of the covenantal relationship with human beings by revealing both His Glory and the Law. Similarly, Sirach describes Moses and the Sinai covenant as follows: "God made him [Moses] equal in glory to the holy ones" (Sir 45:2); God also revealed to Moses His Glory (45:3) and "the law of life and knowledge" which was originally given to Adam at the creation (45:5); and God talked to Moses face to face, just as He did to Adam. For Sirach, Moses' experience is exactly the reenactment of the first manifestation of God's glory and the Law at the creation. In this sense, Moses' encounter with God's glory and his receiving of the Law can be seen as a second creation or new creation of His people.[19] However, the scripture attests that Adam's disobedience along with the loss of the glory is followed by the recurring disobedience of the rebellious people of Israel in the wilderness[20] with the result that both Adam and

---

[17] See also, Hafemann, 197; and Newman, 244.

[18] Cf. 1 Enoch 89:44–45.

[19] Hafemann, 433; and Newman, 111–12, 225.

[20] There is an ongoing Jewish tradition that Israelites could not see the Glory on the face of Moses due to their sin of making a golden calf. This idea is again connected to Adam, who after the Fall was not able to talk to God face to face, because he could not stand God's glory. See Belleville, 66; and cf. Hafemann, 371.

Israel break the Law of God. As a result, the Hebrew Scripture promises "the New Covenant" (cf. Jer 31:31–33) in a future eschatological time.[21]

For Philo, when Moses ascended Mount Sinai, becoming god and king, he saw the invisible God and His image in a vision, which is an incorporeal archetypal essence of existing things (*Mos* I.158f). Moses was transformed into the image and became a paradigm for others to imitate. Philo also claims that this image is the Logos which Moses saw on Mount Sinai (*Conf.* 95–97). At Qumran, the faithful covenanters anticipate, in their renewal of the covenant (1 QS 4:23; CD 3:20; 1 QH 17:15),[22] receiving the glory of God that Adam lost. Also in later Samaritan and Rabbinic materials, the light on the face of Moses is the primordial light of Adam. Furthermore, salvation is understood to be the restoration of the glory and the image that Adam lost and the messiah is expected to come with more glory than Adam (cf. Rom 1:23; 3:23; 2 Cor 4:4, 6).[23]

Fifth and finally, as I already mentioned above, Philo presents the transformed Moses after God's image as a paradigm for others to imitate. According to Wayne Meeks, following Erwin R. Goodenough, this concept of transformative imitation is a common topos of the Hellenistic ideology of kingship. The predominant Hellenistic ideology of kingship viewed the ideal king as a personal presence in unwritten universal law.[24] Human beings' transformation modeled after their transformed leader is, however, well attested in Qumran literature.[25] As is well known, the Qumran community applies the Exodus imagery to themselves with the result that their leader, the righteous teacher, takes up the role of Moses.

In the *Thanksgiving Psalms*, God causes His light to shine on the face of the righteous teacher and in turn, his illumined face causes the faces of the many to shine (1 QH 7:6–25; 2:1–19; 2:31–39; 4:5–5:4).[26] The illumination of their faces also affects their hearts, so that the community who believes to live in the New Covenant of Jer 31:31 (CD 6:19; 1 QpHab 2) comes to acquire a renewed understanding of the Mosaic Covenant of Old

---

[21] It is not surprising that Paul is well aware of this line of thought, so that he presents the covenant on the basis of Jesus Christ' death as the promised new covenant of Jeremiah.

[22] I borrow these examples from Meeks, 105. Also for the bibliographical information on this topic and for further Jewish references, see Newman, 225.

[23] For this discussion on the issue of glory in the Samaritan and Rabbinic materials, see Dunn, 100–5; Meeks, 176–285; Belleville, 48–52, 63–72; and Moses, 66–73.

[24] Meeks, 110–11; Erwin R. Goodenough, *By Light, Light: The Mystic Gospel of Hellenistic Judaism* (New Haven: Yale University Press, 1935); and Erwin R. Goodenough, "The Political philosophy of Hellenistic Kingship," in *Yale Classical Studies*, ed. Austin M. Harmon (New Haven: Yale University Press, 1928).

[25] Fitzmyer, "Glory Reflected on the Face of Christ (2 Cor 3.7–4.6) and a Palestine Jewish Motif," 630–44; and Belleville, *Reflections of Glory,* 44–47.

[26] For more references and their analyses, see Fitzmyer, 639–44.

(1 QS 5:7–9). The language of shining, light/glory, covenant and the Law is clearly reminiscent of Exod 34:28–35 and is powerful evidence of ongoing Jewish exegetical traditions about Moses' transformation at Sinai. In the following exegetical analysis of 2 Cor 3, I will show how these Mosaic traditions reappear in order to help Paul defend his ministry of the New Covenant, especially through the idea of the Corinthians' glorious transformation as the divine credential for his genuine apostleship.

3.4 The Transformed Corinthians as Christ's Recommendation Letter for Paul[27]

3.4.1 The Corinthians as Christ's Recommendation Letter for Paul (3:1–3)

Throughout the Corinthian correspondence, Paul's apostleship is challenged by insiders as well as by outsiders. According to Paul, there are divisions within the Corinthian church and each of them argues for its legitimacy by showing its special ties with different apostles or with Christ (1 Cor 1:12–13).[28] In this situation, it is easily understandable that each group may attempt to invalidate the legitimacy of other groups by attacking their apostolic figures. It seems that what Paul in 1 Corinthians is experiencing is related to this kind of power struggle. Some in the Corinthian church try to repudiate Paul's apostleship by comparing his attitude toward financial issue and marriage with that of Peter and the brothers of the Lord (1 Cor 9:1–7). Paul decides not to receive any financial support from the Corinthian church and to remain single, in order to "make the Gospel free of charge" (9:18) and to focus on the works of the Lord without being distracted (7:32). In his climactic apology in 1 Cor 15:1–11, Paul defends his apostleship by claiming that he also saw the risen Lord like the other apostles (cf. 9:1–5). It was not who he is but through the grace of God that he is called to be an apostle. For Paul, the apostleship is closely tied to both Christology and ecclesiology. For example, by utilizing a metaphor of house building, Paul claims that he is a skilled architect who builds with care a building of the church on the foundation of Jesus Christ (1 Cor 3:10–15).[29] In this logic, if the Corinthian church as the building renounces

---

[27] Throughout the exegetical analysis, the Greek translations will be mine, unless otherwise indicated.

[28] It is likely that the real division is between Paul and Apollo, while Peter and Jesus are there for rhetorical purposes. But it is not our concern to determine the historical situation of 1 Corinthians.

[29] Is Paul responding to a tradition similar to the so-called M tradition in Matthew 16, by claiming Jesus to be the foundation, not Peter?

Paul the builder's apostolic authority, then she ends up being self-destroyed.

In 2 Corinthians, Paul's opponents, who came from outside with a recommendation letter, probably from the Jerusalem church,[30] try to repudiate Paul's apostleship by contending that Paul did not present a commendatory letter to the Corinthian church (2 Cor 3:1). Paul, facing his opponents' attack on the apostleship, builds up his credentials on Christological basis by identifying himself as "servant of the Lord" and "aroma of Christ to God" (2:15; 4:5). Furthermore, answering his own rhetorical question, "[w]ho is sufficient for these things?" (2:16), Paul claims that he was "sent from God to proclaim the good news of Christ" (2:12, 17).[31]

Responding to his opponents' attack on the lack of a recommendation letter (συστατικὴ ἐπιστολή),[32] Paul begins his apology by raising another rhetorical question, "Are we beginning to commend ourselves again?" (2 Cor 3:1), thus recalling his previous question of "who is sufficient (ἱκανός) for these things?" (2:16).[33] Answering the question, Paul, similarly to 1 Cor 3:10–15, presents both ecclesiological and Christological bases for his apostleship: "You yourselves are our letter...a letter of Christ" (2 Cor 3:2–3). Paul here contends that his preaching already produced self-vindicating results in the conversion experience within the Corinthian church, which he will later explain through the idea of the transformative experience of the believers (v.18). In this sense, the Corinthian church is Paul's own recommendation letter. However, Paul does not forget that it is Christ, as the founder of the salvation program, who made Paul's preaching effective – in this way, the Corinthian church is a letter from Christ. In conclusion, Paul distinguishes his special relationship to the Corinthian church "the letter of Christ" as its author from that of "some" of his opponents who have to present recommendation letters (v.1).[34]

---

[30] Paul Barnett, *The Second Epistle to the Corinthians* (Grand Rapids, Michigan: William B. Eerdmans Publishing Co., 1997), 34.

[31] Belleville categorizes 2 Cor 1–7 as an "apologetic self-commendatory letter" in *Reflections,* 120, 131–32. But unlike in a typical self-commendatory letter, Paul boasts of what are regarded from a human point of view as weaknesses (4:8ff; 6:4ff), instead of presenting what others would consider as strengthes.

[32] "The letter of recommendation," of which both Demertius (2 or 1 BCE) and Libanius (4 CE) provide models, is a well-established form in Paul's day. See Furnish, *2 Corinthians,* 180.

[33] Paul already used this Greek term ἱκανός for the discussion of his apostleship in 1 Cor 15:10–11.

[34] Letters of recommendation are advantageous to itinerant Christian teachers or preachers when they present them to already established congregations. See Furnish, 193; and Gerd Theissen, *The Social Setting of Pauline Christianity: Essays on Corinth* (Philadelphia: Fortress, 1982).

Paul further extends the metaphor of commendatory letters to *by what agency* and *on what material* they have been inscribed: "written not with *ink* but with *the Spirit of the living God*, not on *tablets of stone* but on *tablets of human hearts*" (3:3; italics are mine). Although the idea of a letter inscribed into hearts as superior to that written on material stuff is commonly found in Paul's time,[35] it carries within itself a paradoxical irony: the heart which connotes the secrecy of the most interior of human beings, only accessible by God, is claimed by Paul "to be known and read by all" (3:2).[36] Most commentators agree that Paul formulates the above argument by drawing upon passages from Ezek 36:26–27 and Jer 31:31–34, both of which allude to Exod 24:12 and 34:1–4, 27–28.[37] The new heart and Spirit in Ezek 36 are the vehicles of God's inwardly established commandments and the New Covenant in Jer 31 is identified with those commandments inscribed in human hearts.[38] In this association, the stone with the extraordinary value of endurance appears as a condition of a hardened heart. According to Jeremiah, the New Covenant with new heart and Spirit has to come about because of Israel's breaking of the Mosaic Law, the Old Covenant, due to their stubborn hearts.[39] Here, the stone tablets clearly refer to the tablets of the Law which Moses received at Mount Sinai.[40] Paul makes a connection between the letters of his opponents and the engraved tablets of the Law, and places them on the side of negation which stands in opposition to Paul's positive alternatives.[41]

3.4.2 Paul's Confidence as a Minister of the New Covenant (3:4–6)

In 2 Cor 3, Paul moves from one passage to another through the use of catchword connections. I showed above how Paul concluded his argument by presenting the concept of "the Spirit of the living God" (v. 3) as the agent of writing. What is "known and read by all" *outwardly* is a result of what has occurred *inwardly* in the heart by the activity of the life-giving Spirit

---

[35] According to Furnish, Plato's *Phaedrus* provides a good argument that "written words" are only a faint "image" of "the living, breathing word" (276A) (Furnish, 195).

[36] Kuschnerus, 96.

[37] Furnish, 197; Fitzmyer, 635; Hafemann, 156; Harris, 262; and Barnett, *The Second Epistle to the Corinthians*, 165.

[38] Many have argued that Paul is here using the Jewish exegetical method of "rules of analogy" common in his Hellenized Jewish milieu. For more on this issue, see Stockhausen, "2 Cor 3," 154–58. Again, I want to emphasize that Paul, although drawing upon Jewish exegetical traditions and scriptural texts, freely associates those scriptural ideas with his new context of letters of recommendation. Paul controls the narrative logic of his own apology rather than being controlled by narrative logic of scriptural stories.

[39] Hafemann, 210, 330.

[40] Furnish, 198.

[41] Belleville, 148; Kuschnerus, 98.

who has been actively present in the Corinthian church (e.g. 1 Cor 12–13).[42] In the current passage of vv. 4–6, Paul develops and expands the concept of the Spirit of the living God in two ways: (1) the living God is the origin of Paul's competence in being a minister of the New Covenant and (2) this ministry is executed by the life-giving Spirit who manifests God's presence on earth.

In v. 4, Paul makes a transition from the concept of a recommendation letter to that of apostolic confidence by employing a "having-formula" (cf. 3:12; 4:1, 7, and 13): "Such is the confidence that we have through Christ toward God."[43] Having rejected the concept of "self-commendation" (v.1), Paul introduces the theme of "confidence *through Christ* and *toward God*" (v.4) that results from the fact that the Corinthians are Paul's recommendation letter of Christ written by the Spirit of the living God. In v.5, Paul further clarifies the nature of his confidence by reintroducing the theme of sufficiency: it is not because of who he is, but because of God's calling that Paul becomes sufficient (ἱκανός) to be a minister of the New Covenant. In 1 Cor 15:9–10, Paul already stated that he lacked apostolic sufficiency from within himself and that this sufficiency is entirely God-given.[44] Paul's mentioning of sufficiency in the current passage clearly indicates that he attempts an answer to his previous rhetorical question of "who is sufficient for these things?" (2 Cor 2:16). It is now indisputable that Paul is here alluding to Moses' calling narrative in Exod 3–4, where Moses points out his insufficiency as God's agent for Israel.[45] The common theme of sufficiency in both Moses' and Paul's callings further prepares his audience for the following discussion of a comparison in vv. 7–11 between the ministry of Moses and that of Paul.

While most commentators point out in this passage the idea of God as the origin of Paul's sufficiency, they rarely discuss the importance of the Christological expression "through Christ" (3:4; cf. 3:3) or "in Christ" (2:14, 17). In the beginning of 2 Corinthians, Paul identifies himself as "an apostle of Christ Jesus by the will of God" (1:1) and depicts his life as one filled with abundant sufferings and the consolations of Christ (1:5). According to Paul, God called him to proclaim "the Son of God, Jesus Christ" (1:19) or "the good news of Christ" (2:12), the content of which is "Jesus Christ is our Lord" (4:5). For Paul, God's calling is for the "the ministry of

---

[42] In 1 Corinthians, Paul claims that it is only the Spirit of God that can search the thoughts of God and of human beings (e.g. 1 Cor 2:10–12).

[43] For the dividing function of having formulae, see Hans-Michael Wünsch, *Der paulinische Brief 2 Kor 1–9 als kommunikative Handlung: eine rhetorisch-literaturwissenschaftliche Untersuchung* (Münster: Lit Verlag, 1996).

[44] The title "Sufficient One" is applied to God several times in the LXX (e.g. Ruth 1:20–21; Job 21:15; 31:2).

[45] For more on this topic, see Stockhausen, 146–7 and Kuschnerus, 99.

reconciliation," that is, *"in Christ*, God was reconciling the world to Himself" (5:19). Also in the immediate context of our current passage, Paul calls himself "the aroma of Christ to God" (2:15). Any exegesis of 2 Cor 3, if it fails mentioning this Christological edge in Paul's thinking, may turn out to be *insufficient*.

Great numbers of books and articles have been devoted to the topic of the "life-threatening letter" vs. the "life-giving Spirit." Regarding the interpretation of the triple-fold antithesis which seems to exist in v.6 – the New Covenant vs. the Old Covenant (v.14), Spirit vs. letter, and giving life vs. killing, there have been two major schools of interpretation: (1) exegesis along traditional lines on the basis of the contrast between the Law and the Gospel and (2) understanding of the New Covenant as "the Law plus the Spirit," emphasizing continuity between the Old and the New Covenants.[46] Their conclusions are mainly dependent upon differing understanding of Paul's hermeneutical practices, especially regarding the relationship between the Law and the Gospel or between the Old and the New Covenants.[47] It is clear that Paul draws his two key ideas of the New Covenant and the life-giving Spirit from those passages of Ezek 36 and Jer 31. According to these scriptural passages, the New Covenant in Jer 31 seems to be the internalized Law with the knowledge of God in new hearts transformed by the Spirit. Traditionally, v.6 along with the rest of 2 Cor 3 has been interpreted in light of Galatians and Romans, which is believed to have been written by Paul in Corinth, representing his most well-developed theology. For example, in Rom 7–8, while he does not deny that the Law is holy and spiritual (7:12, 14), Paul contends that sin, using the commandment, deceives and kills the one who tries to find life and righteousness through the Law (7:5, 11; cf. Gal 3:21). The law of the Spirit of life in Christ sets free those in Christ from the Law of sin and death (8:2). Also, in Galatians 4, there is a strong antithesis between the two covenants of New and Old. Against his opponents of Judaizers in the Galatian church, Paul exhorts the Galatians not to submit themselves to "the yoke of slavery," that is, living under the Law in the Galatian context. While Paul says in 1 Cor 15:56, "[t]he sting of death is sin, and the power of sin is the Law," in the Corinthian correspondence he does not seem to discuss such ideas as much as he does in Romans and Galatians. This is because the Corinthian situation does not have much to do with the Law.[48]

---

[46] I am borrowing this term from Grindheim, "The Law Kills," 97. Also for a comprehensive survey of various interpretations, see Randall C. Gleason, "Paul's Covenantal Contrasts in 2 Corinthians 3.1–11," *Bibliotheca Sacra* 154 (1997).

[47] For more on this debate and Paul's relevant hermeneutic, see Hafemann, 1–35.

[48] I think it probable that Paul in Corinth had already developed his understanding of the Law and the Gospel in a way similar to his exposition of them in Galatians and Romans. But Paul is here more interested in developing an apology for his ministry and 2

Against this traditional view, some scholars who interpret the New Covenant as the Law plus the Spirit (an idea which is gaining popularity especially among those who embrace the so-called New Perspective), con-
tend that the contrast between the Old and the New Covenants must be understood by seeing the Spirit as that which enables the believers to keep
the Old Covenant Law.[49] The New Covenant comes into the salvation history of God, not because the Law in the Old is defective or wrong, but because Israel cannot keep the Law due to its sinfulness. The Spirit will enable Israelites to keep the Law by transforming their hardened hearts.[50] Similarly, others argue that the letter in v.6 refers not to the Law, but to a
defective understanding of the Law – the Law as something merely written
or the Law as a way of achieving the righteousness before God rather than
receiving the righteous of God as a gift.[51] According to these scholars, Paul
is not making a qualitative evaluation of the Law and the Gospel, nor is he
developing an antithesis between them, but rather, is discussing their effects in God's salvation program in a continuous way that the latter completes the former.[52]

There seems to exist in the outlook of the Qumran community a non-
Christian parallel to this view of the New Covenant as the renewed understanding of the Mosaic Law through the Spirit.[53] In the Damascus document, the members of the Qumran community are claimed to enter a renewed relationship with God through the New Covenant (CD 6.19; 8.21,
33; 20.12) and there is no indication of an abandonment of the Law.[54]
There is also the belief that God has placed the Spirit within them, fulfilling the New Covenant in Jer 31 (1 QH 12.11–12, 17.26–27).[55] However,
this conclusion should be tested by closely examining the two Corinthian

---

Cor 3 should be interpreted in this light. Following this line of thought, I do not believe
that Paul's opponents in the Corinthian correspondence are any kinds of Judaizers, although they may regard Moses highly.

[49] Stockhausen, 73–74; Martin Hasitschka, "'Diener eines neuen Bundes'. Skizze zum
Selbstverständnis des Paulus in 2 Kor," *ZKT* 121 (1999): 92–96; and N. T. Wright, *The
Climax of the Covenant: Christ and the Law in Pauline Theology* (Minneapolis: Fortress
Press, 1993), 182.

[50] This view is championed by Hafemann, *Paul,* e.g. 160–63, 180. For Hafemann, the
New Covenant is the eschatological fulfillment of the Old Covenant (378).

[51] Furnish, 200–01. For more on this topic, refer to James D. G. Dunn, *Christology in
the Making* (London: SCM Press, 1989); *idem.*, *The Theology of Paul the Apostle* (Grand
Rapids: Eerdmans, 1998); and Karl Kertelge, "Buchstabe und Geist nach 2 Kor 3," in
Paul and the Mosaic Law, ed. James D. G. Dunn (Tübingen: J.C.B. Mohr, 1996).

[52] Wright, Climax of the Covenant, 182.

[53] Moses, 62; and Thrall, 236.

[54] Annie Jaubert, *La notion d'alliance dans le judaisme aux abords de l'ère chrétienne*
(Paris: Éditions du Seuil, 1963).

[55] Ibid., 242–43.

letters as to whether both Paul and the Corinthian church share this Qumranic view. Also, while respecting Hafemann, Wright and Hays' emphasis on the importance of the contexts of those scriptural stories in Exod, Ezek and Jer, I again raise the question as to whether those stories are not reinterpreted by Paul in light of the Christ event rather than imposing theological directions on Paul in one direction.

First of all, it is noteworthy that Paul never proclaims the renewed understanding of the Mosaic Law as his gospel message in the Corinthian correspondence, nor does he exhort the new Corinthian converts to keep the Law. Paul clearly understands his calling by God as proclaiming "the Good News of Christ" (2 Cor 2:12), which is God's invitation for the world to reconcile with Him in Christ (5:19).[56] According to the tradition which Paul and the Corinthian church are sharing, the New Covenant does not seem to be "the Law plus the Spirit," but instead is "the New Covenant in the blood of Christ" based on "Christ the Lord's death for their sins" (1 Cor 11:23–26; 15:3; 10:14–16).[57] In his letters, Paul's repertoire of covenantal motifs consistently serves to articulate the rich aspects of God's salvation program *in Christ*, including knowledge, power and manifestation of the Spirit along with the spiritual gifts (cf. 1 Cor 2).[58]

Also, the Corinthians' experience of the Spirit is not limited to the renewed understanding of the Law, but instead, is claimed that they have a rich experience of the life-giving Spirit in various aspects of their lives, including spiritual knowledge and gifts. Furthermore, the activity of the Spirit is intimately related to Paul's Gospel message of "Christ is the Lord" in a way that the former enables the Corinthians to accept the latter. When Paul preached to the Corinthians about Christ the crucified one who is "stumbling block to Jews and foolishness to Gentiles" (1 Cor 1:23), they

---

[56] Krister Stendahl, *Paul Among Jews and Gentiles and Other Essays* (Philadelphia: Fortress, 1976) and J. Christiaan Beker, *Paul the Apostle: The Triumph of God in Life and Thought* (Philadelphia: Fortress Press, 1984), 3–19. Beker tries hard to minimize the effect of the Christ event in Paul's own experience, whether that be calling or conversion, in order to emphasize continuity between Saul the persecutor and Paul the persecuted. Disagreeing with Stendahl, Ralph P. Martin points out what is new in Paul's preaching – Paul was not called to be a prophet, but an apostle of Jesus Christ. See Ralph P. Martin, *Reconciliation: A Study of Paul's Theology* (Atlanta: John Knox, 1980). Also, Newman, *Paul's Glory Christology*, 176–77; and Hans D. Betz, *Galatians* (Philadelphia: Fortress Press, 1979), 74–75.

[57] In the songs of the Suffering Servant in Isaiah (42:6 and 49:8), God gives the Suffering Servant as a covenant for people. Does Paul understand Jesus' death and ministry as that of the Suffering Servant? Both Seyoon Kim (*Paul and the New Perspective* [Tübingen: Mohr Siebeck, 2002]) and J. Jeremias (*Moses*, 864) answer in the affirmative.

[58] Bruce W. Longenecker, "Contours of Covenant Theology in the Post-Conversion Paul," in *The Road from Damascus*, ed. Richard N. Longenecker (Grand Rapids, Michigan: William B. Eerdmans, 1997), 125–46.

came to accept the message through the demonstration of the Spirit of God (2:5). According to Paul, no one understands God's wisdom about "the Lord of glory" the crucified one (2:8), except through the Spirit of God, the mind of Christ (2:16). Paul attests that "no one can say 'Jesus is the Lord' except by the Holy Spirit" (12:3).

Finally, Paul claims that Christ as the last Adam became a life-giving Spirit (1 Cor 15:45) and is offering the Corinthians victory over death (15:56–57). In these references, the Spirit does not appear to reveal the true understanding of the Mosaic Law to the Corinthians, as the camp of the New Covenant as the Law plus the Spirit claims. Instead, it makes effective for them the life-giving salvation program initiated by God and accomplished through Jesus Christ with its climactic transformation of the believers' mortal bodies into immortal glorious bodies like that of Christ, the last Adam.

In my understanding, scholars of 2 Cor 3 have spent too much time and energy on the issue of Paul's understanding of the relationship between the Law and the Gospel, isolating it from the whole context of 2 Cor 3 where v.18 stands as its conclusion. Some have diligently emphasized the continuity between the Law and the Gospel, minimizing Paul's new Gospel message with its Christological edge, while others have read Romans and Galatians into 2 Corinthians in a too hasty manner. Although I side with Furnish and others that Paul in Corinth has already developed similar views to those he holds in Romans, it is not Paul's concern here either to promote or to demote the Law and the Old Covenant in the way he does in Romans and Galatians. However, 2 Cor 3 clearly shows that Paul's transformation experience at the Damascus Christophany, in which he goes from persecutor to advocate for the Gospel (cf. Gal 1:13–23), has changed his perception of Jewish traditions, including those of the Law and of the Covenant. This Christological edge to his theology makes a huge difference between Paul and the Damascus Document.

Why does Paul use the expressions of "tablets of stone" and "the killing letter," seemingly demoting the Mosaic Law and ministry? I remind readers of the nature of 2 Cor 3 – Paul's apologetic defense for his ministry, facing opponents who themselves carried a recommendation letter. On the basis of their written nature on paper and stone, Paul makes an analogy between their recommendation letter and the Mosaic Law, since the Law is the highest form of documentary certification that he can imagine, as it was written by the finger of God. Paul contrasts his ministry with that of his opponents in terms of their origin – the latter from documents written by humans, and the former from the internal work of the Spirit. Comparing his ministry with Moses', thus aligning their ministry with Moses' on the basis of the written nature of their credentials, Paul is saying that just as Moses' ministry with the highest forms of documentary certification resulted in "killing" people due to its inefficiency of transforming them, so also will the ministry of his current opponents, who find their ministerial credentials in a written letter of recommendation, end up being a failure, especially because of its inability to transform the Corinthians.[59] In the following passage of 2 Cor 3:7–11, Paul reinforces this argument by contrasting the results of the two ministries, that of Moses and his own: life vs. death; justification vs. condemnation; transformation vs. blindness.

3.4.3. Comparison between the Ministry of Death and the Ministry of Spirit (3:7–11)

As for the traditions behind Paul's argument in 3:7–18, there exists a scholarly consensus that Paul builds up his argument on the basis of the scriptural tradition of the glory and veil of Moses from Exod 34, as Hafemann demonstrates in a most comprehensive and thorough way.[60] Linda L. Belleville, however, challenges scholars to pay attention to Paul's use of various post-biblical Jewish exegetical traditions regarding Moses' glory, veil and transformation, which I have discussed above.[61] As will be shown in the following analysis of vv. 7–11, I agree with Belleville that Paul makes use of these non-biblical traditions on the Moses' transformation story for his own sake.

2 Cor 3:7–18 has been analyzed in a number of different ways. Some state that it is an independent unit either written by Paul as a Midrash on Exod 34 or Christianized by Paul, having already existed within Judaism in the form of a Midrash.[62] Others suggest that Paul modifies and uses a Midrash composed by his opponents in order to counter their attack on him.[63] However, 2 Cor 3:7–18 is not an insertion without connection to the pre-

---

[59] For a similar line of argument, see Belleville, 148–49.

[60] Scott J. Hafemann, *Paul, Moses, and the History of Israel* (Tübingen: Mohr, 1995).

[61] As exceptions, Stockhausen states that the prophetic texts behind 3:1–6 determine Paul's argument in 3:7–11, in David Renwick, *Paul, the Temple, and the Presence of God* (Atlanta, GA: Scholars Press, 1991). See also C. K. Stockhausen, *Moses' Veil and the Glory of the New Covenant: The Exegetical Substructure of 2 Cor 3.1–4.6* (AnBib 116; Rome: Pontifical Biblical Institute, 1989). David Renwick contends that Paul's allusion to Hag 2 in 3:10 is the key to Paul's thought in our current passage (*Paul, the Temple, and the Presence of God* [Atlanta, GA: Scholars Press, 1991], 109–21).

[62] M. McNamara, *Targum and Testament* (Grand Rapids, MI: Eerdmans, 1972). For more on this topic, see Linda L. Belleville, "Tradition or Creation? Paul's Use of the Exodus 34 Tradition in 2 Corinthians 3.7–18," in *Paul and the Scriptures of Israel*, ed. Craig A. Evans and James A. Sanders (Sheffield: JSOT Press, 1993).

[63] Dieter Georgi, *Die Gegner des Paulus im 2 Korintherbrief* (Neukirchen–Vluyn: Neukirchen Verlag, 1964); and M. Theobald, *Die überströmende Gnade. Studien zu einem paulinischen Motivfeld* (Würzburg: Echter, 1972).

ceding argument in vv. 1–6, nor a Midrash on Exod 34.[64] It functions to
support Paul's previous arguments in two ways: (1) vv. 7–11 further explains Paul's ministerial credentials from God with the aid of a comparison
between his ministry and that of Moses; and (2) vv. 12–18 proves Paul's
claim that his ministry is indeed driven by the life-giving Spirit with its
undeniable result of transforming the Corinthian believers. Just as in 1 Corinthians Paul built up a fundamental unity between himself, the builder,
and the Corinthian church, the building, with Christ as the foundation, so
also does he here defend his apostleship by showing its undeniable effica-
cy in transforming the Corinthians through the Gospel message (μεταμορ-
φούμεθα, v.18).

In our current text of vv.7–11, Paul expands his analogy from the previous contrast between the letter and the Spirit (v.6) to the contrast between the ministry of Moses and his own ministry by raising three rhetorical questions about a new theme of glory. Many have recognized that Paul
is here engaged in an exegetical practice similar to the rabbinic exegetical
rule of *kal va-homer*, "from lesser to greater pattern," as is attested to in
three occurrences of the expression "how much more" (3:7, 9, and 11).[65] In
this practice, the first parts of the assertions present common presuppositions which are also applicable to the second parts and at the same time,
they further amplify the conditions of the second parts through comparison.
By placing his own ministry of the New Covenant in comparison with
Moses' of the Old Covenant, Paul asserts that his ministry has come with
much more (πολλῷ μᾶλλον) glory than that of Moses. In this process, he
not only defends the divine origin of his ministry, but also promotes it
beyond that of Moses. In this way, Paul further supports his previous arguments in 3:4–6 about his confidence as well as sufficiency as the minister of the New Covenant. In the following discussion of the believers'
transformation experience by looking at "the glory of the Lord" in vv.12–
18, Paul will continue to strengthen his argument of how much more abounding or surpassing (ὑπερβαλλούσης, v.10) glory has been accompanying
his own ministry.

According to Paul, there exist sharp contrasts between the two ministries. Paul calls Moses' ministry a "ministry of death" (v.7), a "ministry of
condemnation" (v.9), and "what was set aside (τὸ καταργούμενον)"
(v.11).[66] Paul here maintains an interesting paradox regarding Moses' min-

---

[64] W. C. Van Unnik, "'With Unveiled Face', An Exegesis of 2 Cor 3:12–18," *NovTest*
6 (1963), 168; and Furnish, 230.

[65] Barnett, *2 Corinthians,* 179; and Kuschnerus, 100–1.

[66] Hafemann in *Paul,* 305–7 translates this expression as "what is rendered inopera-
tive in regard to their effects." Furnish renders it as "what was being annulled," expressing a sense of temporariness of Moses' ministry (*2 Corinthians,* 203), and for Thrall, it
means "what is abolished" (*2 Corinthians,* 252).

istry. On the one hand, Moses' ministry is related to the "letters on stone tablets" (v.7) which Paul already defined as life-killing letter in v.6. I agree with Hafemann that Paul is referring here to the Exodus stories where the Law brought condemnation and death to the hard-hearted Israelites due to their inability to keep the Law. Furnish argues that Paul's understanding of the Law and Moses' ministry in our current text is understandable in light of his teachings about the Law in other writings. In Rom 5, for example, Paul claims that the Law brought forth punishment for sin and death as judgment against sin.[67] On the other hand, Paul does not deny that this ministry of Moses, although it resulted in condemnation and death, also came with the divine glory which legitimates Moses' ministry as coming from God. Paul further adds that Israelites could not look at Moses' face due to the brightness of the accompanying glory (v.7).[68]

In contrast to his negative descriptions of Moses' ministry, Paul calls his own ministry a "ministry of the Spirit" (v.8), a "ministry of righteousness" (v.9) and "the permanent (τὸ μένον)" (v.11). As has been noted, the Spirit is claimed by Paul to give life (v.6) and to provide rich spiritual gifts, including the knowledge of his Gospel message "Christ is the Lord" (1 Cor 12:3). As for the term righteousness (δικαιοσύνη), Paul does not explain it here in as much detail as he does in Romans, but simply presupposes that the Corinthians knew what he meant by the term. Paul states in 2 Cor 5:21, "[f]or our sake He [God] made him [Christ] to be sin who knew no sin, so that in him we might become the *righteousness* of God." Also in 1 Cor 1:30, Paul claims that Christ is the Corinthians' "wisdom, power, *righteousness*, sanctification, and redemption." We cannot miss how closely Paul ties the term righteousness to what God has done in Christ or through Christ, regardless of what the term means for Paul and the Corinthians.[69]

In these comparisons, Paul's affirmation of the glory in Moses' ministry becomes a basis for the claim that his ministry of the New Covenant also comes with a glory – even greater glory (v.10). It is noteworthy that Paul does not deny the fact that divine glory also accompanied Moses' ministry. However, Paul promotes his ministry far beyond Moses' by claiming that his ministry possesses "surpassing" and "permanent" glory. He further

---

[67] Furnish, 228.

[68] Hafemann argues that they could not look into Moses face due to fear, as the Glory as God's presence threatened to kill them due to their sinfulness (*Paul*, 280). However, C. Newman contends that the prophets in the Hebrew Bible, when they encounter the glory of God, look beyond the upcoming judgment for a day of forgiveness, deliverance and transformation (*Paul's Glory Christology*, 60).

[69] Cf. Hafemann, 319. He emphasizes the close relationship between the righteousness of God and the Spirit in such a way that the Spirit now enables people in the New Covenant to keep the Law. He, following Stendahl and Beker, tends to ignore the Christological importance of the Spirit's activity in the Corinthian correspondence.

qualifies the glory of his ministry as the "Glory of the Lord" (v.17) who Christ is now for him (4:6). I have already discussed above how widely the story about Moses' glorious transformation was circulating in Second Temple Judaism. Summarizing what I have discussed above, in Jewish exegetical traditions, Moses' glory came to indicate (1) God's legitimization of Moses' mediatory role, especially as the lawgiver, (2) the divine origin of the Law as expression of God's will, (3) God's covenantal presence, and (4) the restoration of the original glory that Adam lost. Likewise, the same glory of God accompanies Paul's ministry, legitimizing his role as a minister of the New Covenant, revealing the divine origin of his Gospel message, manifesting God's presence in his ministry through the life-giving activity of the Spirit, and allowing new creations to happen to those who are in Christ (2 Cor 5:17), reversing what the first Adam has done.

Paul, however, tries to establish a sharp edge between Moses' glory and his own surpassing glory by presenting the contrasting effects of their glory. While Moses' glory only resulted in his own transformation, preventing his audience from being transformed, Paul's own surpassing glory transforms believers by enabling them to see "the light of the Gospel of the glory of Christ, who is the image of God" (2 Cor 4:4). Furthermore, the surpassing glory of Paul's ministry neutralizes the glory of Moses (v.10) with the result that Moses' ministry and its glory are now set aside (καταργούμενον) (v.7, 11).[70]

Paul's opponents as well as the Corinthian readers may wonder: "Where is your proof for the surpassing glory of your ministry, Paul? How can you say that Moses' ministry is now set aside, while yours is still effective?" In answer to these questions, Paul demonstrates, in the following discussion of vv.12–18, that while Moses' veiling of his glory only hardens the minds of his readers and his glory functions as God's punishing power,[71] the glory in Paul's own ministry in his Gospel message continues to transform those who are exposed to it.

3.4.4 Transformation from Glory to Glory (3:12–18)

Since his ministry has come with much more glory than that of Moses, Paul claims, in v.12, that he can "act with great boldness, not like Moses." This sentence sums up his previous comparisons between the two ministries in vv.7–11 and helps him develop the three major points of the current passage, vv.12–18. First, Paul makes a transition from the comparison

---

[70] For the temporality of the Old Covenant, see Grindheim, 102–08. Hafemann argues against Belleville that Moses' glory has been considered permanent in post-biblical traditions (*Paul*, 287).

[71] For the scriptural references and their discussion about glory as punishing power of God, see Hafemann, 222, 280, and 318.

between the two ministries to a comparison between the two different experiences of Israel and the Church.[72] While the former experience a hardening of their hearts due to Moses' veil, the latter experiences transformation through Paul's unveiling of Christ's glory. Second, the transformation becomes the ultimate contrast between the two ministries as well as between the two covenants, and functions as the climactic conclusion of Paul's whole argument in 2 Cor 3:1–18.[73] Third, according to Paul, the transformation results from gazing upon the glory of the risen Christ with an unveiled face, a risen Christ who is now the Lord in Paul's Gospel. In 4:1–6, Paul discusses the third point in more detail, claiming that Christ is the Lord and the image of God.

– Paul's openness vs. Moses' veiling (12–14a)
The Greek term παρρησία generally means boldness, confidence and openness.[74] This term refers to the courage with which Paul acts to fulfill his apostolic commission in relation to others.[75] Van Unnik points out that the Aramaic expression for confidence or boldness, גלה אפין or גלה ראש, which is equivalent to the Greek word παρρησία, literally means "to uncover the face or the head."[76] While to cover the face is a sign of shame and mourning, to uncover the head means to exhibit confidence and freedom. Considering the fact that Paul puts his attitude in contrast to Moses' action of veiling in v.12, the notion of openness better fits the context than that of boldness.[77] Using this term which indicates openness, Paul seems to respond to accusations by his opponents that he has been less than open with his readers (2 Cor 1:17) and that his Gospel message appears to be obscure and hidden (4:2–3).[78]

From Moses' veiling, Paul makes an unexpected turn to Israelites' blindness and hardening of their minds as its result (v.13). In both biblical and extra-biblical literature, the attribution of mental blindness to Israelites

---

[72] Hafemann, 315; and Fitzmyer, 638.

[73] Hafemann, 449.

[74] This Greek term has its etymological origin from a Greek citizen's right to say anything in an assembly. This term belonged to the political sphere of the Greek polis and was an essential mark of the Greek democracy as a sign of the freedom. See Heinrich Schlier, "παρρησία," in TDNT vol. 5, 871.

[75] Furnish, 230.

[76] Van Unnik, 161.

[77] Belleville, 197–8; and Barnett, 188. Hafemann demonstrates that the boldness / openness is the attitude that the righteous will have on the day of judgment (Hafemann, 341–44).

[78] It is interesting to note that in the context of the Transfiguration story in Mark, which I will later compare with 2 Cor 3, Jesus is said to teach "openly" (παρρησία) his suffering and death (cf. Mk 8:32).

is a popular theme, especially in the prophetic and wisdom literature.[79] Hafemann considers the veil to be a theological corollary to the sinful nature
of Israel, both separating and protecting it from God's glory, like the
"fence" around the bottom of Mt. Sinai (Exod 19:12) and the "curtain" before the Holy of Holies.[80] However, in the biblical stories in Exodus, Moses puts a veil on his face, lest the reflected glory continue to frighten the
people (Exod 34:30). To this biblical story, Paul adds that the veil is used
to conceal from Israelites the "end" (τέλος) of "what was fading away"
(τοῦ καταργουμένου), which for Paul refers to both the glory of Moses'
ministry (v.7) and to the ministry itself (v.11).

The meaning of the Greek term τέλος has been at the center of scholarly
debate. This term means either "end" or "goal," depending upon scholarly
perspectives.[81] While the dominant view has been to translate it as "end,"
referring to Moses' veiling of Israelites from seeing the end of the glory on
his face due to its fading nature,[82] A.T. Hanson takes the term to mean
"goal" or the ultimate fulfillment of the glory on Moses' face, which is the
consummation of the Old Covenant in Christ.[83] Agreeing upon its meaning
as goal, but rejecting its reference to Christ, Hafemann argues that the goal
of Moses' veiling refers to "the outcome" or "result" of the glory on his
face, that is, "death-dealing judgment of the glory of God upon His 'stiff-
necked' people."[84] Against Hafemann, I agree with Belleville and Grindheim that it means "end" in our current text, as there exists terminological
parallelism among vv. 7, 11 and v.13.[85] Also in the Corinthian correspondence, the term generally means "end" or "termination" (cf. 1 Cor 1:8;
10:11; 15:24; 2 Cor 11:15).[86]

– the Lord's removal of the veil (14b–16)
In this passage of vv.14b–16, the sense of Moses changes from Moses as
the intermediary in the provision of the Law to Moses denoting biblical
writings ascribed to him, thus alluding to the common reading of the Torah
at the synagogue: "the reading of the Old Covenant" (v.14) and "Moses is
read" (v.15). Through this transition, Paul makes a remarkable shift from

---

[79] Belleville, 222–24.

[80] Hafemann, 223–24.

[81] For bibliographical references to the meaning of the term, refer to Hafemann, 347,
n.38. For a detailed and comprehensive analysis of the term, see Samuel Ngayihembako,
Les temps de la fin: approche exégetique de l'eschatologie du Nouveau Testament
(Genève: Labor et Fides, 1994).

[82] For this view, for example, see Furnish, 207 and Thrall, 1.256.

[83] A. T. Hanson, *Studies in Paul's Technique and Theology* (London: SPCK, 1974).

[84] Hafemann, 357–62.

[85] Belleville, 201–03.

[86] Grindheim, 111.

speaking about the two ministries to speaking about the two texts of the law and the Gospel, and then about two communities of the compared ministers. This shift is accentuated by Paul's use of the contemporizing formulas, "until this very day" (ἄχρι τῆς σήμερον ἡμέρας v.14b) and "to this very day" (ἕως σήμερον v.15).[87] These contemporizing formulas enable Paul to apply the Exodus story to the current situation of Israel and to maintain that the situation has not changed since the days of Moses–"that same veil is still there" (v.14; cf. v.15).

This double temporal clause of "until/to this very day" leads van Unnik to the observation that there exists a parallelism with two antitheses between v.14b–c and vv.15–16 as follows:[88]

Until this very day,
> at the reading of the Old Covenant the same veil is till there (v.14b).
> Since only in Christ, it is removed (v.14c)

To this very day,
> whenever Moses is read, a veil lies over their heart (v.15).
> But, when one turns to the Lord, the veil is removed (v.16).

In this structure, "at the reading of the Old Covenant" (v.14b) parallels "whenever Moses is read" (v.15), while "in Christ" (v.14c) parallels "when one turns to the Lord" (v.16). Also, there are two antitheses marked by ὅτι (v.14c) and δέ (v.16). While the veil still remains at the reading of the Old Covenant/Moses, it is removed only in Christ/the Lord. In these antitheses, Paul seems to promote his Gospel message far beyond Moses' Law by pointing out that the former can remove the veil which the latter is unable to do. Again, due to the stark contrast that Paul puts in between the two, it is hard to accept the view of the New Covenant as "the Law plus the Spirit."

As for the understanding of v.16, Hafemann, following E. Käsemann's typological analysis in Paul,[89] tries to take Moses' own experience in Exod 34:34 as the key to Paul's thought, in that Moses' own transformation experience through turning to the Lord – God in the Hebrew Bible – becomes typical of one whose heart has been changed by the Spirit.[90] According to Hafemann, the contrast lies between Israel's Old Covenant experience and Moses' own experience in the tent of meeting rather than between Israel and the church. It is no wonder that Hafemann understands the Lord in v.16 as Yahweh, not Christ, in order to emphasize the essential continuity

---

[87] Kuschnerus, 102–3. Van Unnik argues that this temporal expression, which is also found in Rom 9:8, is a quotation of Deut 29:4 (Van Unnik, 163).

[88] Van Unnik, 163.

[89] E. Käsemann, "Der Glaube Abrahams," in *Paulinische Perspektiven*, ed. E. Käsemann (Tübingen: Mohr, 1969).

[90] Hafemann, 388.

between the Old and the New Covenants.[91] Although Hafemann is right that Moses' own transformation experience with its various Jewish interpretive traditions becomes a hermeneutical basis for Paul's description of the believers' transformation, Mosaic typology should not be emphasized too much in this passage, as Paul has been putting Moses and his ministry on the side of negation. Also just as there are contrasts between the Old and the New Covenants as well as between the two ministers or ministries, so also does a contrast now exist between the two communities.

The exegetical analysis of v.16 is mostly dependent upon the identification of "the Lord": does it refer to Christ or Yahweh? Or both? While the majority of scholars incline toward its Christological interpretation,[92] some see it as referring to Yahweh, seeking to emphasize a continuity between Exodus and 2 Cor 3.[93] Others think Paul is intentionally ambiguous here in order to have a double reference to God and Christ.[94] I side with the majority of scholars that the Lord here refers to Christ, especially because of the parallelism between v.14c, "since only in Christ, it is removed," and v.16, "when one turns to the Lord, the veil is removed."

My position is further strengthened by Paul's normal use of the term κύριος as a unique title for Christ in his writings. Paul speaks of Jesus as God's son about 17 times, but the Lord about 230 times.[95] With an exclusion of citations of the Hebrew Bible where the term Lord refers to Yahweh, Paul refers to Jesus Christ using the term κύριος. Considering the fact that v.16 is not a citation of Exod 34:34, but is instead Paul's contemporizing of it in the new context with Christological emphasis,[96] it is more likely that here he has Christ in mind. Also, in the Corinthian correspondence, with the exception of three quotations from the Hebrew Bible in 1 Cor 1:31, 2:16 and 3:20 and of one in 2 Cor 3:17, "the Spirit of the Lord," Paul calls Jesus Christ "His Son, Our Lord" (1 Cor 1:2–9) and "the Lord of glory" (2:8). Paul claims that no one can say "Jesus is the Lord except the Holy Spirit" (1 Cor 1:3), which is the core of his Gospel message (2 Cor 4:5). 1 Cor 8:6, "yet for us there is *one God, the Father*, from whom are all

---

[91] Ibid., 392.

[92] Meyer, Plumer, Strachan, Tasker, Wendland, Bruce, Barrett, Bultmann, Danker, Windische, Plummer and Fitzmyer hold this view. As for bibliographical information, see Belleville, 254 n.3 and Fee, *God's Empowering Presence*, 312 n.92.

[93] Hafemann, Belleville, Dunn, Moule, Feuillet, Collange, Thrall and Furnish hold this view. For bibliographical information, see Belleville, 254 n.4 and Fee, 312 n.92.

[94] E. Richard, "Polemics, Old Testament and Theology. A Study of II Cor. III, 1–IV, 6," *RB* 88 (1981): 340–69; and G. Wagner, "Alliance de la lettre, alliance de l'esprit. Essai d'analyse de 2 Corinthiens 2/14 à 3/18," *ETR* 60 (1985): 55–68.

[95] Dunn, *Christology*, 37.

[96] As for the debate upon whether it is a citation or contemporization, see Gordon D. Fee, *God's Empowering Presence* (Peabody: Hendrickson, 1994), 312. He, however, interprets this phrase pneumatologically rather than Christologically.

things and for whom we exist, and *one Lord, Jesus Christ*, through whom are all things and through whom we exist," which is Paul's modification of Jewish *Shema* found in Deut 6:4 (cf. 11:13–21; Num 15:37–41), confirms that for Paul, the Lord is a unique title for Jesus (cf. Phil 2:9–11). The combination of God our Father and the Lord Jesus Christ appears again in 2 Cor 1:2, 3 and 11:32.

It should be emphasized that Paul mentions Christ the Lord, not to the exclusion of God, but including Him in a way that Christ the Lord represents God as His image (cf. 2 Cor 4:4–6). Paul calls his salvation program the "New Creation in Christ" (2 Cor 5:17), but he does not forget to remind his readers that "all this is from God, who reconciled us to Himself through Christ" (5:18–19).[97] As for understanding of Paul's salvation program and the relationship between God and Christ, Larry Hurtado's binitarian model may be promising in this regard.[98]

– believers' transformation into the glory of the Lord (17–18)
In verse 17, which is his contemporization of Exod 34:34, Paul further explains in two ways who the Lord of the previous verse is: (1) the Lord to whom one turns is the Spirit and (2) where "the Spirit of the Lord" is, there is freedom. Paul here repeats earlier key concepts in order to sum up the ideas of the previous passages of 2 Cor 3 and to lead his whole argument into its final conclusion in v.18: the Spirit of the New Covenant (vv. 3–7), the Lord and freedom, which refers back to openness (v.12), expressed with unveiled face.[99]

The difficult phrase, "[n]ow the Lord is the Spirit," has been interpreted in several different ways[100] of which I will list three of the most common: (1) pneumatological[101] and associational – (2) either between Christ and the Spirit[102] or (3) between God and the Spirit.[103] According to the pneu-

---

[97] David Greenwood argues that for Paul, the Lord should be Yahweh in Christ. He tries to include both Yahweh and Christ in Paul's thinking. See David Greenwood, "The Lord is the Spirit: Some Considerations of 2 Cor 3:17," *CBQ* 34 (1972): 464–72.

[98] Larry W. Hurtado, *One God, One Lord: Early Christian Devotion and Ancient Jewish Monotheism* (New York: Continuum, 1998).

[99] For this understanding of the term freedom, see Furnish, 237 and Barnett, 199.

[100] For a summary of major approaches, see Jean-François Collange, *Énigmes de la deuxième épître de Paul aux Corinthiens; étude exégétique de 2 Cor. 2:14–7:4* (Cambridge: University Press, 1972). Also Thrall, 1.278–82.

[101] Fee, *God's Empowering Presence,* 312–20; James D. G. Dunn, "2 Corinthians 3.17 – 'the Lord is the Spirit'," *JTS* 21 (1970): 309–320; Wright, "Reflected Glory," 139–51; and Thrall, 1.274.

[102] For the summary of this view with bibliographical information, see Thrall, 1.280. Also, Barnett, 200–03. For the most comprehensive discussion of it, refer to Ingo Hermann, *Kyrios und Pneuma; Studien zur Christologie der paulinischen Hauptbriefe.* (München: Kösel-Verlag, 1961).

matological interpretation, ὁ κύριος at the start of v.17 bears its anaphoric sense and the phrase reads, "the Spirit is Lord."[104] Wright interprets v.16 in a way that the moment of "turning to the Lord" comes when one opens oneself to the work of the Spirit.[105] He does not, however, justify his claim for the anaphoric sense of ὁ κύριος, nor does he consider Paul's technical use of ὁ κύριος as a title for Christ. It is unlikely that Paul here defines the Spirit in a way that it now becomes the third person of the triune God, as Fee wishes. Although the idea of the Spirit is critical for Paul's understanding of Christ's work, discussing the Trinity and the personality of the Spirit is to raise questions which would not yet have entered Paul's mind.[106]

According to the understanding of the associational view between God and the Spirit, believers now experience God's presence through the works of the Spirit. However, I have already argued above that ὁ κύριος in Paul refers to Christ as a technical title, with an exception of quotations. The phrase in v.17b, "the Spirit of the Lord" (τὸ πνεῦμα κυρίου), seems to argue against my position, as the Lord there clearly refers to God in the Hebrew Bible. The Spirit in the Hebrew Bible is always the Spirit of God, as Paul also attests in v.3, "the Spirit of the living God." Fee is, however, right at the point that τὸ πνεῦμα κυρίου is LXX idiomatic expression, where the term κυρίου refers to Yahweh.[107] While citing LXX, Paul keeps the idiomatic expression as well as the habit of the LXX translators of avoiding the article when using κύριος for Yahweh.

I side with the majority that Paul here identifies Christ and the Spirit, not in a divine substance, but in Christian experience. As Ingo Hermann has already demonstrated, the Spirit for Paul is a means through which Christ is at work in the church. The Spirit represents for believers the reality of experiencing Christ and his continuing work. In this sense, the Spirit is the Spirit of Christ (cf. Rom 8:9; Gal 4:6; and Phil 1:17).[108] Paul in 1 Cor 15:45 already declared that Christ, the last Adam, became life-giving Spirit and will change the bodies of believers into glorious bodies like his own. The rare Greek term ζῳοποιέω appears 4 times in the Corinthian correspondence (1 Cor 15:22, 36, and 45; 2 Cor 3:6) – the first three refer to Christ the life-giving Spirit, while the last one refers to the Spirit of the

---

[103] Furnish, 236.

[104] Wright, 184 and Fee, 311.

[105] Wright, 183.

[106] See also Dunn, 310; Furnish, 236; and Collange, 110.

[107] Fee, 312.

[108] For Paul, the Spirit is a source of experience for believers: of miraculous power (1 Thes 1:5; 1 Cor 2:4–5; Rom 15:19); of moral transformation (1 Cor 6:9–11); of enlightenment (1 Cor 2:12); of joy (1 Thes 1:6); of love (Gal 5:22); and of sonship (Gal 4:6 and Rom 8:15–16).

New Covenant. With the phrase, "[n]ow the Lord is the Spirit," Paul claims that the life-giving activity of the Spirit in the New Covenant is none other than that of Christ the life-giving Spirit.[109] In the following verse 18, Paul demonstrates how the prophecy of Ezekiel and Jeremiah about the transformation of people in the New Covenant is accomplished by the glory of the Lord, Christ the life-giving Spirit.

Verse 18 is the powerful conclusion of Paul's whole argument about the New Covenant ministry, which began at v.1, since it resolves the tension between him and the Corinthian church which resulted from the absence of a recommendation letter. This complex verse can be rearranged as follows:

But
    with unveiled face,
    beholding as in a mirror the glory of the Lord,
  we all are being transformed
    into the same image
    from glory to glory
    as from the Lord Spirit

Until this point, the first person plural has included only Paul and his associates. However, by the emphatic ἡμεῖς δὲ πάντες at the beginning of v.18, Paul deliberately includes the Corinthians in the transformation experience which he describes as result of seeing the glory of the Lord (cf. 4:16).[110] In this way, the common ecclesiological experience of transformation functions in service of establishing unity between Paul and the Corinthians and thereby defends his ministry of the New Covenant as from God.

In regard to ἡμεῖς δὲ πάντες, there seem to exist double contrasts – one implicit and the other explicit: (1) Paul's open proclamation of his Gospel message without veiling stands in contrast with Moses' veiling of God's glory with differing results and (2) more importantly, in their unveiled experience of the glory of the Lord, the believers are opposed to Israelites who cannot see (v.13), whose hearts are blinded (v.14), on whose hearts a veil still lies (v.15), and who don't turn to the Lord (v.16).[111] In these claims, Paul responds to his opponents, "the peddlers of God's word" (2:17) who *hide* shameful things (4:2), by stating that he commends to everyone with "*open* statement of truth" and proclaims his Gospel *openly*

---

[109] It is interesting to note that in Rom 1:3–4, Jesus is declared to be God's Son according to the power of the Holy Spirit. Also, in Acts 9:17–18, Paul became filled with the Spirit right after seeing the Risen Lord. For more on the relationship between the Spirit and Christ, see, Kim, *Paul and the New Perspective,* 128–164.

[110] While some scholars take "we all" to refer to only Paul and his associates, the majority take it to refer to all believers. See Fee, 314; Furnish, 238; Barnett, 204; and J. Lambrecht, "Paul and Suffering," in *God and Human Suffering*, ed. J. Lambrecht and Raymond F. Collins (Louvain [Belgium]: Peeters Press, 1990), 62. Cf. Belleville, 275–76.

[111] J. Lambrecht, "Transformation in 2 Cor 3, 18," *Biblica* 64 (1983), 247.

without veiling it (4:3; cf. 3:12; italics are mine). As a result of Paul's ministry without veiling, the believers can "behold as in a mirror" (κατοπ-τριζόμενοι) the glory of Christ the Lord (cf. 4:4).

The Greek present middle participle κατοπτριζόμενοι, which is a hapax legomenon in the NT, has been understood in three ways:[112] (1) "to behold as in a mirror", (2) "to reflect like a mirror" and (3) "to behold" with no association with a mirror.[113] I agree with the first option, as the participle puts the believers' ability to see without being veiled in contrast with the Israelites' blindness (v.13) and its root contains the notion of a mirror. Also, the participle can best be taken to be causal, since it is through the vision of the glory of the Lord that the believers experience transformation.

Why, then, does Paul use this mirror-image in his description of believers' beholding the glory? Scholars have presented two reasons for this: one Christological and the other ecclesiological. First, according to some, Paul may want to maintain that Christ is the mirror of God as God's glory or God's image (cf. 4:4–6). In Christ, we see God reflected in His Glory as if we were observing a reflected image of an object in a mirror. If the Lord in "the glory of the Lord" in v.18 refers to God rather than Christ, then this option may work better. According to this option, in Christ the mirror, we see the glory of God. However, I have shown that the Lord in v.18 refers to Christ rather than God and therefore, this option may not stand. As an alternative, taking the Lord to be Christ in v.18, Lambrecht maintains that Paul uses the mirror image in order to point out the indirectness of the believers' experience of the glory through his Gospel message.[114] Paul, Peter, James, John, and others had direct vision of the glorious Christ or the risen Lord (cf. Acts 9:3–4, 22:11, and 26:13; Gal 1:15–16; 1 Cor 15:2–11; Mk 9:2–11 and its parallels).[115] Unlike these exceptional cases, Paul claims that it is not directly, but indirectly through their listening to the Gospel which contains and reflects the glory like a mirror (4:4), that believers in their normal experience see the glory of the Lord.

While agreeing with the second ecclesiological interpretation, I would like to add one more aspect of the term κατοπτριζόμενοι, eschatological

---

[112] For bibliographical information, refer to Barnett, 205 n.38. Also, Lambrecht, 246–8; Furnish, 239; Hafemann, 411; and Fee, 314–5. Cf. Wright, "Reflected Glory," 185.

[113] Corinth was famous for its bronze mirrors. See, Henry S. Robinson, *Corinth: A Brief History of the City and a Guide to the Excavations* (Athens: American School of Classical Studies, 1964).

[114] Lambrecht, "Transformation," 249–50.

[115] Although scholars have debates over the nature of Paul's experience at Damascus, recorded in Gal 1 and Acts 9, 22, and 26, there seems to be a consensus that Paul is referring to his own experience of the risen glorious Lord. Regardless of the nature of his experience, it is beyond doubt that that experience drastically changed Paul from the persecutor to the persecuted.

limitation! Already in 1 Cor 13:12, Paul says, "For *now* we see in a mirror dimly, *but then* face to face; now I know in part, but then I will know fully just as I also have been fully known." In Paul's scheme, there is tension between believers' current experience and their final experience at the eschaton. In 2 Cor 3:18, Paul seems to betray similar exegetical limitation in believers' experience of the glory of the Lord. Their indirect limited experience of the glory will be "transformed" into direct full-blown experience of it at the eschaton.

As for the transformation, Paul uses the rare verb μεταμορφόομαι, "to be transformed/transfigured." Paul uses this verb on one other occasion in Rom 12:2 and both occurrences are for a description of believer's transformation. The other two occurrences in the NT are used to refer to the transfiguration of Jesus in Mk 9:2 and Mt 17:2. In the use of this verb, Paul clearly has in mind the Moses parallel at Exod 34 where Moses was glorified and transformed by beholding the glory.[116] It is likely that Paul knows a Jewish tradition of a description of Moses transformation using the same verb, which is attested to in Philo.

There has been scholarly discussion regarding the origin of the phenomenon of transformation: Hellenistic magic ritual or Jewish Apocalypticism or both. The idea of metamorphosis is commonly found in Hellenistic mystery religion, where worshippers claim to experience transformation after beholding their patron god or goddess.[117] For example, in Apuleius' *Metamorphoses* (2 CE), Lucius describes his multiple metamorphoses in the process of initiation into the cult of Isis at Corinth. In this event, Lucius comes to behold the image of the goddess in bright light (XI, 24). Similarly, in the *Corpus Hermeticum*, those who see the image of God are bathed in light and God draws forth their souls from their bodies, and the whole person is transformed into a new substance (X, 6; XIII, 3).[118]

Although both Paul and these examples show a conceptual similarity in their description of transformation into what is beheld, "image of God" or "Glory of God,"[119] the idea is not restricted to Hellenistic mystery religion. J. A. Fitzmyer demonstrates that while we cannot deny the Hellenistic impact of the phenomenon metamorphosis on Paul's account, various Qumran documents witness to the fact that transformation by vision is also a

---

[116] I have shown above how Philo uses this verb for the description of Moses' transformation.

[117] For more on this, see Furnish, 240.

[118] I am borrowing these examples from Furnish, 240.

[119] For more on this, see Richard Reitzenstein, *Hellenistic Mystery-religions: Their Basic Ideas and Significance*, trans. John E. Steely (Pittsburgh: Pickwick Press, 1978).

Palestinian Jewish motif.[120] I have already showed that these Qumran documents also draw upon the Moses' transformation tradition.

Also, the transformation motif is evident in Jewish Apocalypticism in a much more developed form.[121] For example, the prominent theme in 1 Enoch is the transformation of God's elect on the eschatological day when God's glory abides with them (50:1; 38:2–4; 45:4; 58:3–6). Similarly, 2 Baruch 51:3 and 10 attests that the splendor of the righteous will be glorified in changes and the form of their face will be turned into the light of their beauty. It is interesting that these apocalyptic documents have the Son of Man as their hero, who stands in solidarity with his suffering people.

It may be that apart from the Mosaic transformation tradition, both Hellenistic mystery religion with present aspect and Jewish Apocalypticism with future aspect help Paul in such a way that his transformation accounts have both present and future aspects (cf. 1 Cor 15:51–52; 2 Cor 5:2; 4:16–18; Phil 3:21). In order to maintain the eschatological tension between the present and the future aspects of the transformation, Paul introduces in 3:18 an idea of transformation as a process, "from glory to glory." Barnett claims that the first glory refers to that in the Old Covenant, while the second glory refers to the ultimate glory in the New Covenant.[122] It is, however, more likely that Paul, when using the expression "from glory to glory," is maintaining that the destiny of the believers' transformation is to acquire "eternal fullness of glory" (αἰώνιον βάρος δόξης in 2 Cor 4:17) as its climax, in contrast to Moses' glory which experienced extinction (3:7; cf. 3:11, 13).[123]

Considering the fact that the terms glory and image are used so closely by Paul (cf. 1 Cor 11:7; 2 Cor 4:4),[124] it is not surprising that he takes "the same image" (τὴν αὐτὴν εἰκόνα) to be the destination of the glorious transformation process.[125] What is the referent for the expression "the same image"? Whose image or which image does Paul have in mind? In 1 Cor 11:7, Paul calls man the image and glory of God, drawing upon the Genesis story (Gen 1:26–27; 5:1). In 1 Cor 15:49, the believers are said to bear the image of the heavenly Adam (τὴν εἰκόνα τοῦ ἐπουρανίου), i.e. the ris-

---

[120] Fitzmyer, "Glory Reflected on the Face of Christ (2 Cor 3.7–4.6) and a Palestine Jewish Motif." Also, A.D.A. Moses, *Matthew's Transfiguration Story*, 62. It is, however, likely that this motif is from Greek influence.

[121] See A.D.A. Moses, 89 and Hafemann, 412 and 449.

[122] Barnett, 208.

[123] Furnish, 242.

[124] Lambrecht, 245.

[125] Also in the Hebrew Bible, the visible form or image of God is none other than the Glory that Moses, Ezekiel and Isaiah beheld. For more on this theme, see Dunn, *Christology*, 115.

en Christ, who is the image of God (2 Cor 4:4) with God's glory on his face (4:6). Following this line of thought, Paul clearly presupposes that the first image of the earthly Adam was destroyed and his original glory was lost (cf. Rom 3:23; 8:29). For Paul, when anyone is in Christ, there is new creation (5:17), new creation as the restoration of the divine image and glory (cf. Col 1:15–20).

Is it coincidental that the combination of Adam theology/Christology and the idea of transformation occur in Paul's account? We have already observed that in Sirach, Moses, when he receives the Law of life and knowledge at Sinai, is said to restore the glory that Adam lost and to experience his own glorious transformation (cf. Rom 3:23).[126] While the idea of transformation into the divine image is also evident in Hellenistic mystery religion, Paul's heavy use of Exodus stories along with Adam theology indicates that he is aware of various Jewish exegetical traditions about Moses' transformation in light of Adam theology.

Paul, however, goes beyond those Jewish writers by claiming that Jesus Christ is the perfect image, which according to Philo, Moses also saw. While for Philo, Moses, after having seen the perfect image, becomes a model for a mystical ascent and elevation of the righteous at death, for Paul, Christ becomes both the indispensable model and the perfect image through his obedience to God's will – suffering and death (4:10–12).[127] The believers' transformation occurs after the model of Christ and in conformity with his divine image. Moreover, it has an effect of reversing the Fall, including Israel's subsequent fall in the wilderness.

Philippians 3 shows many similar ideas to 2 Cor 3–4. In Phil 3:21, Paul says: "He [Jesus] will *transform* (μετασχηματίζω) the body of our humiliation that it may be conformed to the body of *his glory*, by the power that also enables him to make all things subject to himself." In the same context, Paul claims that the divine power helped Jesus overcome suffering and death through resurrection (Phil 3:10). Following Jesus in the same path of suffering and death, Paul wishes to experience the same divine power, resurrection and glorious transformation. The major difference between 2 Corinthians and Philippians is: while Paul in 2 Corinthians emphasizes the transformation *now in the present time*, he in Philippians anticipates the transformation *in the future*. In the Philippian context, Paul portrays his bodily transformation into Jesus' glorious body as the ultimate goal of his life.

---

[126] For more on this, see Hafemann, 432–36 with n. 305 for bibliographical information.

[127] For more on Adam Christology for Paul, see Dunn, *Christology*, 100–114.

3.4.5 Conclusion

In conclusion, in the above discussion, we have seen that Moses' transformation experience along with his role as the unique mediator between God and Israel provided a rich conceptual framework for Paul in 2 Cor 3. Paul, however, clearly reinterprets the Mosaic tradition through the lens of the Christ event, especially his experience of the glory of the Risen Lord. We saw how five aspects of Moses' legacy are applicable to Paul's account of the New Covenant ministry and how Paul's defense of his ministry could be interpreted in light of or against those aspects of Moses' ideology. First, Moses was remembered in Israel's history as one with the unique experience of theophany at Sinai. Paul compared Moses' experience with the believers' general indirect experience of the glory of the Lord through the Gospel message and his own direct vision of Christophany at Damascus. Second, Moses' theophanic experience gave him divine credentials for his unique role as lawgiver and for his Old Covenant ministry. Likewise, Paul claimed to find credentials for his New Covenant ministry in the abounding glory, "with much more glory" (vv.9–11). Third, Moses experienced his own glorious transformation after having seen the glory of Yahweh, which Philo calls a "perfect image." Paul democratized this unique experience by ascribing it to the transformation experience of normal believers, which would follow from their exposure to Christ's glory. In Paul's account, the transformed Corinthians themselves functioned as Paul's recommendation letter from Christ (vv.1–3). Fourth and fifth, we have seen that Adam theology was applied to Moses ideology in such a way that Moses restored the glory which Adam lost and that he also became the model after which the righteous would be transformed. Paul claimed that the restoration of the lost glory as well as the reversal of the Fall came through Christ's obedience to God's will in his path of suffering and death (cf. 4:10–11). As a result, Christ is now claimed as the divine image as well as the glory of God, in conformity with which the believers would be transformed.

3.5 Comparison between the Believers' Transformation in Paul and Jesus' Transfiguration in Mark and Its Parallels

It will now be useful to compare the transformation account in 2 Cor 3 with Mark 9:2–10 along with its parallels, as both draw on Moses' transformation account in Exod 34 and its later Jewish interpretive traditions. There seem to be many common ideas between them, though these are not without differing interests and motifs. Do Paul and Mark create their accounts independently from each other using their common knowledge of the Mosaic transformation traditions? Or do they draw upon a pre-Markan Transfiguration story? In the following discussion, I examine similarities and dissimilarities between the two accounts in order to explore to what extent they share the Mosaic transformation tradition and relevant Jesus tradition. On the other hand, what are commonly found in both Paul and Mark, but not in the Mosaic transformation traditions, will shed light on the relationship between Paul and Mark. They may help us understand how Jesus' tradition helps Paul and Mark develop distinctive aspects of their theology.

In chapter one, I pointed out similarities between the stories of the Markan Transfiguration and the Mosaic theophanic experiences in Exod 24:1–18 and 34:29–35. It is beyond doubt that the theophanic experience of Moses greatly influenced Mark. Although Paul's account, unlike Mark's, does not line up exactly with the Exodus stories, it clearly draws upon Moses' transformation experience as well as its interpretive traditions. While Mark is in the form of a narrative and Paul in that of a theological discourse, it is nonetheless possible and useful to compare them, given their common use of Moses' transformation.

It is striking that out of four occurrences of the rare Greek verb μετα-μορφόομαι in the NT, one occurs in Paul and one in Mark, with the third occurrence in Matthew's parallel account of the Transfiguration story (Mt 17:2). The fourth occurrence in the NT is found in Rom 12:2, referring to believers' spiritual renewal in the context of transformation. Outside the NT, the verb occurs in Philo's description of Moses' transformation.[128]

The Moses transformation story, while it helps Mark describe Jesus' Transfiguration as an epiphany or Christophany, enables Paul to explain the apostolic as well as ecclesiological implications of the Corinthian believers' general transformation experience. Unlike Moses, however, the Markan Jesus experiences the Transfiguration without being exposed to God's glory and the major message of the Transfiguration is the revelation of his divine identity as God's Son (Mk 9:7). Like the Jesus in Mark and Luke (Lk 9:29–31), but unlike Moses, Paul's Christ is not someone who is to be exposed to God's glory for his transformation, but is himself the glory of God and possesses transformative power. Similar to Mark's Gospel message of Jesus' Sonship, for Paul, Jesus' Sonship is the starting point of his Gospel message. For Paul, however, the transformation experience is not limited to a special few, like the Markan "three," but instead becomes the normal experience for believers as a result of their exposure to the glory of Christ. In this way, the transformation is democratized in

---

[128] For this, see A.D.A. Moses, 51–57.

Paul's thought and bestows upon him ministerial credentials as the undeniable evidence of its effectiveness.[129]

Second, it is also interesting to notice the strong δόξα motif in 2 Cor 3–4 and in the Transfiguration story, which is clearly from the Mosaic transformation tradition. While this particular use of the word δόξα is not paralleled elsewhere in Paul, it is one of the most important themes of the Transfiguration story.[130] Paul insists on the far greater glory which accompanies his New Covenant ministry and as a result of his unveiling of the Gospel of the Lord of glory, "we all" are enabled to see the glory. This revelatory experience of the glory, according to Paul, comes from God's new creation activity of spreading "the light of the knowledge of the glory of God in the face of Jesus Christ" (4:6). The reference to "the glory of God in the face of Jesus Christ" finds its narrative parallel especially in Luke's version of the Transfiguration story. Luke refers to Jesus' altered face in 9:29 and associates it with the δόξα in 9:31; and the three disciples are said to witness the δόξα in 9:32.

Like Luke, Matthew mentions the shining face of Jesus like the Sun, and Mark describes the transfiguration of Jesus' whole being with emphasis upon the dazzlingly white garments, though not using the specific word δόξα. However, the term μεταμορφόομαι in its use at the Transfiguration can be seen in relation to the motifs of εἰκών and δόξα as it is linked to μορφή which, according to R. P. Martin and others,[131] can be associated with εἰκών and δόξα.[132] Since there is a Moses-Jesus parallelism in terms of glory on the face, as is attested to in Paul, Matthew, and Luke, this parallelism suggests that an earlier version of the Transfiguration story contained the idea of glory on the face of Jesus as well. Mark or Mark's source seems to remove this feature in order to surpass Mosaic typology in his Christological claim.[133]

Third, for both Paul and Mark, the glory comes to have legitimizing functions for different reasons. As for Mark, Jesus' Transfiguration in the Caesarea-Philippi context functions to validate his sayings and divine identity in many ways. First of all, the Transfiguration actualizes Jesus' prediction in Mk 9:1 that "some" people will see the Kingdom of God coming in

---

[129] I am using the modern term "democratized" anachronistically, meaning that Paul distributes a prerogative transformation experience to normal believers.

[130] David Wenham, *Paul: Follower of Jesus or Founder of Christianity?* (Grand Rapids; Cambridge: William B. Eerdmans, 1995).

[131] Ralph P. Martin, *Carmen Christi* (Cambridge: Cambridge University Press, 1967).

[132] Moses, *Matthew's Transfiguration Story,* 227.

[133] I will return to this point in the next chapter where I compare Matthew and Luke with Mark.

power before their death.[134] The term "some" implies that this event will be on a somewhat limited, not full scale, and the unusual chronological note "after six days" in the following verse smoothly links the Transfiguration to this saying.[135] The Transfiguration as the actualization of the coming Kingdom of God on a small scale further assures its readers that Jesus' coming as the Son of Man will be realized on a full scale at the Parousia (Mk 8:38). This idea of the Son of Man as the heavenly judge, in turn, draws the readers' attention to Jesus' commandment to follow him on the path of suffering and death (Mk 8:34–37). The Transfiguration, with its Caesarea-Philippi context as a whole, enables Mark to support his main Christological claim that Jesus is God's Son (cf. Mk 1:1, 11; 9:7) as well as the apocalyptic Son of Man (2:10, 28; 8:31, 38; 9:9, 12, and 31).

In comparison to Mark who makes Christological claims on the basis of the Moses parallel, Paul presupposes Jesus to be the divine carrier of the glory and takes advantage of the Mosaic glory tradition for the sake of his own apostolic credentials. Paul claims that his ministry has been accompanied by "much more glory" than that of Moses' ministry. Paul puts himself as the minister of the New Covenant in parallel with Moses the minister of the Old Covenant. Then he promotes his ministry beyond that of Moses by contrasting the amount of glory in his ministry with that in Moses' ministry. For Paul and the Corinthians, Christ as God's glory seems to be a given, as Paul does not try to defend or explain it, but simply presupposes it.

It is, however, interesting to note the apostolic implication of the Transfiguration story in Mark, as it may function to suggest a special status of the three apostles, Peter, James, and John. As I mentioned earlier, if the Transfiguration story fulfills Jesus' saying in Mk 9:1, the prerogative "some" who will live to witness the Kingdom of God in power are the three disciples. Mark and other Synoptic Gospels suggest that Peter, James and John have special status with privilege among the twelve. They are often invited by Jesus to witness particular events (Mk 5:35–43; 14:33–42), they were the first apostles, along with Andrew, to be called by Jesus (Mk 1:16–20), and they stand at the top of the list of the apostles' names (Mk

---

[134] The author of Second Peter, which is another telling in the independent tradition of the Transfiguration story, understands it to be an anticipation of the Parousia (1:16).

[135] For this reading of Mk 9:1, see Wenham and Moses, "'There are Some Standing Here...': Did They Become the 'Reputed Pillars' of the Jerusalem church? Some Reflections on Mark 9:1, Galatians 2:9 and the Transfiguration." Already more than half a century ago, G. H. Boobyer argued for this opinion, in G. H. Boobyer, *St. Mark and the Transfiguration Story* (Edinburgh: T&T Clark, 1942). Boobyer is followed by V. Taylor, C. E. B. Cranefield, J. Gnilka, R. Pesch, W. D. Davies and D. C. Allison, A. McGuckin, and A. D. A. Moses. For the history of the interpretation of Mk 9:1, refer to M. Künzi, *Das Naherwartungslogion Markus 9.1 par. Geschichte seiner Auslegung* (Tübingen: Mohr, 1977).

3:16–17). Jesus gives special names to Simon and John and James, Peter and the Boanerges, respectively.

Along with the Gethsemane event, it is in the Transfiguration story that its readers cannot miss the particular privilege which Jesus provides for the three. It is not surprising that Matthew, the first reader of Mark (Mt 16:16–19), further develops this type of understanding – the Transfiguration as apostolic promotion – by adding the so-called M tradition and softening Jesus' rebuke of Peter (cf. 2 Peter 1). The idea of promoting Peter and the three at the Transfiguration seems to be known to Luke (Lk 9; Acts 9, 22, and 26). The promotion of the three at the Transfiguration is understanda-ble in light of Moses' transformation tradition. Just as Moses' authority (and Paul's authority) is legitimated by the glory, so also is the apostolic authority of the three strengthened by their exposure to Jesus' glory (cf. 1 Cor 15: 2–11).

It is also striking that while preserving the three's special privilege in his narrative accounts in the way he received it from his tradition, Mark tries to negate or neutralize their privilege by continuously mentioning their spiritual blindness. It is in the Caesarea-Phlippi context itself that the Markan Jesus rebukes Peter for setting his mind on "human affairs," not on "God's affairs" (Mk 8:32–33). Jesus also criticizes James and John for seeking to sit at his side in glory (Mk 10:35–45) and delivers a teaching on true leadership found by becoming others' "servants" (Mk 9:35; 10:45). This servant-leadership is exactly what Paul understands the apostleship to be (cf. Rom 1:1; 2 Cor 1:4–5). It is probable that the Transfiguration story already functioned to promote the three, especially Peter, before it reaches Mark; Mark then tries to neutralize this tradition in his gospel accounts by revealing "the veil" of spiritual blindness in their hearts.[136] Matthew and Luke, the first readers of Mark, on the other hand, attempt to neutralize the Markan criticism of the three, especially Peter.[137]

Fourth, both the accounts of Paul and Mark show the paradoxical cha-racter of glorious transformation: glorious transformation only comes after having experienced persecution and suffering. This point is extremely im-portant for us, as it is not found in the Mosaic transformation tradition.[138] What does its common mention in Paul and Mark tell us about the relation-ship between the two, while not being attested to in the Mosaic transforma-tion tradition? In Paul, suffering with Christ is the only way to glory (2 Cor 4:10ff; cf. Rom 8:17ff; Phil 3:10ff). Paul is willing to follow Jesus in

---

[136] While some scholars try to promote Matthean priority by arguing that Mark re-moves the M tradition in Matthew, I agree with the majority view of Markan priority.

[137] I will discuss this in more detail in the following chapter.

[138] I have to mention here that the Suffering Servant is found in Second Isaiah, which is full of Sinai and Exodus motifs. But Mosaic transformation is not explained there, es-pecially in connection with suffering.

the path of suffering and death, so that the life of Jesus may abound in his mortal body and he may acquire the eternal weight of glory (2 Cor 4:11, 17). Also, for Paul, the Gospel of the glory of Christ (2 Cor 4:4) is the very Gospel of the word of the Cross (1 Cor 1:17–18). It is precisely as the crucified one that Christ is "the Lord of glory" (1 Cor 2:8). For Paul, suffering with Christ is never just an apostolic vocation, but is one of the most crucial aspects of being a believer.

Similarly, as I have shown in chapter one, the Markan Transfiguration occurs in the Caesarea-Phlippi context which begins and ends with Jesus' double pronouncement of the necessity of the Son of Man's suffering and death (Mk 8:31; 9:12). I have shown that it is because Jesus has not yet gone through the path of suffering and death that his gloriously transfigured status should be kept secret within the prerogative three. Similar to Paul, Mark seems to create a new Christian dictum: "No suffering, no glory!"

This observation of the paradoxical character of the glorious transformation is, in my opinion, the key to our understanding of the relationship between Paul and Mark regarding the Jesus tradition, especially because of its theological importance for both. Paul and Mark may have developed this idea of paradoxical glorification independently by combining the two different traditions of the glorious transformation and the Suffering Servant, and if so, the similarity between the two accounts is just coincidental. It is, however, more likely that the two ideas reach Mark and Paul, one generation earlier, in a combined form, not only because the idea of the Suffering Servant is so pervasive and crucial for their understanding of glorification in both accounts, but also because the theological frameworks of Paul and Mark and all they imply are almost identical to each other.

We have already seen that a similar combination of the Suffering Servant and the glorious Son of Man is often attested in Enoch, 4 Ezra, and Baruch. Also, in Daniel, we find strong solidarity between the Son of Man in glory and his people in suffering. Already in Second Isaiah, the idea of the Suffering Servant is often followed by glory (Isa 40:1–11; 60:1–3).[139] With this theological background, early believers attempted to understand Jesus' ministry both on earth and in heaven through the lens of those messianic ideas, especially by applying them all to Jesus in a merged form. It seems to me that Paul and Mark are independent witnesses to an early Jesus tradition where an understanding of Jesus' glorious status with its ecclesiological implication has been interpreted through the two key ideas of the Suffering Servant and the Son of Man.

---

[139] For the transformative glory in the prophetic writings, see Carey C. Newman, *Paul's Glory-Christology: Tradition and Rhetoric* (NTSup 69: Leiden: E.J. Brill, 1992).

Fifth, following from the previous point, the glory is both transformative and apocalyptic in both Mark and Paul.[140] As Carey Newman has shown, glory in Second Isaiah functions to transform not only nations, but also individuals, especially on the Day of the Lord.[141] In Paul, it should now be clear that the believers' transformation comes from their exposure to the glory of the Lord (2 Cor 3:18) – God's transforming power. Since the glory in Paul is the glory of the risen Lord, Jesus' own glorious transformation is presupposed in the Corinthian correspondence (cf. 1 Cor 15). The transformation of the believers is an ongoing present reality for Paul and awaits its final climax at the end, in "an eternal weight of glory" (2 Cor 4:17). Also, Paul claims that all will appear before the judgment seat of Christ (2 Cor 5:10),[142] so that they may receive recompense for what they have done in the body. The believers who have been in the process of glorious transformation, says Paul, are to receive the eternal glory on the Day of the Lord (2 Cor 5:5; 1 Cor 1:14). These ideas find their parallels in Jesus' two-fold teaching in the Caesarea-Philippi context with the Transfiguration.

In my analysis of the Transfiguration in the Caesarea-Philippi context, I have argued that the Transfiguration functions as the proleptic revelation of Jesus' coming with angels as the Son of Man in his Father's glory (cf. 8:38–9:2). In Jewish apocalyptic writings, it is believed that the righteous receive transformation as an expression of their vindication by God. This is especially evident in writings about the Son of Man. For example, in Daniel, the suffering righteous, who stand in solidarity with the Son of Man who has received from the Ancient One both glory and power (Dan 7:13–14), are said to be in angelic status after their resurrection (Dan 12:3). Similarly, both 1 Enoch and 2 Baruch attest to the transformation of God's elect on the eschatological day and to the glorification of the righteous through the changing of their form (1 En 50:1; 38:2–4; 45:4; 58:3–6; 2 Baruch 51:3 and 10). Is it coincidental that these writings have the Son of Man as their hero, who will judge at the end of days after having come in glory? It seems that the Son of Man is not only the eschatological judge, but also the harbinger of glorious transformation, an idea which is paralleled in Paul's Christ as the Second Adam.

Similarly to what is expressed in Paul's account, the Markan glory is also apocalyptic as well as transformative, although the transformative aspect for the believers is implicit rather than explicit. In my understanding

---

[140] For the theme of transformation with judgment, see Newman, 45.

[141] Ibid.

[142] It is said that Paul's idea of the judgment seat is from the tradition of the Son of Man as the eschatological judge. Since the term Son of Man does not make much sense to Paul and the Greek-speaking people, he uses the term Son instead of the Son of Man.

of Mark, the gloriously transfigured Jesus tells the readers that he will surely come as the Son of Man in his full glory and change the righteous martyrs in glory.[143] If Moses and Elijah are to be understood as two angel-like attendants of Jesus,[144] as I argued, then they represent the transfigured righteous in angelic status. Mark implies that those who follow Jesus on the path of suffering and death (Mk 8:34–35) will experience similar transformations into angelic beings as their vindication. It is likely that Mark here wants to encourage his readers to endure their current suffering so that they may find consolation in their expectation for similar transformation as an eschatological recompense (cf. Mk 8:38).[145] In their cultural as well as religious milieu, the Markan readers can easily think of sharing the same destiny as that of their hero and readily see their glorious transformation in the transfigured Jesus. It is interesting that one of the apocryphal versions of the Transfiguration story in Apocalypse of Peter (2 CE) claims that the glorious bodies of Moses and Elijah stand for the resurrected bodies of the believers at the Parousia. In conclusion, the readers of Mark and Paul are invited to enter into the same type of discipleship: their glorious transformation through following Jesus in the way of suffering and death.[146]

Sixth, at first glance, readers may think that while Paul's transformation theology is deeply rooted in his unique Adam Christology (cf. Phil 3:2–23), Mark does not seem to manifest any ideas similar to Adam theology: being transformed into the same image by beholding the glory of Christ, who is the image of God.[147] Regarding Adam theology in Mark, however, I have already mentioned above that the term μεταμορφόομαι can be seen in relation to the motifs of εἰκών and δόξα. Furthermore, in Jewish writings, the idea of the Suffering Servant has something to do with God's re-creation activity with His glory and speech, and the Son of Man is described as the author of transformation. Although Mark does not explicitly spell out

---

[143] As for the idea that the Transfiguration is seen as a foreshadowing of the Parousia and the three disciples as witnessing an event with eschatological significance, see Boobyer, *St. Mark and the Transfiguration Story*; T. J. Weeden, *Mark – Traditions in Conflict* (Philadelphia: Fortress Press, 1971), 124–27; W. H. Kelber, *The Kingdom in Mark. A New Place and a New Time* (Philadelphia: Fortress Press, 1974), 72–5; and Smith, *The Petrine Controversy*, 171.

[144] The appearance of two angelic assistants before seers or heroes is common in Jewish apocalyptic writings, which later Christian apocryphal writings inherit (e.g. 1 Enoch).

[145] Most commentators agree that Mark is written around the tragic event of the destruction of the Temple and the Markan community is going through much suffering. Mark develops the theology of the Cross in order to help his readers to get through this troubled time (e.g. Marcus, *Mark*, 28–29).

[146] On the theme of glorious transformation and suffering, see Moses, 236.

[147] See the terminological connection between Gen 1 and 2 Cor 4: light and darkness, God's speaking, image, etc.

Adam theology in the way Paul does, the two key ideas of the Suffering
Servant and the Son of Man may betray similar ideas, even in their new
context of Mark.[148]

In Is 42:6 and 9, God says of the Suffering Servant that he is like a New
Moses, someone who leads Israel in a New Exodus, "I have given you *as a
covenant* for the people, as the *light* to the nations." The Suffering Servant
is given as a covenant, especially through his suffering and death, and
moreover, he becomes the light, a description which alludes to the Genesis
creation story. For both Paul and Mark, this understanding of the Suffering
Servant as God's covenant and light is key not only to their interpretation
of Jesus' life and ministry, but also to the paradoxical nature of glorification through suffering and death. For both, Jesus is the one who establishes
the New Covenant through his suffering and death (cf. 1 Cor 11; Mk
14:22–25). We have also seen in 2 Cor 3 how Paul's New Covenant ministry could transform believers through the glory of Christ, Christ taking the
role of the Suffering Servant (2 Cor 4:10ff; cf. Rom 8:17ff; Phil 3:10ff).
Also in the Markan Caesarea-Philippi context, the Transfiguration story
immediately follows Jesus' two-fold teaching about his own suffering and
death as well as that of his followers', as if the order of suffering-
glorification is something that should be kept.

It is also interesting that this Isaianic Servant is connected to God's new
creation activity in many ways. First of all, in Is 42:6, God presents the
Suffering Servant as the *light* to the nations who are in *darkness*. Moreover,
God's offering of the Servant is the beginning of His new creation activity
which begins with His *speech,* as the first creation started: "See, the former
things have come to pass, and *new things* I now *declare...new songs...*" (Is
42:9ff; italics are mine). Also, in this new creation activity of God, the
coming of the Suffering Servant is followed by God's own theophanic arrival in His glory. In Is 60:1–3, on the dawning of a new day – a dramatic
day of eschatological reversal with judgment – the light of Israel, which is
the glory of the Lord, will be revealed to the nations, reversing the fortunes
of Israel and of the nations (cf. 40:1–11).[149] Like the first day of creation,
the light/the glory of the Lord will offer life-giving healing to His people,
whom He has created for His glory (Is 43:6–7; 58:8).

The idea of eschatological judgment along with the idea of the restoration of God's people, which Isaiah would expect to begin with the coming
of the Suffering Servant and be followed by God's theophanic arrival, is
also found in a much more developed form in Jewish apocalyptic traditions

---

[148] According to C. H. Dodd, the idea of the Suffering Servant is a source of testimo-
nia for the NT. See C. H. Dodd, *According to the Scriptures: The Sub-culture of New Testament Theology* (New York: Scribner, 1953), 88–94.

[149] I am borrowing these examples from Newman, *Paul's Glory-Christology*, 63–66.

dealing with the Son of Man. In those apocalyptic traditions, the Son of Man as God's vice-regent comes to rescue his suffering people from their evil opponents and transforms them in glory. There seems to be scholarly consensus that the Danielic tradition of the Son of Man lies behind the later Jewish apocalyptic traditions of the Son of Man, who is described both as the eschatological judge and harbinger of the transformation of his people (Dan 7:13–14; 12:1–5).[150] In throne visions found in these apocalyptic writings, the Son of Man shares the same throne and functions as God and appears in the same glory.[151] Around the throne(s) of glory, angels or transformed human patriarchs clothed in glory are commonly found.

Many have showed with some success the influence of the throne vision in Ezek 1 on the later apocalyptic revelation of the glory in human form, especially concerning the Son of Man on the throne of God in 1 Enoch.[152] For example, Dan 7 betrays the influence of Ezek 1 and shares many similarities, such as thrones, beasts, winds, wheels, clouds, and the divine being in human form.[153] In Ezek 1:28, God's glory is described in detail and is likened to the divine being in human form who is seated upon the throne: "there was the likeness of a throne, in appearance like sapphire; and seated above the likeness of a throne was a *likeness of a human being*." If the scholarly suggestion that Dan 7:13–14 is drawing upon Ezek 1:28 in the tradition-history of the glory is correct, then the Son of Man is the personification of God's glory in human form. Considering that the glory represents God's image in visible form, we may say that God's glory as God's image becomes personified in the Son of Man.[154] The idea that the Son of Man as God's glory or image transforms his suffering people is not that far from Paul's idea of Jesus as the image/glory of God who will transform the bodies of the believers into his glorious body (1 Cor 15:21–57; 2 Cor 4:4–6). Looked at in this way, Jesus as the Suffering Son of Man in Mark can be considered parallel to Paul's Jesus as the second Adam.

In conclusion, we have seen that Paul and Mark share many similar ideas which are also attested in the Mosaic transformation traditions: the term μεταμορφόομαι, the motif of the glory in the face and its transforma-

---

[150] For this and for bibliographical information, see Ibid., 79–91.

[151] Ibid.

[152] For bibliographical information, see Newman, 92 n.28.

[153] For more on this, see Chrys C. Caragounis, *The Son of Man: Vision and Interpretation* (WUNT 1/38; Tübingen: Mohr–Siebeck, 1986); and D. S. Russell, *The Method and Message of Jewish Apocalyptic 200 B.C. – 100 A.D.* (Philadelphia: Westminster, 1964).

[154] According to Gieschen in *Angelomorphic Christology*, it is a common phenomenon in late Second Temple Judaism that hypostases of God, such as God's names and attributes, become personified into angelic beings. Although they stand in close relationship with God as His representation on earth, they tend to acquire independent personalities in that time period.

tive as well as legitimizing functions. These common themes clearly indicate that both have taken advantage of the Mosaic transformation traditions for their descriptions of the Transfiguration or the transformation. We have seen that the two accounts of transformation stories in Paul and Mark are not isolated phenomena, but are instead closely related to each other in such a way that the transformation of a hero results in that of his people. In several scriptural passages, we find this combination especially in a pattern of Christophany and transformation (e.g. Stephen in Acts 7 and Paul in Acts 9, 22, and 26).

However, it is also true that Paul and Mark share ideas not found in the Mosaic transformation traditions: (1) the paradoxical nature of glorification, (2) in connection with the idea of the Suffering Servant and (3) its apocalyptic implication – standing before the Son of Man (Mk 8:38) or before the judgment seat of Christ (2 Cor 5:10). Since Paul and Mark's transformation accounts are so deeply rooted in these ideas of the Suffering Son of Man and the Mosaic transformation story, it is reasonable to conclude that behind their accounts, there lies an early Jesus tradition where Jesus is glorified through his experience of suffering and death and goes beyond Moses as God's Son with divine glory.

In Mark, Jesus as God's Son takes the role of the Suffering Servant and appears as the glorious Son of Man. In his account, Jesus as the Prophet-like-Moses is presupposed, but surpassed by his Sonship at the Transfiguration event. In Paul, Jesus goes beyond Moses by being the glory of God and enables those who see his glory to be transformed in the same glory. Paul understands Jesus' glorification in light of his suffering and death. I therefore argue that both Paul and Mark develop their accounts not directly from the Mosaic transformation, but from an early Christian understanding of Jesus with a strong glory motif where he becomes glorified through his suffering and death and surpasses Moses as God's Son – the divine carrier of the glory.

Do we have any textual evidence of this Christological tradition other than Paul and Mark? In the process of comparing Jesus with Moses, the author of Hebrews claims that Jesus is faithful over God's house as His Son, while Moses is faithful as a servant (Heb 1:2–3; 3:2–6). Just as the builder has more honor and glory than the house itself, so also is Jesus worthy of more glory than Moses (Heb 3:3). Hebrews also presupposes that Jesus fulfills the prophecy of the Prophet-like-Moses, since it applies Deut 18:15 to Jesus twice (Heb 3:7–8, 15). According to Hebrews, Jesus is crowned with glory and honor because of his suffering and death as atonement for the sins of people (2:9, 17–18). Jesus as the author of salvation will bring the believers to glory (2:10). Jesus is exalted to sit at the right side of God and appears as the eschatological judge (1:13). The Christological sections in the first chapters are the proclaimed faith of its community and are much earlier than its composition.[155] Since Hebrews shows the same complex of ideas arranged in a Christological outlook similar to that of Paul and Mark, we can safely conclude (1) that there is an early Jesus tradition with a strong glory motif where Jesus subsumes the roles of the Son of Man and the Suffering Servant and surpasses Moses as God's Son; and (2) that Mark and Paul develop their transformation accounts from this tradition, Christologically and ecclesiologically, respectively, rather than directly from the Mosaic transformation tradition.

Due to the ample similarities between the two transformation accounts of Paul and Mark, I suspect that the generation following Paul or even Paul himself may have compared the two stories or some of their aspects with one another.[156] Especially because the two stories play an important role in legitimating the apostleship or authority of some Christian leaders, I find this suspicion very probable. For example, there are numerous common ideas found both at the Transfiguration and in Gal 1–2, where Paul seems to allude to his own experience of Christophany at Damascus, though the nature of the experience itself has been debated:[157] (1) the contrast between human approval and divine approval (Gal 1:10; cf. "human affair" vs. "God's affair," Mk 8:33); (2) the revelation of Jesus' divine Sonship (Gal 1:12, 16; Mk 9:7); (3) the Gospel, not of human origin, but of divine origin (Gal 1:11; Mk 9:7; cf. Mt 17:17); (4) the theme of suffering and persecution (Gal 1:13; Mk 8:31; 9:12); (5) life for the sake of Christ and the Gospel (Gal 2:19–20, and 14; Mk 8:35); (6) condemnation of Peter (Gal 2:11; Mk 8:33); (7) three acknowledged pillars (Gal 2:2, 6, 9; Mk 9:2); and (8) the idea of transformation (Gal 1:13, 23; Mk 9:2–3). In addition, in the synoptic traditions, it is in the Caesarea-Philippi context that Peter first appears in a separate role from that of the disciples as a group. Is Paul here comparing his Damascus experience with the three's experience of the Transfiguration? In the following chapter on Matthew and Luke, I will compare the experience of the glory of Jesus by the three and by Paul, especially in the Lukan accounts.

---

[155] Harold Attridge, *The Epistle to the Hebrews* (Philadelphia: Fortress Press, 1989), 9, 26.

[156] See also Wenham and Moses, "'There are Some Standing Here...': Did They Become the 'Reputed Pillars' of the Jerusalem church? Some Reflections on Mark 9:1, Galatians 2:9 and the Transfiguration."

[157] Barnett, 37.

Chapter 4

The Transfiguration Rewritten and Recontextualized in Matthew and Luke

4.1 Introduction

In this chapter, I will analyze the Transfiguration in Matthew and Luke, the first interpreters of the Markan story.[1] Following the scholarly consensus of the two source hypothesis with the Markan priority,[2] I will base my analysis of Matthew and Luke upon their diachronic and synchronic readings.[3] In the diachronic reading, I will compare Matthew and Luke with Mark and flesh out their redactional changes. This reading will demonstrate how Matthew and Luke's new perspectives on Jesus alter the story that they have received from Mark. In the synchronic reading, on the other hand, I will examine how the Christological emphasis of the Transfiguration in Matthew and Luke is related to the rest of their Gospels. This will reveal how they develop or modify the Christological ideas found in the Markan Transfiguration story in order to make the story fit into its new narrative contexts in Matthew and Luke.

---

[1] While adopting the two source hypothesis, I concur with R. T. France and others that a rigid x-copied-y approach does not do justice to the complex relationship among the synoptic Gospels (R. T. France, *The Gospel of Matthew* [Grand Rapids, Mich.: William B. Eerdmans, 2007], 20–21), because it gives a false impression that while Mark is the original writer of the Transfiguration, Matthew and Luke are its mere redactors. It is beyond doubt that before they had access to the Markan story, both Matthew and Luke were already familiar with the story of Jesus, at least in an oral version. This implies that although Matthew and Luke are dependent upon Mark, they still reflect parallel developments of the same story. Their differences from Mark are their own contributions to the ongoing development of the Transfiguration tradition in the first century.

[2] Against this, Barbara Reid, following M. É. Boismard and Jerome Murphy-O'Connor, argues that the Lukan version is a composite of two originally separate pieces of tradition: Luke's special source (9:28–33a, 36b) and Mark (Luke 9:33b–35). See Barbara E. Reid, *The Transfiguration: A Source– and Redaction– Critical Study of Luke 9:28–36* (Paris: J. Gabalda et Cie, 1993). Against Reid, Robert J. Miller, correctly in my opinion, claims that there is insufficient evidence that there is an independent attestation of the tradition from Mark (Robert J. Miller, "Historicizing the Trans-historical: the Transfiguration Narrative," *Foundations & Facets Forum* 10 (1994): 219–48).

[3] For these methods, see Graham N. Stanton, *A Gospel for a New People: Studies in Matthew* (Louisville, KY: Westminster/John Knox Press, 1993), especially part 1.

Matthew and Luke, in the process of making the story tightly fit into the overall contexts of their Gospels, add new motifs or ideas or expand old ones. They also insert catchwords in their retellings of the Transfiguration so that they can add new implications to the story by relating it to the rest of their Jesus stories. I will show that even through small editorial changes, they can greatly alter the flow of the story. These editorial changes often give us hints of the historical settings of Matthew and Luke. Since Matthew and Luke speak to their own communal needs and agendas, their stories should be examined in light of their particular historical situations.

4.2 The Transfiguration in Matthew (17:1–13)

In the Markan Transfiguration story, we have seen that Mark presents a "two-level" Christology, "from above" and "from below," by incorporating various Jewish and Hellenistic ideas and motifs. Responding to Jesus' two questions, "who do people say that I am?" and "who do you say that I am?" (Mk 8:27 and 29), Mark provides the divine answer in two ways: (1) the visible manifestation of Jesus' status in glorious transfiguration and (2) the audible manifestation of his Sonship through God's divine voice. In this Markan narrative scheme, while Jesus fulfills the messianic expectations of the Hebrew Scriptures, he nonetheless surpasses them by being God's Son.

In the Matthean version of the story, the Markan storyline is kept intact, though not without experiencing some redactional changes. Jesus' glorious transformation stands at the center of the Transfiguration event. God confirms Jesus' Sonship and validates his teaching by His voice, being present in a cloud. However, the high mountain, the setting of the Transfiguration, gets new emphasis in the Matthean context by relating the story to the Temptation (ch. 4), the Sermon on the Mount (ch. 5–6), the Gethsemane story (ch. 26), and Jesus' missionary speech on a mountain in Galilee (ch. 28). Also, God's confirmation of Jesus' Sonship is further reinforced by the Incarnation – Jesus is now called Immanuel, "the presence of God."

In his version of the story, Matthew mentions Jesus' brilliant face, which is missing in Mark, and puts additional emphasis on the Moses-Jesus parallel to make the Transfiguration another Sinai event. Matthew also rehabilitates the three disciples by omitting their ignorance of the implications of the Transfiguration in Mark. He calls the event "vision" (ὅραμα), since he considers the knowledge of Jesus' Sonship God's special revelation. In the Caesarea-Philippi context, Matthew emphasizes Peter's role as the foundational rock of the church and includes new material regarding the construction of the church. For Matthew, the Transfiguration

becomes a new Sinai-Theophany event with the making of a covenant between God and His people, now the church.

4.2.1 Matthew's Rewriting of the Markan Transfiguration Story (17:1–13)[4]

– Jesus' Radiant Face

Similarly to Mark, after having predicted that some of the disciples will
witness the Son of Man's coming in his Kingdom (Mt16:28), Matthew narrates the Transfiguration by Jesus' climbing a high mountain with three of
his disciples, Peter, James and John. Jesus is then transfigured (μετεμορφώθη) before them (Mt 17:1–2). Matthew, however, adds a striking detail about Jesus' radiant face, which draws upon the description of Moses'
radiant skin (Ex. 34:39ff; cf. Philo *Vita*. 2.70): "his face shone like the
sun" (ἔλαμψεν τὸ πρόσωπον αὐτοῦ ὡς ὁ ἥλιος; 17:2). In Jewish texts, angels and archangels often appear as brighter than the sun (Dan 10:6; 2 En
19:1; 3 En 18:25; Test. Abr. 7; Apoc. Zepha. 6:11–15; cf. Rev 1:16, 10:1).[5]
Philo in *Mos*. 1.70 compares Moses' facial radiance to that of the sun, thus
making him an angel-like being.[6] In contrast to Mark who does not mention Jesus' radiant face, Matthew includes the face motif and thereby
makes the connection much clearer between the Sinai experience of Moses
and the Transfiguration.[7] Matthew also restores the order of the two prophets' names from "Elijah with Moses" (Mk 9:4) to "Moses and Elijah" (Mt
9:3). While by emphasizing the presence of Elijah in this event, Mark intended to clear away a scribal rejection of Jesus' messiahship on the basis
that Elijah had not returned yet (Mk 9:11–13), Matthew attempts to accen-
tuate the Sinai parallelism by first mentioning Moses before Elijah.

It is beyond doubt that Matthew relies more than Mark on Moses and
Sinai themes in his description of Jesus throughout his Gospel.[8] In the birth
and infancy narratives (Mt 1–2), Jesus flees to Egypt from Herod's persecution. Just as Moses crosses the Red Sea, Jesus crosses water at his bapt-

---

[4] As for Matthew's restructuring and reworking of Mark based on key numerals of
Judaism and Torah, see Anne M. O'Leary, *Matthew's Judaization of Mark: Examined in
the Context of the Use of Sources in Graeco-Roman Antiquity* (London; New York: T &
T Clark, 2006).

[5] For more on this topic, see Craig S. Keener, *A Commentary on the Gospel of Matthew* (Grand Rapids, MI: William B. Eeerdmans, 1999), 437–38.

[6] For Moses–Sinai and his transfiguration in Philo, see A.D.A. Moses, 50–57.

[7] See Stephen C. Barton, "The Transfiguration of Christ according to Mark and Matthew: Christology and Anthropology," in *Auferstehung – Resurrection*, ed. F. Avemarie
and H. Lichtenberger (Tübingen: Mohr Siebeck, 1999), 240–41; and Moses, *Matthew's
Transfiguration Story and Jewish-Christian Controversy*, 122.

[8] For more on this topic, see Allison, *The New Moses. A Matthean Typology*; and John
K. Riches, *Conflicting Mythologies: Identity Formation in the Gospels of Mark and Matthew* (Edinburgh: T & T Clark, 2000), 272.

ism (3); as Moses and Israel wander in the wilderness for forty years, Jesus is tempted by Satan in the wilderness for forty days (4). In the Sermon on the Mount (5–7), Jesus appears as a law-giver and teacher as Moses does on Mt. Sinai. Like Moses, Jesus' journey is from Egypt to the wilderness, to the mountain, and then to Jerusalem, the heart of the Promised Land. Jesus in Matthew clearly recapitulates the stories of Moses and Israel.

However, while Jesus' radiant face at the Transfiguration clearly reminds readers of Moses' experience at the Sinai Theophany, it is questionable whether Matthew, by mentioning his radiant face, intends to legitimize Jesus as the new Moses or affirm his teaching authority.[9] For Jesus was already appointed as God's divine Son in the infancy narrative and at the baptism (3:1–17), and his teaching authority became manifest to the public (7:28). Also, the Mosaic typology cannot be the single dominant hermeneutical key for the entire Matthean Christological project, including the Transfiguration. Against Dale Allison's new Moses Christology, I argue that Matthew reads the scriptural stories, including Moses, on the basis of his understanding of Jesus.[10] For example, although Jesus appears as a teacher and lawgiver like Moses in the Gospel of Matthew, he outstrips Moses by being called God's Son and Immanuel (1:23). While the Moses and Sinai themes provide Matthew with rich theological vocabulary for his description of Jesus, it is his new perspective on Jesus that guides the whole narrative structure of his Gospel. Luz is correct to say that Christology is in the whole story rather than in one title or motif.[11]

In the Transfiguration story, the radiant face of Jesus and his white garments also serve Matthew in his understanding of the story as an apocalyptic "vision" (17:9). In Jewish apocalyptic writings, a facial radiance and white garments are general characteristics of belonging to the heavenly world. For example, angelic beings are often portrayed with radiant faces and white garments (Dan 12:3; 1 En 62:15–16; 4 Ezra 7:97; 2 Apo Bar 51:3).[12] In the resurrection scene of Matthew, an angel of the Lord appears at the entrance of the empty tomb. His appearance is like lightning and his

---

[9] Cf. A.D.A. Moses, *Matthew's Transfiguration Story and Jewish-Christian Controversy*, 122. I here disagree with A.D.A. Moses, since God's voice "listen to him" clearly identifies Jesus as the one who now has to be heard in place of Moses and Elijah. See also Joseph A. Fitzmyer, "The Composition of Luke, Chapter 9," in *Perspectives on Luke–Acts* (Danville, VA: Association of Baptist Professors of Religion, 1978), 146.

[10] See also Ulrich Luz, *Studies in Matthew*, trans. Rosemary Selle (Grand Rapids, MI: W.B. Eerdmans Pub. Co., 2005), 32. Cf. Dale Allison, *The New Moses. A Matthean Typology* (Minneapolis: Fortress, 1993).

[11] *Ibid.*, 96. This can be a criticism of Jack D. Kingsbury's promotion of the Son of God title as the main Christological title of Matthew. Cf. J. D. Kingsbury, *Matthew. Structure, Christology, Kingdom* (Philadelphia: Fortress, 1975).

[12] Luz, *Matthew*, vol. 2, 397.

clothing is white as snow. Also, the cloud out of which God speaks is full of radiant light (17:5). In chapter one, I have argued that there is a sharp contrast between the heavenly three (the transfigured Jesus, Moses and Elijah) and the earthly three (Peter, James and John). By adding the motif of the radiant face, Matthew reinforces this contrast.

Furthermore, the radiant face also connotes an ontological[13] implication for the existence of the righteous in the future. Paul and Jewish apocalyptists speak of the transformation of the righteous into eschatological bodies with glory, which is often symbolized by their receiving of new white garments (1 Cor 15:51–52; 2 Apo Bar 49:2–3; 51:3, 5, 9–12; Dan 12:3).[14] Matthew is aware of this tradition and makes a similar claim in 13:43: "the righteous will shine like the sun in the kingdom of their Father" (οἱ δίκαιοι ἐκλάμψουσιν ὡς ὁ ἥλιος ἐν τῇ βασιλείᾳ τοῦ πατρὸς αὐτῶν). It is very striking that Matthew creates a parallelism between the Transfiguration in the Caesarea-Philippi context and the parable of the weeds of the field (13:36–43). In both stories, Matthew commonly mentions the radiant face, the coming of the Son of Man as the eschatological judge, the presence of angels as his agents of judgment and his kingdom. Due to this striking parallelism, it is likely that Matthew is making a deliberate redactional and thematic connection between the two stories.[15] In light of the parable of the weeds of the field, Jesus' radiant face along with the presence of the resurrected Moses and Elijah at the Transfiguration can be the signs of the reward of the righteous at their resurrection.

In Matthew's theological scheme, righteous believers share the same destiny as Jesus.[16] Like Jesus, they are expected to be persecuted for the sake of righteousness and called "sons of God" (5:9–12; 16:21; 17:5). Like the transfigured Jesus with radiant face, they will also shine like the sun in their Father's kingdom. Matthew, however, further *ethicizes* this idea by claiming that it is now in the present time that the believers should shine like the sun, just as Jesus *is* the light of the world (4:16). In the Sermon on the Mount, Matthew says, "You are the light of the world…Let your light shine before human beings in such a way that they may see your *good works*, and glorify your Father who is in heaven." Matthew further strengthens this message by demonstrating how the believers' ethical life in the present time determines their future destiny when the Son of Man comes to judge (22:11–14; 25:31–46).

---

[13] Following its definition in the Oxford English Dictionary, I mean by this term what is "concerned with the nature or essence of being or existence."

[14] Ibid.

[15] See also Moses, *Matthew's Transfiguration Story and Jewish-Christian Controversy*, 124–26.

[16] See also *Ibid.*, 126–27; and Barton, "The Transfiguration of Christ according to Mark and Matthew: Christology and Anthropology."

– A High Mountain
The two key ideas of a high mountain and Jesus' divine Sonship relate the Transfiguration both *backward* and *forward*: to the Infancy narrative and the Baptism, as well as to the Temptation, the Gethsemane scene, the Passion narrative and the Great Commission on a Galilean mountain. By being related to other stories in the rest of the Gospel of Matthew, the Transfiguration story becomes enriched and gets new emphases in its new context.

The term *mountain* occurs frequently in Matthew as a setting for Jesus' ministry (5:1, 14; 15:29); but only on two occasions (4:8 and 17:1) Matthew speaks of "a high mountain" (ὄρος ὑψηλὸν).[17] Whether the high mountain of the Transfiguration is Mt. Tabor or Mt. Hermon, its location in Caesarea-Philippi is important for Matthew's theological scheme.[18] Jesus' Galilean ministry is surrounded by his two visits to Jerusalem, one under Satan's temptation and the other to accomplish God's divine will – his suffering, death, and resurrection.[19] In Matthew, Jerusalem appears as a place of suffering and death for Jesus and on the pinnacle of its Temple, Satan tempts Jesus to throw him down. On the other hand, on a Galilean mountain, Jesus reveals his divine Sonship at the Transfiguration and God confirms it. After Easter, he is worshipped on a Galilean mountain by his disciples, and he commissions them to continue his earthly ministry (Mt 28:16–20; cf. 26:32). Matthew clearly presents the mountain in Galilee as an alternative for Mt. Zion in Jerusalem or Mt. Horeb. The mountain in Galilee serves Matthew in his polemic against the mainline Pharisaic Judaism.[20]

The term "high mountain" at the Transfiguration reminds the readers of the high mountain in Mt 4:8–10, where Satan offered Jesus all the kingdoms of the world as a reward for worshipping him. At the Temptation, the motifs of the kingdom, the glory, the Sonship and the contrast between the human will and the divine will appear along with the motif of the high

---

[17] As for possible locations of Jesus' Transfiguration, Mt. Tabor and Mt. Hermon have been suggested. Since Mt. Tabor, which is located in lower Galilee, is not very high (588 m) and the city of Caesarea-Philippi is located at the southern base of Mt. Hermon, some scholars consider Mt. Hermon as "the high mountain" of the Transfiguration. See Moses, *Matthew's Transfiguration*, 118; S. Freyne, *Galilee, Jesus and the Gospel* (Dublin: Gill & Macmillan, 1988), 188–89; Nickelsburg, "Enoch, Levi, and Peter: Recipients of Revelation in Upper Galilee," 575–600; and R.J. Clifford, *The Cosmic Mountain in Canaan and the Old Testament* (Cambridge: Harvard University Press, 1972), 187–88.

[18] This city is located about 25 miles north of the Sea of Galilee and at the south-west foot of Mt. Hermon.

[19] See also Freyne, *Galilee, Jesus and the Gospel*, 109.

[20] I agree with Stanton, Luz, Freyne and Riches that Matthew is presenting his church as an alternative for the Pharisaic Judaism by promoting the Galilean mountain over Jerusalem and Mt. Zion or Mt. Horeb. I will discuss this point later.

mountain. In order to establish his kingdom, however, Jesus rejects the sa-
tanic way of bypassing the path of suffering and death. But instead, Jesus
puts himself under the curse of crucifixion – God's way (cf. δεῖ in 16:21)
laid out for him. In view of this, the Transfiguration is a positive counter-
image to the Temptation.[21]

After Jesus' announcement of the necessity of his suffering and death in
the Caesarea-Philippi context, Jesus predicts that some of the disciples
"who are standing here" (16:28) will witness the Son of Man's coming in
his Kingdom. In the immediately following story of the Transfiguration,
Matthew presents Jesus' glorious appearance as a proleptic revelation of
the Son of Man's glory.

I do not think, however, that Matthew intends the Transfiguration to be
an enthronement event for Jesus, since Matthew relates the glory to the
Son of Man rather than the Davidic Messiah. In Matthew's mind, Jesus is
the Son of Man from the beginning of his earthly ministry (8:20; 9:6) and
this Son of Man will come to judge humanity as the eschatological king in
his glory (25:31–34; 16:27–28). Like Mark, Matthew in 22:41–45 problematizes Jesus' identification with the son of David, since David called the
Son of God "my Lord" rather than his son.[22] Although Matthew wants to
ground Jesus in the history of Israel,[23] through the passion narrative he
contrasts Jesus' kingship with worldly forms of royal power. Matthew asserts that Jesus' kingdom is different from the Davidic kingdom, which the
people of Israel have longed for as an expression of their national restoration (cf. 26:52). Instead, Jesus' kingship supports the Matthean community's hope for a final vindication at the last judgment and their own judgment of "the twelve tribes of Israel" (19:27–28).

Stephen Barton finds the pattern of "testing – obedience – confirmation" in the two stories of the Temptation and the Transfiguration and argues that this pattern is repeated in the stories of the Gethsemane (26:36–
56) and the Great Commission (28:16–20).[24] According to Barton, in the
Gethsemane scene, we find the motifs of the divine Sonship, the kingdom,
the glory, the betrayal of the Son of Man, and the contrast between the divine will and the human will. As in Mark, the Gethsemane scene in Matthew is the only other pericope where Jesus appears alone with the three

---

[21] See also Luz, *Matthew*, 398.

[22] For more on Matthew's problematization of Jesus' identification with the Son of
David, see Riches, *Conflicting Mythologies: Identity Formation in the Gospels of Mark
and Matthew*, 282–90.

[23] In his discussion of Jesus' genealogy, Matthew asserts that Jesus accomplishes
Israel's traditional messianic hopes and expectations. Also, through his healings of the
people, Jesus functions as the messiah of Israel.

[24] For more on this, see Barton, "The Transfiguration of Christ according to Mark and
Matthew: Christology and Anthropology," 231–46.

disciples. Just as Jesus at the Temptation rejected Satan's proposal against the divine will, so also does Jesus in the Gethsemane scene decide to obey God's will – drinking "the cup" (26:39) and reject the use of human military power (26:52). As a reward for his obedience to God's will, Jesus on the Galilean mountain after Easter can openly claim to the public, "All authority in heaven and on earth has been given to me" (28:18).

Through Jesus' teaching authority, the term *mountain* also relates the Transfiguration to the Sermon on the Mount and the Great Commission. In the Sermon on the Mount, Jesus recapitulates the role of Moses as a lawgiver and appears as a unique instructor and teacher with authority. B.W. Bacon first presented the fivefold structural dimension of Matthew, which is comparable to the Five Books of Moses.[25] While Bacon neglected the narrative aspect of Matthew, his emphasis on Jesus as a teacher is still important.[26] The Sermon on the Mount (chs. 5–7), the major portion of Jesus' teaching, also happens on a mountain. The Sermon on the Mount shares many common ideas with the Transfiguration: kingdom, Son and Father, light and suffering, persecution and vindication. Jesus' teaching becomes the new Torah for Matthew, since it is not the law written in Deuteronomy (Deut 28:58), but the teachings/commands of Jesus that are to be observed (cf. 5:27–28). This becomes much clearer in the Great Commission (Mt 28:16–20). In this scene, Jesus delivers authoritative words about the disciples' baptizing and teaching ministry, and it is "what Jesus commanded" that the disciples should teach all the nations.

In chapter one, I have argued that God's command of "listen to him" (Mk 9:7; Mt 17:5) at the Transfiguration directs the readers' attention to Jesus' previous teaching about suffering and death, both for him and his disciples. In the Matthean Caesarea-Philippi context, we find another aspect of Jesus' teaching regarding his establishment of the church upon the rock, Peter. Already in Mt 7:24–26, Jesus said that those who hear his words and act on them can be compared to wise men who build their house on the rock. The key ideas of "listen to him," the rock, and the building reinforce the connection between the Transfiguration, the Sermon on the Mount and the Great Commission.[27]

---

[25] B.W. Bacon, *Studies in Matthew* (New York: H. Holt and Company, 1930), 165–249.

[26] For more on Matthew's structural issue, see O'Leary, *Matthew's Judaization of Mark: Examined in the Context of the Use of Sources in Graeco-Roman Antiquity*, especially chapters 4 and 5.

[27] I agree with Luz that the Transfiguration in Matthew is a polyvalent story that permits several possibilities of association (Luz, *Matthew*, vol. 2, 397).

– Jesus' Divine Sonship

As in the Markan version of the story, God at the Matthean Transfiguration speaks out of a cloud and confirms Jesus' divine Sonship (Mt 17:5). While in Mark God's confirmation of Jesus' Sonship may function to correct Peter's half-right understanding of Jesus' identity as the messiah (Mk 9:7), in Matthew God *affirms* Peter's confession of Jesus' Sonship in Mt 16:6: "You are the Christ, the Son of the living God."[28] In contrast to the Markan Peter who partially understood Jesus as Christ, the Matthean Peter correctly identifies Jesus as God's Son. Although Peter in Matthew still hesitates to accept Jesus' teaching about the suffering and death, Jesus, on the basis of Peter's confession, makes him a foundational rock for the church (Mt 16:16–19). Matthew asserts that Peter received this knowledge of Jesus' Sonship directly from God (16:17). For Matthew, understanding Jesus' identity as God's Son is a privilege only given to the disciples by the Father (11:27).[29]

In his rewriting of Mark, Matthew inserts ἐν ᾧ εὐδόκησα ("with whom I am well pleased") in God's confirmation of Jesus' Sonship as follows:

(Mk 9:7) οὗτός ἐστιν ὁ υἱός μου ὁ ἀγαπητός
(Mt 17:5) οὗτός ἐστιν ὁ υἱός μου ὁ ἀγαπητός, ἐν ᾧ εὐδόκησα

Matthew here repeats God's voice at the Baptism (Mt 3:17) and thereby makes the alignment of the Transfiguration and the Baptism more explicit. After God's public announcement of Jesus' Sonship at the Baptism, Satan immediately challenged the Sonship three times at the Temptation. By reasserting the unique filial relationship between the Father and the Son at the Transfiguration, Matthew intends to clear away people's misunderstanding of Jesus as one of the prophets like Moses and Elijah (cf. Mt 16:14). In view of this, while Matthew portrays Jesus as a law-giver drawing upon Mosaic typology, the theme of Jesus as the new Moses is eclipsed or surpassed by the theme of Jesus' divine Sonship.[30]

Matthew, more than Mark, develops the theme of Jesus' Sonship in a very special way that God involves Himself in the birth narrative of Jesus (1:18–25; cf. 2:15). God even announces through the prophets that Jesus is

---

[28] See also Luz, *Studies in Matthew*, 283.

[29] I will later argue that it is not the Law, but the knowledge of Jesus that functions as an identity marker for Jesus' movement in Matthew.

[30] See also Barton, "The Transfiguration of Christ according to Mark and Matthew: Christology and Anthropology." Cf. Celia Deutsch, "The Transfiguration: Vision and Social Setting in Matthew's Gospel (Matthew 17:1–9)," in *Putting Body & Soul Together: Essays in Honor of Robin Scroggs*, ed. Virginia Wiles, Alexandra Brown, and Graydon F. Snyder (Valley Forge, PA: Trinity Press International, 1997), 125–37; and Dale C. Allison, *Matthew: A Shorter Commentary* (London; New York: T & T Clark International, 2004), 281.

Immanuel, "God is with us" (1:23).[31] In Matthew's Gospel, God's presence with His people in the Hebrew Scriptures is now presented by Jesus' presence with his people, that is, "my church" (μου ἡ ἐκκλησία in 16:18). The Transfiguration reveals Jesus' theophanic glory as the visible manifestation of God's presence among His people and thereby, visually reinforces Immanuel ideology. Matthew ends his Gospel story of Jesus – a new story about God's presence with His people, with the promise that Jesus as Immanuel will always be with his people, "even until the end of the age" (28:20).

In chapter one, we observed that Mark narrates his story of Jesus by weaving two seemingly contradictory themes of the glorious Son of God and the suffering Son of Man. He tried to maintain a paradox that Jesus' glory could only be fully revealed after he suffered and died in obedience to God's will. Matthew further develops this theme into a more consistent theological pattern: Jesus' Sonship should be tested through his obedience to God's will and then confirmed to the public. Into Mark's storyline, Matthew adds a new episode regarding Jesus' birth. While God intervenes in Mary and Joseph's marriage in order to reveal Jesus' Sonship, his future as God's Son is immediately threatened by Herod. God publicly announces Jesus' Sonship at the Baptism, but Satan immediately tests his Sonship by enticing him to accomplish the kingdom at the cost of his identity as God's obedient Son. In the Caesarea-Philippi context, Peter takes the role of Satan and rejects Jesus' intention to obey God's will of suffering and death (16:21–22). After Jesus rebukes Peter for the temptation and determines to take up his cross, God at the Transfiguration re-confirms Jesus' Sonship in front of the three disciples (and the readers) (17:5).

The climax of this pattern of testing–confirmation occurs at the narratives of the Gethsemane, the Crucifixion and the Resurrection. Like the Temptation, the Gethsemane narrative is the occasion for the testing of Jesus' obedience to the Father's will. This time, the testing comes not from Satan or from his disciples, but from his human will: "*I* am deeply grieved, even to death...My Father, if it is possible, let this cup pass from *me*; yet not *what I want* but what you want" (26:38–39). In the end, Jesus accepts his destiny of betrayal "in the hands of sinners" (26:45).

This testing of Jesus' obedience to God's will as the Son continues at the Passion and the Crucifixion. The high priest demands to know whether Jesus is the Son of God (26:63) and the passers-by challenge him to "come down from the cross, if you are the Son of God" (27:40). The Jewish leaders also mock him: "He trusts in God; let God deliver him now, if He delights in him; for he said, 'I am the Son of God'" (27:43).[32] Confirming

---

[31] For more on the Immanuel Christology, Luz, *Studies in Matthew*, 84–85.

[32] See also, Barton, 241–43.

again Jesus' obedience to the Father's will as the Son, God at the Crucifixion manifests His presence through apocalyptic events, such as the rending
of the Temple curtain, earthquake, split rocks, opened tombs, and resurrection of the saints (27:51–53). God's confirmation of Jesus' Sonship is
completed by a Gentile centurion's confession. The centurion, after having
watched all these events, confesses with terror, "Truly this man was God's
Son!" (27:54).

Jesus, after having endured all the testing, can now claim to the public
that he is God's Son with all authority in heaven and on earth (28:18–20).
From now on, it is neither God, nor Satan, nor Jesus, nor a Gentile centurion, but the disciples who are to proclaim Jesus' Sonship to all the nations.

– Matthew's Rehabilitation of the Disciples

In comparison to Mark in his rewriting of the Transfiguration, Matthew
rehabilitates the disciples, especially Peter. By removing their spiritual
blindness, Matthew portrays the disciples in a more positive light than
Mark. This is important for Matthew's theological scheme, since he wants
to legitimize the church built upon the rock of the disciple(s) in the Caesarea-Philippi context.

In Mark, the disciples are considered to be spiritually blind about Jesus'
identity and destiny. While Peter in Mk 8:29 only considers Jesus as the
Christ, Peter in Mt 16:16 better understands that Jesus is the Son of the living God. God in the Markan version of the Transfiguration corrects Peter's
half-right answer, but God in the Matthean version confirms Peter's confession of Jesus as God's Son. Matthew already emphasized that this
knowledge of Jesus' Sonship is only possible through God's revelation
(1:26–27; 16:17) and is hidden from "the wise and the intelligent" (11:26–
27).

In the Markan version, Peter proposes to erect three tents for Jesus,
Moses and Elijah. Mark ascribes this proposal to Peter's ignorance and
fear: "For he did not know what to say, for they were exceedingly afraid"
(Mk 9:6). On the other hand, in his rewriting of the Markan story, Matthew
omits Mark's comment about Peter's ignorance and relocates the disciples'
fear immediately after hearing God's voice from the cloud. In Matthew's
version of the story, the disciples' fear appears as a pious human response
to God's presence: "when the disciples heard this, they fell on their faces,
and were filled with awe" (Mt 17:6). In the theophanic scenes in the Hebrew Scriptures, people falling on their faces to express fear and awe are
common responses to divine manifestations. Also, the disciples in the Matthean version not only understand the idea of the resurrection of the dead
(Mt 17:9; cf. Mk 9:10), but also realize that John the Baptist is the returning Elijah (Mt 17:13; cf. Mk 9:13).

Matthew also changes the disciples' attitude toward Jesus. In his proposal to build three tents, Peter in Mt 17:4 humbly seeks Jesus' permission: "If you wish, I will make three booths here." In addition, while Peter in Mk 9:5 calls Jesus "rabbi," Peter in Mt 17:4 elevates Jesus to his Lord. Although it is true that the title Lord (κύριος) can sometimes be an honorary title (Mt 13:27, 21:30, 25:20), simply meaning "master" or "sir," it is more probable that the Lord in the mouths of the disciples has a special religious connotation, betraying their recognition of Jesus' authority and exalted status (3:3; 7:21; 8:2, 6; 15:22; 22:43–45).[33] Matthew in his Gospel deliberately avoids applying rabbi to Jesus, since it is a greatly honored title among the Pharisees (cf. 23:8). Considering that Matthew puts the title rabbi only into the mouth of Judas the betrayer (26:25, 49), it has a negative overtone for Matthew. Judas' calling Jesus "rabbi" reveals his spiritual blindness regarding Jesus' identity and puts him in stark contrast to the other disciples who call Jesus "the Lord."

– Vision

By making two editorial additions in 17:2, "Jesus' brilliant face like the sun" (ὡς ὁ ἥλιος) and "the whiteness of his garments like the light" (ὡς τὸ φῶς), Matthew heightens the apocalyptic flavor of the scene that is already present in Mark. The brilliant faces and clothes are commonplaces in Jewish apocalyptic literature (4 Ezra 7:97; Dan 12:3; 2 Apoc Bar 51:3; 1 En 14:21, 62:15–16; 2 En 22:1–2).[34] Matthew reinforces this tendency of apocalypticizing the Transfiguration by calling it ὅραμα, a "vision." The Greek word ὅραμα is missing in Mark and appears only once in Matthew here at the Transfiguration.[35] Since the word ὅραμα occurs 24 times in the LXX Daniel, the theme of the Danielic Son of Man immediately follows the word in Mt 17:9, and there are so many parallel ideas between Matthew and Daniel, Matthew seems to modify the Transfiguration using the literary model of Daniel. In his vision, Daniel receives special revelations from God and angels regarding the Son of Man and his Kingdom.[36]

After he sees "the vision" and hears "the voice" of an angel, Daniel becomes full of "terror" and "falls on his face" (Dan 8:16–17). But the angel "touches" Daniel and "wakes him up" to make him ready to receive the

---

[33] See also Moses, 131.

[34] For more on this, Deutsch, "The Transfiguration: Vision and Social Setting in Matthew's Gospel (Matthew 17:1–9)," 124–137.

[35] Although Luke does not have this word in his Transfiguration account, he frequently uses it in Acts, referring to various visions (Acts 9:12; 10:3, 17, 19; 11:5; 16:9).

[36] Luz, *Matthew*, vol. 2, 398; and Daniel J. Harrington, *The Gospel of Matthew*, Sacra Pagina Series (Collegeville, MN: The Liturgical Press, 1991), 255. For more on the parallelism between Daniel and Matthew, refer to Moses, *Matthew's Transfiguration Story and Jewish-Christian Controversy*, chapter 4.

interpretation of the vision (Dan 10:9–12). The angel further consoles him by saying "do not be afraid" (Dan 10:16–19).[37] All of these features in Daniel are found in Matthew's narration of the Transfiguration. For example, while Mark has the disciples' fear right after they see Jesus' transfigured glory (Mk 9:6), Matthew relocates the fear motif after they hear God's voice from the cloud (Mt 17:5–6). Hearing God's confirmation of Jesus' Sonship, the disciples "fall on their faces" and are filled with "awe." Jesus "touches"[38] the terrified disciples, "wakes them up," and strengthens them, saying, "Do not be afraid!" These apocalyptic ideas place the disciples' experience of the Transfiguration in continuity with those visionary experiences of the Jewish apocalyptists, and make them the transmitters of apocalyptic mysteries regarding Jesus.[39]

4.2.2 The Transfiguration in Its Immediate Caesarea-Philippi Context

As is the case in the Markan Transfiguration story, through common ideas and key concepts, the Matthean Transfiguration story is also tightly connected to Jesus' previous discourse with the disciples in the Caesarea-Philippi context (Mt. 16:13–28): (1) Elijah appears and becomes a subject of Jesus' discussion with the disciples, (2) Peter is the main speaker as the representative of the twelve, (3) The major theme is about Jesus' identity, (4) Jesus' teaching of suffering and death is emphasized, and (5) Jesus' glory is mentioned and demonstrated. In this sense, Luz is correct to call the Transfiguration "a narrative reprise" of Mt 16:13–28.[40] Matthew, however, adds new material in his retelling of the story: Jesus' blessing of Peter as the foundation of the church. This so-called "M-tradition," whether it is an old tradition or Matthew's creation, indicates the Matthean community's understanding of itself as God's new people.

– Galilee and Jerusalem[41]

For Matthew, geography is full of theological symbolism.[42] Jesus is born in the city of Bethlehem, the city of David and is pursued by all Jerusalem

---

[37] These motifs are also commonly attested to in apocalyptic writings (e.g. Ezek 1:28–2:2; 1 Enoch 14:14, 25; Rev 1:17).

[38] Jesus' touching of the disciples resonates with the healing contacts initiated by Jesus, e.g. the touching of the leper (8:3), the fevered mother-in-law of Peter (8:15), and the eyes of the blind (9:29; 20:34).

[39] Deutsch, "The Transfiguration: Vision and Social Setting in Matthew's Gospel (Matthew 17:1–9)," 135.

[40] Luz, *Matthew*, 394. For a similar opinion, Allison, *Matthew: a Shorter Commentary*, 283.

[41] For an interesting discussion of the geography of restoration, especially in Mark and Q, refer to Sean Freyne, "The Geography of Restoration: Galilee–Jerusalem Relations in Early Jewish and Christian Experience," *NTS* 47 (2001): 289–311.

and its scribes and kings. However, he flees to Egypt and lives in "Galilee of the Gentiles" (4:15), in the city of Nazareth. Jesus fulfills Israel's traditional messianic hopes and expectations, as is shown in his genealogy and activity among the people of Israel. However, Jesus' ministry soon brings forth a division in Israel. After his numerous conflicts with Israel's leaders, "the real family of Jesus," who accomplish the will of God, comes into being (12:46–50). And the circle of his disciples appears as the new people of God – the church (13:36–16:20). The mountain in Galilee replaces the mountain in Jerusalem, Mt. Zion, as a center for Jesus' major activities – the Sermon, the Transfiguration and the resurrection appearance.[43] In Matthew's account of Jesus' story, Galilee becomes a place not only of a starting, but also of an ending of his ministry and mission, while Jerusalem is a place for his suffering and death (16:21; 17:22; 19:1; 20:17).[44]

From the beginning of his career, Jesus faces opposition from Israel's leaders (e.g. 9:32–34; 12:1–8, 14), whom he labels as "hypocrites" and "blind guides" (3:7; 6:2; 7:28; 15:14; 23:1–39). The conflict between Jesus and Israel's leaders leads to the formation of a new group of leaders – the twelve disciples. The twelve are reminiscent of the original Israel with the twelve tribes. The twelve Galilean followers share Jesus' rejection by Israel and are promised to be the judges of the twelve tribes of Israel in the future (19:28). In Matthew's theological scheme, it is around the twelve and their leader Peter that Jesus gathers his church (ἐκκλησία); and in the midst of the church, Jesus will be present as Immanuel to the end of the age (16:18; 18:17–20; 28:18–20). Considering that the term ἐκκλησία refers to the people of God in LXX, Matthew claims that Jesus' faithful community is now the new alternative for the unfaithful Israel.[45]

In Matthew's polemical scheme, the disciples are set in contrast to the Jewish leaders in many different ways. While the scribes and the Pharisees shut off the Kingdom of heaven from people, the disciples are claimed to have an authority to bind and loose both on earth and in heaven (18:18; 23:13). Due to their spiritual blindness, the Jewish leaders reject Jesus' identity as God's Son (23:16–26) and ascribe his healings to Beelzebul the ruler of the demons (12:24). On the contrary, the disciples, as the recipients of the Father's revelation of the secret, firmly grasp Jesus' Sonship (11:25–30; 21:15–16; 26:63–64; 27:43) and know "what the rising from the dead means" (Mt 17:9; cf. Mk 9:10). They also understand that it is

---

[42] O'Leary, *Matthew's Judaization of Mark: Examined in the Context of the Use of Sources in Graeco-Roman Antiquity*, 125.

[43] For more, Luz, *Studies in Matthew*, ch. 8; and Freyne, *Galilee, Jesus and the Gospel*, 188–89.

[44] For the implication of Jerusalem for Jesus' movement, see John Nolland, *The Gospel of Matthew* (Grand Rapids, MI: William B. Eerdmans, 2005), 684–86.

[45] Freyne, *Galilee, Jesus and the Gospel*, 88; and Luz, *Studies in Matthew*, 244–45.

John the Baptist who fulfils the returning Elijah (Mt 17:13). In his polemic against the Jewish leaders, Matthew attempts to color in a more positive way Mark's portrayal of the disciples in Galilee.

– Peter the Rock and the Birth of the Church
Following Peter's confession, Jesus appoints Peter as the rock of the church and announces that he will build his church on this rock (Mt 16:18–19). Peter's acknowledgement of Jesus' Sonship creates a stark contrast between the two groups of people: the disciples with Peter as their spokesperson and the Pharisees who reject Peter's confession of Jesus' Sonship. This contrast further relates to the legitimacy of the institutions that each group represents – "my church" (16:18)[46] and "their synagogues" (4:23; 9:35; and 10:7). Graham Stanton presents four different options of understanding of the relationship between the church and the synagogue in Matthew.[47] I agree with Stanton, Luz, Harrington and Allison that the Gospel of Matthew was written in the wake of its community's recent painful parting from Judaism.[48] Stanton further argues that like the Damascus Document, Matthew is written for a sectarian community as a foundation document, legitimating its separation from the parent body.[49] In view of this, Matthew offers the Caesarea-Philippi incident as the foundational story for the church on the basis of two major elements: (1) Jesus' teaching as the new Law and (2) his Transfiguration as the new Sinai Theophany.

The word ἐκκλησία appears twice in Matthew (16:18 and 18:17). In 16:18, Matthew provides evidence of a group that defines its boundaries and its leadership. The church in Matthew does not simply find its identity in the descent from the forefathers of Israel or their attachment to the Promised Land, but also (and more importantly) in Jesus' teaching as the New Torah and his presence among them as Immanuel.[50] In 18:17, Matthew presents a rule for regulating the life of believers in the church in terms of including or excluding a brother who has sinned. In this passage,

---

[46] The term ἐκκλησία is a common Greek term for an assembly of people (political, social and religious), but in a Jewish context, it means the assembly of the people of God. See France, *The Gospel of Matthew*, 623. The possessive adjective "my" in Mt 16:18 adds a further emphasis to Matthew's understanding of the church as God's new people.

[47] Stanton, *A Gospel for a New People: Studies in Matthew*, ch. 5.

[48] See Luz, *Matthew*, vol. 2, 356–62; *idem. Studies in Matthew*, ch. 1; and Allison, *Matthew: A Shorter Commentary*, 265.

[49] Stanton, *A Gospel for a New People: Studies in Matthew*, 88.

[50] See also Riches, *Conflicting Mythologies: Identity Formation in the Gospels of Mark and Matthew*, 291.

the authority to "bind and loose," with which Jesus invested Peter in 16:18, is given to the assembly of the church as a whole.[51]

Scholars have discussed the implication of the name Cephas–Peter. Dale C. Allison presents a parallelism between Peter and Abraham.[52] In Gen 17:1–8, Abram acquires a new name Abraham from God, which means "a father of a multitude of nations." In Isa 51:1–2, Abraham is called "the rock" from which the people of God originate. According to Allison, Peter the rock functions as a new Abraham for the church; and his faith is the means by which God brings a new people into being.[53] It is possible that Matthew intends the Abraham-typology to be operative in his presentation of Peter as the rock of the church. It is, however, doubtful whether Peter is the new Abraham, since the image in Isa 51:1–2 is not that of a building and Peter's confession is commonly shared by all the other disciples.[54]

Allison's presentation of another parallelism between the church and the Temple is more convincing to me. In the Jewish tradition, the rock at the base of the Temple on Zion is at the center of the world.[55] Likewise, the church at the rock stands at the center of the cosmos, sitting above "the gates of the dead" (Mt 16:18). It is likely that Matthew sees in the church the new Temple that Jesus promises to build in three days (cf. 26:61; 27:40).[56]

Mt 16:18–19 is Matthew's major addition to the Markan parallel. Luz argues that this passage is a re-interpretation of the surname Cephas by a Greek-speaking community in Syria in the post-apostolic era.[57] Peter's role in Matthew is, however, both unique and typical.[58] In Mt 13–18, that is, the story of the formation of the church out of Jesus' conflicts with Israel's leaders, Peter appears frequently as a unique figure as the first apostle and as the rock of the church. But at the same time, Peter is typical of the disciples in his confession and behavior. His confession of Jesus' Sonship becomes possible through the revelation from God the Father, which the other disciples commonly share (16:17; 11:25–27; 14:33). Peter's authority "to bind and loose" is what all the disciples also share as the members of the church (16:19; 18:18). Both Peter and the other disciples subject themselves to the destiny of martyrdom as a genuine expression of their dis-

---

[51] Dennis C. Duling and Norman Perrin, *The New Testament: Proclamation and Parenesis, Myth and History*, 3rd ed. (Fort Worth: Harcourt Brace College Publishers, 1994), 337.

[52] Allison, *Matthew: A Shorter Commentary*, 267–70.

[53] *Ibid.*, 272.

[54] Luz, *Matthew*, vol. 2, 362.

[55] Allison, *Matthew*, 370. Cf. Luz, *Matthew*, vol. 2, 363.

[56] See also, Luz, *Matthew*, vol. 2, 363.

[57] *Ibid.*, 357–60 and 366–68.

[58] *Ibid.*, 365.

cipleship.[59] In Mt 10, they all accept Jesus' task as theirs and reflect Jesus' lifestyle, including the martyrdom. Like Jesus, they all will shine like the sun (13:43; 17:2). Just as Jesus is the light of the Gentiles, so also are the disciples the light of the people (4:16; 5:14–16).

4.3 The Transfiguration in Luke (9:28–36)

Luke, from the beginning of his story, claims through Gabriel (1:32), Zechariah (1:69) and an angel of the Lord (2:11) that Jesus is the Davidic Messiah. On the other hand, God and angels appear as important protagonists in the birth narrative and confirm Jesus' divine Sonship. The demonic beings also recognize Jesus as God's Son (4:34, 41; 8:28). Contrary to these divine beings, humans in Luke's story fall short of understanding the true identity of Jesus. The Jewish people and their leaders are perplexed by Jesus' authority and power, but they reject Jesus or reluctantly accept him as a prophet like Elijah. Even John the Baptist is not sure about who Jesus is, since he asks whether Jesus is the "Expected One" (7:19). People's misunderstanding of Jesus' identity culminates at Herod's perplexed question: "Who is this about whom I hear such things?" (9:7–9). Jesus' disciples are marveled at his supernatural powers revealed through his miracles (8:21), but their best answer to the Christological debates among people is "the Christ of God" (9:20).

At the Transfiguration, God's voice confirms Jesus' Sonship as the final answer to the Christological debates in Jesus' Galilean ministry and emphasizes Jesus' suffering ministry as the "Chosen One" (9:35). God's voice at the Transfiguration, however, further promotes the divine credentials of the Son's voice. It is not Moses and Elijah, but Jesus who all should now "listen to." While in Mark, God's voice directs the disciples' attention to Jesus' previous teaching about the martyrdom, Luke further directs their attention to Jesus' farewell speeches at the end of his Gospel (24:44–49) and in the beginning of his second volume of Acts (1:4–5). In Jesus' final command, Luke expands the disciples' mission from Jerusalem to all the nations; and this mission to all the nations culminates in Paul's mission to the Gentiles. Is it by coincidence that Luke, on three occasions, narrates Paul's experience of the risen Lord with glory on his way to Damascus (Acts 9, 22 and 26)? What is the implication of the *three* occurrences of Paul's experience of the risen Jesus' glory and voice in Acts in comparison to the *three* at the Transfiguration in Luke? Why does Luke narrate stories about the three Hellenists, Stephen, Philip and Paul, back to back in Acts 6–8? I suspect that Luke tries to make the visionary expe-

---

[59] In 7:21–23, Matthew makes it clear that confession without praxis is useless.

rience of the Hellenists comparable to that of the three in order to harmonize their ministries to different groups of people.[60]

4.3.1 Luke's Rewriting of the Markan Transfiguration Story (9:28–36)[61]

Luke's account of the Transfiguration is based mainly on Mark,[62] but he still introduces a number of significant changes.[63] Luke does not use the verb μεταμορφόομαι to describe Jesus' transformation, but instead, he speaks of how Jesus' face has changed. Luke omits Mark's detailed description of Jesus' clothes. Luke does not directly link the Transfiguration with the returning Elijah and leaves out Jesus' conversation with the disciples regarding Elijah and John the Baptist (cf. Mk 9:11–13). Contrary to Mark, Luke mentions Jesus' glory as well as that of Moses and Elijah. Luke also reveals the content of the conversation between Jesus and the two ancient prophets, that is, Jesus' "exodus," which he will fulfill in Jerusalem. Luke introduces the theme of the sleepiness of the disciples, which he borrows from the Gethsemane scene. God in Luke's version calls Jesus "My Chosen One" (ὁ ἐκλελεγμένος), which is an allusion to Is 42:1 (ὁ ἐ κλεκτός; cf. Lk 25:35), while the disciples call him "master" (ἐπιστάτα).

---

[60] Marianne Bonz argues that the Transfiguration points to the disciples' future roles as authoritative witnesses (*The Past As Legacy: Luke–Acts and Ancient Epic* [Minneapolis: Fortress Press, 2000], 142). And at the same time, in my opinion, Luke presents Paul and Stephen as authoritative witnesses to the risen Lord on the basis of their visionary experience. In view of this, I suggest that Luke compares the visionary experiences of the representative of both groups in order to harmonize their ministry, which scholars have already discussed.

[61] As for the reading of the Lukan Transfiguration from a feminist perspective, refer to Sharon H. Ringe, "Luke 9:28–36: the Beginning of an Exodus," *Semeia* 28 (1983): 83–99.

[62] Some suggested that Luke has access to a source other than Mark. See Tim Schramm, *Der Markus-Stoff bei Lukas: Eine Literarkritische und Redaktionsgeschichtliche Untersuchung* (Cambridge [Eng.]: University Press, 1971), 136–39; and Reid, *The Transfiguration: A Source- and Redaction- Critical Study of Luke 9:28–36* . For a critical assessment of their position, see I. H. Marshall, *The Gospel of Luke* (Grand Rapids: Eerdmans, 1978), 381; and Miller, "Historicizing the Trans-historical: the Transfiguration Narrative," 219–48.

[63] For the minor agreements between Matthew and Luke against Mark, refer to F. Neirynck, "Minor Agreements – Matthew–Luke in the Transfiguration Story," in *Orientierung an Jesus; Zur Theologie der Synoptiker. Für Josef Schmid*, ed. Paul Hoffmann (Freiburg: Herder, 1973), 253–66. Neirynck, after having analyzed in detail the minor agreements at the Transfiguration, concludes that there is no reason to posit a second source (Neirynck, 264). Bovon concurs with Neirynck that both Luke's own peculiarities as well as the similarities to Matthew can be more convincingly explained on the basis of redactional tendencies (see Bovon, *Luke*, vol.1, 370). Similarly, Joseph A. Fitzmyer, *The Gospel According to Luke*, vol. 1 (Garden City, NY: Doubleday, 1981), 791–92.

Luke relocates the disciples' fear immediately after their entering into the cloud rather than after their seeing the transfigured Jesus as in Mark.[64]

Luke, by adding new ideas or themes or by expanding old ones, recasts the Markan Transfiguration to make it interact with the various Christological affirmations in his Gospel story. This is similar to Matthew's effort to alter the Markan Transfiguration in order to relate the story backward and forward to other Christological events in his Gospel. Through the word "form" (εἶδος) and God's voice, the Transfiguration is related to the Baptism (Lk 3:22; 9:29). The term "glory" relates the Transfiguration to the Birth narrative (2:9), to the Temptation (4:4, 5), and the Son of Man's glory at the Parousia (9:26; 21:27). Also, the themes of prayer and sleepiness of the disciples help readers of the Transfiguration recall the Gethsemane scene (22:40–46). The Lukan phrase "behold two men" draws together the Transfiguration, the Resurrection and the Ascension (9:30; 24:4; Acts 1:10).[65]

– The Change of Jesus' Face in Glory and the Two Men
In contrast to Mark, who describes Jesus' transfiguration through the term μεταμορφόομαι, Luke explains his transfiguration by saying that "the appearance of his face suddenly became different" (τὸ εἶδος τοῦ προσώπου αὐτοῦ ἕτερον in Lk 9:29). While Matthew keeps both the Greek term μεταμορφόομαι and Jesus' radiant face (Mt 17:2), Luke simply replaces the Markan term μεταμορφόομαι with Jesus' altered face. Fitzmyer and many other commentators argue that Luke, writing for Gentile Christians, avoids the Markan term, since he does not want Jesus to be identified as one of the Hellenistic gods.[66] However, by mentioning Jesus' glorious face, Luke may want to emphasize the contrast and parallelism between Moses' Sinai experience and Jesus' transfiguration. This is probable because in 9:31, Luke also introduces Moses' appearance in glory, clearly recalling Ex 34:30–35. Throughout his two volume work, Luke portrays Jesus with prophetic features and often legitimates Jesus' messiahship by referring to the promised Prophet-like-Moses (e.g. Acts 3:22–23; 7:35).[67] In Lukan

---

[64] For more on the synoptic comparison, Bovon, *Luke*, vol.1, 370.

[65] For more on this correlation, refer to Allison A. Trites, "The Transfiguration in the Theology of Luke: Some Redactional Links," in *The glory of Christ in the New Testament*, ed. L.D. Hurst and N. T. Wright (Oxford: Clarendon Press, 1987), 71–81.

[66] Fitzmyer, *The Gospel According to Luke*, 798; and Neirynck, "Minor Agreements – Matthew–Luke in the Transfiguration Story." Against this view, Bovon, *Luke,* vol.1, 374 n.39; and Heinz Schürmann, *Das Lukasevangelium* (Freiburg: Herder, 1969), 556.

[67] For Moses in Acts, see F. Bovon, "La figure de Moïse dans l'oeuvre de Luc," in Robert Martin-Achard, *La figure de Moïse : écriture et relectures* (Genève: Geneva Labor et Fides, 1978).

theology, however, although Jesus fulfills the promise of the Prophet-like-Moses, he goes beyond the concept as God's Son.

In the Lukan writings, the word "face" occurs 13 times in Luke and 11 times in Acts. In most of the occurrences, the word is part of an idiomatic expression. Only in the transformed faces of Jesus (Lk 9:29) and Stephen (Acts 6:15), does it carry a literal connotation of "face" or "countenance." The change of face physically reveals something about Jesus' identity or status. I already mentioned that in the Jewish apocalyptic traditions and the Hellenistic epics, those with shining faces belong to the heavenly realm. It is likely that at the Transfiguration of Luke, a glimpse of the true nature of Jesus' divine status is seen alongside his humanity.

In Lk 9:32, through the term "glory" Luke recapitulates the implications of Jesus' altered face or appearance and radiant garments. Luke introduces the word glory at the Transfiguration, which Mark and Matthew only mention in Jesus' prediction of the Son of Man's coming (Mk 8:38; Mt 16:27). While Matthew and Mark call the Son of Man's glory "the glory of his Father," in 9:26 and 32, Luke calls Jesus' transfigured glory "his glory." Luke indicates that Jesus' glory is his own permanent possession, unlike Moses' glory that temporarily reflects God's glory.

Glory is used three times in Luke before the Transfiguration: twice on the lips of the angels (2:9, 14) and once in Simeon's prophecy (2:32). In 2:9, the angel of the Lord appears with "the glory of the Lord" and announces to the shepherds the birth of "Christ the Lord" (2:11). Simeon claims that the child Jesus is God's glory that He prepared for the people of Israel. After the Transfiguration, Luke says that Jesus should pass through suffering and death to enter into the glory (24:26). As God's Son, Jesus is the prophesied carrier of the divine glory, but with the exception of the Transfiguration, he will assume it only after his suffering.[68] It is especially in his Parousia that it will finally be manifest to all humanity (9:26; 21:27).[69]

There are two interesting things regarding the Lukan theme of glory. First, Luke in Acts describes in detail the glory of Jesus in Stephen and Paul's experience of the risen Lord. Similarly to the three disciples, Peter, James, and John, who observe Jesus' glory at the Transfiguration, both Stephen and Paul are claimed to witness his glory. It seems that Luke wants to create a parallelism between the experience of the Jewish Chris-

---

[68] Bovon, *Luke*, vol.1, 374.

[69] A.A. Trites argues that through the term *glory*, Luke skillfully presents the interconnections of the passages of the Birth Narrative, the Temptation, the Transfiguration, the Parousia, the Resurrection and the Exaltation (Trites, "The Transfiguration in the Theology of Luke: Some Redactional Links," 76–77).

tian leaders and that of the Hellenist leaders. Second, it is noteworthy that in Luke's account of the Transfiguration, not only Jesus, but also Moses and Elijah appear in glory. Whereas Mark and Matthew simply mention their appearance beside Jesus, Luke speaks of their glorious appearance. Since Luke calls the two old prophets "two men," which is the Lukan way of referring to angels (Lk 24:4; Acts 1:10), Luke intends to reveal their angel-like status through their glorious appearance; and thereby, Luke emphasizes the contrast between the heavenly three and the earthly three, which is already manifest in the Markan version.[70]

Like Mark and Matthew, at the Transfiguration Luke also reports the presence of the two old prophets, Moses and Elijah. There is a strong parallelism between Jesus and Moses/Elijah in Luke's stories. Both Jesus and Elijah are portrayed as men of prayer (Lk 3:21; 5:16; 6:12; 9:18, 28–29; 10:21–22; 1 Kgs 17:21–22; 18:36–37; 19:9). Luke's statement of Jesus' being taken up and his ascension in Acts 1:9 recall Elijah's being taken up into heaven (2 Kgs 2:11). Jesus' saying about putting one's hand to the plow as a metaphor for discipleship is reminiscent of Elijah's call of Elisha while plowing (1 Kgs 19:19–21). Jesus' saying about casting a fire on earth (Lk 12:49) and the desire of James and John to bid fire come down from heaven to consume the Samaritans (Lk 9:54), recall Elijah's calling down of fire from heaven to consume the delegations from King Ahaziah (1 Kgs 1:10–12).[71] Since Luke in 9:8 and 19 clearly rejects people's perception of Jesus as the returning Elijah, his comparison of Jesus with Elijah is to highlight the continuity of God's work of salvation from the prophets of old to Jesus.[72]

Similarly, Jesus in Luke shares many features with Moses in his life and ministry. Both are said to possess the spirit (Num 11:17, 25; Lk 4:12, 14). Both spend forty days in the wilderness as a time of testing (Deut 8:2; Lk 4:2; Acts 7:36). They are portrayed as the mouthpiece of God (Exod 4:15–16; Lk 4:32, 43; 5:1). Each selects a group of seventy to share in his mission (Num 11:17, 25; Lk 10:1, 17). Jesus' feeding of the multitude in the deserted countryside in Lk 9:10–17 has echoes of Moses' provision of manna in the desert for Israelites (Exod 16:1–36). The whole journey of Jesus from birth to death in Jerusalem has numerous parallels to Moses'

---

[70] Jindrich Mánek, "The New Exodus in the Books of Luke," *Novum Testamentum* 2 (1958), 10.

[71] For these parallels, see Reid, 119.

[72] Joel B. Green, *The Gospel of Luke* (Grand Rapids, MI: William B. Eerdmans, 1997), 381. Bovon argues that Moses and Elijah in the Lukan account represent the Law and the Prophets, who had foreseen Christ's fate, above all his suffering (*Luke*, vol. 1, 376). Luke is familiar with a division of the Hebrew Scripture into three parts (24:44) alongside the division into two (24:27; Acts 26:22).

journey to the Promised Land.[73] In Acts 3:20–23, Peter presents Jesus as the Prophet-like-Moses. In Stephen's speech (Acts 7), the lives of Moses and Jesus show similar patterns.[74]

The importance of the portrayal of Jesus as a prophetic figure like Moses and Elijah cannot be denied in Luke's stories. It is underscored by the pervasiveness of echoes of Moses and the prophetic traditions in Luke, making Jesus appear as "the eschatological prophet in might and power" (Lk 4:16–30; 24:19). However, for Luke, this perspective is in need of significant modification, since Jesus is more than a prophet – he is God's Son.[75] In Lk 1:17, an angel announces to Zacharias that his son, John the Baptist, will be the forerunner of Jesus "in the spirit and power of Elijah," and John the Baptist is presented as the "prophet of the Most High" (1:76). But Luke claims that Jesus is even greater than John the Baptist (1:5–2:52). At the Transfiguration, Jesus clearly goes beyond the two prophets as God's beloved Son, since God singles him out as the one to whom the disciples should listen. Although Luke claims that Jesus consummates the prophecy of the Prophet-like-Moses in the sermons of Peter and Stephen in Acts, he presents in these sermons a new criterion for deciding who belongs to the people of God, that is, whether one *listens to* Jesus (Acts 3:22–23; 7:37).[76] This criterion implies that Jesus' teaching now replaces that of Moses as the new Torah. In the sermons of Peter (Acts 15:10–11) and Paul (13:38–39), Luke reinforces this aspect of Jesus' teaching in contrast to the Mosaic Law.[77]

At the Transfiguration, the appearance of Moses and Elijah definitively clears away people's understanding of Jesus as one of the prophets (9:18). Rather, their appearance implies a basic continuity between their work on God's behalf and Jesus' own. The presence of these great prophets from Israel's past serves to interpret and to legitimate Jesus' mission.[78] Furthermore, through the idea of Moses as a prototype of Jesus, Luke fleshes out that there is continuity between the old Exodus and the new Exodus, which

---

[73] For this comparison, see David P. Moessner, "Luke 9:1–50: Luke's Preview of the Journey of the Prophet like Moses of Deuteronomy," *JBL* 102 (1983): 575–605; Robert F. O'Toole, "The Parallels between Jesus and Moses," *Biblical Theology Bulletin* 20 (1990): 22–29; and Mánek, "The New Exodus in the Books of Luke," 8–23.

[74] See R. O'Toole, "The Parallels between Jesus and Moses," 22–29.

[75] Mark L. Strauss, *The Davidic Messiah in Luke–Acts: the Promise and Its Fulfillment in Lukan Christology* (Sheffield: Sheffield Academic, 1995), 261–305; and Green, *The Gospel of Luke*, 353.

[76] Jerome H. Neyrey also opines that Jesus' word constitutes a boundary marker between the church and all others in the Lukan accounts. See J. H. Neyrey, "The Symbolic Universe of Luke–Acts: "They Turn the World Upside Down," in *The Social World of Luke–Acts*, ed. J. H. Neyrey (Peabody, MA: Hendrickson, 1991), 301.

[77] For more, O'Toole, "The Parallels between Jesus and Moses," 23–28.

[78] Green, *Luke*, 381.

Jesus accomplishes in Jerusalem for the salvation of God's people, both the Gentiles and the Jews (Lk 9:31).[79]

Luke further twists the implication of the presence of Moses and Elijah by calling them "two men" in glory (9:30–32). Since the expression "two men" often refers to angelic beings in the Lukan writings, Luke presents them as resurrected humans, possibly functioning like angelic attendants of Jesus, and assumes their role as the *angelus interpres*, who reveal the implication of Jesus' journey as the "exodus" (9:31).[80] Since angels signal events of greater importance for Luke, he introduces angels in the key stages of Jesus' life:[81] the birth of his predecessor John the Baptist (1:5–23); Jesus' birth (1:26–38; 2:8–15); his resurrection (24:1–11); his ascension (Acts 1:6–12); and the extension of his mission to the Gentiles (Acts 10:1–8). Especially in Acts, the appearance of angels continues to mark turning points in the ministry of the disciples (e.g. 1:6–12; 10:1–8). In all these instances, Luke highlights that God orchestrates the drama of the salvation history through angelic interventions.[82] Luke's calling the two prophets "two men in glory" brings the Transfiguration into close contact with these critical events in the salvation history and heightens the significance of the Transfiguration as divinely planned.

– Jesus' Prayer at a High Mountain
Many have noticed that it is characteristic of Luke, the evangelist of prayer, to describe Jesus as constantly at prayer.[83] In his rewriting of the Transfiguration, Luke not only adds a new element of prayer, but also emphasizes its importance by mentioning it twice. First, Jesus goes up the mountain "in order to pray" (προσεύξασθαι in 9:28); and second, it is when Jesus is praying (ἐν τῷ προσεύχεσθαι αὐτὸν in 9:29) that he is transfigured. Prior to Peter's confession of Jesus' messiahship immediately before the Transfiguration, Jesus is portrayed as being in prayer (9:18).[84] Through the theme of prayer, Luke emphasizes Jesus' intimate union with God and the

---

[79] See also O'Toole, "The Parallels," 28.

[80] Bovon, *Luke*, vol.1, 375.

[81] Reid, 95.

[82] Reid, 116.

[83] For a comprehensive analysis of this theme in Luke–Acts, refer to Bovon, *Luke the Theologian*, 453–57.

[84] David M. Crump argues that it is Jesus' prayer that enables Peter to acquire the spiritual knowledge of Jesus' messiahship. See David Michael Crump, *Jesus the Intercessor: Prayer and Christology in Luke–Acts* (Tübingen: J.C.B. Mohr, 1992), 21.

unfolding of the course of Jesus' life and ministry in accord with God's divine plan.[85]

Luke uses the term *prayer*, both noun and verb, 47 times, contrasted with 17 in Matthew, 12 in Mark, and none in John.[86] This indicates that prayer is a theme of considerable significance in the Lukan writings. Jesus is at prayer especially at critical turning points of his ministry: at his baptism (3:21), before his choice of the twelve (6:12), before Peter's confession of him as the Messiah (9:18), at the Transfiguration (9:28), before his arrest on the Mount of Olives (22:39–46), and on the cross (23:46). Jesus instructs his disciples to pray (6:28; 10:2; 11:1–4; 20:45–47), and pious individuals, such as Zechariah (1:8–23) and Anna (2:36–38), are depicted at prayer. According to David M. Crump, in his biographical portrayal of Jesus as one in constant prayer during his life on earth, Luke creates a narrative explanation of and/or justification for how Jesus can be conceived of as the church's heavenly intercessor.[87] Although Crump is right in connecting Jesus' prayer with Christology and paraenesis, it is hard to find in Acts the idea of the risen Lord as an heavenly intercessor (cf. Rom 8:34; Heb 7:25).[88]

In Acts, the early Christians are also portrayed as constantly at prayer (1:14, 24; 2:42, 46, 47; 3:1; 6:4, 6; 8:15; 9:11, 40; 10:9, 30)[89] and the birth of the church is the result of their prayer (Acts 1:4–5; 1:8, 13, and 14). In Luke's eyes, prayer is an integral part of the Christian movement from its outset (Acts 2:41–42) and its vitality is closely related to the growth of the church (2:47).[90] For Luke, prayer is the instrument by which God directs the course of the salvation history, both in the life of Jesus and in the development of the Christian church.

The expression "to the mountain" (εἰς τὸ ὄρος) occurs four times in Luke (6:12; 9:28; 21:37; 22:39). In all these occurrences, Luke tells his readers that Jesus is in prayer or that Jesus goes up the mountain to pray. In Luke's mind, the mountain provides Jesus with solitude and separation from the crowd, so that he enjoys a time of more intimate communion with

---

[85] Reid, 104; and Allison A. Trites, "The Prayer Motif in Luke–Acts," in *Perspectives on Luke–Acts*, ed. Charles H. Talbert (Danville, VA: Association of Baptist Professors of Religion, 1978), 169. See also, Bovon, *Luke the Theologian*, 457.

[86] Trites, "The Prayer," 169.

[87] Crump, *Jesus the Intercessor: Prayer and Christology in Luke–Acts*, 238–39.

[88] F. Bovon, *Luke the Theologian*, 2nd ed. (Waco, TX: Baylor University Press, 2006), 533.

[89] O'Toole, *The Unity of Luke's Theology*, 72–73; and Reid, 104.

[90] Trites, "The Prayer," 179.

God the Father.[91] In the last two occurrences of the expression, the mountain refers to the Mount of Olives. The Mount of Olives is represented by Luke as the point of departure for the entry into Jerusalem (19:29, 37), the place where Jesus would lodge for the night after teaching all day in the Temple (21:37, and implied in 22:39), and the place of the ascension (implied in 24:50 and made explicit in Acts 1:12).

Right before his arrest by the Jewish rulers at the Mount of Olives, Jesus prays so fervently that "his sweat became like drops of blood, falling down upon the ground" (22:44). In the same moment, Jesus also asks the disciples to pray so that "they may not enter into temptation" (22:40). According to Luke's report, since the disciples do not pray, but fall asleep, they fail this time in following Jesus in the path of martyrdom. Luke suggests that Peter's failure to pray causes him to deny Jesus three times, although he announces that he will not leave Jesus (22:61).

– Jesus as the Son of God and the Chosen One, and His Exodus in Jerusalem

God's confirmation of Jesus' Sonship at the Transfiguration differs slightly in the Synoptics as follows:

(Mk 9:7) "This is My beloved Son,"
(Mt 17:5) "This is My beloved Son, with whom I am well pleased"
(Lk 9:35) "This is My Son, My Chosen One"

It is interesting that Luke substitutes "My Chosen One" (ὁ ἐκλελεγμένος) for "My beloved" (ὁ ἀγαπητός), both of which are Greek equivalents in competition with the Hebrew verb בחיר.[92] Although by this expression Luke emphasizes Jesus' prophetic mission,[93] he still presents Jesus' Sonship as the concluding message of the Transfiguration. Compared to Mark and Matthew, Jesus as God's Son in Luke becomes much more filial and physical. Especially in the annunciation of Jesus' birth to Mary (Lk 1:26–38), the transcendent mode of Jesus' conception is highlighted: "the Holy Spirit will come upon you, and the power of the Most High will overshadow you" (v.35). This conception uniquely relates him to God in filial terms, "vastly outstripping any conventional expectation concerning the Davidic Messiah and...drastically transforms his messianic mission and behavior."[94] Luke clears away any ambivalence concerning Jesus' filial

---

[91] In Acts 7:30–38, Mt. Sinai occurs as the place of the apparition of an angel to Moses. In this passage, Luke presupposes that mountain is a place for the communication between God and human beings.

[92] Marshall, *The Gospel of Luke*, 388; and Bovon, *Luke*, vol.1, 379.

[93] Bovon, *Luke*, vol.1, 379.

[94] Brendan Byrne, "Jesus as Messiah in the Gospel of Luke: Discerning a Pattern of Correction," *CBQ* 65 (2003), 85.

status in the story of the child Jesus in the Temple (2:41–52). In response to Mary's complaint, "your father and I have been searching for you in great anxiety" (2:84), Jesus replies, "Why is it that you were looking for me? Did you not know that I had to be in my Father's house?" (2:49).[95] Again in the conversation between Jesus and the Jewish people in the synagogue of Nazareth, the phrase "Son of God" stands in stark contrast to the phrase "Joseph's son" (4:22). Although they are impressed by Jesus' "gracious words," the Nazarenes' response, "Is this not Joseph's son?,", is inadequate. In the subsequent episode about Jesus' healing, however, the demons recognize Jesus as "God's Son" (4:41).

The Lukan addition of "My Chosen One" (ὁ ἐκλελεγμένος) is an allusion to the Suffering Servant in Isa 42:1 (ὁ ἐκλεκτός). The phrase "the Chosen One" as the Isaianic servant reinforces Jesus' undergoing his "exodus" in Jerusalem, that is, his suffering, being mocked, and then crucified. The connection between Jesus' "exodus" in Jerusalem and his identity as God's Chosen One becomes much clearer in Lk 23:35 (ὁ ἐκλεκτός), since the scoffers at the cross taunt Jesus by calling him "the Chosen One." Bovon argues that the immediate context of the Transfiguration and the parallel at 23:35 show that Luke connects Jesus' chosen status with his suffering mission.[96] In chapter one, I argued that the story of the binding of Isaac in Gen 22 lies behind the Markan expression of "beloved one"; and the expression signifies God's sacrifice of His Son Jesus. By replacing the "beloved one" with "the Chosen One," it seems that Luke wants to emphasize the martyrdom aspect of Jesus' mission as God's Suffering Servant. Luke reinforces his emphasis on Jesus' martyrdom by revealing the conversation between Moses and Elijah about Jesus, his "exodus" in Jerusalem (9:31).

It is only Luke among the Gospel writers who discloses the conversation between Moses and Elijah on the subject of Jesus' mission as his "exodus" (ἔξοδος). Scholars have presented different options of understanding the word "exodus." Two of their suggestions seem most probable, with which I concur:[97] it is a euphemism for death (cf. 2Pet 1:15; Wis 3:2, 7:6; Josephus *Ant.* 4.8.2 §189) and all of the events of Jesus' life, including his resurrection and ascension.[98] In the Lukan account, Jesus' life has similarities to Moses' Exodus: threats to his life during his infancy, wandering in the wilderness, performing miracles and rejections by the people of Israel. In contrast to Moses' Exodus, in which Jerusalem is the end place as the

---

[95] For the variant meanings of the phrase ἐν τοῖς τοῦ πατρός μου δεῖ εἶναί με, refer to Bovon, *Luke*, vol.1, 114.

[96] Bovon, *Luke*, vol. 1, 380.

[97] Reid, *The Transfiguration*, 125–6.

[98] Bovon, *Luke*, vol. 1, 376; and Fitzmyer, *Luke*, 167.

Promised Land, for Jesus, the city of Jerusalem is the place for his martyrdom.

The term "exodus," although it is closely related to the idea of Jesus' death in Jerusalem, may not have to be translated into "death," since his exodus is also related to his resurrection and ascension. According to Jindrich Mánek, the appearance of the "two men" at the empty tomb is the Lukan key for understanding of the word "exodus" at the Transfiguration.[99] The exodus in Luke is Jesus' *departure from* the tomb, the realm of death, through the resurrection. At the Transfiguration pericope, Jesus predicts his resurrection, immediately following his death (9:22). The idea of Jesus' resurrection is the major topic in Acts. The apostles are defined as the witnesses of his resurrection (Acts 1:22) and Peter and Paul deliver sermon after sermon on his resurrection.

Moreover, for Luke, it is not Jerusalem, but heaven that is the end point of Jesus' exodus. Since in the Lukan accounts, heaven is "the eternal dwelling place" for Jesus and his disciples, Jesus' exodus is consummated at his ascension.[100] As Luke narrates in Lk 9:51, it is "when the days are approaching for his ascension" that Jesus determines to set out his journey to Jerusalem. At the end of Luke (Lk 24:50–51) and in the beginning of Acts (Acts 1:9–11), Luke depicts Jesus' ascension into heaven as the end point of his exodus.

In the Luke's theological scheme, however, Jesus' ascension as the end of his exodus is the beginning of the disciples' exodus. Immediately following Jesus' ascension in Acts, the disciples begin to experience their own exodus: suffering and persecution and miracles. The disciples are assured that the death is not the end of their exodus, but their exodus journey will lead them to their ascension, like Jesus.[101] In view of this, the term *exodus* in Luke not only refers to Jesus' individual journey, but also to God's redemptive work for the church revealed through his journey. This recalls the ancient redemptive act of God for Israel.[102]

---

[99] Mánek, "The New Exodus in the Books of Luke," 12.

[100] See Moessner, "Luke 9:1–50: Luke's Preview of the Journey of the Prophet like Moses of Deuteronomy," 595; Bovon, *Luke*, vol.1, 376; Fitzmyer, *Luke*, 800; and O'Toole, "The Parallels between Jesus and Moses," 24.

[101] In Luke–Acts, fulfillment of a prophecy becomes in turn a prophetic sign and gives a new impetus to the promise. For this, Luke uses two literary procedures, "the effect of realism" and "prophetic ambiguity." See F. Bovon, "The Effect of Realism and Prophetic Ambiguity in the Works of Luke," in *New Testament Traditions and Apocryphal Narratives* (Allison Park, PA: Pickwick Publications, 1995), 97–104.

[102] See also Walter L. Liefeld, "Theological Motifs at the Transfiguration Narrative," in *New Dimensions in New Testament Study*, ed. Richard N. Longenecker and Merrill C. Tenney (Grand Rapids: Zondervan Pub. House, 1974), 173; I. H. Marshall, *Luke: Historian and Theologian* (Exeter: Paternoster P., 1970); and Bovon, 376.

While Mark does not mention Jerusalem in the Caesarea-Philippi Transfiguration context, Matthew clearly mentions it as a place for Jesus' suffering, death, and resurrection (Mt 16:21). Luke also designates Jerusalem as the place of Jesus' exodus in the conversation between Moses and Elijah at the Transfiguration (Lk 9:31). In the geographical schema of Luke–Acts, Jerusalem plays an important role as the center of Luke's theological universe.[103] Luke has a double attitude toward Jerusalem. (1) Negatively, Jerusalem is a place of danger for Jesus, since it is "the killer of prophets" (Lk 13:34), and symbolizes a realm of lack of faith.[104] (2) Positively, it is a location where God will vindicate Jesus through resurrection, and from which God's salvation program should start all the way to the ends of the earth (Acts 1:8).[105]

From the beginning of Jesus' life to its end, Jerusalem appears as the center of his mission and identity. At the Temple in Jerusalem, God's special revelation about the messiah is made to Zechariah (Lk 1:5–23), and Simeon and Anna observe its accomplishment in the baby Jesus (2:25–38). Jerusalem is the place of pilgrimage for Jesus and his family (2:41) and the place where the child Jesus reveals his wisdom and status as God's Son (2:46–47). But, the picture of Jerusalem changes its tone from the Temptation where the pinnacle of the Temple in Jerusalem becomes a site for Jesus' temptation (4:9). In Jesus' Galilean ministry, people from Jerusalem constitute the audience in Jesus' healing of the paralytic (5:17) and for the Sermon on the Plain (6:17). From the Transfiguration on, Jerusalem becomes the place of Jesus' death (9:51) and becomes the symbol of all who reject Jesus (9:53; 13:4, 33–34). When Jesus enters the city, he weeps over it and foretells its destruction (19:41–44 and 21:20–24). The Temple in it is no more the place of prayer, but "the den of thieves" (19:46); and in it the leaders of Israel plot to kill Jesus (19:47).

In contrast to Mark and Matthew, however, Luke locates all the post-resurrection stories in Jerusalem (24:1–53) rather than in Galilee. Also, the Lukan Jesus commands the disciples to remain in the city of Jerusalem until they are clothed with power from on high (24:49; Acts 1:8). They are equipped with the power of the Spirit in Acts 2:1–13 to preach the Gospel from Jerusalem to the ends of the earth. For Luke, Jesus' Gospel should be preached first in Jerusalem, and then to the nations; and although the followers of Jesus are first called "Christians" in Antioch (Acts 11:26), in Luke's view it is Jerusalem where Christianity originated. Despite a

---

[103] Conzelmann, *Luke*, 17–94; Reid, "The Centerpiece of Salvation History…," in *The Bible Today* 29 (1991): 20–24; and Freyne, *Galilee, Jesus and the Gospel*, 97–120.

[104] See also Mánek, 14 and 18.

[105] See also Green, 382.

prophecy of his suffering in Jerusalem, Paul feels obliged to visit Jerusalem in order to seek harmony between his mission and that of the twelve.

– God's Voice and Jesus' Voice

Like Mark and Matthew, the Lukan Transfiguration reaches its climax at "God's voice" from a cloud (9:35). The phrase "God's voice" occurs in the Baptism (Lk 3:22) apart from the Transfiguration. For their contents, both occurrences have Jesus' Sonship, revealed first to Jesus and then to the three disciples. In Lk 9:35, God's voice not only reveals Jesus' Sonship, but also draws the disciples' attention to Jesus' voice, "listen to him!" In the immediate context of the Transfiguration, Jesus' voice has as its content his teaching about the martyrdom and resurrection (9:22–26). By introducing the phrase "after these words" in the beginning of the event (9:28), Luke relates Jesus' voice at the Transfiguration to his previous teaching.[106]

In Luke, Jesus' words are mentioned many times and often represent his teachings or authoritative commands (4:22, 32, 36; 6:47; 7:7; 9:26, 44; 10:39; 20:20; 21:33; 24:19, 44). In 7:7, a Gentile centurion requests Jesus simply to "say the word" so that his servant may be healed. In 10:39, Luke reports that Mary wisely listens to Jesus' words in contrast to Martha, who is distracted with the preparations for serving him. After the resurrection, Jesus' voice concludes the Gospel story with the commissioning of the disciples and opens their stories of continuing Jesus' mission in Acts. While Luke speaks of God's voice that came to Moses from the burning bush (Ex 3:4), he reports that in their visions, Jesus' voice comes from heaven to Peter (Acts 10:13, 15; 11:7) and to Paul (Acts 9:4, 7; 22:7, 9; 26:14) in order to guide their ministry according to the divine will. In these stories, Jesus takes over God's role of pronouncing the divine will and his voice becomes an audible aspect of Christophany. More specifically, in the Lukan narrative scheme, Jesus' divine voice functions to harmonize both the experience of Peter and Paul and their ministry to people in different geographical areas.[107]

4.3.2 The Transfiguration in Its Immediate Context

Lk 9 with the Transfiguration is a transitional unit between Jesus' Galilean ministry and his "exodus" in Jerusalem, functioning as a prelude to the Travel Account (9:51–18:14).[108] As the closing of the Galilean section, Lk

---

[106] See also Reid, 99.

[107] I will come back to this point later when I discuss Stephen and Paul.

[108] This section is considered one of the central problems in Lukan studies. For the former scholarship on this topic and four different approaches to it, refer to Moessner,

9 deals with Jesus' identity and mission, and at the same time, shows his concentrated instruction on the nature of discipleship. In Luke's mind, the two motifs of Christology and discipleship are closely intertwined and mutually interpretive. In the rest of his Gospel, Luke will demonstrate how Jesus' exodus will be fulfilled in Jerusalem. In Acts, he will show how the disciples actively share in Jesus' exodus by following him in the same path of suffering and glorification.

By removing most of Mk 6:45–8:26, including Mark's designation of the city of Caesarea-Philippi as a location for the Transfiguration, Luke brings the Transfiguration into close contact with Herod Antipas' perplexed question: "Who is this about whom I hear such things?" (9:7–9).[109] In contrast to Mark, Luke highlights Herod's perplexity when he hears about people's reports of Jesus as John the Baptist, Elijah, or one of the old prophets. While in both Mark and Matthew Herod concludes without any hesitation that Jesus is John the Baptist *redivivus* (Mk 6:16; Mt 14:2), he remains inconclusive in the Lukan account: "'John I beheaded; but who is this about whom I hear such things?' And he tried to see him [Jesus]" (Lk 9:9). Herod's perplexity creates a tension regarding Jesus' identity until God's testimony at the Transfiguration finally resolves it.

Jesus' conversation with the disciples about his identity in Lk 9:18–20 recapitulates Herod's speculation over the reports about Jesus. By acknowledging Jesus as the Christ of God, Peter and the disciples go beyond people, who understand him merely as a prophet. Furthermore, the disciples' answer to Jesus' question contrasts them to Herod, who is confused.[110] Unlike Matthew and Mark, however, Luke does not accord any praise or blessing to Peter for his confession and does not record Jesus' rebuke of Peter for his misunderstanding of Jesus' destiny of martyrdom, either. It seems that Luke wants to tighten chapter nine around Herod's question of who Jesus is, in order to make the entire chapter one continuous story about Jesus' identity.[111]

At the Lukan Transfiguration, the presence of Elijah and Moses visibly refutes Herod's speculation about people's understanding of Jesus as Elijah *redivivus* or one of the ancient prophets (Lk 9:7–9), since they appear and speak with Jesus as distinct individuals. In the Lukan account of the Transfiguration, although Elijah and Moses appear in glory, they still remain distinct from and inferior to Jesus. Jesus is uniquely qualified to be

---

"Luke 9:1–50: Luke's Preview of the Journey of the Prophet like Moses of Deuteronomy," 575–79. Also, Fitzmyer, "Composition of Luke 9," 150–51.

[109] Robert F. O'Toole, *The Unity of Luke's Theology* (Wilmington, DE: Michael Glazier, Inc., 1984), 218. See also, Fitzmyer, "The Composition of Luke, Chapter 9," 139–52; and Bovon, *Luke*, vol.1, 353.

[110] Crump, *Jesus the Intercessor: Prayer and Christology in Luke–Acts*, 29.

[111] See also Fitzmyer, "The Composition of Luke, Chapter 9."

called God's Son and the two are not worthy of sharing this appellation with him.[112] God's testimony to Jesus' divine Sonship in Lk 9:35 answers Herod's question, and trumps any other opinions about Jesus' identity, bringing the Christological debate to a conclusion. In order to emphasize God's voice as the conclusion of the Transfiguration, Luke in his account removes Jesus' discussion of John the Baptist as the returning Elijah in Mk 9:11–13.[113]

4.3.3 The Transfiguration in the Context of Acts

I concur with Robert C. Tannehill that while it is possible to read Luke apart from Acts, reading it as part of Luke–Acts will enrich our understanding of it.[114] In the beginning of his Gospel, Luke indicates the comprehensive saving plan of God for both Gentiles and Jews (Lk 2:30–32; 3:6). In this next volume of Acts, he shows how God's universal salvation program is fulfilled in the ministry of the apostles, both Jewish Christians and the Hellenists.[115] While Mark and Matthew end their Gospels with Jesus' commissioning of the disciples, Jesus in Luke asks them to remain in Jerusalem to "be clothed with power from above" (24:49). This Lukan ending anticipates its fulfillment at the Pentecost in Acts 2.

According to Peter's speech on the replacement of Judas (Acts 1:21–22), the requirements for the apostleship are twofold: the apostle (1) must have

---

[112] Cf. D.A.S. Ravens, "Luke 9.7–62 and the Prophetic Role of Jesus," *NTS* 36 (1990): 119–29. According to Ravens, the presence of the prophets at the Transfiguration and in its immediate context is to reaffirm the prophetic role of Jesus. Bovon, agreeing with Conzelmann, argues that Luke deletes the ending of the Markan Transfiguration, because he does not equate the Baptist with Elijah (Bovon, 370).

[113] James M. Dawsey analyzes the Gospel of Luke through an idea of conflicting voices and considers God's voice as the final victor. See James M. Dawsey, *The Lukan Voice: Confusion and Irony in the Gospel of Luke* (Macon, GA: Mercer University Press, 1986). Applying Dawsey's model to his analysis of the Lukan Transfiguration story, Thomas W. Martin argues that Luke at the Transfiguration erases the glorious Jesus – the visible aspect of the story, through God's voice of commanding the disciples to listen to Jesus' voice (Thomas W. Martin, "What Makes Glory Glorious? Reading Luke's Account of the Transfiguration over against Triumphalism," *JSNT* (2006): 3–26). I, however, disagree with Martin, since Jesus' glory receives more emphasis in Luke than in Matthew and Mark. The Lukan emphasis on Jesus' glory is further confirmed in Paul's experience of the risen Lord.

[114] Robert C. Tannehill, *The Narrative Unity of Luke–Acts: A Literary Interpretation*, 2 vols. (Philadelphia: Fortress Press, 1994), vol. 2, 7.

[115] There has been scholarly debate regarding the division between the Hellenists and the Jewish Christians. Recently, some have tried to erase a dichotomy between them, suggesting a range of perspective among the early Christian groups. For more on this view, Craig C. Hill, *Hellenists and Hebrews: Reappraising Division within the Earliest Church* (Minneapolis: Fortress Press, 1992).

participated in Jesus' whole itinerant ministry and (2) must be a witness of his resurrection. Stephen and Paul do not have these qualifications, but they are still called Jesus' witnesses in Acts (22:15, 20; 26:16). What makes Luke call these Hellenists the witnesses of Jesus' resurrection? In the accounts of Stephen's martyrdom (Acts 7) and of Paul's Damascus experience (9; 22; 26), Luke argues that since both of them have experienced the divine glory and the risen Jesus in their visions, they are qualified to be the witnesses of Jesus' resurrection (cf. 1 Cor 15: 2–11). In the following, I will show that the contents of the visions of Stephen and Paul are similar to what the three apostles experienced at the Transfiguration. Luke, I suspect, wants to emphasize the continuity between the ministry of the Jewish Christians and that of the Hellenists on the basis of their common experience of Jesus' glory. For Luke, it does not matter whether they experience Jesus' glory before Easter or after, since it is the same glory of Jesus.

– *Stephen*

Stephen's speech and vision in Acts 6–7 show many interesting parallel ideas to the Transfiguration incident with Jesus' teaching of the martyrdom and Parousia in Lk 9.[116] Immediately before the Transfiguration, replying to Peter's answer, Jesus reveals and teaches his martyrdom, resurrection and return as the Son of Man with glory (Lk 9:22–26). Moreover, Jesus expects his disciples to be willing to sacrifice their lives for his sake as an expression of genuine discipleship. In his speech, Stephen mentions how the Jews and their ancestors not only rejected Moses and Jesus, the Prophet-like-Moses, but also the prophets who prophesied the coming of "the Righteous One Jesus" (Acts 7:52). He also mentions the tent in the wilderness (σκηνή in Acts 7:43) and announces that God does not dwell in the Temple made by human hands.[117] In my reading of Luke–Acts, this part of Stephen's speech resonates with Peter's proposal to erect the tents (σκηνή in Lk 9:33) at the Transfiguration and God's implicit rejection of it.

In his vision, Stephen sees the heavens opened up and Jesus as the Son of Man standing at the right hand of God with divine glory (Acts 7:55–56). While the opened heavens, along with Stephen's being filled with the Spirit, recalls the scene of Jesus' baptism, the Son of Man with glory reminds readers of the Transfiguration incident. Since the three disciples' experience of Jesus' Transfiguration is a proleptic revelation of the Son of Man's glory at the Parousia, Stephen's vision of the Son of Man with glory is identical to their experience. In Stephen's vision we find that Jesus' promise of his return as the Son of Man, to vindicate his righteous follow-

---

[116] For the later reception of Stephen's martyrdom, refer to François Bovon, "The Dossier on Stephen, the First Martyr," *HTR* 96 (2003): 279–315.

[117] Ibid., 284–85.

ers, is fulfilled for Stephen on an individual level. Moreover, Luke describes Stephen's transformation into someone with an angelic face, while confronting his martyrdom (Acts 6:15). By this transformation, Luke claims that the Son of Man's vindication of his righteous martyrs, which is promised to take place in the future in Lk 9, is actualized in Stephen's present experience of martyrdom and his personal vindication and transformation. Regarding Stephen's vision, C. K. Barrett maintains, "It is an actual but personal and individual Parousia taking place for the benefit of Stephen himself."[118] According to Barrett, this individual Parousia is distinct from the universal Parousia of the last day and in this way, Luke offers to his community a solution to the delay of the Parousia. In my opinion, for the Lukan readers, "the individual Parousia" still functions as strong evidence for "the universal Parousia."[119]

It is significant that Luke presents Stephen the Hellenist as the first martyr who experiences, even prior to Peter, James and John, Jesus' prediction of his coming as the Son of Man with glory. Also, since Stephen's announcement of the Son of Man standing at the right hand of God corresponds to Peter's witness to the exalted Lord at God's right hand (Acts 2:33–35; 5:31), in Luke's mind, Stephen is well qualified to become a witness of Jesus' resurrection like Peter and the twelve.[120] Luke states this more clearly in the case of Paul, whose role as a witness is more extensively discussed than Stephen's (Acts 22:14–15; 26:16).

– Paul

As soon as Stephen is killed, Philip carries on Stephen's preaching about Jesus in Samaria and makes first contact with a representative of the people at the end of the earth, an Ethiopian eunuch (Acts 8). Then, Paul takes over the Gentile mission and Stephen's (and Jesus') role of the suffering servant[121] and like Stephen, encounters Jesus the risen Lord in a vision and sees his glory. In Paul's vision, Jesus announces that Paul "must suffer" for his sake (δεῖ παθεῖν; 9:16); this is exactly the same message that Jesus taught immediately before the Transfiguration (Lk 9:22). In Luke's description of Paul's final journey to Jerusalem, Paul accepts his coming suffering in the same city where Jesus fulfilled his own "exodus."

At his Damascus experience, Paul receives from the risen Lord the mission to preach the Gospel to "the Gentiles, kings and the sons of Israel"

---

[118] C. K. Barrett, "Stephen and the Son of Man," in *Apophoreta: Festschrift für Ernst Haenchen zu Seinem Siebzigsten Geburtstag* (Berlin: Töpelmann, 1964), 35–36.

[119] For a brief survey of the theme of the Son of Man in Acts with bibliographical information, see Bovon, *Luke the Theologian*, 205–06.

[120] See Tannehill, *The Narrative Unity of Luke–Acts: A Literary Interpretation,* vol. 2, 80–101.

[121] Ibid.

(Acts 9:15). This experience resonates with the Transfiguration incident in many ways.[122] Paul sees the light, which represents the glory of the risen Jesus, and hears his voice (9:3–4). The risen Jesus mentions his suffering by Paul (9:5) and predicts Paul's own suffering for his sake in the future (9:16). Responding to the light, Paul falls on the ground (9:4; 22:7; and 26:14) and raises a question as a response to the vision. Paul hears a divine instruction with commission (9:6; 22:10; and 26:16). Immediately after the Damascus experience, Paul begins to proclaim that Jesus is God's Son (Acts 9:20), which is the central message of the Transfiguration. In his preaching throughout Acts, Paul argues that Jesus the Messiah had to suffer and be raised from the dead (17:3; 18:5; cf. Lk 9:22). Interestingly, Paul is called Jesus' "chosen instrument" (σκεῦος ἐκλογῆς in Acts 9:15), which recalls God's calling Jesus "the Chosen One" (ὁ ἐκλελεγμένος in Lk 9:35).

While all these elements are commonly found in two other accounts of the same event in Acts 22:6–15 and 26:12–13,[123] in Acts 26:17–18, Luke further develops the implication of the light in God's salvation program. The light connotes a salvation implication that Jesus "the light" will send Paul to open the eyes of both the Jews and the Gentiles, so that they may turn from darkness to light.[124] In Acts 13:47, Jesus calls Paul "the light of the Gentiles," which is a quotation of Isa 49:6 that Simeon ascribes to the infant Jesus in Lk 2:30–32. In the Lukan portrayal of Paul, he takes over not only Jesus' fate as the Suffering Servant, but also his mission as the light of the Gentiles.

In the Lukan accounts, the three Hellenists, Stephen, Philip and Paul, have both a similar role to that of the twelve and a special role that goes beyond theirs. In contrast to the twelve, the Hellenists are not the witnesses of Jesus' earthly ministry (Acts 1:21–22; 10:39, 41).[125] Like the twelve, however, the three Hellenists are called the apostolic witnesses of the resurrection of Jesus and complete Jesus' command in Acts 1:8: "You will receive power when the Holy Spirit has come upon you; and you will be my witnesses in Jerusalem, in all Judea and Samaria, and to the ends of the earth." Philip preaches the Gospels to people in Samaria and the end of the earth; and in his defense before the king Agrippa, Paul highlights the wide geographic scope of his mission to Damascus, Jerusalem, all the district of Judea and the Gentiles. Paul and Philip, however, have a special role that

---

[122] See also Moses, *Matthew's Transfiguration Story*, 232.

[123] There are discrepancies among the three accounts of Paul's Damascus experience in Acts. Tannehill argues that the three reports are slanted for the speaker's benefit and that slight conflicts of detail are of little consequence as long as central affirmation does not rest on them (Tannehill, 321).

[124] For more, see Tannehill, vol. 2, 119–21.

[125] See Tannehill, vol. 2, 280–81.

goes beyond that of the twelve. While the twelve focus on the Jews (13:31), Paul and Philip will witness to "all people, both the Jews and the Gentiles" (22:15). Also, Paul (and Stephen) follows Jesus in the same path of suffering and trial in Jerusalem (6–7; 21:11–14; 22:22). Like Jesus, Paul must appear before the Jewish council, the Roman governor and a Jewish king. Like Jesus, Paul is repeatedly declared innocent, but is not released.[126]

4.4 Conclusion

In this chapter, we have seen how Matthew and Luke modify the Markan Transfiguration story to make it more meaningfully answer their particular agendas and theological needs. Both keep the base story line of the Markan Transfiguration: Jesus' transformation before the three; appearance of Moses and Elijah; Peter's proposal to build three tents; and God's confirmation of Jesus' Sonship from a cloud. However, Matthew adds a new motif in his description of Jesus' transformation – Jesus' brilliant face. Luke also explains Jesus' transformation through the change of his face, while removing the Greek term μεταμορφόομαι. In contrast to Mark, both Matthew and Luke want to rehabilitate the disciples, especially Peter. Matthew omits Peter's ignorance of Jesus' mission in Mark and the Matthean Peter correctly understands Jesus' identity as the Lord and God's Son. Luke also portrays Peter in a more positive light by removing both his rejection of Jesus' message of suffering and Jesus' rebuking of him.

Both Matthew and Luke introduce new ideas and terms at the Transfiguration in order to relate the story backward and forward to the rest of their Gospel stories. For Matthew, Jesus' brilliant face like the sun recalls his prediction of the believers' future existence like the sun. Also, the second part of God's confirmation of Jesus' Sonship, "with whom I am well pleased," tightly relates the story to the Baptism. Since the revelation of Jesus' Sonship comes directly from God, Matthew calls the story "a vision." On the other hand, Luke introduces a new word, "glory," in his description of the transfigured Jesus with Moses and Elijah. While in Mark and Matthew, Jesus' glory is called "the glory of his Father," Luke calls it "his glory." Also, Luke reveals the content of the conversation between Moses and Elijah, that is, Jesus' exodus, which he will fulfill in Jerusalem. Luke calls the two old prophets "two men," which refers to angelic beings in the Lukan accounts. God in the Lukan accounts calls Jesus "the Chosen

---

[126] For more on this comparison between Jesus and Paul, refer to Walter Radl, *Paulus und Jesus im lukanischen Doppelwerk* (Bern: Herbert Lang, 1975), 211–21; and J. Neyrey, *The Passion According to Luke: A Redaction Study of Luke's Soteriology* (New York: Paulist Press, 1984), 104–5.

One," which refers to Isaiah's Suffering Servant. Although Luke removes the Markan expression "beloved," he heightens the intimacy between the Father and the Son through his emphasis on Jesus' constant prayer.

In its immediate context of the Transfiguration, Matthew adds Jesus' establishment of his church on Peter, the rock. Matthew sees at the Transfiguration a new Sinai event between God and His people in two ways: (1) Jesus' teaching as the new Torah and (2) Jesus' transfigured glory as the Theophanic glory. Matthew uses this story to legitimate his community's recent separation from mainline Judaism. In this sense, the Transfiguration is a foundational story for Matthew and his community. For Luke, the Transfiguration resolves the tension raised by Herod's perplexity about Jesus' identity. By removing most of Mark 6–8, Luke makes chapter nine of his Gospel one single scene about Jesus' identity. Furthermore, Jesus' exodus at the Transfiguration functions as a prelude to the Travel Account (Lk 9:51). The fulfillment of Jesus' exodus in Jerusalem is, however, not the end of the Lukan story, but it starts the exodus of the disciples who are commissioned to preach the Gospels from Jerusalem to the end of the earth. In Luke's theological scheme, he wants to reconcile the ministry of the Twelve and that of the Hellenists, especially by making the visions of Stephen and Paul comparable to the three disciples' experience of the Transfiguration.

Chapter 5

The Transfiguration Accounts in the Early Second Century: 2 Peter and the *Apocalypse of Peter*

5.1 Introduction

We have seen so far how the Transfiguration story served the first century Christians by providing meaningful solutions for their various Christological, ecclesiological, anthropological, apologetic and eschatological issues. They resisted simply *re*-presenting the story in the traditional form that they received, but reinterpreted or rewrote it to meet their particular needs. Similarly, in the second century, the Transfiguration tradition does not stop growing, but acquires new elements and emphases in order to answer second century Christian readers' contemporary issues. What are those new elements and emphases of the story in the second century? How do second century Christians interpret the story similarly or differently? We can only answer these questions by examining specific texts, which offer new contexts for the story, and then putting them in dialogue with their predecessors of the first century.

2 Peter and the *Apocalypse of Peter* (ApoPt), both of which are dated to the early second century, have often been examined together by scholars, as they show great similarity in terms of vocabulary, themes and the pseudonym Peter.[1] It is especially interesting to notice that both present the Transfiguration as relevant to the Parousia in their confrontation with false messiahs and false teachers. Do they belong to the same pro-Petrine community? Or do the similar understandings of the Transfiguration in two independent texts represent a similar religious milieu in the second century Christianity? Or do they witness a certain Petrine tradition regarding Parousial understanding of the Transfiguration?

Readers of 2 Peter and ApoPt experience similar challenges in their exegesis of each text: their pseudepigraphic nature, distinctive vocabulary, and difficulty in dating and locating them geographically and chronologically. Because of these challenges, I find it very useful to compare both

---

[1] For the dating of 2 Peter and ApoPt, see Richard J. Bauckham, *Jude, 2 Peter, Word Biblical Commentary* (Waco, Texas: Word Books, 1983),157–58; and Daniel J. Harrington, *Jude and 2 Peter*, *Sacra Pagina Series* (Collegeville, Minnesota: A Michael Clazier Book), 235–37.

texts, since this comparison may help us locate them in the development of early Christian history. Although we may not reach a definitive conclusion about their historical contexts, we may at least obtain their relative contexts within the spectrum of the second century Christianity.

It is, however, necessary to hear their distinctive voices first, before we can make any profitable use of comparing and contrasting them with each other. We should allow them to speak about their understanding of the Transfiguration on their own terms. Also, since we lack certain evidence of specific contexts for 2 Peter and ApoPt, our reading of them has to start with the texts themselves rather than with any hypothetical scenarios or theoretical contexts.[2]

In this chapter, I will first examine the literary and historical context of 2 Peter; then explain how the Transfiguration story functions for the author of 2 Peter to resolve his crisis caused by false teachers; then I will move on to an analysis of the literary and historical context of ApoPt and its understanding of the Transfiguration story; and finally, I will compare both texts in terms of their contexts and their interpretations of the Transfiguration story.

My comparison of both texts will show that they understand the story as a key element of the Parousia, though with different emphases. It is interesting to note, first, that while 2 Peter takes the Transfiguration as an event where Jesus receives honor and glory as the eschatological judge (Christological), ApoPt focuses on the transfigured bodies of Moses and Elijah, which represent the resurrected glorious bodies of the believers at the Parousia (ecclesiological/anthropological). Second, we can detect two distinctive forms of presenting the story: 2 Peter in a form of theological discourse and ApoPt in a narrative discourse. Do different forms serve the readers differently and with different rhetorical functions? This development in two literary forms also finds its earlier parallel in Mk 9 and 2 Cor 3. Third, their understanding of the Transfiguration as a part of or an evidence for the Parousia will speak against some scholars who tend to argue that Christian eschatological expectation for the Parousia substantially waned in the second century. Instead, the expectation of the Parousia was vividly alive in the second century, at least within some groups of people who venerated Peter as their apostle. Fourth, we will notice that the name Peter is tightly connected with the Transfiguration tradition, as if he is the guarantor of the correct understanding of the story. Being remembered with the name Peter, the story becomes a part of the apostolic tradition.

---

[2] Speculation with specific hypotheses often permits texts to say more than is there. Moreover, readers' specific choices of contextual and methodological hypotheses may import modern readers' values into the ancient texts, where these modern values are not simply operative.

Although the story also appears in the *Apocryphon of John* and the *Acts of John*, this time in a form of polymorphy,[3] it exclusively finds its patron in the apostle Peter, while completely forgetting James, one of the three witnesses.

As the general corollary of these conclusions, I will show that the boundary between canonical and non-canonical (or apocryphal) is not helpful for our reconstruction of early Christian thought during the first two centuries, and that the non-canonical version of the story in ApoPt is not that different from the canonical version in 2 Peter and from the synoptic stories. The author of ApoPt seems to rewrite the synoptic stories, filling the gaps with new materials, in a way that the story becomes *transformed* to tell much more to its new readers in the second century. In a similar line of thought, it is not meaningful in our examination of the history of early Christianity to relegate 2 Peter and ApoPt to the fringe of the early Christian texts, not least because both texts are pseudepigraphic writings. Their marginalization is further exacerbated by the fact that 2 Peter is much different from the rest of the New Testament in terms of style, theology and vocabulary,[4] and that ApoPt is apocryphal, not canonical. 2 Peter and ApoPt are, in my opinion, as important evidence for our understanding of early Christian thoughts as the Gospels and Paul, although the former draws upon the latter.

5.2 2 Peter

Confronting false teachers' eschatological skepticism, 2 Peter presents the Transfiguration story as a promise of the Parousia, Jesus' second coming. According to its description of the story in a form of theological discourse, Jesus is claimed to receive "honor" (τιμή) and "glory" (δόξα) on the holy mountain. These, in turn, represent the divine manifestation of his powerful coming as the eschatological judge (1:16–18; 3:7–10). In the theological scheme of 2 Peter, its Christological Parousial understanding of the Transfiguration has something to do with the believers' existence in a new life; those divine attributes of Christ, such as honor, glory, power and virtue, become guiding principles for their present journey to "the eternal kingdom" (1:11). In this theological scheme, the journey to the eternal kingdom is best accomplished by becoming "participants of the divine na-

---

[3] I will come back to these texts in the following chapter, when I analyze the *Acts of Peter*.

[4] For more on this, Lauri Thuren, "Style Never Goes out of Fashion: 2 Peter Re-Evaluated," in *Rhetoric, Scripture and Theology: Essays from the 1994 Pretoria Conference*, ed. Stanley Porter and Thomas Olbright (Sheffield: Sheffield Academic Press, 1996), 341.

ture" (θείας κοινωνοὶ φύσεως) (1:4). Thus, the three major questions that I would like to answer in this part of discussion are: (1) What is the literary and historical context of 2 Peter? What is its crisis? Who are the opponents? (2) How does its understanding of the Transfiguration resolve the tension inside the church of 2 Peter? And (3) what does the transfigured Jesus have to do with the idea of believers as participants of the divine nature?

5.2.1 Literary and Historical Context

– False Teachers' Eschatological Skepticism and Rejection of the Parousia
In my analysis of 2 Peter, rather than imposing any hypothetical historical situations on it, I would like to first examine how the text describes those false teachers who reject the Parousia message. Then I will explore how 2 Peter develops its argument in order to overcome the crisis. After having understood the text's literary description of the inscribed opponents and their claims, I may then attempt to identify who those false teachers are.[5]

2 Pet 2:1–3 and 2:20–22 explicitly acknowledge that there are false teachers (ψευδοδιδάσκαλοι) with "destructive opinions" (αἱρέσεις ἀπωλείας) inside the church of 2 Peter.[6] Their destructive teaching is especially based upon eschatological skepticism: "Where is the promise of his [Christ] coming? For ever since our fathers died, all things continue as they were from the beginning of creation" (3:4–5). According to these false teachers, the early Christian eschatological expectation of the Parousia is mistaken and there will be no eschatological judgment (2:3b). They further claim to liberate people from the fear of divine judgment (2:19), which is a part of the apostles' "concocted myth" from their perspective (1:16). They promote an immoral lifestyle and ethical libertinism (2:2, 10a, 13–14, 18). They are also accused by 2 Peter of exploiting the believers with their false words out of a desire for their own financial gain (2:3).[7] From the perspective of the author of 2 Peter, their character is best summarized in two verbs, "denying" (2:1) and "distorting" (3:16).

According to 2 Peter, they tend to slander angelic powers (2:10) and disrespect the teachings of the apostles and the scriptures about the Parousia message. The false teachers further argue that the Parousia message,

---

[5] It is, however, difficult to identify the opponents of 2 Peter, not least because its accusations of the false teachers are full of common literary topos. Furthermore, its extensive use of Jude 6–18 in its polemical description of these false teachers makes the identification even harder.

[6] For more on the false teachers, see Bauckham, *Jude, 2 Peter*, 154–57; Jerome H. Neyrey, *2 Peter, Jude, The Anchor Bible* (New York: The Anchor Bible, 1993), 122–28; and Harrington, *Jude and 2 Peter*, 233–35.

[7] This ethical charge is such a common literary motif that we may not deduce any historical importance from it.

"the power and coming of the Lord Jesus Christ," is a myth the apostles devised (1:16) for their moral control of the believers. Although it goes beyond the evidence to speak of their relationship with Paul,[8] from the perspective of the author of 2 Peter, they have misinterpreted Paul along with other scriptures (3:15–16; cf. 1:19–21).[9]

It is noteworthy that 2 Peter creates a sharp contrast between the apostles and the false teachers in two major ways: (1) while the former cherishes scriptural teachings about the Parousia of Christ, the latter rejects it; and (2) as its corollary, the former promotes an ethically oriented lifestyle, while the latter advocates libertinism. As for candidates for these false teachers, the references to "myths" (1:16) and "knowledge" (1:2, 3) prompted an old hypothesis that it is the Gnostics whom the author of 2 Peter faces in his church (cf. 1 Tim 1:4; 4:7; 2 Tim 4:4; Tit 1:14).[10] But the term "myths" is the opponents' charge against the apostles, not the author's charge against his opponents.[11] Also, the term "knowledge" in 2 Peter is free of polemical overtones. More importantly, the hypothesis of the false teachers as the Gnostics becomes unwarranted due to insufficient data in 2 Peter and the problem of defining the term Gnosticism, which Karen King deals with in more detail.[12]

On the other hand, Jerome H. Neyrey makes a hypothesis that it is either the Epicureans, who rejected traditional theodicy, or Jewish "scoffers," who espoused a similar attitude to that of the Epicureans.[13] However, the dearth of information in 2 Peter does not allow us to reach a definitive conclusion about the identity of the false teachers. What 2 Peter allows us to conclude at this moment is: (1) there are ongoing debates regarding the genuineness of the Parousia message in the post-apostolic age around the beginning of the second century and (2) this Parousia message is somehow associated with a specific understanding of the Transfiguration – in the

---

[8] It is possible that the false teachers are some sort of Paulinists who overemphasize present aspects of Paul's teachings to the exclusion of all future eschatological emphases. See also, Harrington, 235.

[9] It seems that 2 Peter takes Paul's writings to be of equal value to other scriptural writings (cf. 3:15–16).

[10] E. Käsemann, "An Apologia for Primitive Christian Eshatology," in *Essays on New Testament Themes* (London: SCM, 1964), 169–95 and W. Grundmann, *Der Brief des Judas und der zweite Brief des Petrus* (Berlin: Evangelische Berlagsanstalt, 1974). More specifically, Terrence V. Smith proposes that 2 Peter's opponents are the Gnostic Basilideans (*Petrine Controversy*, 92–93). But against them, see Tord Fornberg, *An Early Church in a Pluralistic Society* (Uppsala: Gleerup, 1977).

[11] See also, Bauckham, *Jude, 2 Peter*, 157.

[12] King, *What is Gnosticism?*

[13] Neyrey, *2 Peter*, 122–28. Also, *idem.*, "The Form and Background of the Polemic in 2 Peter," *JBL* 99 (1980): 407–32.

case of 2 Peter, the transfigured Jesus is the coming eschatological judge with honor and glory.

– Peter the Pseudonym, His Death and Farewell Speech
It has been noticed by many scholars that 2 Peter adopts a form of "epistolary testament" or "farewell speech," which is commonly attested in Second Temple Judaism.[14] Pseudepigraphers especially find this literary genre useful for their purposes, as they can transmit advice about present dangers, which they are currently confronting, by having a certain renowned figure in the past speak for themselves.[15] The author presents those dangers along with their solutions as if Peter prophesied in his farewell speech. In a typical pseudepigraphal setting, the chosen hero in the past, facing his death, delivers revelations of the future crises as well as their solutions, and offers the following generations some ethical admonitions as well.

By adopting the epistolary testament form, the author of 2 Peter locates its pseudepigraphical setting in Peter's imminent death (1:14–15; cf. Jn 21:19) and deliberately juxtaposes Peter's prophecies of false teachers with their present accounts in the church. In this way, the author intends his letter to be relevant to the controversy of his own time and legitimates the credibility of his own solution for it by ascribing it to Peter's authoritative teaching delivered in the form of prophecy.

Why does the author of 2 Peter put his work in the name of Peter?[16] Does his church understand itself as a part of a Petrine school or community? Not only is the existence of the Petrine school doubted, but also it is less likely that 2 Peter belongs to a Petrine school, since the vocabulary and themes are much different from those of 1 Peter. Instead, they are closer to those of the Pauline writings, especially the Pastorals.[17] Also, its audiences are the Gentile churches to which Paul also wrote his own letters (3:15). So, what we have here in 2 Peter may be a Petrine teaching for a pro-Pauline community.[18]

---

[14] Bauckham, *2 Peter*, 131–32; Smith, *Petrine Controversies*, 69–70; Harrington, *Jude and 2 Peter*, 252–3; and Neyrey, "The Apologetic Use of the Transfiguration in 2nd Peter 1:16–21," 506.

[15] Harrington, 252.

[16] For more on the concepts and functions of real reader, inscribed reader, and pseudonyms, refer to Richard J. Bauckham, "Pseudo-Apostolic Letters," *JBL* 107 (1988): 469–94.

[17] For this, see Michael J. Gilmour, *The Significance of Parallels between 2 Peter and Other Early Christian Literature* (Leiden; Boston: Brill, 2002), 130.

[18] It is no wonder that the Tübingen school sees here the early Catholic church's endeavor to reconcile Peter and Paul in the beginning of the second century. See more on this, Smith, *Petrine Controversy*.

The author's choice of Peter as the pseudonym has to do with the church's memory of the apostle Peter and traditions pertaining to him rather than the old idea of Peter as the apostle *par excellence*.[19] Facing the problem of the delayed Parousia and his enemies' attack on it, the author brings anew his teaching about the Transfiguration with much more eschatological flavor. However, the enemies, some teachers inside the community, reject this tradition, calling it "devised myth" of the apostles (1:16). In his apologetic defense against the false teachers, the author needs someone to authenticate this traditional teaching. Peter is the best person to bolster its authenticity, because he is remembered as the unique eyewitness of the event in the memory of the church – this is well attested in the synoptic versions of the story. In this way, the author can make his eschatological understanding of the Transfiguration as old and genuine as Peter the apostle. 2 Peter shows that in order to buttress its truth claim, its community needs a specific apostolic figure as its guarantor, who is often associated with the tradition in the memory of the church. In our current case, Peter serves as the guarantor of the truth claim of the Transfiguration as a key proof for the Parousia discourse due to his privileged status as an eyewitness of the event. Peter functions as the center of the gravity of the Transfiguration story, acquiring new elements which are lacking in the synoptic versions.[20]

– Reminding through Key Words
The form of farewell speech or epistolary testament often makes use of the catchwords "reminding (ὑπομιμνῄσκειν)" and "refreshing (διεγείρειν)" (1:12, 13). These catchwords serve the purpose of Peter's farewell speech well both by foretelling the dangers after his death and presenting Peter's authoritative teaching as a defense against the false teachers (cf.

---

[19] François Bovon, "Apostolic Memories in Early Christianity," in *Studies in Early Christianity* (Tübingen: Mohr Siebeck, 2003), 1–16.

[20] It is clear that 2 Peter is not interested in venerating the person Peter or his work, unlike hagiographa, which manifest various legends about specific apostolic figures for their veneration. For example, 2 Peter clearly maintains in its opening verse that Peter is called to be an apostle by Christ and that there also exists an apostolic/exclusive group of "we" (1:16). However, in the same opening verse, 2 Peter goes quickly to erase the distinction between "the apostolic/exclusive we" and "the inclusive/ecclesiological we" by making their faith of the same value as well as from the same origin (M. Eugene Boring, "Gospel and Church in 2 Peter," *Mid-Stream* 35 (1996): 402–5): "To those who have received *a faith as precious as ours through the righteousness of our God and Savior Jesus Christ*" (v. 1; italics are mine!). 2 Peter, however, tries to bolster both Peter's authority as the eyewitness to the Transfiguration and his eschatological understanding of it in two ways: (1) the message is also confirmed by the prophecies of the scriptures (1:19–21) and (2) it stands well in harmony with other apostolic traditions, especially Paul (3:16–17).

Mk 13).[21] In addition to his previous teaching in vv. 3–11, Peter's "reminding" verifies the Parousia-judgment message which is reinforced by his eyewitness experience of the Transfiguration, although it is delayed. In the process of reminding, the author makes use of such key words as *power*, *glory*, *virtue* and *promise* in 1:3–5 in order to prepare the audience for his upcoming teaching about the Transfiguration story as a proof for the coming Parousia in vv. 16–18, where these terms will reappear.

Peter's death (ἡ ἀπόθεσις τοῦ σκηνώματος in v. 14; cf. Jn 21:19) with the use of Greek term σκήνωμα for body, which is interchangeable with σκηνή for "tent," further helps the readers remember the Transfiguration story in three ways (cf. 2 Cor 5:1). First, Peter offered to build up three *tents* in the Synoptic version of the story. Second, Jesus said right before the Transfiguration, "there are some standing here who will not taste *death* until they see that the kingdom of God has come with power" (Mk 9:1 and its parallel). And finally, the Transfiguration in the Synoptics is surrounded by Jesus' prediction of his own suffering and *death*. All these may indicate that the framework of the Caesarea-Philippi context lies behind the Transfiguration account of 2 Peter.[22]

5.2.2 The Transfiguration (1:16–18)

16 For we did not follow cleverly devised myths when we made known to you the power and coming of our Lord Jesus Christ, but we had been eyewitnesses of his majesty. 17 For when he received honor and glory from God the Father, such a voice as this was delivered to him by the Majestic Glory, saying, "This is My son, My beloved, with whom I am well-pleased." 18 We ourselves heard this voice come from heaven, when we were with him on the holy mountain.[23]

In 2 Peter, Peter begins his farewell speech by reiterating the salvation history on the axis of time: (1) Christ's salvation work in the past (1:1–2), (2) its implication for the believers in the present (vv. 3–10), and (3) their future entry into the eternal kingdom (v. 11). And then, by introducing the necessity of "reminding" the later generations of his teaching as well as "refreshing" their memory in a form of farewell speech (vv. 12–15), he makes a transition from the summary of his previous teaching in 1:3–11 to an apologetic defense of the certainty of the Parousia in vv.16–18. This last point was hotly contested at the time of 2 Peter, as I have already shown.

---

[21] See more, Charles H. Talbert, "2 Peter and the Delay of the Parousia," *Vigiliae Christianae* 20 (1966): 138–40.

[22] I will later show that the author is well aware of the synoptic version, especially the Matthean one.

[23] Translation is mine.

– Jesus' Receiving of Honor and Glory at the Transfiguration

Responding to the opponents' labeling the Transfiguration as "devised myth (σεσοφισμένοις μύθοις)" (v.16), 2 Peter grounds the certainty of the promised Parousia in Peter's eyewitness experience of the Transfiguration. Most commentators now agree that the term "myth" refers to 2 Peter's tradition of the Transfiguration event, which has been slandered as a myth, rather than the author's polemic against Gnostic mythmakers.[24] The Greek term ἐπόπτης[25] for eyewitness, emphasizes the veracity of the Transfiguration event and provides an historical basis for the expectation of the Parousia, the powerful second coming of Jesus Christ (2 Pet 3:4–5; cf. Acts 1:21–22).[26] In the theological mind of the author of 2 Peter, Jesus' "majesty" as the future eschatological judge at the Parousia has already become manifest on a limited scale in his receiving honor and glory at the Transfiguration. However, the readers of 2 Peter must wait until the Parousia to witness the full-blown majesty of Jesus.

At the Transfiguration event, Peter claims to have seen Christ receiving "honor" and "glory" from God and to have heard God's voice from heaven regarding the revelation of Christ's special relationship with God as His son. For 2 Peter, Christ's "majesty" is expressed through his divine attributes of honor and glory which come from God the Father.[27] It is evident that 2 Peter also calls God the "Majestic Glory (μεγαλοπρεπής δόξα)" (v.17; cf. Heb 1:3; 8:1; 1 En 14:20; 102:3; T. Levi. 3:4). In these two examples, it is clear that the glory, power and the majesty are synonymous, expressing the divine nature of God (cf. Ps 68:34; 96:6; 111:3).[28] In addition, Jesus' sharing those qualities with God offers him a special status right next to God in the heavenly hierarchy.[29] In 2 Pet 2:10–11, the author

---

[24] See, Neyrey, "The Apologetic Use of the Transfiguration in 2nd Peter 1:16–21," 506; Fornberg, *An Early Church,* 60; Smith, *Petrine Controversy,* 78; and Bauckham, *2 Peter,* 213–14. On the contrary, see C. Spicq, *Les epîtres de saint Pierre* (Paris: Gabalda, 1966), 580–82.

[25] Jerzy Klinger, "The Second Epistle of Peter: An Essay in Understanding," *St. Vladimir's Theological Quarterly* 17 (1973): 152–69.

[26] Bauckham also says in *2 Peter,* 216, "a stress on the apostolic eyewitnesses occurs when there is a need for apologetic defense of the Christian message in some way by reference to its historical basis." Similarly, Neyrey, *2 Peter,* 176.

[27] The idea that Jesus' divine glory reflects the glory of God is somewhat similar to Paul's understanding of Jesus as the image/glory of God in 2 Cor 3:18–4:6.

[28] See F. W. Danker, *Benefactor* (St. Louis: Clayton Publishing House, 1982).

[29] The phrase τοῦ θεοῦ ἡμῶν καὶ σωτῆρος Ἰησοῦ Χριστοῦ in 1:1 is interesting, as there is only one definite article, making "God" and "saviour Jesus Christ" one and the same figure. Does the author of 2 Peter have only Jesus in his mind in this verse or both God and Jesus? Or did a later copyist happen to omit the definite article before "savior" by mistake? It is likely that 2 Peter calls Jesus God, as Jesus is for him not only the Lord,

calls the angels "the glorious ones (δόξας)" who possess might and power similar to the Father and the Son. 2 Peter makes it clear that the angels are to be considered lower than Jesus Christ in the heavenly hierarchy, as Jesus is also the Lord of these angels.[30] It is beyond doubt that in 2 Peter, Jesus' possessing the majestic glory elevates his status, placing him next to God the Father as His Son.

How is the Transfiguration related to the Parousia? The apologetic importance of the term "glory" lies in the fact that Jesus' glory at the Transfiguration, which has been shown only to the three disciples, will become manifest to the whole universe at the Parousia, which may not be imminent in the opinion of 2 Peter.[31] In this sense, the glory of the transfigured Jesus in 2 Peter is the Parousia-glory. These similar words of honor, glory and majesty in 2 Peter are generic equivalents of the specific details of glory in the Synoptics, such as his transfiguration, shining garments and face.[32] Even in the Synoptics, the glory was tightly related to the Parousia, as if it was the eschatological glory.[33] For example, in Mk 8:38 and 13:26 (and its equivalents), the Son of Man is promised to come in glory at the Parousia. I have also shown in chapter one how Mk 9:1 relates the Transfiguration to Jesus' promise of coming in glory at the end of times.[34]

Similarly to the Synoptics, 2 Peter reinforces Jesus' divine commissioning and special relationship with God by introducing God's divine interruption through the heavenly voice: "This is My son, My beloved one, with whom I am well pleased" (1:17). This phrase is, as I already discussed in chapter one, a pastiche of the Hebrew Bible phrases: "you are my son" (Ps 2:7), referring to the Kingly Messiah, "your only son whom you love" (Gen 22:2), referring to Isaac, and "My chosen one, with whom my soul delights" (Is 42:1), referring to the Suffering Servant. While the two texts of Psalm and Isaiah have to do with divine commissioning, the Genesis passage implies God's deliverance of His only son to death for a certain purpose. In the Synoptics, however, while the Transfiguration has something to do with the theophanic revelation and future vindication of Jesus

---

but also one to whom the doxology is to be offered (3:18), both of which belong to God's prerogatives in the Hebrew Bible.

[30] The identification of Jesus with the Lord is also an important idea of Paul. This does not necessarily make 2 Peter dependent upon Paul, but attests how popularly that identification was made in the Gentile churches.

[31] François Bovon, my *Doktorvater*, keeps drawing my attention to the delay of the Parousia in 2 Peter's theological scheme.

[32] Although only Luke mentions the term glory (9:32), the descriptions of Matthew and Mark are exactly what the ancient people would think of the divine glory.

[33] There lies behind this the Danielic tradition of the Son Man in glory (Dan 7:13–14).

[34] See also, Bauckham, *2 Peter*, 211; and Harrington, *2 Peter*, 258.

and his disciples, it is at the Baptism that God commissioned Jesus to preach and perform powerful miracles (Mk 1:7–15 and its parallels).

It is worthwhile comparing 2 Peter's version of the contents of God's testimony with those in two occasions of the Synoptics, since the comparison may shed light on their literary relationship.

Transfiguration
Mk 9:7   Οὗτός ἐστιν ὁ υἱός μου ὁ ἀγαπητός
Mt 17:5   Οὗτός ἐστιν ὁ υἱός μου ὁ ἀγαπητός, ἐν ᾧ εὐδόκησα
Lk 9:35   Οὗτός ἐστιν ὁ υἱός μου ὁ ἐκλελεγμένος
2 Pet 1:17 Ὁ υἱός μου ὁ ἀγαπητός μου οὗτός ἐστιν εἰς ὃν ἐγὼ εὐδόκησα

Baptism
Mk 1:11   Σὺ εἶ ὁ υἱός μου ὁ ἀγαπητός, ἐν σοὶ εὐδόκησα
Mt 3:17   Οὗτός ἐστιν ὁ υἱός μου ὁ ἀγαπητός, ἐν ᾧ εὐδόκησα
Lk 3:22   Σὺ εἶ ὁ υἱός μου ὁ ἀγαπητός, ἐν σοὶ εὐδόκησα

It seems that the version of 2 Pet 1:17 is almost identical to that of the Matthean version of the Transfiguration (Mt 17:5), which has exactly identical wordings to those at the Baptism (Mt 3:17). There are, however, two minor differences between 2 Pet 1:17 and Mt 17:5: (1) addition of μου after ὁ ἀγαπητός and (2) the prepositional phrase εἰς ὃν instead of ἐν ᾧ in 2 Peter. Since there is an exact agreement between 2 Pet 1:17 and *Clem. Hom.* 3:53 (οὗτός ἐστιν μου ʼο υἱός ὁ ἀγαπητός εἰς ὃν εὐδόκησα) and both have the voice ἐξ οὐρανοῦ "from heaven" instead of ἐκ τῆς νεφέλης "from the cloud" (Mk 9:7; Mt 17:5; Lk 9:35), Bauckham argues that there is an independent tradition behind 2 Peter and *Clem. Hom.*, which is not dependent upon the synoptic versions.[35] Bauckham further argues that it is from his own knowledge of Peter's preaching or from the oral traditions current in the Roman church that the author of 2 Peter knew this independent version.[36] However, the two minor elements of mou after ὁ ἀγαπητός and the prepositional phrase εἰς ὃν, found in 2 Pet 1:17 but not in Mt 17:5, *are present* in Mt 12:18 (ὁ ἀγαπητός μου εἰς ὃν εὐδόκησεν ἡ ψυχή μου).[37] This indicates that 2 Peter may be dependent upon Matthew. *Clem. Hom.* 3:53 also lacks the second μου in its phrase and the expressions ἐξ οὐρανοῦ and ἐκ τῆς νεφέλης can be interchangeable in their meaning and literary function. The difference between "from heaven" and "from the cloud" is too minor to warrant an independent tradition of the Transfiguration. As a result, Robert J. Miller says,

---

[35] Bauckham, *2 Peter,* 206–10.
[36] Ibid., 210.
[37] Robert J. Miller, "Is There Independent Attestation for the Transfiguration in 2 Peter?," *NewTestStud* 42 (1996): 620–25.

"It is thus simpler to understand 2 Pet 1:17 as dependent on Matthew, either as a literary conflation of the wording in Matt 17.5 and 12.18, or as an understandable mistake in transcribing 17.5, or as a result of the author recalling Matthew from memory."[38]

Agreeing with Miller, Michael J. Gilmour, after having compared synoptic parallels with the Transfiguration in 2 Peter, concludes that although there are no clear citations of the Synoptics in 2 Pet 1:16–18, several clear allusions to the Gospel narratives presuppose no other source than the Gospels in a written form.[39]

It is striking that 2 Peter is not interested in presenting such fascinating details of the story as the description of the transfigured Jesus and the appearance of Moses and Elijah, but simply summarizes Jesus' transfiguration in two key ideas of glory and honor. Also, the author is silent about another important part of the event, God's intervention, "listen to him" (Mk 9:7 and its parallels). It is, however, understandable that since his interest is different from that of Mark, the author of 2 Peter does not feel the need to keep the phrase "listen to him."[40] 2 Peter has to deal with the eschatological skepticism of the false teachers, while it is the nature of discipleship in the midst of suffering that is the issue that Mark engages. It is likely that 2 Peter omits many other details, simply because its readers are familiar with the story and do not question the historicity of the Transfiguration.[41] The main issue of 2 Peter is not a defense of the Transfiguration event, but of the Parousia.[42] In his apologetic argument for the validity of the promised Parousia, the author makes use of undisputed evidence (the Transfiguration), so that it functions to prove the validity of the disputed matter (the promise of the Parousia).

Another interesting omission is related to Peter. In the Synoptics, Peter's anti-passion stance is undeniably manifest throughout the stories, and Jesus often rebukes him for his misunderstanding of the divine mission. Since Peter denied Jesus three times (Mk 14:66–72), it is not Peter but another Simon of Cyrene (the father of Alexander and Rufus who followed Jesus) who takes up Jesus' cross (Mk 15:21). The Synoptics imply in this story that Peter failed in "listening to him" and understanding his teachings about suffering and discipleship (Mk 8:34). However, the absence in 2 Pe-

---

[38] Ibid., 625.

[39] Michael J. Gilmour, *The Significance of Parallels between 2 Peter and Other Early Christian Literature* (Atlanta: Society of Biblical Literature, 2002), 99–100. Bauckham also maintains that the brevity and allusiveness of the account in 2 Peter presupposes a story well-known to the readers, in *2 Peter*, 210.

[40] As I already discussed in ch. 1, this phrase draws the attention of the disciples and Mark's readers to Jesus' two-fold teaching of suffering and death in the Markan context.

[41] See also Bauckham, *2 Peter,* 205–10, 215 and Miller.

[42] See also Denis Farkasfalvy, "The Ecclesial Setting of Pseudepigraphy in Second Peter," *The Second Century* 5 (1985/1986): 3–29.

ter of these derogatory remarks about Peter is necessary to make Peter a conscious and intelligent eyewitness of the sacred event of the Transfiguration. The fact that 2 Peter does not identify the other two apostolic eyewitnesses of James and John, but simply subsumes them into "we," further reinforces Peter's unique position as its eyewitness.[43]

The author of 2 Peter not only omits some details of the synoptic story, but further expands the possible meanings of the story by filling a gap between its earlier implication in the Synoptics and his current needs. He does that by emphasizing the eschatological implication of the Transfiguration that Jesus' glory in the event verifies his coming as the Son of Man for judgment. After having defended the authenticity of Christ's Parousia, 2 Peter asserts the certainty of Christ's eschatological judgment against the false teachers. For the author, the delay of the Parousia does not make the prophecy of Christ's coming and judgment wrong, as the false teachers claim. Its delay expresses God's generosity for them (3:9). As the scripture has predicted, there will certainly be judgment against those who don't respond to God's generous patience at the right time. In order to emphasize the judgment at the Parousia, 2 Peter not only draws upon Jewish apocalyptic material from Jude, but also adds his own traditions about eschatological judgment, including that of the angels (2:4–16).

It is very likely that through the concept of the Son of Man with glory, 2 Peter sees a thematic link between the Transfiguration in its Caesarea-Philippi context (Mk 8:27–9:13 and its parallels) and the Olivet discourse (Mk 13 and its parallels). In the Synoptics, the apocalyptic Olivet discourse greatly expands the theme of the Parousia, the coming Son of Man and his judgment, which Jesus only briefly mentioned in the Caesarea-Philippi context. I have already argued in chapter one that the threefold theme of suffering–death–glory correlates the Transfiguration with the Olivet discourse as well as the Gethsemane story. This link also helps 2 Peter understand the Transfiguration as a proof for the prophecy of the Parousia, followed by the judgment (2 Pet 1:19). From the perspective of the author's scriptural understanding, the Transfiguration as the prophecy of the Parousia further confirms the prophecy of the Day of the Lord in the Hebrew Bible (1:19; 3:2, 7, 10).

---

[43] While the Synoptics often portray Peter as a champion of misunderstanding Jesus and his ministry, they also ascribe to him a prerogative of becoming a beneficiary of heavenly revelations (Mk 13 and its parallels; Lk 24:34; also cf. Acts 2 and 10), including the Transfiguration, and offer him a privileged access to important events in Jesus' life and ministry (Mk 5:37; 14:33).

In order to expand the Parousial implication of the Transfiguration as a promise of the Parousia with an aspect of judgment, the author adopts a chiastic structure in 1:16–2:3a as follows:[44]

(A) the apostles with their genuine message (1:16–18)
   (B) the genuine prophets in the Hebrew Bible (1:19–21)
   (B′) the false prophets in the Hebrew Bible (2:1a)
(A′) the false teachers with destructive opinion (2:1b–3)

In this structure, there is a strong contrast between the apostles/the genuine prophets and the false prophets/the false teachers. While the former group is guided by the Holy Spirit, the latter is guided by "human will" (1:21). Adopting this chiastic structure, 2 Peter warns the readers that just as the false prophets in the Hebrew Bible were condemned by God's judgment, so also will the false teachers and their followers surely experience eschatological judgment at the Parousia (2:3a, 9; 3:5–10).

– The Transfigured Jesus and the Sharers in Divine Nature
So far, I have explained how 2 Peter takes the honor and glory of Jesus at the Transfiguration as what he, as the eschatological judge, will fully reveal at the Parousia. At first sight, it seems to be the case that 2 Peter does not mention any implication of the Transfiguration for the believers. However, through the key term "promise," 2 Peter makes a tight connection between the Transfiguration of Jesus / the Parousia and the believers' new existence in "the knowledge of Jesus the Lord" / their entry into the eternal kingdom. In 2 Peter, the term ἐπάγγελμα is used twice: for the promise of their becoming "participants of the divine nature" (1:4) and for the promise of "the New Heavens and Earth where righteousness dwells" (3:13). Another Greek term ἐπαγγελία is also used twice for the promise of Jesus' coming on the Day of the Lord (3:4, 9), once by the false teachers and once by the author of 2 Peter.

In the theological scheme of the author, the coming Parousia, the Day of the Lord, is the time when the New Heavens and Earth come into existence on a cosmological level. On the ecclesiological level, already in the present the individual believer begins to experience the Parousia or the New Heavens and Earth by becoming a participant of the divine nature. What does it mean to become participants of the divine nature in 2 Peter? What is the divine nature like? How is the concept of becoming participants of the divine nature related to the Transfiguration of Jesus?

In 3:11–12, the author relates his eschatological expectation of the New Heavens and Earth to the present lifestyle of believers:

---

[44] See Ben Witherington, "A Petrine Source in Second Peter," in *Society of Biblical Literature 1985 Seminar Papers*, ed. Kent Harold Richards (Atlanta, Georgia: Scholars Press, 1985), 189. Also, Bauckham, *2 Peter*, 236–37.

"Since all these things are to be dissolved in this way, what sort of persons ought you have to be in *holy conduct* and *godliness* (ἐν ἀγίαις ἀναστροφαῖς καὶ εὐσεβείαις), waiting for and hastening the coming of the Day of God, because of which the heavens will be set ablaze and dissolved, and the elements will melt with fire?" (italics are mine).

In the following verse, 2 Peter indicates that the major moral principle of the New Heavens and Earth is the *righteousness*, which the author already claimed to be a part of the divine attribute of God and Jesus in 1:1. It is striking that in 1:3–11, all these terms of *holy conduct, godliness* and *righteousness* appear in Peter's teaching of the new lifestyle to those who possess the *knowledge* of Jesus. In this passage, the author explains the believers' new life in three-fold form along the axis of time. Their new existence started in the past with the acquisition of the knowledge of Christ as Savior and Lord (vv. 3–4). In the present, they are encouraged to acquire new moral virtues as a part of their transformation, including *godliness*, which is not only Jesus' divine attribute, but also what the believers should strive to acquire (vv. 3, 5–10). Their new existence is completed in the future when the eschatological promises are accomplished and they enter into the eternal kingdom (v.11).[45]

Jesus' divine nature is expressed through the cluster of these key words: *righteousness, divine power, glory, godliness,* and *majesty* (1:1, 3; 2:16–17).[46] In 2 Peter, Jesus' divine nature not only enables the believers to experience a new existence in life, but also it becomes the very *goal* of their new lifestyle, which finds its expression in various moral virtues (1:5–10). Eventually, their ethical struggle to acquire the divine nature in the present will result in their future entry into the eternal kingdom (1:11) and their experience of immortality (1:4). In its description of the sharing of the divine nature, 2 Peter is close to the Stoic ideas. Both envision this sharing happening partly through a moral change and partly through a promised new life after death; and for both, the knowledge of the divine plays a key role.[47] However, 2 Peter differs from the Stoics in presenting Jesus the Lord as the source of knowledge rather than reason, which permeates the cosmos as a wise god for the Stoics.

The last question to answer is: how is this discussion of the believers' participating in the divine nature in their new lifestyle related to the Transfiguration of Jesus? According to the author of 2 Peter, the believers, who have no access to the historical Jesus, are enabled to live this kind of lifestyle only through the knowledge of him as the Lord and his divine power

---

[45] See also, James M. Starr, *Sharers in Divine Nature: 2 Peter 1:4 in Its Hellenistic Context* (Stockholm, Sweden: Almqvist & Wiksell International, 2000), 47.

[46] See also, Ibid., 40–45.

[47] Ibid., 165.

(1:3, 10).[48] His divine power has given them "everything needed for life and godliness" after having called them, and is further expressed through the concepts of his glory and godliness (v.3). According to 2 Peter, it was at the Transfiguration that the divine nature of Jesus was revealed *historically* to "we" (1:16). When the believers accept this knowledge about the Transfiguration of Jesus as the proof for the promise of Parousia, which Peter verifies as its eyewitness, the divine nature of Jesus becomes operative as the divine power within the believers' life. In this way, the key concepts of the promise and the divine nature of Jesus function to help the author correlate with the ideas of the Transfiguration, the Parousia, the believers' own transformation and their entry into the eternal kingdom. They appear as different aspects of the entire event of Jesus' salvation program. James M. Starr well summarizes this kind of sophisticated theological thinking of 2 Peter as follows:

> Briefly, the initial *knowledge* of Christ in his capacity as sovereign and rescuer inaugurates the Christ believer on a journey intended to give him safe passage through the *coming eschatological judgment* into Christ's *eternal kingdom*. The Christ believer's well-being is dependent on his sharing in *divine nature*, seen at present in the taking on of moral virtues (Christ's *righteousness* and *virtue*) and seen ultimately in the rescue from corruption and the worlds' destruction (Christ's *glory* and *eternity*). Progress in taking on Christ's nature is dependent throughout 2 Peter on the reality of the *knowledge* of Christ, so that the Christian's theology (i.e. who they know God in Christ to be) is finally inseparable from his ethics (i.e. who Christ has called them to be). (italics are mine)[49]

Concluding this part of the discussion, I believe that this theological thinking of 2 Peter is almost equivalent to both the Markan discipleship of following Jesus in his suffering, death and glorification (Mk 8:27–9:13) and Paul's understanding of the believers' continuous transformation into the image of Christ (2 Cor 3:18–4:6).[50] Although each author has different emphases for different needs, they all show similar theological framework.

5.3 The *Apocalypse of Peter*

The *Apocalypse of Peter* (ApoPt), which enjoyed a short life of canonicity in the Muratorian canon, has been traditionally examined in comparison

---

[48] The false teachers' failure in acknowledging Jesus as Lord leads them into moral corruption in 2:1–3.

[49] Starr, *Sharers in Divine Nature: 2 Peter 1:4 in Its Hellenistic Context*, 49.

[50] I will return to this point later when I compare the Transfiguration accounts of 2 Peter, ApoPt, Mk and Paul with one another, after having analyzed the account of ApoPt.

with 2 Peter.[51] Former scholarship on ApoPt focused upon four of its aspects: (1) its literary relationship with 2 Peter, (2) the tour of hell, which is the oldest account found in Christian literature, (3) Bar Kokhba as a candidate for its single most important anti-Christ and (4) its unique description of the Transfiguration as revealing the resurrected bodies of the believers.

According to Bultmann and others, the Transfiguration account in ApoPt is not only older than the Synoptics', but also strong evidence of their opinion that the original Transfiguration account is about the resurrected Jesus.[52] They further argue that the Transfiguration has been misplaced or predated in the midst of Jesus' ministry by the synoptic authors.[53] This view has been almost crippled by C.H. Dodd and R.H. Stein. In ApoPt, the Transfiguration story seems to be postdated after the resurrection and right before the ascension, inasmuch as the Olivet discourse, which is a part of Jesus' teachings before his suffering and death, has been postdated after the resurrection.[54]

Also, until the discovery of the Ethiopic text, scholars used to argue that ApoPt was dependent upon 2 Peter in a way that the former borrowed from the latter the concepts of false teachers, their judgment, the Parousial understanding of the Transfiguration, and the way of righteousness. However, ApoPt and 2 Peter not only make use of Matthew, but also draw upon other Petrine traditions.[55] What is striking in ApoPt is that two synoptic traditions of the Transfiguration and the Olivet discourse, where Peter stands as a recipient of Jesus' special revelations, are combined in a way that the Transfiguration account becomes a part of the Olivet discourse, revealing the glorious destiny of the believers at the Parousia.

In terms of the genre of ApoPt,[56] I suggest that we can call it a rewritten bible with expansions – a huge expansion of the tour of hell with punishments and another expansion of the paradisiacal garden.[57] The au-

---

[51] As for the bibliographical information of ApoPt, refer to Jan N. Bremmer, "Bibliography of the Apocalypse of Peter," in *The Apocalypse of Peter*, ed. Jan N. Bremmer and Istvan Czachesz (Leuven: Peeters, 2003), 200–03.

[52] Bultmann, History of the Synoptic Tradition, 259ff.

[53] I will later return to this issue in my discussion of the Transfiguration account and try to show why this Bultmanian view is not popular any more in the Transfiguration scholarship.

[54] I want to emphasize that Jesus' own transfiguration is not mentioned in the account of ApoPt.

[55] Gilmour, *The Significance of Parallels between 2 Peter and Other Early Christian Literature,* 99–100. Also, Smith, *Petrine Controversy,* 49–51.

[56] Since there exists a scholarly consensus that the Ethiopic version is much closer to the original than the Greek Akhmim, I intend to mean the Ethiopic version by ApoPt throughout this chapter, unless otherwise specified.

[57] As for the so-called rewritten Bible, refer to P.S. Alexander, "Retelling the Old Testament," in *It Is Written. Scripture Citing Scripture.*, ed. D.A. Carson and H.G.M.

thor of ApoPt clarifies in the prologue that his writing contains Peter's revelation of "the second coming of Christ" and "the resurrection of the
dead." By rewriting the two scriptural stories of the Olivet discourse and
the Transfiguration in a combined way and with two major additions, the
author tries to explain what will happen at the Parousia in terms of the destiny of believers as well as sinners. In this way, ApoPt attempts to solve a
theological problem regarding the issue of theodicy.

5.3.1 Literary and Historical Context

– Which Apocalypse of Peter?
ApoPt is preserved in two Ethiopic manuscripts and three Greek fragments.
The full text of ApoPt is left to us only in old Ethiopic (Ge'ez) with two
manuscripts: manuscript P (number 51 in the collection of Antoine
d'Abbadie in Paris at the Bibliothèque Nationale) and manuscript T (Tana-
see 35, catalogued by Hammerschmidt).[58] ApoPt is embedded in a pseudo-
Clementine work, entitled *The Second Coming of Christ and the Resurrection of the Dead*, followed by another pseudo-Clementine writing, *The
Mystery of the Judgment of Sinners*.[59]

There are two more fragmentary Greek manuscripts of B (Bodleian) and
R (Rainer), which are believed to belong to the same manuscript, and
another longer later Greek text of Akhmim with a full description of hell
and paradise.[60] Also, our ApoPt should be distinguished from the Coptic
Apocalypse of Peter found at Nag Hammadi and the Arabic *Book of the
Rolls*, which A. Mingana, its editor, has given exactly the same title, *Apocalypse of Peter*.

M.R. James already maintained that the two fragmentary Greek manuscripts of B and R, though they contain different sections of ApoPt, are
from the same manuscript and are much closer to the Ethiopic than the

---

Williamson (Cambridge: Cambridge Press, 1988), 99–121; G. Vermes, *Post-Biblical
Jewish Studies* (Leiden: Brill, 1975), 60–91; and Jacques Van Ruiten, *Primaeval History
Interpreted: the Rewriting of Genesis 1–11 in the Book of Jubilees* (Leiden: Brill, 2000).

[58] See Dennis D. Buchholz, *Your Eyes Will Be Opened: A Study of the Greek (Ethiop-
ic) Apocalypse of Peter* (Atlanta, Ga: Scholars Press, 1988), 119–54; and C.D.G. Müller,
"Apocalypse of Peter," in *The New Testament Apocrypha*, ed. Wilhelm Schneemelcher
(Westminster: John Knox Press, 1991–1992), 620–22.

[59] ApoPt of the manuscript P was edited by Sylvain Grébaut, "Littérature Éthiopienne
pseudo-clémentne," *Revue de l'Orient chrétien* 15 (1910), 198–214, 307–23, 425–39. For
the discussion of these Pseudo-Clementine works, refer to Monika Pesthy, "Thy Mercy,
O Lord, is in the Heavens; and Thy Righteousness Reacheth unto the Clouds," in *The
Apocalypse of Peter*, ed. Jan N. Bremmer (Leuven: Peeters, 2003), 40–51.

[60] As for the description of the Akhmim manuscript, see Peter Van Minnen, "The
Greek Apocalypse of Peter," in *The Apocalypse of Peter*, ed. Jan N. Bremmer and Istvan
Czachesz (Leuven: Peeters, 2003), 15–39.

Akhmim.[61] The general reliability of the Ethiopic version as faithful to the original is confirmed by its similarity to the two Greek fragments and the patristic quotations.[62] While the Ethiopic seems to be a word-for-word translation of the Greek original, the Akhmim is a rewriting of the original with more changes and scribal freedom.[63] Also, the Ethiopic version is more about the eschatological *future* fate of the previous *Jewish Christian* believers, but the revised version of the Akhmim is about the *present* fate of the *previous Christian* believers who had passed away.

Furthermore, the Akhmim removes all other features of the Greek original, including the setting of the Olivet discourse and Peter's martyrdom, in order to focus on the description of the hell and paradise. The Akhmim also removes references to Moses, Elijah and other patriarchs at the Transfiguration account and thereby makes the story more applicable to the general believers than to the Jewish believers. We can conclude from this observation that the Ethiopic must have originated in the Jewish milieu in Palestine, while the Akhmim originated outside Palestine where the patriarchs were less relevant to its readers.

– The Olivet Discourse and the Transfiguration

The prologue of ApoPt reads as follows: "The *second coming of Christ* and the *resurrection of the dead* which he [Christ] told to Peter...And this he [Peter] pondered that he might know their mystery."[64] ApoPt clearly directs its readers' attention to the two major topics from the beginning, as if they are two aspects of the same event. It is on Mt Olivet that ApoPt begins to explain the first theme of the Parousia by introducing an apocalyptic dialogue between Jesus and the disciples. Here, it is more than clear that ApoPt is using the material found in the so-called Olivet discourse, recorded in Mk 13 and its parallels. According to Richard Bauckham and Pheme Perkins, ApoPt is closer to Matthew than Mark and Luke.[65] Buchholz further claims that the form of the sayings in ApoPt 1–2 is often so close to the Matthean version that the author of ApoPt must have had this

---

[61] M.R. James, "A New Text of the Apocalypse of Peter I–III," *JTS* 12 (1911): 36–54, 362–83; and *idem.*, "The Rainer Fragment of the Apocalypse of Peter," *JTS* (1931): 270–79. See also, Van Minnen, 34–39; Buchholz, 142, 417; and Richard J. Bauckham, "The Apocalypse of Peter: A Jewish Christian Apocalypse from the Time of Bar Kokhba," *Apocrypha* 5 (1994): 10–12.

[62] M.R. James, "A New Text," 367–75, 573–83; Buchholz, 145–52, 418–22; Richard J. Bauckham, *The Fate of the Dead: Studies on the Jewish and Christian Apocalypses* (Leiden; Boston: Brill, 1998), 163; and Gilmour, 107.

[63] Buchholz, 427.

[64] I am using the translation of the Ethiopic by Buchholz throughout this chapter.

[65] Pheme Perkins, *Peter: Apostle for the Whole Church* (Columbia, S.C.: University of South Carolina Press, 1994), 133; and Bauckham, "The Apocalypse of Peter: A Jewish Christian Apocalypse from the Time of Bar Kokhba," 22.

part of Matthew before him in written form or was very familiar with its oral reading.[66] For example, while Mark and Luke consider their apocalyptic descriptions as Jesus' answer to the disciples' request about the sign of the destruction of the temple (Mk 13:4; Lk 21:7), for Matthew, the discourse is more of a sign of Jesus' second coming at the Parousia and the end of the age (Mt 24:4).

In both accounts of ApoPt (chs. 1–14) and Matthew 24 (and its parallels), there are common themes found in similar storylines: the signs of Jesus' coming, the end of the world, the appearance of the Son of Man in glory, who is the eschatological judge, the fig tree as a key sign, the appearance of false messiahs, the judgment of the wicked and the suffering/persecution of the believers. Although, responding to the disciples' request (ApoPt 1:2), Jesus of ApoPt takes up the same subjects in the synoptic versions, he not only goes into more detail on aspects of the apocalyptic discourse, but also introduces new materials not found in the Synoptics. Apart from the fig tree parable (ch.2),[67] the most striking addition is ApoPt's portrayal of the eternal punishment of sinners in hell (chs 7–12).[68] Also, the ideas of the punishment "according to their deed" and of the following reinforcement of ethical codes are not found in the Olivet discourse of the Synoptics. In the Matthean version, the phrase "according to their deed," is found in Jesus' teaching about his coming as the Son of Man right before the Transfiguration rather than in the Olivet discourse (Mt 16:27). It is the case that both events, the Olivet discourse and the Transfiguration, are merged into one and inspire the author to understand them in light of each other.

I propose that the two major themes of the judgment of the sinners and the resurrection of the dead are ApoPt's narrative expansion of Jesus' concluding remark in the Olivet discourse, which Matthew leaves unexplained: "[a]nd they will go away into *eternal punishment,* but the righteous into *eternal life*" (Mt 25:46). ApoPt finds a need to fill in the gap and tries to explain what this phrase means or may mean for its current readers. Al-

---

[66] Buchholz, 398.

[67] Cf. Lk 13:6–9. According to Bauckham, ApoPt is drawing this parable not from Luke, but independent tradition. See Richard J. Bauckham, "The Two Fig Tree Parables in the Apocalypse of Peter," *JBL* 104 (1985): 281–83.

[68] Jan N. Bremmer argues that behind the description of hell, there is the Jewish origin of the genre of the tour of hell, which has been influenced by Orphic and Eleusinian stories. See *idem.,* "The Apocalypse of Peter: Greek or Jewish?" in *The Apocalypse of Peter,* ed. Jan N. Bremmer (Leuven: Peeters, 2003), 1–14. For the description of hell and judgment, see Istvan Czachesz, "The Grotesque Body in the Apocalypse of Peter," in *The Apocalypse of Peter,* ed. Jan N. Bremer and Istvan Czachesz (Leuven: Peeters, 2003), 108–126; and L. Roig Lanzillotta, "Does Punishment Reward the Righteous? The Justice Pattern Underlying the Apocalypse of Peter," in *The Apocalypse of Peter,* ed. Jan N. Bremer and Istvan Czachesz (Leuven: Peeters, 2003), 127–57.

though the eternal punishment is well developed in its description of the tour of hell, how does ApoPt explain the eternal life of the righteous in what specific forms and for what specific purposes? In chs. 15–17, we have descriptions of two heavenly men, Moses and Elijah, and the garden of paradise, where the righteous will have rest with honor and glory. While the description of the garden seems to have its parallel in 1 Enoch,[69] it is beyond doubt that for the description of the beautiful form of Moses and Elijah, ApoPt depends upon the synoptic Transfiguration story. In my analysis of the synoptic Transfiguration story, I have argued that it is closely related to the Olivet discourse because the Olivet discourse further explains Jesus' prediction of the Son of Man's coming and his judgment at the Parousia (cf. Mk 8:38).[70] Also, we have seen that one of the implications of the Transfiguration is that the transfigured form of Jesus is what the righteous sufferers are expected to acquire as their vindication by the Son of Man. In a narrative form, chapters 15–17 of ApoPt emphasize and expand this specific aspect of the Transfiguration. Before going into a detailed analysis of ApoPt's use of the Transfiguration, let us first discuss the revolt of Bar Kokhba to explore whether ApoPt could be located in this milieu.

– Bar Kokhba, Jewish Christian Martyrdom and Peter's Death

In the past century, scholars focused their attention on the parable of the fig tree in chapter two of ApoPt. They believed that it might contain crucial information of the date and provenance of ApoPt. There are two major theses about the parable. In the first view, the false messiah in ch. 2 specifically refers to Bar Kokhba around the Jewish revolt in 132–35 CE in Palestine, either during the revolt or after it.[71] In the second, the false messiah in ch. 2 is a generic apocalyptic motif, which is popularly and commonly found in apocalyptic discourses and does not necessarily refer to Bar Kokhba. Rather, references to specifically Egyptian elements, such as

---

[69] Nickelsburg, "Enoch, Levi, Peter," 600; and Eibert Tigchelaar, "Is the Liar Bar Kokhba? Considering the Date and Provenance of the Greek (Ethiopic) *Apocalypse of Peter*," in *The Apocalypse of Peter*, ed. Jan N. Bremer and Istvan Czachesz (Leuven: Peeters, 2003), 76. Also, T. Adamik, "The Description of Paradise in the Apocalypse of Peter," in *The Apocalypse of Peter*, ed. Jan N. Bremer and Istvan Czachesz (Leuven: Peeters, 2003), 78–90.

[70] See that there are five occurrences of the expression, "each according to his deed," in the description of judgments by ApoPt. This idea is found at the Transfiguration pericope of Matthew (16:27). It is clear that ApoPt sees a tight relationship between the Olivet discourse and the Transfiguration story.

[71] Tigchelaar, 63.

idols of cats or reptiles (ch.10), suggest an Egyptian provenance around the time of Jewish revolt in 115–117 CE in Egypt.[72]

As a good example of the former view, Dennis D. Buchholz reconstructs the historical situation from the fig tree parable, especially 2:7–13, as follows:

> The predicted events as I can reconstruct them from this terse account are: (1) a particular false Christ arises who does an evil deed (v.8); (2) some Christians (specifically Jewish Christians perhaps, "the House of Israel only" in v. 11) will join the cause of this man (v. 8); (3) this will be considered a denial of the crucified one [Jesus Christ] (v. 9); (4) when they realize that he is not the messiah, they will desert his cause (v. 10); (5) the false messiah will persecute and kill many of his former followers; (6) Enoch and Elijah will come to let people know that this is the end-time deceiver who had to come.[73]

Following Heinrich Weinel, Buchholz argues that this false messiah, or the end-time deceiver, must refer to Bar Kokhba, who later became known as Bar Koziba, "son of a liar." When the Jewish Christians refused to take part in his revolt against Rome, Bar Kokhba persecuted and killed them. According to Buchholz, ApoPt is written in this context in order to explain the issue of theodicy regarding punishment of the evil persecutors as well as vindication of the righteous martyrs.

It is, however, Bauckham who has become a champion of this Bar Kokhba hypothesis by publishing a series of articles.[74] Bauckham presents five major reasons why he sees in this parable references to Bar Kokhba and Jewish Christian martyrdom and moreover, to the origin of ApoPt in Palestine.[75] First, he begins by defending the view that Bar Kokhba was seen by many of his supporters as the messiah, as is shown in the well known tradition that Rabbi Aqiva declared him to be the kingly messiah (*y. Ta'an.* 68d).[76] In support of Bauckham, J. Bolyki asserts that the false prophet in ApoPt 1–3, who disseminates propaganda on behalf of the false

---

[72] And also, Tigchelaar, "Is the Liar Bar Kokhba? Considering the Date and Provenance of the Greek (Ethiopic) *Apocalypse of Peter*," 63, 71. Cf. Bauckham, *The Fate of the Dead: Studies on the Jewish and Christian Apocalypses.*

[73] Buchholz, 409.

[74] Bauckham, "The Two Fig Tree Parables in the Apocalypse of Peter," 269–87; *idem.*, "The Apocalypse of Peter: A Jewish Christian Apocalypse from the Time of Bar Kokhba," 7–111; *idem.*, "Apocalypse de Pierre. Introduction," in *Écrits apocryphes chrétiens*, ed. François Bovon and P. Geoltrain (Paris: Gallimard, 1997); Bremmer, "Bibliography of the Apocalypse of Peter," 200–03; and *idem.*, *The Fate of the Dead: Studies on the Jewish and Christian Apocalypses*, 160–258.

[75] Bauckham, "The Apocalypse of Peter: A Jewish Christian Apocalypse from the Time of Bar Kokhba," 36–43.

[76] For more on this tradition, see P. Schäfer, *Der Bar-Kokhba-Aufstand* (Tübingen: Mohr Siebeck, 1981), 55–57; and P. von den Osten-Sacken, *Rabbi Akiva* (Berlin: Institut Kirche und Judentum, 1987).

messiah, is none other than Rabbi Aqiva ben Josef.[77] Second, we have evidence from Justin (*1 Apol.* 31.6) that Bar Kokhba ordered the Christians who did not deny Jesus as the messiah to be punished severely. Third, ApoPt may have understood Bar Kokhba's military success as "the signs and wonders" of the false messiah (2:12). Fourth, the derogatory nickname of Bar Kokhba, Bar Koziva meaning "liar," is found in 2:10: "as for that *liar*, he is not the Messiah." Finally, the phrase, "one tent, not made by human hand, which my heavenly Father has made for me and for my elect" (16:9), may be ApoPt's criticism of Bar Kokhba's intention of rebuilding the temple in Jerusalem. For Bauckham, his proposal that the false messiah is Bar Kokhba seems to be a necessary conclusion, since "we know of no other Jewish messianic pretender who persecuted Christians in the period A.D. 80–160."[78]

Bauckham claims that ApoPt was written in the milieu of the Jewish revolt in Palestine around 132–35 CE and the persecution of the Jewish Christians by Bar Kokhba. He also reads the two major themes of ApoPt, the punishment of the persecutors (chs. 3–24) and the vindication of the righteous martyrs (chs. 15–17), from the perspective of another important rabbinic movement in Palestine, which is well shown in the so-called *birkat ha-mînîm* (benediction of God for cursing the *mînîm* [heretics or sectarians]).[79] In the version known from the Cairo Genizah manuscripts, it reads:

For the apostates let there be no hope, and uproot the kingdom of arrogance, speedily and in our days. May the *Nazarenes* and the sectarians perish as in a moment. Let them be *blotted out of the book of life*, and *not be written together with the righteous*. (italics are mine)[80]

In this benediction, the cursing of the *mînîm*, including the *Nazarenes*, is linked with prayer for the downfall of the kingdom of arrogance, i.e. the Roman empire. Jewish Christians who resisted supporting Bar Kokhba's movement for the liberation from the Gentile power could be seen as taking the side of the kingdom of arrogance and consequently their names would be removed from the book of life. According to Bauckham, while the punishment scene (chs. 3–14) is a Christian response to Bar Kokhba's persecution, the Transfiguration with Paradise is their counter response to *the birkat ha-mînîm*. ApoPt counterclaims against *the birkat ha-mînîm* that

---

[77] J. Bolyki, "False Prophets in the Apocalypse of Peter," in *The Apocalypse of Peter*, ed. Jan N. Bremmer and Istvan Czachesz (Leuven: Peeters, 2003), 52–62. However, notice that there are false prophets in ApoPt 1–3, without singling out any one specific false prophet.

[78] Bauckham, "The Two Fig Tree Parables," 286.

[79] Bauckham, *The Fate of the Dead*, 236–240.

[80] Ibid., 236.

God's righteous people, Christians in ApoPt, will share the same destiny with the righteous patriarchs: they will have rest along with glory and honor in paradise, like Moses, Elijah, Abraham, Isaac, and Jacob (16:1, 5), and their names will remain written in the book of life (17:7).

Although the Bar Kokhba hypothesis is very attractive to our analysis of ApoPt, it is questionable whether one can definitely prove it from the internal textual evidence. It is true that Bar Kokhba may be the single most distinctive Jewish messianic pretender in that time period, but this argument has several shortcomings.[81] First, while Bauckham claims that ApoPt 1–2 is drawing from Mt 24, which speaks of false messiahs (Mt 24:24), his Bar Kokhba hypothesis is based too heavily upon ApoPt's redactional change from multiple false messiahs in 2:7 to a single false messiah in 2:8. The single messiah as the persecutor of the fig tree parable leads Bauckham to a conclusion that ApoPt is dealing here with its contemporary single Jewish messianic pretender, namely Bar Kokhba. However, although the Ethiopic text is faithful to the Greek in general, it is often corrupt and confused in gender and number.[82] Even Bauckham acknowledges that these problems of the Ethiopic text make it difficult for him to draw a concrete conclusion from specific details of the text.[83]

Second, it is right that Eusebius and Justin mention Bar Kochba and his killing of Christians. However, while ApoPt 2:10 speaks of "many martyrs" by the false messiah, there is no evidence in Eusebius and Justin that "many" were killed by Bar Kokhba.[84] Moreover, according to Buchholz's reconstruction from the fig tree parable, it is those who renounced the crucified Christ, then joined Bar Kokhba, and then deserted his cause, that the false messiah persecutes (2:8–10). However, Justin and Eusebius describe the very opposite: Bar Kokhba persecuted Christians who refused to deny Christ the crucified one (*Apol.* 1, 31, 6; *Chron.* Hadrian's Year 17). If ApoPt's description of the false messiah and his persecution is different from those of Justin and Eusebius, it is hard to accept Bar Kokhba as the false messiah of our text.[85]

Finally, the motifs, such as false messiahs, signs and wonders, *liar* which Bar Kokhba happens to have as his nickname, persecution, and de-

---

[81] As for a comprehensive criticism of the Bar Kokhba hypothesis, refer to Tigchelaar, "Is the Liar Bar Kochba?" and L.J. Lietaert Peerbolte, *The Antecedents of Antichrist: a Traditio-Historical Study of the Earliest Christian Views on Eschatological Opponents* (Leiden; New York; Köln: E.J. Brill, 1996), 56–61.

[82] P. Marrassini, "Note sur le texte éthiopien," in *Écrits apocryphes chrétiens*, ed. François Bovon and P. Geoltrain (Paris: Gallimard, 1997), 750–52. See also, Tigchelaar, 66.

[83] Bauckham, "Two Fig Tree Parables," 210–21; *idem.*, *The Fate*, 254.

[84] See also, Tigchelaar, 67.

[85] See also, Lietaert Peerbolte, 59 and Tigchelaar, 67–68.

struction of the temple are too commonly attested in apocalyptic discourses. If they are generic features of apocalyptic discourses, then it is hard to determine that they only refer to Bar Kochba in our text (cf. Mk 13; Mt 24–25). In this sense, reading ApoPt from the perspective of the Bar Kokhba hypothesis may assume more than is warranted by the textual evidence.

We may not reach a definitive conclusion that Bar Kokhba is the false messiah of ApoPt, but from the internal evidence of the text, we may say with some certainty that ApoPt and its readers had to come to terms with a historical person from whom they experienced persecution and martyrdom.[86] Bauckham is right that the motif of martyrdom is prevalent throughout the text (2:10–13; 9:2–4) and the two major themes of judgment and resurrection are ApoPt's expectation of God's final resolution for its crisis: eternal judgment for one group and eternal bliss for the other group (3:3). In this context of Christian martyrdom, it is more than appropriate to mention Peter's death in Rome in ApoPt 14:1–4, which stands in between ApoPt's description of the hell and its upcoming description of the glorious bodies of Moses and Elijah.[87] According to the Rainer fragment,[88] which is closer to the original than the Ethiopic, it is striking that Peter's death is not only an example of imitation, but also the very beginning of the apocalyptic events which ApoPt has been explaining.[89]

5.3.2 The Transfiguration: the Beautiful Bodies of Moses and Elijah[90]

In the previous section, we have seen that the author and readers of ApoPt may be experiencing or have just gone through martyrdom under a Jewish messianic pretender, though it is not certain whether he is Bar Kokhba or not. In order to resolve the issue of theodicy and in an effort to understand their experience of hardship as a sign of the end times, ApoPt combined two synoptic stories of the Olivet discourse and the Transfiguration. In the Synoptics, both are linked to each other through the concept of the Son of Man with glory. In the synoptic versions, the Olivet discourse describes in

---

[86] See also, Lietaert Peerbolte, 60; and Julian V. Hills, "Parables, Pretenders, and Prophecies: Translation and Interpretation in the *Apocalypse of Peter* 2," *RB* (1991): 572–73.

[87] There is a textual problem regarding the city Rome in the Rainer fragment. I am following James' reconstruction in this matter. See M. R. James, "The Rainer Fragment of the Apocalypse of Peter," JTS 32 (1931), 270–29.

[88] For the discussion of the Rainer fragment, see Buchholz, 152–54, 342–62.

[89] This is the oldest Christian reference to Peter's martyrdom in Rome. As for the tradition of Peter's martyrdom, refer to Perkins, *Peter: Apostle for the Whole Church*, 131–50.

[90] In ApoPt, unlike the synoptic stories, Jesus's transfiguration is not discussed. However, since the story in ApoPt is clearly a rewriting of the tradition, I still call it the Transfiguration story.

detail the coming of the Son of Man in glory as the eschatological judge on a full scale, followed by various cosmic signs. On the other hand, the Transfiguration within its Caesarea-Philippi context manifests this heavenly glory on a limited scale in a sense that it is only revealed to three disciples. Moreover, the appearance of Moses and Elijah rhetorically functions to help the suffering believers to *visually* confront the future glory of the righteous sufferers which Jesus promises as their reward (Mk 8:34–38 and its parallels). They are assured that they will experience the Son of Man's acknowledgment at the Parousia, followed by their glorification similar to that of Jesus, Moses and Elijah. Since the destiny of the Jewish Christian martyrs has become a theological issue of its community, ApoPt makes more explicit this specific aspect of the Transfiguration by focusing on the glorious bodies of Moses and Elijah at the expense of the details of Jesus' own transfiguration.

– Brief Description of Former Scholarship on the Transfiguration in ApoPt
In the scholarship on the Transfiguration, ApoPt has played a controversial role.[91] F. Spitta compared the synoptic Transfiguration accounts with the Akhmim fragment of ApoPt and demonstrated that the latter account is not about his glorious transfiguration, but about the heavenly world.[92] It is M. Goguel who first compared the Ethiopic text with the synoptic Transfiguration account.[93] Goguel argued that since Jesus is not transfigured in the stories of the Akhmim and the Ethiopic, they are more primitive than the synoptic Transfiguration stories. Following J. Wellhausen, he argued that the synoptic version is a misplaced resurrection account which Mark predated as an event in the ministry of Jesus before his suffering and death.[94] While C. E. Carlston joined them in his defense of the theory that the Transfiguration was originally a misplaced resurrection account,[95] R. H. Stein and C.H. Dodd, correctly in my opinion, refuted the view of Goguel, Wellhausen and Carlston by comparing the resurrection accounts with the Transfiguration story and then showing their differences in themes and ge-

---

[91] For more, refer to Buchholz, 109–13.

[92] Friedrich Spitta, "Die evangelische Geschichte von der Verklärung Jesu," *Zeitschrift für Wissenscaftliche Theologie* 54 (1911): 97–167.

[93] Maurice Goguel, "A propos du texte nouveau de l'Apocalypse de Pierre," *Revue de l'histoire des religions* 89 (1924), 208–09.

[94] Maurice Goguel, *La Foi en la Résurrection de Jésus dans le christianisme primitif* (Paris: Ernest Leroux, 1933), 326–330. For the adherents to this view, refer to Robert H. Stein, "Is the Transfiguration (Mark 9:2–8) a Misplaced Resurrection-Account?," *JBL* 95 (1976), 79.

[95] Carlston, "Transfiguration and Resurrection," 233–40.

nres.[96] Subsequently, Stein's position was embraced by the majority of the Transfiguration scholars and commentators.[97]

Agreeing with G.H. Boobyer, I believe that the Transfiguration story in ApoPt is more developed than the synoptic versions, because it seems to remove abrupt features and explain some features of the latter in more detail.[98] Since ApoPt concludes its description of the Transfiguration by Jesus' ascension, it is beyond doubt that it has given a post-resurrection setting to the two accounts of the Olivet discourse and the Transfiguration. The postdating of the Olivet discourse, which is an event before the passion and resurrection of Jesus in the Synoptics, also strongly suggests a similar postdating of the Transfiguration rather than the other way around.[99]

Also, in this Transfiguration debate, the brief summary of the Transfiguration in 2 Pet 1:16–18 has often been compared to that of ApoPt and to the synoptic versions as well. For some, the details of 2 Pet 1:16–18 are in harmony with those in ApoPt over against the synoptic accounts.[100] While there are some common features between the two accounts of 2 Peter and ApoPt, such as the Parousial understanding of the Transfiguration, the themes of glory and honor, judgment, and false prophets/messiahs/teachers, ApoPt does not mention Jesus' Transfiguration, as 2 Peter does. However, from the beginning of its account, Jesus of ApoPt is "the glorious God" and "the eschatological judge with glory," which is exactly the same Jesus of 2 Peter. Obviously, both texts are emphasizing different aspects of the Transfiguration, while sharing similar theological framework. Since this issue was discussed in the previous scholarship regarding the literary relationship between 2 Peter and ApoPt, I will return to this issue after having examined in detail the Transfiguration account of ApoPt 15–17.

– Glorious Bodies of Moses and Elijah and the Paradisiacal Garden
I have argued above that for the author of ApoPt, the two narrative accounts of the Olivet discourse and the Transfiguration story are not two separate events, but two tightly connected parts of one and the same event, that is, Jesus' second coming as the eschatological Son of Man and his

---

[96] Stein, "Is the Transfiguration (Mark 9:2–8) a Misplaced Resurrection-Account?", 79–96; and C. H. Dodd, "The Appearances of the Risen Christ: An Essay in Form-Criticism of the Gospels," in *Studies in the Gospels*, ed. C. H. Dodd (Oxford: Blackwell, 1955), 25.

[97] E.g. Schweizer, *The Good News According to Mark*, 180.

[98] See Boobyer, *St. Mark and the Transfiguration Story*, 13–14.

[99] Robert Gundry, *Mark: A Commentary on His Apology for the Cross* (Grand Rapids, Mich.: Eerdmans, 1993); Stein, "Is the Transfiguration (Mark 9:2–8) a Misplaced Resurrection-Account?," 87–88; and Bauckham, "The Two Fig Tree Parables," 275.

[100] Buchholz, 110–112.

judgment for both the righteous and the wicked. In its literary structure, the appearances of the false messiahs and their deceiving and persecuting of the believers serve as one of the major signs of the Parousia (chs. 1–2). In the following chapters, ApoPt explains this sign to the believers and the wicked: (1) the evil persecutors will experience severe punishments in hell (chs. 4–13), but (2) the persecuted righteous people of God will enjoy rest in paradise with honor and glory (15–17). Ch. 14 serves as a transition between the two sections and leads the readers to the Transfiguration account, which follows by introducing those key ideas of "the portion of the righteous ones," "the eternal kingdom," "the promise" and "Peter's imminent martyrdom." Taking up and expanding these key ideas, the Transfiguration account of ch.15–17 functions well as a beautiful conclusion to the whole story by revealing in its narrative the strong contrast between the eternal punishment and the eternal bliss of the two groups of people (cf. Mt 25:46).[101]

In ApoPt's version of the Transfiguration story, as in the synoptic versions, Jesus takes the initiative in leading the disciples onto a mountain. Unlike the synoptic versions, however, it is not the prerogative three, but the unspecified disciples who accompany Jesus this time. Also the location is not simply a high mountain, but the "holy mountain" (15:1). While ApoPt is closer to Matthew than Mark and Luke, as will become clearer later, the motif of praying seems to be an adaptation to Luke (9:28). In his use of the Transfiguration account, the author of ApoPt removes the exclusive group of three so that his revelation may become a general experience more applicable to his readers than a limited prerogative experience of the three.[102] While reading the text, the ancient readers are encouraged to follow the unspecified disciples in their experience of the glorious bodies of Moses and Elijah. Also, while Mark has to introduce the motif of secrecy here until Jesus completes his mission at the cross, ApoPt does not feel the need to keep the secrecy motif in its account of the Transfiguration (Mt 17:9; Mk 9:9; Lk 9:36), especially because ApoPt intends to give a full revelation of the end time story on a cosmic level.

It is also interesting to note that 2 Peter and ApoPt agree over against the Synoptics that the upcoming event is happening on the "holy mountain." Although other mountains like Horeb are sometimes called the holy mountain in Israelite traditions, it is Mt. Zion which is the holy mountain *par excellence,* since God is believed to reside there in the temple. It is not just coincidental that ApoPt has the holy mountain as its setting for the Transfiguration scene. For ApoPt later links the holy mountain with the

---

[101] The Akhmim version shows this contrast in a much clearer way by removing all other features except for the two descriptions of the hell and the paradise.

[102] In the Akhmim, the twelve disciples are claimed to go up the mountain with Jesus.

heavenly temple in Jesus' response to Peter's proposal of three tents, "one tabernacle which the hand of men has not made, which my Heavenly Father has made for me and for my elect" (16:9; cf. Mk 14:58; 2 Cor 5:1; 2 Pet 1:13–14; Heb 9:11). Bauckham here makes a suggestion that ApoPt is dealing with the question of the true temple in its historical context where Bar Kokhba intends to rebuild the temple.[103] Although I am hesitant about reading the Transfiguration story from the Bar Kokhba hypothesis, Bauckham's conjecture of ApoPt's criticism of the temple is interesting, since the Olivet discourse in Mk 13 clearly has Jesus' denunciation of the temple in Jerusalem.[104] If I am right that the author of ApoPt sees the two accounts of the Olivet discourse and the Transfiguration story as two closely related parts of one event, then he can easily correlate Jesus' rebuke of Peter's proposal of the tents (Mk 9:5) to his rebuking of anonymous disciple's praise of the beauty of the temple in Jerusalem (Mk 13:1–2).

Moses and Elijah appear again, as in the Synoptic story, but without the transfigured Jesus (15:2; 16:1). Since ApoPt describes the glorious forms of two men one after another, it is clear that the author is not interested in describing Jesus' transfigured form, but the transfigured form of the two patriarchs. The Akhmim version makes the purpose of the appearance of the two heavenly men much clearer. It ascribes the revelation of two glorious men to Jesus' direct answer to the disciples' request for "the glorious form of one of the righteous brothers who died, so that they may be encouraged through their glorious form" (A 1–5). Unlike 2 Peter, in whose church the false teachers challenged the validity of the Parousia and Jesus' coming as the eschatological judge, for both the author and the readers of ApoPt, Jesus' coming in glory at the Parousia is a given factor from the beginning: "I will come in my glory while giving out light seven times brighter than the sun" (1:7). Since the author already described Jesus' glory and his glorious throne (6:1–2), he finds no compelling reason to describe Jesus' glory in addition to that of the two heavenly beings. Rather, since it is not Jesus' destiny, but that of the righteous martyrs that has been an issue for the readers of ApoPt, his main intention is to teach his readers about their future glorious rest (cf. 1:2–3).

The heavenly status of the two men is further emphasized by the disciples' (the earthly inhabitants) inability to observe and describe their glorious forms (15:2–4). As for the first man's appearance, there comes a light from his face which shines more brightly than the sun. His clothing

---

[103] Richard J. Bauckham, "Jews and Jewish Christians in the Land of Israel at the Time of Bar Kochba War, with Special Reference to the Apocalypse of Peter," in *Tolerance and Intolerance in Early Judaism and Christianity*, ed. Graham N. Stanton and Guy G. Stroumsa (Cambridge: University Press, 1998), 233.

[104] Also, if ApoPt has originated in the Palestine in the first half of the second century after 135, it may at least be aware of the Bar-Kokhba revolt.

does not belong to this world and the beauty of his form is indescribable. The motifs of face shining like the sun and the white garment like light, "which no fuller on earth could bleach," are both found in Matthew's description of the transfigured Jesus (Mt 17:2).[105] While the three disciples' response in the synoptic stories can best be described by fear, the disciples in ApoPt are astonished and amazed at the beauty of the heavenly splendor, but not terrified (15:4, 7).

On the other hand, ApoPt describes the appearance of the second heavenly being by elaborating on each specific part of the body (15:5–7). The color of his bodily appearance is like rose; his long hair is like a crown of beautiful flowers and a rainbow; and his face is adorned with every ornaments. While the author of ApoPt wants to intensify the appearances of the two heavenly beings by recounting one at a time, he finds that the synoptic stories do not have enough materials for his description of the second heavenly being. For this, the author of ApoPt resorts to another source, which is similar to 1 Enoch in its description of the newborn Noah:[106]

"His body was white as snow and *red as a rose*; the *hair of his head* as white as wool and his *demdema*[107] [*long and curly hair*] beautiful; and as for his eyes, when he opened them the whole house glowed like the sun...whose *image and forms* are not like unto the characteristics of human beings; and *his color* is whiter than snow and *redder than a rose*, *the hair of his head* is whiter than white wool, and his eyes are like the rays of the sun" (1En 106: 2, 10).

Is it by coincidence that ApoPt's descriptions of the heavenly temple, the garden and the second heaven along with the heavenly man's appearance, are also found in 1 Enoch and that the Akhmim version of ApoPt was found together with 1 Enoch along with the *Gospel of Peter* in a tomb of a monk? In fact, the Akhmim's description of the two heavenly beings is much closer to that of 1 Enoch than the Ethiopic. Also, the Akhmim further says that the two heavenly beings were covered with glory (7).

In this scene, Peter again singles himself out as the spokesperson of the twelve, as he often does in the Synoptics by raising a question: "My Lord, who is this?" Answering his question, Jesus says that they are Moses and Elijah. Previously in 2:12, Elijah appeared with Enoch to teach the believers that the false messiah will appear as a sign of the end time, as has been predicted, and will perform signs and wonders to deceive the believers.[108] Elijah in ApoPt functions to serve as a link between the Transfiguration

---

[105] Both Mark and Luke lack any description of Jesus' face (Mk 9:2–3; Lk 9:29).

[106] I am quoting this from James H. Charlesworth, *The Old Testament Pseudepigrapha*, 86–87. I got this reference from Buchholz, 365.

[107] E. Isaac says that this Ethiopic word has no equivalent in English. It refers to long and curly hair combed up straight. See Isaac, "1 Enoch," 86.

[108] There are also two witnesses in Rev 11:3–13, but they have traits of Moses and Elijah.

account and the apocalyptic discourse, just as the phrase, "each according to his deed," did.[109]

Why is Enoch in 2:12? In the Israelite traditions, there are three heroes who are claimed to ascend to heaven without experiencing death: Moses, Elijah and Enoch. This has caused so many Transfiguration scholars and commentators of the synoptics to wonder why in the Transfiguration story only Moses and Elijah appear, without Enoch. Because of this Jewish tradition about Enoch's ascension without death, he has been considered as one of the prerogative few who have experienced a heavenly tour along with special revelations. Perhaps, the author of ApoPt has the same question about Enoch in his reading of the Transfiguration story that modern interpreters often have – why not Enoch? Since he is familiar with the Enochic traditions, he decides to include Enoch in his rewriting of the Transfiguration story. As a result, the author puts Enoch here right next to Elijah as a witness against the false messiah. Moreover, the author makes use of the Enochic materials in his description of the glorious appearances of Moses and Elijah.[110] Although I have no proof for this conjecture, it is undeniable that ApoPt seems to pay considerable attention to Enoch and there are many parallel ideas between ApoPt and the Enochic traditions.

After Jesus' answer to the first question, Peter raises his second question: "[w]here are Abraham, Isaac, Jacob, and the other righteous fathers?" (16:1). As an answer to this, Jesus, now *God* Jesus Christ in ApoPt,[111] shows them a paradisiacal garden with trees and fruits and filled with fragrance (16:2–3). The description of the garden is very close to 1 Enoch's description of the holy mountain with trees with fragrances (1 En 24:4; 32:3–6).[112] The presentation of the garden is followed by Jesus' enigmatic declaration: "You have seen the patriarchs, and like this is that which is their rest" (16:4). According to the Ethiopic text that we have, it is not the patriarchs, but the paradise that the disciples saw. To solve the problem presented by this difficult sentence, Müller renders it as an interrogation: "Have you seen the companies of the fathers?"[113] Against Müller, Buch-

---

[109] As for the function of this phrase, refer to footnote 114.

[110] Buchholz maintains that an originally short account of the paradise of ApoPt on the basis of 1 Enoch has been expanded in the Akhmim by material found in other descriptions of paradise, such as a tradition found in Theophilus of Antioch, *Ad Autolycum* 2:19: "God chose for Adam as paradise a place in the eastern region, marked out by light, illumined by shining air, with plants of wondrous beauty." See *idem.*, 368.

[111] Buchholz considers "God" as later addition, as the Akhmim has the Lord, which is older in his opinion (Buchholz, 363). It is a little odd to me that he considers the Akhmim text more original than the Ethiopic only in these Christological expressions.

[112] See Buchholz, 367–68. Also for the Greek nature of the paradise in ApoPt, refer to Adamik, "The Description of Paradise in the Apocalypse of Peter."

[113] Müller, "Apocalypse of Peter," 633.

holz claims that a question is not really appropriate from Jesus at this point.[114] Instead, Peter's request for the present status of the patriarchs has been answered by ApoPt in two ways: first, their "honor and glory" (16:5) will be exactly the same "honor and glory" that Moses and Elijah now manifest;[115] and second, the garden is the very place for their rest.[116] In ApoPt's theological scheme, the other patriarchs are surely among "people in the flesh" (17:3) who are the righteous people of God and greet Jesus with Moses and Elijah during their ascent to the second heaven.

The Greek Akhmim explains this difficult phrase differently from the Ethiopic. First of all, the Akhmim does not specify the two heavenly beings as Moses and Elijah; they are simply the righteous Christian brothers who have passed away (A 5, 13). Also, it does not mention the names of the righteous patriarchs, Abraham, Isaac, and Jacob. They are all subsumed anonymously under Peter's righteous brothers. Furthermore, unlike the Ethiopic, the Akhmim does not describe their forms separately, but deals with them together as one entity. What is especially noteworthy is that the Akhmim claims that the two heavenly beings are covered with glory (A7, 14), which symbolizes their heavenly citizenship like angels (cf. A 17, 19). Also, the Akhmim's description of the garden is much longer than that of the Ethiopic. The Akhmim's garden not only has the fragrant trees, but also is full of gleaming light, fresh air, flower, spices, and blessed fruits (A.15).[117] In this comparison, it is clear that the Ethiopic is written in Palestine in a Jewish milieu. In this Jewish milieu, Israelite patriarchs matter to its readers, because the destiny of the readers will be exactly the same of the patriarchs. However, in the Akhmim, which is written in Gentile Christian milieu outside Palestine, the names of the patriarchs don't matter any more to their salvation history.

Then, Peter says that he "understood what is written in the book of my Lord Jesus Christ" and offers to build three tents (16:6–7), which is the same proposal that is found in the synoptic versions. It is likely that the book of Jesus Christ refers to Matthew, which ApoPt has been quoting

---

[114] Buchholz, 369–70.

[115] It is interesting that ApoPt agrees with 2 Peter in retaining the terms, "honor and glory," in their Transfiguration accounts, though while the former ascribes them to Moses and Elijah, the latter ascribes to the transfigured Jesus. Also, for ApoPt, they mean the righteous' heavenly status, but for 2 Peter, they refer to Jesus' status as the eschatological judge.

[116] The *rest* is often designated as the coming eschatological reward in eschaton in the NT, especially in Hebrews (cf. 2 Th 1:7; Heb 3:11, 18; 4:1–11).

[117] Buchholz already presented that the Akhmim's description is similar to that found in Theophilus. See no. 96.

from.[118] The first part of Peter's response seems to indicate what the author of ApoPt has been doing throughout his writing: he has been *interpreting* the Gospel, especially two synoptic accounts of the Olivet discourse and the Transfiguration story! Likewise, he also expects his readers to *understand* what he, in the name of Peter, has *understood*.

Peter's offer of building three tents and Jesus' rebuke of him are found in all three synoptic stories of the Transfiguration. While in the Synoptics, Peter is rebuked, as he is against the imminent suffering and death of Jesus, in ApoPt, Peter is rebuked because he does not accept the promise of the heavenly tabernacle which has been made, not by human hands, but by the Heavenly Father (16:8–9). Also, Jesus' rebuke of Peter for siding with Satan, which appears in Jesus' teaching *right before* the Transfiguration story in the Synoptics, *follows* the Transfiguration account in ApoPt. This clearly shows that for the author of ApoPt, the Transfiguration story is understood within its immediate context of the Caesarea-Philippi incident.

In ApoPt, Peter's misunderstanding is due to Satan's shutting his eyes and ears. This motif is commonly found in the Jewish prophetic traditions regarding people's obstinate rejection of God's message, now put in the mouth of prophets. Also in the Synoptics, there are traditions about Peter's misunderstandings of Jesus' message (e.g. Mt 16:23; Mk 8:32) and they stand in sharp contrast with a healed blind man at Bethsaida (Mk 8:22–26). The key ideas of opening eyes and ears (16:9), understanding (16:6; 1:2, 3), knowing (1:2), pondering (prologue) and teaching/preaching (1:3), which happen to occur especially in the beginning and at the conclusion of ApoPt, may tell us that the contents of ApoPt have been taught as important sources of the eschatological traditions within its community.

Following the storyline of the synoptic Transfiguration, ApoPt then introduces the Father's heavenly voice, "This is My son whom I love, and I have been pleased with him. Obey him!" (17:1). This phrase is exactly the same that is found in Mt 17:5 (cf. Mk 9:7; Lk 9:35) and 2 Pet 1:17. It functions to direct the disciples' attention to Jesus' teaching of the heavenly Tabernacle, not to his suffering and death. Unlike the Synoptics, the scriptural verses behind this phrase, such as Ps 2:7, Is 42:1 and Gen 22:2, don't play an important role in ApoPt, because its interest lies not in Christological inquiry, but in the believers' destiny. This is easily understandable, as while ApoPt respects the synoptic storyline of the Transfiguration and decides to keep God's testimony intact in its narration, it changed the focus of the Transfiguration from Christ to Moses and Elijah.

---

[118] See also, Buchholz, 370; and Jacques Van Ruiten, "The Old Testament Quotations in the Apocalypse of Peter," in *The Apocalypse of Peter*, ed. Jan N. Bremmer and Istvan Czachesz (Leuven: Peeters, 2003), 158–9 no.3.

There then comes an exceedingly white cloud which carries away Jesus with Moses and Elijah into the second heaven (cf. 1 En 13–16; *Test. Levi* 2.6–12; 5:1).[119] In this context, the cloud functions as a carrier of heavenly beings, as is the case of the Danielic Son of Man. Peter, with other disciples, hails Jesus' ascension by quoting Ps 24 which was intended for God in the Hebrew Bible[120] and praises God for writing their names in *the book of life* (cf. Dan 12:1; Rev 17:8).[121]

Concluding this part of discussion, we have seen that ApoPt describes the glorious bodies of Moses and Elijah in much more detail than do the Synoptics and places them in the paradisiacal garden, which is not mentioned in the synoptic stories. ApoPt intends the patriarchs' glorious bodies to serve as an encouragement to the righteous believers that they will be clothed with the same glory after having endured their hardship. In addition to this honor and glory, ApoPt presents the garden (of Eden) with various trees with fruits as the place for their eternal rest.

We have also seen that the Transfiguration account of ApoPt is closer to Matthew than Mark and Luke due to five points.[122] (1) First, Peter in ApoPt and Matthew calls Jesus "Lord," while Mark has "Rabbi" and Luke "Master." (2) Second, both ApoPt and Matthew have the phrase "if you wish" in Peter's proposal to build up three tents, which is missing in Mark and Luke. (3) Third, it is only Peter who offers to build tents in Matthew and ApoPt, while in Mark and Luke, the three disciples offer to build tents. (4) Fourth, the form of God's testimony to Jesus' Sonship in ApoPt is exactly the same that Matthew has. (5) Fifth, in the description of the Transfiguration, both ApoPt and Matthew use a motif of shining face, which is absent in Luke and Mark.[123] This suggestion that Matthew lies behind ApoPt is further strengthened by the fact that the beginning of ApoPt (1–3) is much closer to Mt 24 than Mk 13. Also, the phrase, "each according to his deed," which occurred five times in ApoPt as a concluding remark on the judgments, is found in the Matthean version of the Transfiguration story (Mt 16:27).[124] This last point again reinforces my argument that the au-

---

[119] For the parallels between ApoPt and 1 Enoch, refer to Tigchelaar, 76–77.

[120] For the discussion of the Hebrew Bible quotations in ApoPt, refer to Van Ruiten, "The Old Testament Quotations," 158–73 and Richard J. Bauckham, "A Quotation from 4Q Second Ezekiel in the Apocalypse of Peter," *RQ* 15 (1991–92): 437–64. Also, Bauckham, *The Fate of the Dead*, 242–43.

[121] While the Ethiopic ends with the disciples' praise, the Akhmim puts the tour of hell right behind the description of the garden.

[122] See also, T. Smith, 46.

[123] The term glory (in the Akhmim) and motif of praying (in both the Ethiopic and the Akhmim) are only found in Luke, not Matthew and Mark.

[124] For more on the discussion of the function of the phrase, "each according to his deed," see Bauckham, "Apocalypse of Peter," 44–47.

thor of ApoPt sees a close link between the Transfiguration pericope and the Olivet discourse.

5.4 Comparison between the Two Transfiguration Accounts

So far, we have examined the two Transfiguration accounts within their own contexts. In this part of discussion, I would like to compare both accounts to explore how early Christian believers in the second century interpreted the Transfiguration story with parousial emphasis. It is M.R. James[125] who first detected 15 resemblances between 2 Peter and ApoPt, followed by Harnack who also made a similar observation. Some concluded that 2 Peter is dependent upon ApoPt, while others claimed that they derive from the same school or the common author.[126] The most prevailing view has been that of A.E. Simms and F. Spitta that the author of ApoPt borrowed some key ideas from 2 Peter. However, the former scholarship has only compared the Akhmim with 2 Peter, not the Ethiopic, which is closer to the original.

Bauckham tries to compare the Ethiopic with 2 Peter and presents eight common ideas for possible contacts between them. They cluster in two passages of "Peter's martyrdom" (ApoPt 14:1–4; cf. 2 Pet 1:4–15), and "the Transfiguration" (ApoPt 15–17; cf. 2 Pet 1:16–18).[127] Following Spitta and Simms, Bauckham concludes that since the Transfiguration story of 2 Peter is from an independent tradition and ApoPt is dependent upon Matthew, "it is clear that the dependence must be of the Apocalypse of Peter on 2 Peter, not *vice versa*."[128] However, Bauckham's conclusion becomes substantially weakened, if his hypothesis that 2 Peter draws the Transfiguration account from an independent tradition turns out to be problematic. As I have shown above, Robert Miller has demonstrated that 2 Peter draws from Mt rather than an independent tradition. Also, Bauckham maintains that ApoPt has put the Transfiguration tradition to "a secondary use," as a revelation of the glory of the redeemed rather than Jesus Christ.[129] I wonder whether labeling ApoPt's use of the Transfiguration story "a secondary use," simply because it does not contain anything about the transfigured Jesus, can do justice to its function in the overall narrative structure. On

---

[125] J. A. Robinson and M.R. James, *The Gospel according to Peter and the Revelation of Peter* (London: C.J. Clay, 1892), 819–20.

[126] For the history of scholarship on the relationship between 2 Peter and ApoPt, refer to Richard J. Bauckham, "2 Peter and the Apocalypse of Peter," in *The Fate of the Dead* (Leiden; Boston: Brill, 1998), 290–93.

[127] See Bauckham, "2 Peter and the Apocalypse of Peter," 294–302.

[128] Ibid., 303. See also, T. Smith, 53–54.

[129] Bauckham, "2 Peter and the Apocalypse of Peter," 302–03.

the contrary, in my understanding, the Transfiguration account as the revelation of Parousial glory of the righteous well serves the whole narrative
scheme of ApoPt as its beautiful and powerful conclusion. In ApoPt's version, we have a very serious theological use of the Transfiguration by a
second century writer, although it is "a secondary use" of it.

In addition, Jesus' prediction of Peter's martyrdom in ApoPt 14 is different from 2 Peter's mention of his death in Peter's farewell speech. The
themes and structures of two stories of Peter's death don't show any re-
semblance at all, except the prophecy of Peter's imminent death. It seems
that 2 Peter is not aware of the tradition about Peter's martyrdom in Rome,
as is recorded in ApoPt 14. Also, it is hard to imagine that in his description of the Transfiguration, the author of ApoPt is picking up a few words
and phrases, such as "the holy mountain" and "honor and glory," from
such a brief summary of the Transfiguration in 2 Pet 1:16–18, when he has
such rich sources as Matthew, Enochic materials and other Christian traditions.[130] It is more likely that both texts share some common traditions,
which may be called Petrine, rather than that they are dependent upon each
other on a literary level.[131]

Having said that 2 Peter and ApoPt are written independently from each
other, while sharing some common traditions, including Matthew, it is now
more interesting to compare them to each other to see how they develop
the synoptic Transfiguration story similarly and differently. First of all, it
is noticeable that ApoPt does not mention anything about the transfigured
Jesus in its own retelling. For 2 Peter, the Transfiguration has much to do
with Jesus' commissioning as the eschatological judge by God the Father.
Jesus' receiving of honor and glory at the Transfiguration reveals to 2 Peter and its readers his divine majesty and power as the coming eschatological judge (2 Pet 1:16–17). It is, however, striking that ApoPt ascribes this
"honor and glory" to those who pursue God's righteousness (16:5). In other words, the "honor and glory" in ApoPt becomes the heavenly condition
of the vindicated righteous people of God.

However, these seemingly divergent accounts are not that different from
each other. I have shown in the first part of this chapter how 2 Peter describes the believers' present life and destiny into the eternal kingdom with
the help of Jesus' divine nature of majesty, power, honor and glory. Jesus'
divine nature becomes not only the motivating power of their present life,
but also the very goal of the believers' destiny. Also, while ApoPt does not
devote any time to arguing for Jesus' status as the eschatological judge, we
have seen that from its very beginning, Jesus is the Son of Man in glory,

---

[130] See also, Gilmour, 114–15..

[131] See also, David Henry Schmidt, "The Peter Writings: Their Redactors and Their
Relationships" (Ph.D dissertation, Northwestern University, 1972), 115–16.

which is seven times brighter than the sun (ApoPt chapters 1 and 6). 2 Peter and ApoPt commonly show how Jesus' identity as the Son of Man with glory is tightly related to his followers' glorious destiny.

Second, I have argued that in ApoPt, the Olivet discourse is combined with the Transfiguration, constituting two different aspects of the same event of Jesus' second coming at the Parousia: judgment for the sinners and vindication for the righteous. The two stories are already related to each other in the synoptic stories. I have shown that 2 Peter is drawing apocalyptic themes from the Olivet discourse in Mt 24, which also lies behind the Olivet discourse of ApoPt. As a result, both ApoPt and 2 Peter manifest some common literary topos of apocalyptic discourse, such as false messiahs, false teachers, deceivers, and signs and wonders. Most importantly, just as Jesus' Transfiguration account assures the readers of 2 Peter that the false teachers inside their church will be put under Jesus' judgment on the Day of the Lord, so also will the wicked persecutors of the readers of ApoPt be tortured in hell. In both texts, it is clear that the idea of the Son of Man's coming inspires the two authors to maintain the idea of two-fold judgment.

There is, however, a difference in their eschatological reflections on the destiny of the believers. While ApoPt points to the future for their glorious vindication, as is typical of the genre of apocalypse, 2 Peter emphasizes that the glorious transformation finds its expression in the present, in the lifestyle of the believers, though it has its own consummation at the Parousia. In this sense, 2 Peter is very close to Paul's idea of continuous transformation ("from glory to glory") with its eschatological tension of "already but not yet" (2 Cor 3:18).

Third, in relation to the previous comment on the Parousial implication of the Transfiguration, both accounts locate the Transfiguration on the *holy mountain*, not simply the high mountain of the synoptic versions. The common existence of the single term, "the holy mountain," is not enough evidence of the literary dependence of the two accounts, but rather that they may share a common tradition. I have already pointed out that the Olivet discourse of the synoptic version contains Jesus' criticism of the temple in Jerusalem on Mt. Zion, the holy mountain *par excellence*. ApoPt presents Jesus' criticism of the Temple built by human hands by directing the readers' attention to the heavenly tabernacle made by the divine hands. 2 Peter is silent about the temple. This is understandable if we recall their provenances and audiences. While 2 Peter can be located in the Gentile world, far removed from Palestine where the temple in Jerusalem has no effect on the everyday life of the gentile believers, ApoPt is written in Palestine in the first half of the second century where the Jewish believers should come to terms with the ruined temple or some messianic pretender's attempt to rebuild the temple.

Fourth, both texts mention Peter's imminent death immediately before their retelling of the Transfiguration story (2 Pet 1:14–15; ApoPt 14; cf. Jn 21:19). I have claimed that Peter's death (ἡ ἀπόθεσις τοῦ σκηνώματος) with the use of Greek term σκήνωμα for body, which is interchangeable with σκηνή for "tent," reminds the readers of 2 Peter of the Transfiguration story. For, in the Synoptics, it is the theme of Jesus' death that precedes and follows the Transfiguration story. However, in contrast to ApoPt, Peter's death in 2 Peter has no eschatological or ecclesiological implications (e.g. like a model for imitation). For the readers of 2 Peter, his death simply provides the pseudepigraphical setting for the farewell speech. However, in ApoPt 14, especially in the Rainer fragment, Peter's death in Rome ("a city ruling over the west") is understood as a part of the spiritual Eucharist – Peter should drink the cup which Jesus promised (R 14:4). Moreover, Peter's martyrdom is the first eschatological sign of Jesus' judgment as its beginning.

Fifth, it is interesting to note that both Transfiguration accounts of 2 Peter and ApoPt have something to do with the creation story and the Garden of Eden. In the Genesis story, Adam and Eve eat from the tree of the knowledge of good and evil (Gen 3:22) and attempt to become immortal by eating of the tree of life. Their very human desire to be like God is inappropriate in His eyes, since it does not originate from God Himself (Gen 3:5). As a consequence of their human desire to acquire divinity, they are expelled from the Garden.[132]

In 2 Peter, the Greek term ἐπίγνωσις or γνῶσις for knowledge occurs eight times (1:2, 3, 5, 6, 8, 20; 2:20; 3:18) and is crucial for 2 Peter's understanding of the salvation program. In 2 Peter, the term *knowledge* takes as its object Jesus Christ, who called them by his own glory and goodness (2 Pet 1:3). The knowledge enables the believers to escape from corruption by acquiring immortality and to become participants in the divine nature. The divine nature, which Adam and Eve desperately desired, finds its expression in Jesus' glory and the moral excellence (1:4–5). Jesus' divine nature is claimed by the author of 2 Peter to have become manifest at the Transfiguration (1:16–18). While Adam and Eve's desire to become divine is rejected due to its improper direction *from below to above*, the divine attributes are granted to the readers of 2 Peter, as God takes the initiative of providing them *from above to below*.[133]

---

[132] For more on this topic and its comparison with 2 Peter, refer to Starr, *Sharers in Divine Nature: 2 Peter 1:4 in Its Hellenistic Context*, 65–82.

[133] The term *knowledge* and its implication for human acquisition of immortality in process in 2 Peter is very close to Paul's idea of New Creation in the Lord (cf. 2 Cor 3–4; Phil 3).

ApoPt is quoting Ezekiel 37 or its later Jewish interpretation, which is similar to what is found in 4Q Second Ezekiel.[134] Ezek 37:1–14 is believed to be the oldest Jewish evidence of the idea of resurrection in the Hebrew Bible. Although the Ezekiel account has something to do with God's bringing Israelites out of the graves of Babylon and their subsequent exile, the story clearly speaks of physical resurrection along with transformation. Also, the Spirit of God, the transformative agent of the resurrection, seems to contain three overlapping dimensions in the Ezekiel context:[135] (1) the breath necessary for human life, (2) the cosmic creative divine Spirit, and (3) the eschatological divine Spirit. Along with the resurrection of individual people, their wasted and desolate land will also be transformed into the Garden of Eden (Ezek 36:56). It is beyond doubt that Ezekiel sees the resurrection phenomenon as God's new creation activity and the reversal of the Fall.

It is interesting to note that in ApoPt 4, we also have a prophecy of resurrection through a quotation of Ezek 37:4 or its later interpretation. Interestingly, this prophecy becomes true at the Transfiguration account (ApoPt 15–17): the gloriously transformed bodies of Moses and Elijah are none other than the future resurrected bodies of the believers. Moreover, they are located in the paradisiacal Garden with lots of trees and fruits. The resurrected righteous will live in the Garden of Eden! Is it by coincidence that both 2 Peter and ApoPt somehow create a connection between the Transfiguration and the creation story? What do they have to do with Paul's transformation of the believers according to the image of God, Christ, which is the New Creation? I wonder whether they are evidence of early Christian thought in which the Transfiguration account is not only connected to the Parousia, but also to the creation or new creation idea.

Finally, I want to point out that both texts express all these similarities in two different forms of literary genre: (1) one in a form of narrative discourse (ApoPt) and (2) the other in a form of theological discourse, contained in a letter (2 Peter). At first sight, the form of theological discourse seems to deal with theological issues of *here and now* in the readers' lives in a more direct way, while the form of narrative discourse presents more *distant* stories of *there and then* in the life of Jesus and his disciples. The latter seems to have only an indirect effect on the life of its later readers.

However, I argue that the story in a narrative form is equally and directly dealing with its readers' contemporary issues in a different way. As for

---

[134] Bauckham, "A Quotation from 4Q Second Ezekiel in the Apocalypse of Peter," 437–64; and Van Ruiten, "The Old Testament Quotations in the Apocalypse of Peter," 159–68.

[135] Andrew Chester, "Resurrection and Transformation," in *Auferstehung – Resurrection*, ed. F. Avemarie and H. Lichtenberger (Tübingen: Mohr Siebeck, 1999), 50.

the readers of 2 Peter, the author interprets the Transfiguration story in a way that it provides a direct solution for their current parousiac crisis. Although the pseudonymous Peter functions as a link between its contemporary readers in the present and the teaching of Jesus in the past, the temporal focus of the theological discourse of 2 Peter is definitely on the present. On the other hand, ApoPt is silent about its readers' current conditions and crisis. We only have vague hints about its current readers in its description of the false messiah and his persecution. Even these hints are hidden behind the conversation of Jesus and his disciples in the past. However, in its narration of the Olivet discourse and the Transfiguration, although the stories are all about Jesus and his teaching a century prior to ApoPt, the author of ApoPt intends them to speak directly for the readers and their contemporary issues. While they read the story retold by the author, the readers see their very destiny in Moses and Elijah at the Transfiguration. Although the story may have happened a century ago in the life of Jesus, in the story the readers find the very solution for their current crisis.

The theological discourse of 2 Peter guides its readers' thought in a direct and concrete way by explaining the contemporary implications of the past story. Similarly, the narrative discourse of ApoPt speaks about the solutions for its current readers' crises in a seemingly indirect (but powerful) way. In the case of ApoPt and 2 Peter, we have a parousiac understanding of the Transfiguration in two different forms, but they all function similarly and powerfully to serve their readers' current needs.

5.5 Conclusion

We have seen that there was a lively apocalyptic expectation of the Parousia at the beginning of the second century. The old hypothesis that the Parousial expectation had waned due to its delay may not be true at least for some segment of second century Christianity. ApoPt and 2 Peter witness an interesting theological interpretation of the Transfiguration by two second century Christian thinkers, in which the Transfiguration becomes concrete evidence of the Parousia. For some it assures Jesus' coming as the eschatological judge and for others it reveals the resurrected bodies of the believers at the Parousia. Both texts also adopt different forms of literary genre: one with a narrative discourse and the other with a theological discourse. Regardless of these different literary forms, both deliver their messages to their readers in the same powerful and direct way.

Also, in their interpretations, these second century writers do not hesitate to make use of their own extra-canonical traditions along with the scriptures.[136] They not only take advantage of Jewish scriptural and pseu-depigraphical traditions, especially the Enochic, but also draw from Christian synoptic traditions, especially the Gospel of Matthew. They attempt to reinterpret some parts of the scriptures and also add new materials to them in order to make the scriptural passages more applicable to their current readers. In ApoPt, we have an excellent piece of Christian rewriting of the two synoptic stories with huge additions of the tour of hell and the paradisiacal Garden.

In their use of the Transfiguration tradition, Peter the apostle appears as the major human character. It is not because he is the apostle *par excellence*, but because the church has remembered the story with his role as the spokesperson of the disciples. While John is mentioned in the *Apocryphon of John* and the *Acts of John* in relation to the Transfiguration, James is totally forgotten in the church's memory. This again shows how church traditions are transformed into apostolic traditions and in turn, apostles become legitimate guarantors of traditions. In our case, Peter appears as the very guarantor of the Transfiguration story or its legitimate version.

While ApoPt seems to be unaware of Paul, 2 Peter clearly gives him and his writings authority comparable to the scriptures. Moreover, against the false teachers who were pro-Paulinists and had misinterpreted parts of Paul's writings, Peter tries to defend a necessity of correct interpretation of Paul, just as they are carefully engaged in interpreting other scriptures (2 Pet 3:15–16). Why does 2 Peter mention the name Paul in its discussion of the Parousial understanding of the Transfiguration? What passages of Paul do the false teachers misinterpret against the Transfiguration tradition of 2 Peter? Paul in 2 Cor 3 advocates for believers' continuous transformation. I conjectured in chapter two that the story can be compared to the synoptic Transfiguration. Both developed from similar Mosaic transformation traditions with the aid of the hermeneutical lens of Jesus' event. But Mark focuses on Jesus' transformation and Paul on the believers' transformation. Also, it seems that Paul is regarded as a lower class apostle and that his Gospel message is not as genuine as that of Peter in Gal 1–2. In that Galatian context, is Paul arguing against his pro-Petrine enemies who presented Peter's experience of the transfigured Jesus as evidence of Petrine supremacy? Does Paul argue that both he and Peter have seen the same glorious Jesus? Are their Gospels of equal value, because they come from the same Jesus Christ? Moreover, does 2 Peter happen to respond to the false teacher's misuse of Paul, more specifically his teachings in 2 Cor 3 and Gal 1–2? Although we have no concrete support for this conjecture, the historical picture of early Christians' engagement with the Transfiguration story may

---

[136] For these texts, the scriptural boundaries are still blurry and the numbers of their scriptures may be different from each other.

have been much more complicated due to its multiple and powerful implications for the lives of its readers.

Chapter 6

Polymorphy in the *Acts of Peter* 20–21:
The Transfiguration Remembered, Reinterpreted and Reenacted

6.1 Introduction

In Peter's sermon in APt (*Acts of Peter*), we have an interesting account of the Transfiguration. In his sermon, the Transfiguration story is interpreted in light of the incarnation idea[1] and Greco-Roman mythology with polymorphism, and is reenacted as a form of polymorphy among the members of APt's community. While the incarnation represents Jesus' taking on human form, the Transfiguration speaks of his temporary revelation of his divine form. In APt the two events constitute a unified story of Jesus and assert that Jesus keeps appearing on earth in multiple forms (polymorphy) and with multiple names (polyonymy). Through polymorphy and polyonymy, Jesus reveals his mercy toward the believers by his active and diverse interventions in the salvation history. Furthermore, since the Transfiguration testifies to Jesus' on-going care for his people, it does not stop being reenacted as a present reality in the lives of the believers. As a narrative proof for this claim, Jesus again manifests himself in a polymorphous way to the old widows of the community of APt.[2]

I hypothesize that the polymorphy in APt has the Transfiguration as its generative narrative and draws upon both Greco-Roman mythology and the idea of the incarnation as its two major interpretative stimuli. The three earliest polymorphy accounts of the *Apocryphon of John* 1–2 (ApoJn), the *Acts of John* 88–90 (AJn), and APt 20–21 are the results of their authors' dynamic participation in a continuous development of the polymorphy tradition. It is more likely that each author reshapes the polymorphy tradition to meet with his particular needs than that they are dependent upon one another on a textual level. In the polymorphy account of APt, Jesus appears in the divine light and then in three human forms as a boy, a young

---

[1] I am using the term incarnation for the sake of convenience, referring to Jesus the divine's appearance on earth in human form in APt. Throughout the chapter, I will avoid downloading the incarnation theology not found in our current text of APt.

[2] For the history of former scholarship on APt, refer to Matthew C. Baldwin, *Whose Acts of Peter?* (WUNT 196; Tübingen, Germany: Mohr Siebeck, 2005), 26–62.

man and an old man (trimorphy). I also propose that for APt, the polymorphy *visually* recapitulates the two events of the Transfiguration and the incarnation, while the polyonymy *narratively* accounts for them. At first sight, the readers who are familiar with the Transfiguration story are surprised at the polymorphy because of its differences from the synoptic versions. They are left wondering where this new account comes from and why they read the story this way. I believe our analysis of polymorphy will tell us about the community of APt, their interpretative strategies and their socio-cultural background.

In this chapter, I will first discuss the text and date of APt, its literary context and the definition of the term polymorphy. Second, I will analyze APt 20–21 in order to explore how the Transfiguration story is remembered, reinterpreted and reenacted as a form of polymorphy. By comparing APt's account of polymorphy with the early Church Fathers, I will demonstrate that APt participates in an on-going development of the Transfiguration into polymorphy. Finally, I will discuss the formation of polymorphy by examining its former scholarship and cultural and traditional backgrounds: Greco-Roman mythology, the Hebrew Bible (and Jewish traditions) and the New Testament (and Christian traditions). I will explore how these traditions help APt read the Transfiguration as polymorphy.

6.2 Text and Date, Literary Context, and Polymorphy Defined

6.2.1 Text and Date

APt (Acts of Peter) was originally written in Greek. Two thirds of it has survived in a Latin manuscript, the *Actus Vercellenses* (Act.Verc.), a codex at Vercelli (Cod. Verc. CLVIII, 6th–7th century). Act. Verc. is a copy of Rufinus' translation of the Pseudo-Clementine *Recognitions*, which includes an appendix of APt without a title. This manuscript is thought to be a third or fourth century Latin translation of the original Greek text, which was written around the end of the second century.[3] It has been suggested that the missing first third of the manuscript contains stories of Peter and Paul in Jerusalem and their contest with Simon the magician (cf. APt ch. 23).[4]

---

[3] Wilhelm Schneemelcher, *The New Testament Apocrypha*, trans. R. McL. Wilson, Rev ed., 2 vols. (Louisville: Westminster/John Knox, 1991–1992), vol. 2, 277; and J. K. Elliot, *The Apocryphal New Testament* (Oxford: Clarendon Press, 1993), 391. Also, for a comprehensive study of the issue of text, see Matthew C. Baldwin, *Whose Acts of Peter?*, 1–25.

[4] Elliot, 391.

In addition to this Latin translation, there are three Greek manuscripts detailing Peter's martyrdom story: (1) Cod. Patmiacus 48 (9th CE, = P), (2) Cod. Athous Vatoped. 79 (10th/11th CE, = A), and (3) Cod. Ochrid. Bibl. Mun. 44 (11th CE, = O).[5] Along with these three Greek manuscripts, there is a further reference to the Greek original of APt in P. Oxy. 849, corresponding to Act.Verc. 25–26.[6] Another Latin text, *Vita Abercii* (4 CE), contains speeches by Peter and Paul found in Act.Verc., but transfers them to the life of St Abercius of Hierapolis.[7] Comparison of these Latin and Greek manuscripts shows that the Act. Verc. is generally a reliable and faithful translation of the Greek text.[8]

While there are references to the Petrine traditions of miracles and martyrdom in Clement of Alexandria, Origen and the Didascalia, it is Eusebius who most clearly mentions APt in his canon list (*Ecc. His.* 3.3.2), declaring it to be heretical. By the end of the fourth century, Philaster of Brescia speaks of the use of APt by the Manichaeans (*Haer.* 88).[9] Although the relationship between APt and the Pseudo-Clementine literature is complicated, the latter helps us locate the former as being written earlier than 260 CE. In addition, the mutual relationship among APl (*Acts of Paul*), APt and AJn (*Acts of John*), along with their use of similar theological themes and literary motifs, help us situate APt around the turn of the third century, at a time when Christians were composing the apocryphal acts. The common motifs of encratic tendency and sexual continence are popular in 2nd and 3rd century Christian texts. Since a reference in Tertullian fixes the date of APl at the end of the second century, APt is likely to have originated right before or after the composition of APl, depending upon how the relationship between the two texts is established.[10]

---

[5] François Bovon and Bertrand Bouvier recently presented the critical edition of a Greek fragment entitled "From the Acts of the saint apostle Peter," which is a part of a manuscript preserved in the library Angelica in Rome. See François Bovon and Bertrand Bouvier, "Un fragment grec inédit des actes de Pierre?," *Apocrypha* 17 (2006): 9–54.

[6] Schneemelcher, 278; and Elliot, 391.

[7] Schneemelcher, 276.

[8] Ibid., 278. Matthew C. Baldwin, however, maintains that the original second century Greek APt never existed and that we should treat the Latin Act. Verc. as a new and independent text. Accordingly, the study of APt is relevant to the historical study of the time of its translation and translator. See Baldwin, *Whose Acts of Peter?*, 2–10. However, since we have one or two Greek fragments which are similar to the Latin in content, it is probable that there was an original Greek manuscript from which the Latin was translated. For the study of the Latin editions and the analysis of problematic passages, see A. Hilhorst, "The Text of the *Actus Vercellenses*," in *The Apocryphal Acts of Peter*, ed. Jan N. Bremer (Leuven: Peeters, 1998), 148–60.

[9] Schneemelcher, 275 and Elliot, 390.

[10] While Dennis R. MacDonald argues that APl is a literary source for APt and AJn, Robert F. Stoops, Jr., counter-argues that APl took the voyage to Rome, the *quo vadis*

6.2.2 The Literary Context of Jesus' Transfiguration and Polymorphy (APt 20–21)

APt consists of three major sections: (1) the contest between Peter and Simon in Jerusalem along with the stories about Peter's daughter and a gardener's daughter (cf. ch. 23; Acts 8:9–24), (2) Peter and Simon's contest in Rome, and (3) Simon's tragic death and Peter's martyrdom. The second major section of APt, where the Transfiguration story is found, starts with Paul's departure from Rome, followed by Simon's arrival in Rome. Simon the magician brings a great challenge to the Christian community in Rome and causes many believers to stray from their faith. As the divine response to the community's prayer for help, God sends Peter to Rome so that he may defeat Simon and consolidate the community in crisis (chs. 1–29).

The story of Jesus' Transfiguration (chs. 20–21) appears in the middle of the second major section. This section also relates the story of Peter's healing miracles of the blind widows, preceded by the accounting of his first defeat of Simon in Rome (12–18) and followed by the story of the second contest with Simon in the forum (chs. 23–29). This sandwich structure suggests that the Transfiguration should be interpreted in the context of the stories surrounding it, that of Peter's healing miracles and his contests with Simon.

In ch. 19, after Peter's first defeat of Simon the magician, Marcellus the senator, who allowed Simon to stay in his house, cleanses it and invites Peter and the old widows to pray for him. When Peter arrives at Marcellus's with Narcissus the presbyter[11] and other brothers, he performs his first healing miracle by healing the blindness of an old widow who has been led there by her daughter. Then, having entered the dining room, Peter hears the Transfiguration account of the Gospel being read in a worship service and delivers a sermon on it (ch. 20).

According to Peter's sermon on the Transfiguration recorded in APt 20, it is Jesus' majesty with brilliant light that was revealed on the "holy mountain." Jesus' majesty shown in the light is the very divine form which he hid in the incarnation. Peter confesses that he could not take in the divine form with his human eyes and felt that he might lose his sight due to its brightness. Jesus then reappeared in the human form that Peter had seen

---

scene and the martyrdom story from APt. See Dennis R. MacDonald, "Which Came First? Intertextual Relationships Among the Apocryphal Acts of the Apostles," *Semeia* 80 (1997): 11–41; and Robert F. Stoops, "The *Acts of Peter* in Intertextual Context," *Semeia* 80 (1997): 57–86. Interestingly, Eric Junod and P.J. Lalleman, who wrote monographs on AJn, prioritize AJn over APt and APl.

[11] This is the only ecclesiastical office mentioned in APt. Possibly, the "virgins of the Lord" (ch. 22) are another ecclesiological order in the community of APt. However, we don't have any description of it in the text.

many times before and could take in with his physical eyes. Peter asserts that Jesus showed "his *mercy* and *goodness*" toward human beings by appearing in human form in the incarnation, and that he lived, died and resurrected from the dead for the sake of the believers (ch. 20). Peter further illustrates this point by discussing the list of Jesus' multiple epithets with contradictory values and names. According to Peter, Jesus keeps appearing in human history in different forms (polymorphy) and with different names (polyonymy). Both the polymorphy and the polyonymy show that God (Jesus in APt) is greater than human thoughts and is more than one – this is the concluding message of Peter's sermon in ch. 20.

When Peter finishes his sermon, other blind widows' request to experience, as Peter had, Jesus' mercy and goodness. Responding to Peter's prayer for them, Jesus again appears in the light. Again, as at the Transfiguration account, Peter confesses that those present at the polymorphy event can neither see nor endure Jesus' divine form. Then, the light enters into the eyes of the blind widows and causes them to see Jesus in three different human forms: an old man, a young man and a boy – a polymorphy (ch. 21). It is striking that for the community of APt, the Transfiguration is not simply an one-time event of the past, but that it can be continuously reenacted in the lives of the believers. Praising Jesus for allowing them to experience his mercy through the polymorphic event, Peter proclaims, "God is greater than our thoughts." This is the central message of Jesus' polymorphic appearances in APt.

In the overall context of APt, Jesus' Transfiguration/Polymorphy reinforces his divine status as well as the idea of Jesus' continuing care for the believers. God's caring for the people is accomplished directly by His own miraculous interventions in human history and by His working through Peter the apostle. Peter, as God's agent, performs the healing and resurrection miracles for the community in Rome, especially for the old widows, the most wretched group of people in APt's context. In addition, Jesus' Transfiguration/Polymorphy is APt's answer to Simon's challenge regarding Jesus' divinity and his benevolent mercy (cf. chs. 14 and 23). Apart from God's benevolent care and Jesus' divinity, the idea of Transfiguration/Polymorphy is closely related to the various themes of APt, such as miracles, apostolic function, and the patronage system.[12]

6.2.3 Polymorphy Defined

Since I will use the term polymorphy throughout the chapter, I define it here before proceeding to analyze the text. Eric Junod first attempted to define the term polymorphy. He writes that polymorphy is the deliberate

---

[12] Robert F. Stoops, "Christ as Patron in the *Acts of Peter*," *Semeia* 56 (1992): 143–57.

appearance of someone in multiple forms either *simultaneously* or *successively*; however, the change of forms (metamorphosis) is not concealed, but becomes manifest to the public for the testimony of its miraculous nature.[13] In Junod's definition, while metamorphosis (transfiguration / transformation) refers to a general phenomenon of changing forms, polymorphy is a specific instance in which one's multiple forms are presented for the sake of testimony. Pieter Lalleman agrees with Junod that polymorphy is "part of wider concept of metamorphosis or shape shifting, which is the idea that a person or a deity can at any moment assume another form, stature or age."[14] However, Lalleman makes a distinction between polymorphy and metamorphosis. He argues that while polymorphy is a kind of metamorphosis in which a person or a deity can be seen differently by different people *at the same time*, metamorphosis refers to a person's taking multiple forms *consecutively*, and not at the same time.[15] Lalleman clearly prioritizes the polymorphic account of AJn 88–90 over the polymorphic account of APt 20–21. While calling the latter a mere metamorphosis, not a polymorphy, he presents the former as the genuine polymorphy. Lalleman substantially reduces not only the definition of the polymorphy by Junod, but also the list of texts with polymorphic phenomenon.

Hughes Garcia problematizes Lalleman's definition of the polymorphy, pointing out that such a rigid and fixed definition as Lalleman's cannot explain the various types of polymorphy, as polymorphy is by nature a very fluid and diverse phenomenon.[16] However, Garcia also makes a strange division between polymorphy and metamorphosis. While polymorphy refers to gods and angels' *divine* power to take multiple forms, human or animal, metamorphosis refers only to humans' changing of forms into the divine.[17] I believe that it is unnecessary to create too sharp and rigid a distinction between polymorphy and metamorphosis, attributing one to the divine and the other to the human realm. In the Greco-Roman literature, polymorphy refers exclusively to the divine power to change forms, and humans are enabled to change forms only by the gods' divine intervention (e.g. Odysseus' transformation by Athena).[18] It is exclusively gods and

---

[13] Eric Junod, "Polymorphie du Dieu Sauveur," in *Gnosticisme et monde hellénistique*, ed. J. Ries (Publications de l'institut orientaliste de Louvain 27; Louvain-La-Neuve: Université catholique de Louvain, 1982), 39.

[14] Pieter J. Lalleman, "Polymorphy of Christ," in *The Apocryphal Acts of John*, ed. Jan N. Bremmer (Kampen, The Netherlands: Kok Pharos, 1995), 99.

[15] Ibid., 99 and 102.

[16] Hughes Garcia, "La polymorphie du Christ. Remarques sur quelques définitions et sur de multiples enjeux," *Apocrypha* 10 (1999): 17–18.

[17] Ibid., 20.

[18] The magicians were said to change their forms and those of others through magical tricks. But the epithet "polymorphous" is not ascribed to them.

goddesses, such as Athena and Isis, who are called "polymorphous." In my opinion, Junod's definition of polymorphy in relation to metamorphosis best explains the various occurrences of polymorphy in the texts in our possession. Polymorphy is the result of multiple metamorphoses by gods. Gods have divine power to change their forms through the process of metamorphosis and therefore, can always appear in multiple forms, resulting in polymorphy.

6.3 The Analysis of the Transfiguration and the Polymorphy in APt 20–21

6.3.1 The Transfiguration in APt 20

– Peter's Healing of an Old Blind Widow
The Transfiguration account of APt 20 is preceded by Peter's healing of an old blind widow. When Peter sees the widow led by her daughter to Marcellus' house, he says, "Mother, come here; from this day onward Jesus gives you his right hand, through whom we have *light unapproachable*, which no darkness hides; and he says to you through me, 'Open your eyes and see, and walk on your own.'" Instantly, with her healed eyes, the widow can see Peter laying his hand on her. Within the context of APt 20–21, the healing of the blind widow indicates that the understanding of the Transfiguration requires inner spiritual eyes, since the Transfiguration, according to Peter's sermon, is evidence of God's divine will of mercy toward humanity. In the following chapter, Peter clarifies this point by underscoring the need for spiritual eyes when other blind widows request to share the same experience of Jesus' divine and human forms. In his healing of the blind widow, Peter prepares the readers of APt for the upcoming interpretation of the story both by awakening their spiritual insight and by calling Jesus "the light unapproachable."

It is very likely that this story about the blind widows at the Transfiguration account of APt 20–21 is APt's rewriting of Jesus' healing of the blind man that occurs right before the synoptic Transfiguration story (cf. Mk 8:22–26). In the Markan story, the disciples bring a blind man to Jesus to be healed. Interestingly, the healing is completed in two steps: first, the blind man sees human beings as if they were trees and then, he sees everything clearly. This story has a deep theological implication in the Markan context. Since Peter and the disciples keep failing in understanding Jesus' true identity as God's Son, through Jesus' double-staged healing of the blind man, Mark emphasizes that it is the disciples who are spiritually blind and who need Jesus' healing to understand his ministry and teaching. By changing the blind man into the blind widows, APt makes the widows,

who have become the recipients of special miracles and monetary assistance, the first group of believers who experience the greatest miracle of
Jesus – his polymorphic appearances.

It is striking that APt pays such great attention to widows throughout
the narrative. In general, there are two different treatments of the widows
by APt. First, the widows are expected to devote themselves to prayer (ch.
19) and are called "the virgins of the Lord" (ch. 22).[19] Second, the widows
are the first group of the poor to be taken care of by God, along with the
orphans. The Senator Marcellus is praised for being the patron of widows
and orphans (ch. 8). Eubula, having recovered all her property, gives alms
to the widows and the orphans in gratitude for acquiring faith in Christ (ch.
17).[20]

The healing of the blind widows resonates with the major themes of APt
such as God's care for the people, the apostles as God's agent and the truth
claim for the Gospel message. In the second century, miracles are an important tool for religious propagandistic purposes. Writings by the early
Church Fathers, such as Justin, Irenaeus, Tertullian, and Origen, as well as
references in the apocryphal acts reveal second-century cultural expectation about miracles: miracles function as convincing proofs for the validity
of religious messages.[21] It is interesting to note that the storyline of APt is

---

[19] Stevan Davies argues that the widows in APt are a particular group of Christians
with a collective identity. See Stevan L. Davies, *The Revolt of the Widows: the Social
World of the Apocryphal Acts* (Carbondale: Southern Illinois University Press, 1980),
74–78. However, the fact that the descriptions of the widows in APt are all attested to in
the New Testament makes it harder to conclude whether there is a group of widows with
a collective identity and with ecclesiological office in the community of APt.

[20] APt is drawing this double-fold attitude toward the widows from the New Testament and the Hebrew Bible. In the New Testament, widows appear as objects of care and
have a devout attitude to God (1 Tim 5). In Acts, there is a dispute between the Hellenists
and the Hebrews regarding their alms giving to widows (6:1) and a concern about caring
for the poor widow (9:36–43). In Luke 2:36–38, there is an account of Anna, a widow
prophetess. In the synoptic stories, there are also numerous healing and resurrection miracles by Jesus for widows and their sons/daughters. Similarly in the Hebrew Bible, widows, along with orphans, appear as the prototypes of the socially underprivileged. The
widow becomes a symbol of human desolation and of dependence on God. And at the
same time, the true widow is devout, wise, and chaste; wisdom and chastity are traditional characteristics of widows in the public's eyes. God is also called "the Father of the
orphans and the Judge for the widows" (Ps. 68:5). For more on widows in Israelite traditions, refer to Karel van der Toorn, "The Public Image of the Widow in Ancient Israel,"
in *Between Poverty and the Pyre: Moments in the History of Widowhood*, ed. Jan N.
Bremmer and Lourens van den Bosch (New York: Routledge, 1995), 19–30. Also, Jan N.
Bremmer, *The Apocryphal Acts of Peter* (Leuven: Peeters, 1998), 5.

[21] Davies, *The Revolt of the Widows: the Social World of the Apocryphal Acts*, 22–32;
and Paul J. Achtemeier, "Jesus and the Disciples as Miracle Workers in the Apocryphal
New Testament," in *Aspects of Religious Propaganda in Judaism and Early Christianity*,

mainly framed by contests pitting the miraculous power of Simon the magician against Peter. Since Peter turns out to be the potent, true miracle worker with power, his message is heard by the Romans, while Simon's derogatory remarks about Jesus are eventually rejected: "Is God born? Is he crucified? He who owns a Lord is no God!" (ch. 23).

According to APt, both "words" and "deeds" should go together to encourage faith in Jesus as a Savior (chs. 7 and 17). Blaming Simon for perverting believers with empty words, Peter says, "We must put no faith in *words*, but in *actions* and *deeds*. So we must go on with what we have begun" (ch. 17; italics are mine).[22] Already in the Hebrew Bible, Elisha's miracle in 2 Kgs 5:15 does not simply verify him as a true prophet, but more importantly, proves that the God of Israel is the true God.[23] Miraculous deeds confirm the validity of the spoken words.

In APt, the role of the apostle is multifaceted. Peter is established as an important carrier of God's divine power by his ability to perform miracles. He also delivers a Christian Gospel message and embodies heroic virtues in his life-style.[24] In this sense, Peter the apostle in APt shares some common features with the so-called divine man tradition.[25] According to Robert F. Stoops, Jr., Peter functions as a broker in the patron-client system, as Jesus, the patron, speaks and works through Peter for the believers, the clients.[26] In APt, God cares for the believers through Peter's ministry (ch. 4). Jesus speaks through Peter to Eubula and the blind widow (chs. 17 and 20). Jesus performs signs and wonders through Peter for the conversion of the sinners (ch. 26). And Jesus even appears in the form of Peter in Marcellus' dream (ch. 22). Peter is only an intermediary between God, the ultimate patron, and the believers however, and never acts as a patron in his own right. In the scheme of APt, the human patronage system is modified in a way that all the honors have to be paid only to Christ, since he is the ultimate patron who empowers the apostle to care for the believers.[27]

---

ed. Elisabeth Schüssler Fiorenza (Notre Dame: University of Notre Dame Press, 1976), 171–72. For the discussion of miracles stories in the *Acts of Andrew* and Irenaeus, refer to David W. Pao, "Physical and Spiritual Restoration: The Role of Healing Miracles in the *Acts of Andrew*," in *The Apocryphal Acts of the Apostles*, eds. François Bovon, Ann Graham Brock, and Christopher R. Matthews (Cambridge: Harvard University Press, 1999), 259–80.

[22] See also, Bremmer, *The Apocryphal Acts of Peter*, 37–38; and Achtemeier, "Jesus and the Disciples as Miracle Workers in the Apocryphal New Testament," 158.

[23] For more on this, refer to Efraim Elimelech Urbach, *The Sages: Their Concepts and Beliefs*, 2nd ed. (Jerusalem: Magnes Press, 1987), 103–05.

[24] See also, Davies, *The Revolt of the Widows: the Social World of the Apocryphal Acts*, 32.

[25] Bremmer, *The Apocryphal Acts of Peter*, 37–38.

[26] Stoops, "Christ as Patron in the *Acts of Peter*," 147.

[27] Robert F. Stoops, "Patronage in the Acts of Peter," *Semeia* 38 (1986): 91.

In the overall context of APt, the miracle stories manifest God's benevolent care for the believers, especially for the poor. In his final confrontation with Simon the magician, Peter preaches that God showed His compassion through signs and wonders (ch. 36). In APt 25–28, we have two
resurrection stories: (1) the poor widow and her only son and (2) the senatorial son. It is true that while the first story appeals to the poor, the second
appeals to the rich benefactors. However, in these two resurrection stories,
APt emphasizes the responsibility of the rich to take care of the poor, especially the slaves and the widows. Right before resurrecting the senatorial
son, Peter asks his mother to set free the slaves who carried the son and to
distribute the funeral expenses to the poor widows in gratitude for her
soon-to-be-restored son (ch. 28). When the resurrected senatorial son and
Chryse bring gold pieces to Peter (chs. 29–30), Peter commands that they
be distributed to the poor, especially to the widows. It is interesting that
Chryse brings gold pieces to the poor as "a debtor to Christ" or as a recipient of Christ's benefit, rather than as a patron of the poor.[28] Again, human benefactors/patrons for the church become relativised in this Christian
patron-client system because of their indebtedness to Christ.

– "The Holy Scriptures of the Lord" May Appear Weak to Your Eyes
After having healed the blind widow, Peter goes into the dining-room of
Marcellus' house and becomes aware that the Transfiguration story of the
gospel is being read in a worship service. Peter *rolls up* the book and ne-
cessitates a proper declaration of the scriptures. The occurrence of the participle "rolling up" (*involvens*) is surprising, since most of the New Testament texts come to us in the form of codex.[29] Both H. Gamble and D. Trobisch agree that, despite the fact that until the fourth century, the codex
form is rarely used in the Roman literature, the New Testament manuscripts are written in the codices, not in the scrolls, from the beginning of
their productions.[30] Disagreeing, J. Bremmer argues that the occurrence of
"rolling up" in APt 20 is an illustration of the continuing use of the scrolls

---

[28] See also, Stoops, "Christ as Patron in the *Acts of Peter*," 151.

[29] Bremmer, *The Apocryphal Acts of Peter*, 4; Harry Y. Gamble, *Books and Readers
in the Early Church* (New Haven: Yale University Press, 1995), 42–81; and David Trobisch, *The First Edition of the New Testament* (Oxford; New York: Oxford University
Press, 2000), ch. 2.

[30] Although they agree upon the early Christians' use of codices for the New Testament from its beginning, they present different reasons for the prevalence of the codex
form. Trobisch notes several advantages of the codex over the scroll (Trobisch, 74–76).
For example, the codex can hold more texts than the scroll and can be used to distinguish
the New Testament from its competitor, the Jewish biblical scrolls. Gamble, however,
posits that the codex form becomes authoritative, since a primitive edition of Paul's "letters to seven churches" is first published in the form of a codex and then becomes the
model Christian text (Gamble 58–65).

in some Christian circles. Agreeing with Gamble and Trobisch that the Gospels exist exclusively in the form of codex, I argue that the occurrence of the participle "rolling up" in APt 20 has something to do with the way in which APt wants to portray Peter in connection with Jesus: Peter *imitates* Jesus in his "rolling up" (πτύξας) of the scroll of Isaiah at the synagogue (cf. Lk 4:20).

Responding to the reading of the scriptural passage of the Transfiguration, Peter asserts that believers should learn how to declare the scriptural text:

> You men who believe and hope in Christ, you must know how the holy scripture of our Lord should be declared. What we have written by his grace, so far as we were able, although it seems weak to you as yet, yet (we have written) according to our powers, so far as it is endurable to be implanted in human flesh. We should therefore first learn to know the will of God, or (his) goodness (ch. 20).[31]

In this pericope, APt reveals an interesting attitude of the second century Christian community toward the Gospels.[32] They call the Gospels "the holy scripture of our Lord" (*sancta scriptura domini nostri*) and consider them to be objects of veneration and interpretation since they contain God's divine will (*dei voluntatem*). The community of APt reads the written texts in their public worship service and remembers the scriptural stories as their foundation stories. As possible criteria for the scriptural authority of the Gospels, APt presents the apostles as their authors and Jesus' grace as the divine power motivating them to write.

On the other hand, APt finds that the written texts may appear "weak" (*infirma*) to the eyes of some members, since in the process of being written, the divine message has to accommodate the limited capacity of human beings to understand it.[33] The reasoning behind their considering the written texts weak is interesting, since it is exactly the same reason that gods (and Jesus) must appear in human form. Since the written texts may appear *weak* to human eyes, in order to see the divine will hidden behind the writ-

---

[31] *Viri, qui in Christo creditis et speratis, scitote, qualiter debeat sancta scribtura domini nostri pronuntiari. Quae gratia ipsius quod coepimus, scribsimus, etsi adhuc uobis infirma uidentur, capaciter tamen quae perferuntur in humana carne inferre. Debemus ergo prius scire dei uoluntatem seu bonitatem.*

[32] For APt's use of the New Testament texts and other non-canonical writings, refer to Stoops, "The *Acts of Peter* in Intertextual Context," 65–71; Christine M. Thomas, "Canon and Antitype: the Relationship between the *Acts of Peter* and the New Testament," *Semeia* 80 (1997): 189–202; and Pieter J. Lalleman, "The Relation between *the Acts of John* and *the Acts of Peter*," in *The Apocryphal Acts of Peter*, ed. Jan N. Bremmer (Leuven: Peeters, 1998), 162–63.

[33] See also, Thomas, "Canon and Antitype: the Relationship between the *Acts of Peter* and the New Testament," 188; and Stoops, "The *Acts of Peter* in Intertextual Context," 68–69.

ten stories, APt has to interpret the scriptural stories by drawing upon their interpretive traditions. The community believes that their interpretative traditions reveal the *strong* spiritual implications about God's "divine will" and "goodness." In this process of interpretation, APt does not hesitate to introduce its extra-canonical traditions outside of the written Gospels. In our current text, by putting in Peter's mouth their traditional interpretation of the Transfiguration story, APt makes it as old and genuine as the apostle Peter.[34] By claiming that it is Peter who teaches the polymorphic under-standing of the Transfiguration as the *strong* meaning of the *weak* text, APt can now promote its own interpretive tradition to the equal status with or even higher than the scriptures.

This treatment of the Gospels by APt is comparable to that of other second-century Christians. Papias of Hierapolis collects and expounds upon the words and deeds of Jesus, preferring these oral traditions to the written Gospels. In the so-called 2 Clement (middle of the second century), we find the first indication that the authority of the Lord and his words are transferred to the Gospel writings (2 Clem. 2.4; 5.2; 8.5).[35] It is Justin the martyr (mid second century) who attests to the use of the Gospels in public worship in Rome (*Apol.* I.65ff). In Justin's account, the Gospels are consi-dered authoritative writings of equal value with the Hebrew Bible. Howev-er, he still shows some freedom with respect to the written texts and har-monizes the synoptic accounts.[36] Tatian's *Diatessaron* also shows that, on the one hand, the Gospel writings are the authoritative scriptures, but that, on the other hand, the texts can be harmonized and supplemented with ex-tra-canonical materials.

– The Transfiguration: the Revelation of Jesus' Majesty on the Holy Moun-tain
In the context of APt, the charge that the written text may appear weak is deeply grounded in the presumption that the divine will (*dei voluntas*) goes beyond the human capacity to understand it. Peter declares that this human incapacity to fully understand is demonstrated by peoples' ignorance of the implication of Jesus' appearance on earth as a human being:

for when error was in full flood and many thousands of men were plunging to destruction, the Lord in *his mercy* was moved to show himself *in another shape* and to be seen *in the form of a man*, on whom neither the Jews nor we were worthy to be enlightened. For each one of us saw (him) as he was able, as he had power to see (ch. 20).

---

[34] See also, Christine M. Thomas, "Word and Deed: the *Acts of Peter* and Orality," *Apocrypha* 3 (1992): 163.

[35] Schneemelcher, *The New Testament Apocrypha*, vol.1, 19.

[36] Ibid., 20.

According to Peter, neither the Jews nor the disciples could understand the real implication of Jesus' incarnation – his appearance in another shape (*alia figura*) and his taking on the human form (*effigie hominis*) – that is, "his mercy" to deliver human beings from destruction. In chapter 7, Peter also claims that God sent His son into the world so that he could remove human "ignorance" and "weakness" which cause them to fall into death. In the logic of APt, once human beings understand the implications of Jesus' merciful appearance in human form, they are able to overcome their ignorance and weakness and accept the Gospels as the depository of God's divine will.

This way of understanding the incarnation clearly draws upon the idea that gods should appear in disguise on earth because of humans' inability to take in the divine form. What is interesting in the context of APt is: (1) Jesus' appearance in human form reinforces the charge that humans are incapable of recognizing the written texts of the scriptures as the depository of the divine will, and (2) Jesus' incarnation presumes that, like the Homeric gods, he is a divine being who can take on and appear in any forms he likes. In our current text, this incarnation idea helps APt interpret the Transfiguration as a revelation of Jesus' divine form and as a part of his polymorphic appearances on earth. The polymorphic appearances, in turn, confirm Jesus' divine capacity to take on as many forms as he would like.

Having mentioned Jesus' appearance in human form, Peter then claims that at the Transfiguration, Jesus showed him and the sons of Zebedee (James and John) his "majesty" (*maiestatem*) that he had hidden behind the human form:

> And now I will explain to you what has just been read to you. Our Lord wished me to see *his majesty* on the holy mountain; but when I with the sons of Zebedee saw *the brilliance of his light*, I fell as one dead, and closed my eyes and heard his voice, such as I cannot describe, and thought that I had been blinded by *his radiance*...I said to myself, "Perhaps my Lord willed to bring me here to deprive me of my sight." And I said, "If this be thy will, Lord, I do not gainsay it" (ch. 20).

In Peter's sermon, the divine majesty is equivalent to the brilliance of Jesus' light and radiance. These references to majesty, brilliance of the light, and radiance are synonyms and represent the divine form, namely the glory. Peter admits that he cannot describe the divine form that he has seen and the divine voice that he has heard. As is the case of the epiphany stories in the Homeric epics and the Hebrew Bible, the revelation of the divine form goes beyond the human capacity of understanding; it fills the three disciples with extreme fear. They experience near-blindness, as well. As a human response to the divine epiphany, just as Peter in the Synoptics offered three tents as the spokesperson of the three disciples, so also does Peter in APt say that if Jesus the Lord brought him to the mountain to deprive him of sight, he would not gainsay it. Jesus touches Peter and lifts him up, and then reappears in the human form that Peter is used to seeing: "And when I stood up I saw him in such a form as I was able to take in." As in the stories of the Homeric gods, Jesus' human disguise functions to protect the disciples from the danger of encountering Jesus' divine form face to face, and it allows him to speak with the mortal disciples at their level.

In comparison to the synoptic stories, we find both old and new motifs in APt's version of the story. As in the account of the Synoptics, the Trans-figuration event in APt is the epiphany in its literary genre, since it reveals Jesus' divine nature and form: the scene is full of the bright light; disciples hear the divine voice; the event is happening on the holy mountain; the disciples fall and are struck with awe and fear; and it is Peter who responds to this divine revelation as the spokesperson. However, unlike the synoptic versions, APt explains the Transfiguration in light of the incarnation in terms of the divine and human forms. While the main message of the Syn-optic story (cf. Mk 9:7) is Jesus' divine Sonship that God confirms with His voice, in APt's version, the revelation is more about Jesus' own divine majesty and form which he kept hidden in the incarnation. In APt, it is not God's voice but Jesus' that the three hear with awe. Also, in the story of APt, both Moses and Elijah are forgotten, nor is there any mention of Je-sus' radiant clothes and face. Unlike the Synoptic Peter, who is spiritually blind, the Peter of APt is spiritually enlightened.

The most noticeable difference between the Synoptic Peter and the Peter of APt is found in his attitude toward the martyrdom. While Peter rejected Jesus' message of suffering and death in the Synoptics, the Peter of APt not only accepts the message, but also willingly accepts crucifixion as his destiny. In ApoPt and 2 Peter, the Transfiguration story is remembered to-gether with the apostle Peter and his death. In these Petrine traditions, there is an apologetic tendency to not mention Peter's misunderstandings and refusal of Jesus' teaching of suffering and death (cf. Mk 8:33–34; 9:6). Instead, in 2 Peter, Peter's death becomes a setting for his farewell speech about the Transfiguration; in the Apocalypse of Peter, it becomes an escha-tological event as the beginning of the Parousia. In APt 20–21, Peter's mi-sunderstanding of Jesus' teaching of suffering and death and Jesus' rebuk-ing of him are not mentioned. Instead, unlike the synoptic Peter who avoids the martyrdom in a cowardly fashion, the Peter in APt heroically faces his martyrdom even with his head downwards (chs. 35–40). Peter's crucifixion with head downwards symbolizes Adam's birth and the Fall, which caused the whole cosmic system to be out of order (ch. 38).[37] As a

---

[37] For more on the meaning of Peter's martyrdom in APt, see J. Bolyki, "'Head Downward': The Cross of Peter in the Lights of the Apocryphal Acts, of the New Testa-

contrast, the cross of Christ, "who is the Word stretched out," represents the restoration of the world back into the correct order.[38]

It is interesting that both APt and 2 Peter mention "Jesus' majesty" and "the holy mountain" (cf. 2 Pet 1:16–18), which are not attested to in the synoptic versions. Also, the key concepts of the glory and the goodness appear together in APt 20 and 2 Pet 1:3. The occurrence of this combination is interesting because in Exod 33:19, God shows Moses not only the glory, but also His *goodness*, *names*, and *compassion* as well, responding to Moses' request to experience the divine glory. In all these accounts, God's revelation of the divine glory is the very expression of His goodness and compassion toward His human favorites. However, while APt and 2 Peter commonly show these ideas, rather than both texts being dependent upon each other on a textual level, they belong to the same broad stream of Petrine traditions about the Transfiguration.[39] Also, in the two motifs of "touching" and "light" APt 20 is close to the Matthean version of the story (cf. Mt 17:7), which also lies behind the Transfiguration story of 2 Peter 1:16–18.[40]

– The Transfiguration and the Incarnation: His Divine Form vs. Human Form

The most interesting aspect of APt's version of the Transfiguration is its interpretation of the story in the context of the incarnation. Both events constitute a unified story of Jesus' ministry on earth. In its explanation of the Transfiguration in light of the incarnation, APt quotes Isa 53:2 and Jn 10:18:

---

ment and of the Society-transforming Claim of Early Christianity," in *The Apocryphal Acts of Peter*, ed. Jan N. Bremmer (Leuven: Peeters, 1998), 111–22; and Monika Pesthy, "Cross and Death in the Apocryphal Acts of the Apostles," in *The Apocryphal Acts of Peter*, ed. Jan N. Bremmer (Leuven: Peeters, 1998), 123–33.

[38] Peter's martyrdom and the *Quo Vadis* scene have been at the center of the debate regarding the relationship between the Acts of Paul and the Acts of Peter. For this debate, refer to Robert F. Stoops, "Peter, Paul, and Priority in the Apocryphal Acts," *Society of Biblical Literature Seminar Papers* 31 (1992), 225–33; Dennis R. MacDonald, "Which Came First? Intertextual Relationships Among the Apocryphal Acts of the Apostles"; McGuckin, *The Transfiguration of Christ in Scripture and Tradition*; Dennis R. MacDonald, "The Acts of Paul and the Acts of Peter: Which Came First?," *Society of Biblical Literature Seminar Papers* 31 (1992), 214–24; and Willy Rordorf, "The Relation between the *Acts of Peter* and the *Acts of Paul*: State of the Question," in *The Apocryphal Acts of Peter*, ed. Jan N. Bremmer (Leuven: Peeters, 1998), 178–91.

[39] See also, Stoops, "The *Acts of Peter* in Intertextual Context," 70–71; Thomas, "Word and Deed: the *Acts of Peter* and Orality," 159–60; and David R. Cartlidge, "Transfiguration of Metamorphosis Traditions in the Acts of John, Thomas, and Peter," *Semeia* 38 (1986), 62.

[40] See also, MacDonald, "Which Came First? Intertextual Relationships Among the Apocryphal Acts of the Apostles," 29.

So, my dearest brethren, as God is merciful, he has borne our weaknesses and carried our sins, as the prophet says, "He bore our sins and is afflicted for us; yet we thought him to be afflicted and stricken with wounds." For "he is in the Father and the Father is in him," he also is himself the fullness of all majesty, who has shown us all his goodness. He ate and drank for our sakes, though himself without hunger or thirst, he bore and suffered reproaches for our sakes, he died and rose again because of us (ch. 20).

A similar understanding of the incarnation is already present in the New Testament, in John 1, Phil 2:6–11 and Hebrews 1–2, for example. These New Testament texts commonly explain the concept of the incarnation through the contrast between the divine form and the human form. In Phil 2, for example, Jesus' human form is called the form of a slave/servant, which the Suffering Servant in second Isaiah is said to possess in his outer appearance.[41] Considering that in the synoptic versions Jesus' suffering and death at the Transfiguration pericope have a clear resonance with the Suffering Servant, I argue that the concept of the Suffering Servant with a loathsome *form* helped the Christian thinkers see a close connection between the two events of the Transfiguration and the incarnation. APt's quotations of the Isaiah and John passages seem to demonstrate that APt is engaged in an ongoing theological discussion of the two events of the Transfiguration and the incarnation as one unified story of Jesus.

As APt's quotation of Isa 53:4 indicates, Jesus' existence as a human being has the clear goal of saving the believers. However, unlike the short visits on earth by the Homeric gods and the God of the Hebrew Bible, APt claims that Jesus' mission lasted throughout his human life, including his tragic death on the cross and his resurrection (cf. chs. 7 and 23).[42] However, APt does not ascribe any physical human needs to Jesus during his existence on earth: "He ate and drank for our sakes, though himself without hunger or thirst." This shows APt's endeavor to make Jesus belong to the divine realm by nature rather than to the human realm (cf. chs. 2, 5, 6, 10, 24, and 28).[43]

---

[41] Stroumsa argues that the description of Jesus as the servant in the form of a slave and with the name of God (cf. Phil 2:6–11) takes its origin in the Jewish tradition on the superior angel Yahoel-Metatron, who is the servant of God and who also carries the name of God. See Gedaliahu G. Stroumsa, "Polymorphie divine et transformations d'un mythologème: l'apocryhon de Jean et ses sources," *Vigiliae Christianae* 35 (1981): 425. However, since the dating of the Jewish tradition on Metatron is still in debate, it is safe to say that both Christian and Jewish traditions betray common ideas of the time.

[42] "I urge you through the faith in Jesus Christ, that none of you should expect another (savior) than him who was despised and mocked by the Jews, this Nazarene who was crucified and died and rose again the third day" (ch. 7).

[43] We have to be cautious about the concept of Docetism in the context of APt, since the definition of the term is illusive. We should pay attention instead to how these seemingly docetic elements function in APt's narrative context, especially in its apology for Jesus' divinity. Regarding the relationship between Polymorphy and Docetism in Acts of

During the first centuries of the Christian era, the early Church Fathers explain the implications of the Transfiguration by focusing on the following topics: the revelation of the divinity of Jesus, the implication of the appearance of Moses and Elijah, the three disciples, the Resurrection, the Kingdom of God, and the divine glory and the glorification.[44] For example, Irenaeus asserts that Moses and Elijah appeared at the Transfiguration, since they wished to see God face to face; they see Jesus in glory as the divine response to their desire to see God (*Adv. Haer.* 4.20.9). However, some Fathers read as one story the two events of the Transfiguration and the incarnation through the concepts of the Suffering Servant and his loathsome form. For example, Origen argues against Celsus that at the Transfiguration, Jesus revealed his glorious form and the splendor of his garments that he hid in the incarnation (*Contra Celsum* 6.68). Origen also explains Jesus' human form by discussing the form of a slave in Isaiah 53:2 (*Contra Celsum* 6.76). Unlike Celsus, who does not understand the changes and the transformation of Jesus in the events of the incarnation and the Transfiguration, Origen explains the dynamics between Jesus' divine and human forms by quoting Phil 2:6–11 (*Contra Celsum* 4.14–16). In his *Comm. on Matt* 12, Origen again explains the divine and human forms of Jesus by expositing two passages of the Transfiguration and the Philippian hymn. APt clearly participates in this type of ongoing interpretive tradition of the Transfiguration with the incarnation.

– The Binary Sets of Epithets and the Polyonymy
Peter continues his preaching on the Transfiguration in terms of Jesus' divine and human forms by discussing (1) binary sets of epithets about Jesus with contradictory values/actions and (2) his multiple names/designations (polyonymy).[45] As for the binary sets of epithets, APt 20 narrates:

this God [Jesus] who is both great and little, beautiful and ugly, young and old, appearing in time and yet in eternity wholly invisible...beauteous, yet appearing among us as poor and ugly.

John, see Pieter J. Lalleman, *The Acts of John: A Two-stage Initiation Into Johannine Gnosticism* (Leuven: Belgium, 1998), 204–12.

[44] For these interpretations, refer to McGuckin, *The Transfiguration of Christ in Scripture and Tradition* .

[45] The *Acts of John* has similar lists in chs. 94–97. See Eric Junod and Jean-Daniel Kaestli, *Acta Iohannis*, 2 vols., *Corpus Christianorum* 1–2 (Turnhout: Brepols, 1983); Paul G. Schneider, *The Mystery of the Acts of John* (San Francisco: Mellen Research University Press, 1991); and Lalleman, *The Acts of John: A Two-stage Initiation Into Johannine Gnosticism* , 64–65. However, the list in the *Acts of John* is quite different from that of the *Acts of Peter*, so it is hard to determine a textual relationship between them. Also, it should be critically examined whether these lists are typically a part of the "Gnostic" movement.

At first sight, as a part of his sermon on the Transfiguration, these binary sets with *contradictory* values appear strange. The Hebrew Bible describes God with similar binary features, not with *contradictory* attributes, but with *synonymous* values such as "transcendence and immanence" and "justice and mercy." Why does APt portray Jesus as someone with these contradictory values?

First, these contradictory epithets further Peter's sermon on the Transfiguration in terms of Jesus' existence in two different forms: one in the divine form with superior values ("great, beautiful, and young" and "invisible"); and the other in the human form with inferior values ("little, ugly, and old" and "visible"). Peter says at the end of the list that although Jesus was beautiful, he appeared among us as poor and ugly (ch. 20). Also, in his confrontation with Simon in the forum, Peter, quoting Isa 53:2, says, "and we saw him [Jesus], and he had no grace *nor beauty*" (ch. 24; italics are mine). It is no wonder that for Simon the magician, Jesus is simply the son of a carpenter and a carpenter himself, since he has only been exposed to Jesus' human form. The binary epithets with the contradictory values recapitulate in a poetic way APt's previous discussion of Jesus' two forms found in the two stories of the Transfiguration and the incarnation.

Second, the epithets reflect the spiritual conditions of the observers. Peter declared in the beginning of his sermon that neither the Jews nor the disciples were worthy to be enlightened to grasp Jesus' appearance in human form. While Jesus benevolently allows Peter to see his divine form at the Transfiguration and to understand the salvific implication of his appearance in human form, Simon the magician remains spiritually blind throughout his life. Simon challenges Peter, saying, "Show us, Peter, who is your god, or what is his greatness, which has given you such confidence?" (ch. 23). When Peter declares that Jesus is the true God, Simon ridicules him:

"Jesus the Nazarene, the son of a carpenter and a carpenter himself, whose family comes from Judaea...you men of Rome, is God born? Is he crucified? He who owns a Lord is no God!" (ch. 23).

In APt's narrative scheme, to the unenlightened eyes of Simon and the Romans, Jesus may appear merely "poor, ugly, little and old," and he is a criminal who faced a tragic death on the cross. This is the reason Peter, in the following chapter and responding to the blind widows' request for sharing Jesus' mercy and goodness, raises the necessity of spiritual "inner eyes" in order to recognize Jesus in his full divine majesty, that is, "young, beauteous, and great" (ch. 21).

Peter continues his discussion of Jesus' appearance in divine and human forms through the binary lists of his activities:

whom [Jesus] no human hand has *grasped*, yet is *held* by his servants, whom no flesh has *seen*, yet now he is *seen*; whom no *hearing* has found yet now he is *known* as the word that is *heard*; whom no *suffering* can reach, yet now is (*chastened*) as we are; who was never *chastened*, yet now is *chastened*; who is before the world, yet now is *comprehended* in time; the beginning greater than all princedom, yet now *delivered* to the princes (ch. 20).

While the binary epithets describe Jesus' two forms in a poetic way, the binary lists of activities narrate what happened to Jesus during the two different modes of his existence – the divine and the human. In these lists, Jesus' existence in the divine mode before his incarnation is categorized both by his transcendence beyond human comprehension and his perfect condition free from human suffering. On the other hand, in the human mode of his existence, he is known, touched, heard, and chastened by other human beings. Both the binary epithets with contradictory values and the binary lists of the activities summarize the paradoxical nature of Jesus' existence using two different forms and modes: the divine and the human.

While the above epithets and lists beautifully narrate Jesus the divine's involvement in human history in general, the following list of Jesus' multiple titles and designations (polyonymy) speak specifically of his various functions in salvation history:[46]

the door, the light, the way, the bread, the water, the life, the resurrection, the refreshment, the pearl, the treasure, the seed, the abundance, the mustard-seed, the vine, the plough, the grace, the faith, the word. He is all things, and there is no other greater than he.

Most of these titles and designations are attested to in the New Testament, especially in John, and connote a variety of theological understandings of Jesus among the believers. Unlike the previous epithets and lists, the designations are positive and numerous.

In the Hebrew Bible, God often reveals his names intentionally, and they have much to do with His prior actions in Israel's history. Likewise, the polyonymy refers to Jesus' salvific actions for his people in many different ways.[47] In this list of polyonymy, Jesus appears differently in human history according to the situations and needs of the individual believers, and Jesus' multiple manifestations have to do with the recipients' power to see and to take. However, there is still a unity of Jesus' identity behind the multiple appearances[48] and the multiple designations express his merciful

---

[46] In the Greco-Roman religions, the Greek term πολυώνυμος is often used as an epithet for deities like Isis and Pluto (cf. Plut. *Is. et Os.* 372 E; Apu. *Meta.* XI.4). Also, Philo calls the Logos πολυώνυμος (cf. *De Conf. Ling.* 146–48).

[47] As for the discussion of names and numbers in early Christianity, see François Bovon, "Names and Numbers in Early Christianity," *NewTestStud* 47 (2001): 267–88.

[48] Vernant argues that the perfection, plenitude and eternity are the exclusive attributes of a totally unified being. Every fragmentation of the One, every dispersion of

attempt at including among his people all the believers who have different experiences of him. In APt's theological scheme of polyonymy (and polymorphy in the following chapter), no one is left out because of his or her particular opinion about Jesus. Instead, everyone is allowed to experience Jesus' merciful manifestation according to one's own spiritual power and need. Peter concludes his sermon by praising Jesus for manifesting his greatness in such diverse ways.

In his sermon on the Transfiguration in light of the incarnation, Peter maintains that Jesus has appeared in multiple forms and names in the salvation history. Both the polymorphy and the polyonymy represent Jesus' merciful care for the believers in diverse ways and his divine power and greatness which go beyond human recognition. These ideas are also found in the writings of the early Church Fathers. Irenaeus speaks of the incarnation, saying that Jesus, although he is "the invisible, incomprehensible and boundless," made himself visible and comprehensible for life. But his *greatness* is past finding and his *goodness* is beyond telling (*Adv. Haer.* 4.20–5–6). The Clementine literature asserts that Jesus changed his *forms* and *names* from the beginning of the world and reappeared again and again in the world. When his own time came in the incarnation, he was anointed with mercy for the salvation works of God (*Homilies* III, 20).

It is Origen who espouses exactly the same ideas as APt regarding this type of interpretation of the Transfiguration. The three disciples are chosen to accompany Jesus at the Transfiguration since they possess the power to witness Jesus' divine form and nature (*In Matt* 12.37). Those who remain on the plains do not possess the spiritual power and see Jesus according to their physical eyes. Origen also mentions similar lists of Jesus' titles and names in *Contra Cels.* 2.64. He believes these lists represent the various aspects of Jesus from different viewpoints and that Jesus is more than one. Jesus does not appear in the same way to all who see him, but is seen differently according to an individual's capacity to receive him (*Contra Cels.* 2.64 and 6.77).

6.3.2 The Polymorphy in APt 21

– The Transfiguration Reenacted in Jesus' Polymorphic Appearances
As soon as Peter finishes preaching on the Transfiguration, some old blind widows ask Peter to pray for them so that they may share the same "mercy and goodness":

---

the Being, and every distinction among parts, signifies death's entrance on the stage. To rid themselves of death and to fulfill themselves in the permanence of their perfection, the Olympian gods renounce their individual bodies and dissolve themselves in the *unity* of a great cosmic god, Zeus, or are absorbed in the person of the orphic Dionysus. See Vernant, 48.

We sit here together, Peter, hoping in Christ Jesus and believing (in him). So as you have now made one of us to see, we beg you, sir Peter, let us also share his mercy and goodness.

Although Peter would prefer they come to see Jesus with spiritual eyes, he nonetheless prays that Jesus may touch their physical eyes for healing:

If there is in you the faith which is in Christ, if it is established in you, then see *with your mind* what you do not see with your eyes; and (though) your ears be closed, yet let them open in *your mind* within you. These eyes shall again be closed, that see nothing but men and cattle and dumb animals and stones and sticks; but only *the inner eyes* see Jesus Christ. Yet now, Lord, let thy sweet and holy name assist these women; do thou touch their eyes, for thou art able, that they may see with their own eyesight (italics are mine).

As in the miracle stories of the Synoptics, APt mentions the widows' faith and Jesus' touch as the two key healing elements. Peter emphasizes that it is the widows' faith in Christ that enables the inner spiritual eyes to be opened wide. Peter here creates a contrast between the physical eyes and the spiritual eyes, stressing that it is the latter that makes them see Jesus. The contrast reminds readers of APt's previous claim that spiritual awakening is necessary in order to understand the divine will hidden behind the written texts. In the overall context of APt, the contrast further exhorts readers to be on Peter's side in their high evaluation of Jesus rather than on Simon the magician's.

Responding to Peter's prayer, Jesus again appears in the "ineffable (*inenarrabilem*) and invisible (*inuisibilem*)" light to Peter and the old blind widows. As in the previous Transfiguration event, in this reenacted Transfiguration story, Peter confesses that he can neither endure nor see the light: "[h]ave mercy on us thy servants, Lord. Let thy gift to us, Lord, be such as we can endure; for this we can neither see nor endure." Then the bright light enters the eyes of the blind widows and enables them to see Jesus in three different human forms (trimorphy): an old man, a young man, and a boy. The sequence of Jesus' divine form and then his human form in this event is exactly the same as what Peter witnessed at the Transfiguration. According to the widows, Jesus in the form of a boy gently touches their eyes, instantly restoring their sight.

In this polymorphy account, we have a reenactment of the Transfiguration event that Peter remembered and reinterpreted in his sermon as the revelation of Jesus' benevolent appearance in multiple forms and names. Jesus' polymorphic appearance to the blind widows shows that for APt, the Transfiguration should not remain an event belonging to the past, but can still be reenacted in the current believers' lives as a present reality.[49] Since Jesus' various manifestations of himself are the expression of his ongoing

---

[49] In this sense, the Transfiguration story can be called "inclusive narrative." See Luz, *Studies in Matthew*, 238.

care for the believers, he does not stop appearing to them in a polymorphic way. Similarly in his sermon, Peter calls Jesus "the merciful God, the Lord" and confesses, "God is greater than our thoughts as we have learnt from aged widows, how they have seen the Lord *in a variety of forms*."

The polymorphy reveals that Jesus has the divine power to take multiple forms and that his whole is much greater than what humans can understand of him. This is the reason Peter speaks of the necessity of opening one's inner spiritual eyes for the right understanding of Jesus. In the overall context of APt, this conclusion constitutes APt's apology for Jesus' divine identity in confrontation with Simon's challenge. Simon has questioned Peter's Gospel message that "Jesus Christ the Nazarene who was despised and mocked by the Jews, is the Savior and God the Lord" (chs. 7, 14, 23 and 32). APt asserts that Jesus' identity and mission belong to the divine realm and thus go far beyond Simon's human power of recognition.

– A Structural Parallelism between the Transfiguration and the Polymorphy

There is a structural parallelism between the *remembered* and *reinterpreted* Transfiguration story in ch. 20 and the polymorphy, the *reenacted* Transfiguration in ch. 21, as follows:

the Transfiguration (ch. 20)	the polymorphy (ch. 21)
mentioning of a blind widow	mentioning of the blind widows
motif of God's goodness and mercy	motif of God's goodness and mercy
necessity for spiritual awakening	necessity for spiritual eyes to open
revelation of the light	revelation of the light
list of multiple epithets/designations	polymorphous forms of Jesus
Peter's praise for Jesus' greatness	Peter's praise for Jesus' greatness

In both accounts, APt begins by mentioning the presence of old widows who wish to be healed by Jesus' brilliant light. In APt's narrative structure, the widows' blindness highlights how it is necessary to open the spiritual eyes in order to understand the following stories. The idea of blindness emphasizes that these stories have to do with deep spiritual truths about God's goodness and mercy toward humanity. The motif of God's mercy and goodness functions as the hidden spiritual message of the two accounts. APt maintains that only those with spiritually enlightened eyes can have access to this truth.

As for God's response to the human request, in the first account, Peter explained that Jesus as the divine showed his mercy and goodness by appearing in human form. Peter further explained this idea by discussing the binary sets of epithets and the list of Jesus' various designations. Similarly, in the second account, Jesus shows his mercy and goodness by *re*-appearing among his worshippers in both divine and human forms. When the light of Jesus, the divine form, enters the eyes of the blind widows, it enables them to see Jesus in three different human forms. APt does not forget to emphasize the transcending quality of Jesus' divine form, the light, by qualifying it as something ineffable (*inenarrabilem*) and invisible (*inuisibilem*). It is interesting that the widows tell Peter that they cannot even describe Jesus' human form of an old man.

In this structural parallelism of the two accounts, Jesus' trimorphic appearance in the second account (ch. 21) becomes equivalent to the polyonymy with the list of the epithets in the first account (ch. 20). Both the polyonymy and the polymorphy carry the same message about Jesus' benevolent care for the believers expressed in *particular* and *multiple* ways. In this regard, the polymorphy *visually* represents Jesus' mercy and goodness shown in the stories of the Transfiguration and the incarnation, while the polyonymy *narratively* accounts for how Jesus' mercy and goodness have become manifest in human history. Both accounts end similarly by having Peter proclaim that "God [Jesus] is greater than human thoughts" and that "there is no other greater than he [Jesus]."[50]

– Jesus' Trimorphic Appearance in the On-going Interpretive Traditions
Clearly, Jesus' polymorphic appearance in three human forms represents APt's visual recapitulation of Jesus' life on earth and its salvific implication, which Peter accounted for in detail in his sermon on the Transfiguration. Those who are familiar with the interpretive traditions of the Transfiguration story may find Jesus' three age specific forms surprisingly foreign to the story. However, the trimorphy is not unexplainable. If the trimorphy is read in light of Greco-Roman mythology, Jesus' age specific forms may represent his taking on different human forms throughout his life on earth rather than simply getting old as a normal human being. This idea is not far from ideas included in Peter's discussion of Jesus' appearance in multiple forms and under multiple names in his sermon. Also, considering the scriptural tradition that three is a large enough number of witnesses to validate a truth claim, the three forms can be considered enough to represent the whole life span of Jesus. Finally, the number three is drawn from the presence of the *three* disciples and the *three* heavenly beings of Jesus, Moses and Elijah in the Transfiguration story.[51]

There are Christian interpretive traditions regarding Jesus' age specific forms in the theological discourses by the early Church Fathers. Some Church Fathers discuss the implications of Jesus' different ages in relation to the Incarnation. For example, Irenaeus argues that Jesus sanctified dif-

---

[50] It is interesting that similarly to APt, Irenaeus also discusses Jesus' manifestation in a visible and comprehensible manner in terms of his greatness and goodness (*Adv. Haer.* 4.20.5–6).

[51] In AJn 90, John sees another being in the form of Jesus talking with him.

ferent ages of human life by passing through every age in order to save all human beings (*Adv. Haer.* II. 22.4). Jesus became an infant for infants, thus sanctifying them. Similarly, he became a child for children, a young man for young adults, and on old man for old men. The scriptures clearly mention Jesus' different ages, but not his old age: Jesus' being new born and infant (Mt 2:11; Lk 2:7, 16–17), child (Lk 2:42), and adult around thirty (Lk 3:23; cf. *Adv. Haer.* II.22.5). Because Jesus' old age is not mentioned, Irenaeus argues that John, the other Gospels, and the elders, assert that Jesus was still teaching from the 40th to the 50th year of his life (*Adv. Haer.* II.22.5). For Irenaeus, even the Jews who disputed with Jesus clearly demonstrate Jesus' old age, which he defines as between the ages of 40 and 50. For when Jesus said to them, "Your father Abraham rejoiced to see my day; and he saw it, and was glad," the Jews answered him, "You are not yet *fifty* years old, and have you seen Abraham?" (Jn 8:56–57). This reply is fitting only to one who has already passed the age of forty, but not yet reached his fiftieth year (*Adv. Haer.* II.22.6).

For Origen, Jesus' appearance in human form in the incarnation has the clear goal of saving human beings who cannot behold him in the divine form (*Contra Cels.* VI.68). Since people have different capacities for seeing Jesus, he appears in multiple forms so that all people can see and receive him (II.64; and VI.77). Origen also mentions the changing relationship between Jesus' body and the capacity of the spectators (VI.77). The different stages of Jesus' life in different ages, which manifest a variety of Jesus' age specific forms, have exactly the same function for Origen and for APt: the inclusion of people with different understandings of, or relationships with, Jesus among his own people.

It is possible that for Gentile readers who don't know much about Moses and Elijah, the three heavenly beings in glory at the Transfiguration are the result of the single divine being's different manifestations to the three apostles according to their spiritual power.[52] It is likely that in order to uphold the incarnation theology of Jesus' merciful act of embracing all humanity in different ages, APt chooses the *three* representative forms of child, adult, and old man in its polymorphic presentation of Jesus at the Transfiguration. The three forms are enough to represent the full cycle of human life from birth to death. In any case, the comparison between APt and the early Church Fathers indicates that in its interpretation of the Transfiguration in terms of the polymorphy, APt participates in an ongoing dialogue with the church Fathers and other apocryphal writings, including AJn.

---

[52] See also Bovon, *Luke*, vol.1, 372.

6.4 How to Explain the Emergence of the Tradition of Jesus' Polymorphy?

6.4.1 Former Scholarship on Its Origin

Polymorphy has been at the center of debate in regard to the relationship among the apocryphal acts, especially between AJn and APt. Its illusive nature and difference from the Transfiguration have prevented scholars from reaching a definitive conclusion about its origin and function. Several scholars present various religious ideas as the possible candidates for the origin of the polymorphy. Jacques E. Ménard argues that the polymorphy tradition goes back to Daena, the goddess in the Persian mythology, who changes her stature in relation to the works of those who contemplate her.[53] Although Jesus appears in different statures in some Christian writings (e.g. the *Gospel of Peter*; AJn), Daena's appearances with different statures cannot explain the polymorphous Jesus of APt, since it is not in different statures but in different ages that APt's polymorphous Jesus appears.

Eric Peterson refers to Aeon, the eternal time, in *the Discourse to the Greeks* by Tatian. The eternal Aeon appears to humans in the forms of the past, present, and future.[54] Henri-Charles Puech, following Peterson, maintains that the polymorphous Jesus is a personification of Aeon and the three forms signify his eternity.[55] However, in APt 20–21, polymorphy is more about Jesus' mercy and goodness than his eternity. As I have shown above, Jesus' trimorphy in APt visually recapitulates its discussion of how Jesus manifested his merciful intervention in human history. Also, we are left wondering how Jesus' three forms in different ages in APt can represent the three fold temporal division of the past, the present, and the future.[56]

G. Stroumsa argues that the trimorphy of Jesus is the result of the development which adds the form of the servant/child to those of a young and an old man. According to him, the bimorphy of young man and old

---

[53] Jacques E. Ménard, "Transfiguration et polymorphie chez Origène," in *Epektasis*, ed. Jacques Fontaine and Charles Kannanengiesser (Paris: Beauchesne, 1972), 367.

[54] Eric Peterson, *Frühkirche, Judentum und Gnosis* (Rome; Fribourg; Vienne: 1959), 183–208.

[55] For the bibliographical information on Puech, refer to Stroumsa, "Polymorphie divine et transformations d'un mythologème: l'apocryhon de Jean et ses sources," 412, n.3–4.

[56] Already in the Scriptures, both God and Jesus are claimed to be "who was, is, and will be" (Rev. 1:4, 8; 4:8). Especially, the expression "who will be" becomes a technical term for Jesus as the coming eschatological judge. If the polymorphous Jesus has something to do with the eternity, then these scriptural traditions are more likely to have inspired that idea.

man takes its origin in the esoteric Jewish tradition on the figure of Song of Songs 5:11[57] and the Ancient of Days in Dan 7.[58] However, since the Jewish esoteric tradition on Metatron is hard to date, we can not definitively say that the Christians are drawing upon the Metatron tradition in the polymorphy. It is also hard to prove how the development of the polymorphy moved from bimorphy to trimorphy. There is a Jewish speculation on the polymorphous presentation of God and angels in the second and third centuries which are contemporaneous with the apocryphal acts, to which I will soon return.[59] Although it is not impossible that this Jewish speculation goes much earlier and has contributed to the Christian formulation of the polymorphy, it is more likely that this Jewish tradition is a parallel development to APt's polymorphous Jesus.

A. Jacoby, followed by Peter Weigandt[60] and E. Junod, ascribes to the origin of polymorphy the Egyptian cult of Horus the sun god.[61] According to this tradition, Horus the sun god appears in a polymorphous way as regards his age: child, boy, young man, and old man. His four different forms represent four different seasons, and his two or three forms stand for the positions of the sun during a day, such as sunrise and sunset. The different ages express the eternity and the absolute permanence of Horus the sun god. Weigandt argues that ApoJn introduces this Egyptian tradition into Christianity by applying it to Jesus' polymorphy. Junod further supports Weigandt's thesis by asserting that both ApoJn and AJn, two second

---

[57] There is an idea of macrocosmic representations of the divinity in Jewish traditions, similar to the divine forms of Greco-Roman mythology which are greater than life sizes and more beautiful than human forms. Since Justin Martyr, Origen and Basil the Great criticize this idea of Jewish macrocosmic anthropomorphism, the original Jewish speculation on the macrocosmic divine body is pre-Christian (See Gedaliahu G. Stroumsa, "Form(s) of God: Some Notes on Metatron and Christ," *HTR* 76 (1983): 277). While its dating is still debated, *Shi'ur Qomah* ("measurement of the divine stature") exposits Song of Songs 5:11–16 and offers the measurement of the limbs of the divine figure who is identified with the Beloved and called Metatron. In this text, Metatron, the archangelic hypostasis of God, appears as a *child* and an *old* man, and both in the form of God and in the form of a servant (cf. Phil 2:6–11).

[58] Stroumsa, "Polymorphie divine et transformations d'un mythologème: l'>>apocryphon de Jean<< et ses sources," 426.

[59] See Judah Goldin, *The Song at the Sea; Being a Commentary on a Commentary in Two Parts* (New Haven: Yale University Press, 1971), 124–38; and Urbach, *The Sages: Their Concepts and Beliefs* , 89.

[60] Peter Weigandt, *Der Doketismus im Urchristentum und in der theologischen Entwicklung des zweiten Jahrhunderts* (Doctoral Dissertation; Heidelberg, 1961), 45.

[61] A. Jacoby, "Altheidnisch-Aegyptishes im Christentum," *Sfinx* (1903), 110; F Stanley Jones, "Principal Orientations on the Relations between the Apocryphal Acts (Acts of Paul and Acts of John; Acts of Peter and Acts of John)," in *Society of Biblical Literature Seminar Papers* (1993), 485–505; and Junod, "Polymorphie du Dieu Sauveur."

century documents with polymorphic accounts, find their origin in Egypt.[62] Junod clearly prioritizes the polymorphic accounts of ApoJn and AJn over that of APt.

The polymorphic appearance of Horus in different ages is similar to the polymorphous Jesus in APt 21. It is, however, for many reasons, hard to conclude decisively that Horus the sun god is the unique origin of the Christian polymorphy. First, except for the Egyptian origin of ApoJn and AJn, which may be still debatable,[63] there is no concrete evidence that compels us to conclude that the apocryphal writers are directly dependent upon the Egyptian sun cult in their formation of the polymorphy. Apart from the forms in different ages, there are no elements of the sun cult in the apocryphal accounts of Jesus' polymorphy.

Second, the polymorphic appearance in different ages is commonly attested to in Greco-Roman mythology rather than the unique characteristics of Horus the sun god. For example, Odysseus calls Athena the polymorphic goddess, who appears as a young boy and an old woman. Isis is also called polymorphous and even "of many names" (polyonymous), similarly to the polymorphous and polyonymous Jesus in APt. Third, the polymorphy in ApoJn (2), AJn (90), and APt (21) do not betray the idea of eternity or permanence of Jesus as the primary message of Jesus' polymorphy.[64] For ApoJn and AJn, the main message of the polymorphy is about Jesus' unity within diverse appearances similar to God's unity within His diverse anthropomorphic appearances in the *Mekilta*. It is Jesus' greatness of being more than one thing or of going beyond human thoughts that APt stresses as the main message of the polymorphy. Fourth, since ApoJn and AJn have much more developed aspects of the polymorphy tradition not only regarding ages, but also regarding stature and gender, it is hard to defend the trajectory from Horus the sun god to ApoJn and AJn to APt. If the Egyptian sun cult was available to the Christian thinkers – at least in its visual presentation of Horus in different ages, it was not as the unique origin of the polymorphy, but as a part of the Greco-Roman religious complex where gods can appear in multiple forms. Horus was one of the many gods who have power to take different forms.

---

[62] Junod, "Polymorphie du Dieu Sauveur," 42.

[63] See Lalleman, "Polymorphy of Christ," 111; and cf. Karen King, *The Secret Revelation of John* (Cambridge, Ma: Harvard University Press, 2006), 7–24.

[64] While ApoJn mentions the idea Aeon, it discusses his imperishability or indestructibility, not the eternity (ApoJn 1.28). While King has the indestructible Aeon in her translation, Frederik Wisse has the imperishable Aeon in "The Apocryphon of John," in *The Nag Hammadi Library in English*, 105. Also, it is Jesus the undefiled and incorruptible one, not Jesus the eternal one that ApoJn explains in detail (2.15).

6.4.2 Alternative Suggestion

I have a reservation about whether one single author, either of ApoJn, or of AJn, or of APt, is the first creator of the polymorphy account from a single source. The polymorphy must be the product of an on-going process of Christian presentation of Jesus within a complex network of several different ideological motifs. It is more likely that all three polymorphic accounts of ApoJn, AJn, and APt (and others) are the result of their authors' various and dynamic participations in the development of the polymorphy tradition.[65] The different polymorphy accounts of these writings manifest the different trajectories that the polymorphy tradition takes in its transmission.[66] In regard to APt's understanding of the polymorphy, I propose that the Transfiguration story functions as the generative narrative,[67] and the idea of the incarnation – Jesus' merciful appearance on earth in human form and Greco-Roman mythology are the two major interpretative stimuli.

APt, while drawing its narratives from the Scriptural traditions,[68] appropriates the literary and cultural conventions of its time: the collections of miracles for religious propaganda, the patron-client system, the literary ge-

---

[65] Christine Thomas also considers the polymorphy as the shared tradition by AJn and APt. See Thomas, "Word and Deed: the *Acts of Peter* and Orality," 159–60.

[66] Those three writings of ApoJn, AJn, and APt all show some similar ideas in regard to the Transfiguration, the incarnation, and the polymorphy. ApoJn 1–2 has similar topics to the Transfiguration/polymorphy of APt: the ineffable light, the discussion of Jesus' identity, the misunderstanding of Jesus as a mere Nazarene, the mentioning of John and the sons of Zebedee, the mountain setting, the idea of incarnation, and Jesus' polymorphous appearances. Also Jesus in ApoJn appears as the ineffable light in the forms of a young man, an old man, and a servant/child. He is also the Father, the Mother, and the Son. Similarly, AJn 90–91 clearly shows that the setting for its polymorphy is the Transfiguration: the presence of John, James, and Peter on the mountain; Jesus' appearance in the ineffable light; the motif of fear; and mentioning of Jesus' clothes. It is interesting that AJn presents Jesus' polymorphy as the content of his glory, that is, his divine form. In AJn, the polymorphy account prioritizes John over Peter and challenges the Petrine primacy at the Transfiguration tradition. AJn's apologetic presentation of John as the unique recipient of special revelation on the mountain presupposes its familiarity with the Petrine primacy at the Transfiguration tradition.

[67] See also MacDonald, "Which Came First? Intertextual Relationships Among the Apocryphal Acts of the Apostles," 29–30; Judith B. Perkins, "The Acts of Peter as Intertext: Response to Dennis MacDonald," in *Society of Biblical Literature Seminar Papers no. 32* (1993), 627; and Richard I. Pervo, "Egging on the Chickens: A Cowardly Response to Dennis MacDonald and then Some," *Semeia* 80 (1997), 51.

[68] For more on APt's use of the scriptures, see Thomas, "Canon and Antitype: the Relationship between the *Acts of Peter* and the New Testament," 185–205; Christopher R. Matthews, "The *Acts of Peter* and Luke's Intertextual Heritage," *Semeia* 80 (1997): 207–202; and Stoops, "The *Acts of Peter* in Intertextual Context," 57–86.

nre of romance,[69] and Greco-Roman mythology. It is clear from our analysis of APt 20–21 that in its presentation of the polymorphic Jesus, APt keeps the synoptic Transfiguration story as its base story. However, in its complex relationship with the surrounding culture, APt reshapes the Transfiguration story in order to meet with its cultural expectations of gods. And at the same time, APt attempts to challenge these cultural expectations by claiming that only the Christian God is the true God who is worthy of worship. Answering Simon and the Romans' question, "Show us, Peter, who is your god, or what is his greatness, which has given you such confidence" (ch. 23), APt presents Jesus as the God whose greatness is found in his ability to appear in multiple forms which escape human recognition (ch. 21). For this polymorphic presentation of Jesus, APt especially draws upon Greco-Roman mythology of gods and their polymorphic appearances on earth, which has already influenced the portrayal of Jesus in New Testament.[70]

In the following, I will explore the phenomenon of divine appearances in human forms both in APt's cultural and scriptural traditions: (1) Greco-Roman mythology, (2) Hebrew Bible (and Jewish traditions) and (3) New Testament (and Christian traditions). I acknowledge that this division may appear somewhat artificial, since the Christian scriptures are also a part of the Greco-Roman world.

– Greco-Roman Mythology

Gods and goddesses in the ancient world who wanted to communicate with human beings had to modify their presence so as not to endanger them. However, since their visual encounter with humans was extremely dangerous, humans had to respond to the gods' benevolent manifestations in a proper manner. This situation poses serious questions: (1) if gods are not corporeal or cannot be seen by humans, how can they be recognized by their mortal worshippers? (2) if gods appear in forms which humans can recognize, does this not strain the gods' transcendent nature? And (3) what is the divine body/form like in contrast to the human body/form that the deities temporarily take on for their short visits on earth?[71]

In order to explain the divine body, the ancient cannot but compare it with the human body and create extreme contrasts between the two. The two bodies are situated between the two poles of contrasting values: limitation and transcendence, darkness and luminosity, ugliness and beauty, and

---

[69] Judith B. Perkins, "This World or Another? The Intertextuality of the Greek Romances, the Apocryphal Acts and Apuleius' *Metamorphoses*," *Semeia* 80 (1997): 247–60.

[70] See my chapter 1 on the Markan Transfiguration story.

[71] See Vernant, *Mortals and Immortals:Collected Essays*, 27–47.

foulness and purity.[72] The human body is qualified with limitation, deficiency, darkness and incompleteness, and is confined by the axes of time and space. The human body should pass through successive phases of growth and decline: after childhood and youth, human beings experience old age with weaknesses, and then death. Human beings are vulnerable to the changes of *time* flowing on without return. Human beings recognize that they are mere ephemeral creatures.[73] Also, a human body positions every individual in one location, only one location in *space*. However, a god's body transcends these limitations of space and time by being here and there at the same time[74] and by escaping the natural cycles of aging in time. Gods' bodies are always young, gigantic, luminous and beautiful, and their vitality extends across past, present and future.[75] In this thought world, the eternal nature of the divine body stands at the opposite ends of the poles to the ephemeral nature of the mortal body, although the boundary between the two is porous so that some heroes can achieve divinity through heroic actions or virtues.

Since the ancients believed that the divine body possessed extreme qualities and luminosity, it was dangerous for human beings to see the divine body face to face (e.g. *Hymn. Aphr.* 172–5; 181–3; *Hymn. Dem.* 188–90; 275–80; *Il.* 1.47; 24.170; 24.533).[76] In order for the divine to appear to human beings for regular exchanges of homages and benefits, the divine should accommodate their appearances to human beings' capacities either by clothing their luminous bodies in a mist or by hiding them behind multiple disguises.[77] For example, Athena, in her struggle against the suitors with Odysseus, appears to him in the form of a *very young boy* (*Od.* 13.221); she then takes on the appearance of a *tall and beautiful woman* (*Od.* 13.288). As a response to Athena's polymorphous appearances, Odysseus asserts that it is the gods' power to take on different shapes and he calls Athena one who "takes all manners of shapes" (*Od.* 13.312–14). The divine body can take on so many forms, because not one of them can encompass within itself the transcendent nature of the divine body. If the divine body could be identified with any one form, it would impoverish and limit the divine body's surpassing power.

---

[72] See Dietrich, "Divine Epiphanies in Homer," 71.

[73] Vernant, 32.

[74] Although the Homeric gods sometimes travel from one place to another, their speed is like that of lightning.

[75] Ibid., 46. See also, Fox, *Pagans and Christians*, 141.

[76] See Ibid. , 109.

[77] Vernant, 45.

In their visits to human beings, gods take on human disguises in three ways apart from animal shapes.[78] First, the disguise is simply generic: gods are claimed to look like human beings with no further descriptions of their human forms (e.g. Ares in *Iliad* 5.604, 13.357). Second, gods often resemble someone from a particular age group. For example, Poseidon looks like "an old man" (*Iliad* 14.135–6), and Hermes puts on the form of "a young man" (24.137). Third, gods sometimes choose to look like particular individuals with whom the human addressees are familiar. For example, Apollo takes a form of Periphas (*Iliad* 17.323–5) and Poseidon looks like Calchas (13.45). Also, Athena, when she persuades Hector to fight Achilles, disguises herself as Deiphobus, who is Hector's favorite brother.

The gods' disguises in human forms shield their divine identity from humans and protect mortals from risking their lives by encountering gods with their bare eyes.[79] Furthermore, the disguise permits the gods to intervene in human history in order to help their favorite heroes and to trick their opponents as well. Gods' appearance in human disguise is their expression of *mercy* and *goodness* toward their favorite mortals. However, the disguise cannot hide the divine body completely. Even behind the disguises, there still lies something of their divine nature which shines through whatever disguises they choose to take on. Achilles can still see the terrible gleam in the eyes of Athena (*Iliad* 1.199) and Poseidon leaves gigantic footsteps (13.20).

Summarizing the discussion, in Greek religion, the deity is believed to have divine forms and appears in visible human forms to mortals. Especially in Homer, gods such as Athena, Demeter, Dionysus, and Aphrodite are believed to possess a power to take and change forms. While the Homeric epics pick up everyday language and beliefs of the time, the epics enhance and pass them on to their readers in a more vividly narrative way.[80] Although philosophy challenges the idea of a physical manifestation of the deity, the divine appearance in human form as a concrete phenomenon remains current in the Roman world.[81] For example, in the Isis initiation in *Apul. Met.* XI. 23, the initiate experiences a twelve-fold change of form which happened to a god. According to Robin L. Fox, the revived Platonism of the second and third centuries, which is contemporaneous with APt, accepts the visible appearances of gods as a fact to be explained.[82] In the Hellenistic Roman world, the phenomenon of metamorphosis develops itself into a whole literary genre, as is attested to in Ovid,

---

[78] I borrow these examples from Warren Smith, "The Disguises of the Gods in the *Iliad*," *Numen* 35 (2004), 163.

[79] Ibid., 165–6.

[80] Fox, *Pagans and Christians*, 110.

[81] Behm, "μορφή," 746. Also, Dietrich, "Divine Epiphanies in Homer," 69.

[82] Fox, 164.

Apuleius and Pseudo-Lucian.[83] Dennis MacDonald further demonstrates how popular the Homeric idea of gods' appearances in human forms is in Christian thought in the first centuries of Christian era.[84]

If Greco-Roman mythology is a part of the religio-cultural context of APt, what can we tell in terms of similarity and dissimilarity between the Homeric gods and APt's Jesus? First, like the Homeric polymorphous gods, Jesus of APt appears as a polymorphous God, taking on multiple forms to accommodate his presence to the believers' capacities. He takes on a human form in his incarnation and reveals his divine form at the Transfiguration. He appears to the blind widows in three different forms as a boy, a young man, and an old man. Throughout the narrative stories of APt, the polymorphous Jesus appears in the forms of Peter (ch. 22) and a young man in order to intervene in the lives of the believers.[85] The polymorphic appearance is his willingness to intervene in human crisis and his expression of *mercy* and *goodness* toward the believers. In the context of APt, this polymorphic appearance especially prepares Peter and the church for the upcoming contest with Simon by reassuring Peter's victory over him. However, there are a couple of major differences between the Homeric gods and Jesus: (1) while the visits of the Homeric gods are temporary, lasting only for a short amount of time, APt claims that Jesus lives on earth as a permanent resident, from his incarnation to the resurrection (cf. chs. 7 and 20); (2) unlike the Homeric gods who are not susceptible to the tragic fates of the mortals,[86] Jesus, after having taken on human form – "ugly, little and old," suffers and dies at the cross, the most tragic human death of the time (chs. 7 and 20); and (3) while the Homeric gods only appear to their heroes, Jesus appears to ordinary people like the blind widows.

– Hebrew Bible and Jewish Traditions
Similarly to Greco-Roman mythology, in Jewish tradition there exists a tension between God's willingness to reveal Himself to humanity and humanity's incapacity to see God face to face. Just as the Homeric gods should accommodate their appearances to human capacity in disguise, so

---

[83] Behm, 756.

[84] For this topic in general, refer to Dennis R. MacDonald, *The Homeric Epics and the Gospel of Mark* (New Haven & London: Yale University Press, 2000); and Dennis R. MacDonald, *Christianizing Homer: The Odyssey, Plato, and the Acts of Andrew* (New York: Oxford University Press, 1994).

[85] It is also interesting that just as a particular hero possesses the same power and quality that his patron god has in Homeric epics, so also does Peter perform the same miracles, especially healing the blind and resurrecting the dead, that Jesus performs in the Synoptics.

[86] Although the Homeric gods are sometimes wounded, there is no serious damage to their immortality.

also does God in the Hebrew Scriptures appear in the disguise of a human form or in the divine form of Glory or behind the angelic beings.

In the Hebrew Bible, it is mostly angels who, as God's agents, appear in human forms to take care of God's people.[87] In Gen 16 the Angel of the Lord appears to Hagar during her fleeing away from Sarah and promises to multiply her descendants. Interestingly, the Hebrew Scripture asserts that it is God Himself whom Hagar saw in her encounter with the Angel of the Lord (cf. Gen 16:13). In this story, the Angel of the Lord clearly represents God's presence before Hagar and is even identified with God. At the same time, however, the Angel of the Lord has his own independent identity distinctive from that of God. The distinctive identity of the Angel of the Lord helps the Hebrew Scripture maintain the tension between God's transcendent nature and His involvement in human history. Daniel also reports that an angelic interpreter appears in a human form and reveals the meanings of the visions he has seen (cf. Dan 10:16, 18). In the anthropomorphic appearances of the angels, Daniel still sees their divine nature shining through the human disguise. Daniel is caught in awe and fear.

In the Hebrew Bible, God manifests Himself in several different ways: directly in His glory, disguised in human form and using an angel as a surrogate. What does God's divine form look like in the Hebrew Bible? It is the glory that only some prerogative humans are allowed to witness in God's theophanic appearances. In Israelite Theophany traditions, God often appears before His favorite individuals, revealing His divine form of glory in full. The glory strikes human recipients with awe (cf. Exod 34). In the prophetic traditions, it is in the context of God's calling of the prophets that He allows them to witness His divine form of glory (cf. Isa 6:1–6). This idea is well shown in the calling stories of Moses, Isaiah and Ezekiel. It is interesting that in Ezekiel's vision, God's glory on the throne appears in a human form: "and seated above the likeness of a throne was something that seemed *like a human form*" (כמראה אדם; ὁμοίωμα ὡς εἶδος ἀνθρώπου; Ezek 1:26). According to Gen 1, God created human beings in His divine image. If human's physical form has something to do with God's divine image, then it is not surprising for God to appear in human form.[88]

While the Hebrew Bible explains God's presence mostly through His divine glory without mediation or by hiding Himself behind angelic mediators, God sometimes appears in human disguises to patriarchs and to the

---

[87] As for the functions of angels in the Hebrew Scriptures and Second Temple Judaism, refer to Loren T. Stuckenbruck, *Angel Veneration and Christology: A Study in Early Judaism and in the Christology of the Apocalypse of John* (Tübingen: J.C.B. Mohr, 1995) and Gieschen, *Angelomorphic Christology*.

[88] John Kenneth Kuntz, *The Self-Revelation of God* (Philadelphia: Westminster Press, 1967), Chapter 5; and James Barr, "Theophany and Anthropomorphism in the Old Testament," *Vetus Testamentum* 7 (1959): 33 and 38.

later generations of Israel. In Gen 18, God appears to Abraham in a human form with two other angelic beings by the oak trees of Mamre (cf. Gen 19:1). In this story, the scripture does not offer any particular attributes in describing God's human form. God delivers a prophecy regarding Sarah's pregnancy and the birth of Isaac. Through His appearance in human form and the following conversation with Abraham, God resolves the biggest problem of Abraham and Sarah: the dilemma between God's promise to Abraham of the countless descendants and Sarah's physical inability to become pregnant due to her age.

The exceptions to this generic appearance are God's appearances as the Warrior in Exodus (e.g. Exod 15:1) and the Ancient of Days in Daniel (Dan 7:13). In their original contexts, these appearances of God as the Warrior and the Ancient of Days are not to be taken too literally, as they may simply express in anthropomorphic language the idea of God's various activities in the salvation history. God's appearances in these forms are not about the scriptural authors' endeavor to explain God's *human forms*, but about God's *functions* relevant to each occasion in human history. However, according to *Mekilta de-Rabbi Ishmael*, the halakic Midrash to the book of Exodus, the Jewish rabbis in the second and third centuries CE, who are contemporaneous with APt, discuss the tension between God's immutability and His manifestations in these human forms. According to *Mekilta de-Rabbi Ishmael* 4, God revealed Himself in the form of a warrior at Exodus – a *young* man, making battle with enemies (cf. gods in battle in the *Iliad*); at Sinai He revealed Himself as an *elder* full of wisdom and compassion; and in Daniel's vision, He appears as an *Ancient of Days* as well as a fiery stream (Dan 7:9–10).[89] In this *Mekilta*, the anthropomorphic languages in the Hebrew Bible become statements about God's various self-manifestations in physical human forms. It is interesting to note that the rabbis see a close relationship between these physical forms and human occasions, so that God's forms are dependent upon His functions/roles in specific human situations.[90]

What is at issue to these rabbis is not the possibility of God's polymorphic appearances in the human history, but the opponents' claim for the duality or plurality in God's nature. The rabbis presuppose that God can appear in a polymorphous way to intervene in human matters. The rabbis in the *Mekilta* protest against the idea of plurality of God's nature by quoting Isa 44:6, 48:12 and Deut 32:39: God is "the same in Egypt, the same at the Sea; the same in the past, the same in the age to come; the same in this

---

[89] I am borrowing these examples and their analyses from Goldin, *The Song at the Sea; Being a Commentary on a Commentary in Two Parts*, 124–38.

[90] Ibid., 124–6. See also, Urbach, *The Sages: Their Concepts and Beliefs*, 89.

world, the same in the world to come."[91] God is at all times one and the same God, possessing unity within diverse appearances.[92] According to the *Mekilta,* God's unique name "the Lord" confirms the idea of God's unity and immutability (cf. Mal 3:6). Their use of the name "the Lord" as an expression of God's transcendence and immutability is striking. For in the Theophanic appearances of the Hebrew Scripture, God delivers His Names as a part of self-revelation in order to remind the readers of His prior promises, interventions and actions in Israel's history.

There are some interesting comparisons to make between the Homeric gods, God of the Jewish traditions and the polymorphous Jesus of APt. Like the Homeric gods and Jesus, God's appearances in Israelite history are an expression of His love and concern for the people.[93] Similarly to the Homeric gods, the God of the Hebrew Scripture does not subject Himself to the phases of the life cycle in time nor does His divine power as a warrior wane: "the longer he [the human warrior] lives, the more his strength declines. But it is not so with Him [God] who spoke and the world came to be."[94] Also, similarly to the divine forms of Greco-Roman mythology which are greater than life size and more beautiful than human forms, there is an idea of macrocosmic representations of the divinity in Jewish traditions. Since Justin Martyr, Origen and Basil the Great criticize this idea of Jewish macrocosmic anthropomorphism, the original Jewish speculation on the macrocosmic divine body is pre-Christian.[95] While its dating is still debated, *Shi'ur Qomah* ("measurement of the divine stature") exposits the Song of Songs 5:11–16 and offers the measurement of the limbs of the divine figure who is identified with the Beloved and called Metatron.[96] In this text, Metatron, the archangelic hypostasis of God, appears as a *child* and an *old* man, and both in the form of God and in the form of a servant (cf. Phil 2:6–11).

The rabbis' relating various God's physical manifestations to human occasions in the *Mekilta* is similar to APt's portrayal of Jesus' multiple manifestations pertinent to the needs of the believers. While the Hebrew Scripture does not mention the connection between God's forms and human capacity to see them, Philo asserts that God reveals Himself according to the capacities of human beings: to the incorporeal soul, God appears as He is; to the corporeal soul, God appears in angelic form (*De Somniis* I 232–7). Similarly in APt 20, Peter asserts, "[f]or each one of us saw (him)

---

[91] Goldin, 128.

[92] The unity within the diverse appearances of Jesus is the central message of the polymorphic accounts of ApoJn 1–2 and AJn 88–90.

[93] Goldin, 133.

[94] Ibid., 130.

[95] Stroumsa, "Form(s) of God: Some Notes on Metatron and Christ," 277.

[96] For detailed analysis of it, see Ibid., 277–80.

as he was able, as he had power to see." I have shown above that Origen had exactly the same idea. However, since APt explains the idea of Jesus' polymorphy in light of his incarnation, which is lacking in the rabbis' discussion of God, it is hard to prove that APt is dependent upon the Rabbis in its discussion of Jesus' polymorphy. It is more likely that they share some common ideas regarding the polymorphy and apply them differently to their understanding of God and Jesus.

– New Testament and Christian Traditions
The Hebrew Bible resolves the tension between the transcendent God and His manifestation in sensible appearances to His people by describing Him appearing in the visible form of a human being, through the angels, in the burning bush, or behind the luminous clouds. Some New Testament writers in the first century interpret these divine appearances on earth in a "Christianized" way that Christ as God's Son or God's Word represents God in a recognizable form.[97] I will discuss John, Philippians and Hebrews, since APt is quoting Jn 10:38 and shows similar ideas to Phil 2:6–11 and Heb 1–2.

The incarnation as the revelation of the Father in the Son is well explained by John the evangelist. In the Johannine prologue, John claims that the preexistent Word became flesh in Jesus and lived among human beings (Jn 1:14).[98] John further asserts that while no one has ever seen God, it is Jesus the only begotten Son who has made God known to human beings in a human form (1:18). Replying to Philip's request that Jesus show him God the Father, Jesus says, "Whoever has seen me has seen the Father" (14:9). Through the idea of the incarnation of the preexistent Word, John tries to resolve the tension of the Hebrew Bible regarding the transcendent God and His manifestation in sensible appearances. In this process, John reformulates the tension of the Hebrew Bible into a tension between the invisibility and the visibility of God.[99] For John, the Son is the visibility of the invisible Father.[100] APt is quoting Jn 10:38 in its discussion of the Transfiguration, mainly because John supports APt's claim for Jesus' possession of the divine majesty through his filial relationship with the Father.

It is the Philippian hymn that interprets Jesus' incarnation as a metamorphosis from "the form of God" to "the form of a slave" (Phil 2:7),

---

[97] See also Joseph Moingt, "Polymorphisme du corps du Christ," *Le temps de la réflexion* 7 (1986): 49.

[98] It is beyond doubt that John accomplishes this idea of incarnation through the Jewish concept of the preexistent Word. However, applying the preexistent Word to a human being, called Jesus, is a Christian innovation.

[99] See also, Moingt, "Polymorphisme du corps du Christ," 50.

[100] Irenaeus later develops this idea in a reciprocal way: "the Son is the visibility of the Father, and the Father is the invisibility of the Son" (*Against the Heresies* IV. 6.6).

which, according to APt, the Transfiguration reverses. Jesus, who existed in divine form, came into the world by taking on a human form. In the hymn, Jesus' taking on "the form of a slave" is equivalent to his being born in human likeness and his being found in human form. Behind the idea of "the form of a slave" there certainly lies "Christian" application of the servant songs of the second Isaiah to Jesus' incarnation: "For he grew up before him like a young plant, and like a root out of dry ground; he had *no form* or *majesty* that we should look at him, nothing in his *appearance* that we should desire him...My servant" (Isa 52:2, 11; italics are mine).[101] Is it by coincidence that APt is quoting these Isaianic passages in its discussion of Jesus' divine and human forms?

I, however, believe that Jesus' incarnation as his taking on the form of a slave can be explained not only by Isaiah, but also by Greco-Roman mythology, especially with the idea of the contrast between the superior divine form and the inferior human form. For Paul, Jesus' taking on a human form is the expression of his humbleness, because he, as the divine, condescends to the level of humans by taking their inferior form. This is why Paul finds in Jesus the best example for the Philippians to imitate. Jesus' earthly life, which is marked by his taking on of a human form, starts from the incarnation and ends with his experience of death at the cross, followed by his exaltation (Phil 2:8). I argue that the Philippian hymn is the most critical passage that has inspired the Fathers and the author of APt to interpret Jesus' appearances in multiple forms in light of the incarnation.

Similarly, Hebrews claims that Jesus was helping God at the Creation as a preexistent divine being. Jesus is the radiance of God's glory and the exact representation of His divine nature (Heb 1:2–3). It is striking that for Hebrews, Jesus is the very divine form of God. Hebrews explains the idea of incarnation in a way that God brings His firstborn Son into the world by making him appear lower than angels temporarily (1:6, 4, 14; 2:7–9). In this context, Jesus' appearing lower than angels means his incarnation in a human form. Hebrews further claims that in the incarnation, Jesus does not simply appear in the human form, but also partakes of human nature, "flesh and blood" (2:14). According to Hebrews, Jesus the divine's partaking of human nature has a clear goal of saving God's children from the devil who has power through death (2:14–17). By dying and rising up again, Jesus "frees those who have been held in slavery by the fear of death."

---

[101] Stroumsa argues that the description of Jesus as the servant, carrying the name of God in Phil 2:6–11, is from Jewish traditions on the superior angel Yahoel-Metatron. Metatron is the Servant of God, carrying God's name. See Stroumsa, "Polymorphie divine et transformations d'un mythologème: l'>>apocryhon de Jean<< et ses sources," 425–34.

This idea is similar to Peter's understanding of Jesus' incarnation in APt in many ways.

These New Testament passages betray a common "Christian" interpretation of Jesus' incarnation not only as the metamorphosis from the divine form to the human form, but also as the manifestation of the invisible God.[102] The idea of incarnation as metamorphosis continues to develop in the second century. For example, in the *Ascension of Isaiah,* when Jesus descends through seven heavens into earth, he changes his forms from the divine to the angelic to the human, so that he can hide his incarnation from the angelic beings and the archons. Here, the Transfiguration story of the Synoptics can be easily related to the incarnation in a way that the former reveals Jesus' divine form hidden at the latter event. Although the Synoptics do not mention the idea of Jesus' metamorphosis in the incarnation event, I have shown that some Church Fathers (and APt) interpret the Transfiguration story in light of the incarnation, especially through the concept of the divine/human forms.

Like the Homeric gods, Jesus in the Gospel stories takes multiple forms and also transcends temporal and spatial limitations. As Behm has already shown in his article on μορφή, the Greek word μεταμορφόομαι means "to change into another form" and the phenomenon *metamorphosis* connotes an outward change of forms perceptible to the senses (cf. Mk 9:2).[103] The metamorphosis constitutes a possibility of the polymorphous capacity of a god.[104] In Mark 16:12, after the resurrection, Jesus appears in another form (ἐν ἑτέρᾳ μορφῇ) to two of his disciples. In the Markan context, this form of the resurrected Jesus is different from both his previous human form and the divine form revealed at the Transfiguration. For the Gentile readers of Mark, Jesus may appear as a polymorphous god like Athena in the *Odyssey*.

In the Lukan story, the risen Jesus appears to two disciples on their way to Emmaus (Lk 24:13–31), but they don't recognize him. Although Luke does not mention Jesus' other form, the fact that the two disciples fail in recognizing Jesus indicates that the risen Jesus appears in a different form than his previous human form that they used to see. In this Lukan story, as soon as the two recognize Jesus, he suddenly disappears with extreme speed like the Homeric gods (24:31); then he suddenly reappears among the other disciples (24:36).

Similarly, in the resurrection story of John, Mary only finds two angels in Jesus' tomb and begins weeping (John 20:11–18). Jesus suddenly appears and stands beside her, but she cannot recognize him. She thinks that

---

[102] See also, Moingt, "Polymorphisme du corps du Christ," 48–52.

[103] Behm, "μορφή," 755.

[104] Garcia, "La polymorphie du Christ. Remarques sur quelques definitions et sur de multiples enjeux," 44.

he is a gardener who stole Jesus' body.[105] In the immediately following story, where the disciples gathered with the doors shut for fear of the Jews, Jesus suddenly appears among them, coming through the wall like a ghost (20:19). Would the readers of the Gospels who are familiar with the Homeric epics find any difference between these appearances of the risen Jesus and those of the Homeric gods? One of the challenges that the readers of the Gospels have to resolve is how to distinguish Jesus from the Homeric gods.

6.5 Conclusion

In the second century C.E., the Transfiguration tradition continues to develop in multiple ways, and the polymorphy as its most distinctive development is attested to in some apocryphal writings and in writings by the early Church Fathers. The polymorphy of APt is the result of the interpretation of the Transfiguration in light of the incarnation idea and of Greco-Roman mythology. Already in the New Testament, some biblical writers discuss Jesus' appearance on earth in multiple forms. Also, some Jewish traditions discuss God's manifestations in physically sensible ways. I argue that along with the Church Fathers, APt (and ApoJn and AJn) engages in conversation with the ongoing Christian discussion of polymorphy, though not without adapting it to its new contextual need – Peter's defense of Jesus' divinity against Simon. In APt, the polymorphy *visually* recapitulates Jesus' benevolent mercy toward humanity shown by the incarnation and the Transfiguration, while the polyonymy *poetically* accounts for it. While the Fathers discuss the idea of the polymorphy in a theological discourse, APt portrays it in the form of a narrative, but with the same theological emphasis. APt not only interprets the scriptural story of the Transfiguration as Jesus' polymorphous appearance, but also demonstrates that the believers participate in the scriptural story in a new and creative way, so that the story of the past becomes continuously re-enacted in the current lives of the readers. Since Jesus of the Gospels is the same Jesus who is present in APt's community, the old stories about his saving act should be present reality among the current readers' experience.

Similarly to ApoPt and 2 Pet, APt betrays the apologetic tendency of not mentioning Peter's failure in understanding Jesus' teaching of the suffering and death. Instead, Peter in APt emphasizes Jesus' role as the Suffering Servant and follows him in the path of martyrdom, experiencing the crucifixion with his head downwards. The motif of the Suffering Servant

---

[105] See also, Lalleman, "Polymorphy of Christ," 115–16; and Garcia, "La polymorphie du Christ. Remarques sur quelques definitions et sur de multiples enjeux," 23–24.

with the loathsome form functions to connect the two events of the Transfiguration and the incarnation. Moses and Elijah are forgotten and are subsumed under Jesus' three human forms. In APt, Jesus becomes God on his own rather than the visible manifestation of the invisible God in the Synoptics and John. Jesus manifests his divinity by showing his great power to take multiple forms like the Homeric gods. Apart from APt's description of Jesus' polymorphous forms in different ages, Christian thinkers continue to develop Jesus' polymorphy in terms of substance (AJn), stature (the *Gospel of Peter*), and the Trinity (the *Acts of Philip*; cf. AJn 2). Jesus often appears in the forms of the apostles. Jesus' appearance in the forms of his apostles asserts that Jesus in heaven still works in the lives of the believers through his human agents on earth.[106]

---

[106] Even in some of the apocryphal writings, the demonic powers imitate Jesus by appearing in a polymorphous way.

Chapter 7

Conclusion

When readers of the synoptic Gospels reach the end of the Gospel stories, they are often surprised at the lack of description of Jesus' glory at his resurrection. The synoptic writers do mention an angelic figure in luminous clothes, but they do not attempt to describe Jesus' resurrected body, and the risen Jesus simply appears in one place like a ghost and then suddenly disappears. This makes it all the more amazing to read the synoptic's description of Jesus' glorious appearance at the Transfiguration. Before coming to the Transfiguration story, readers often find Jesus described as being misunderstood, hungry, and threatened by his fellow countrymen. When Jesus appears in his glory at the Transfiguration, readers realize that there is much below the surface of Jesus' life, that his true identity has, up until now, been hidden from human eyes. With its powerful messages and symbols, it is no wonder that the Transfiguration story has enjoyed great popularity among Christian believers.

Due to this popularity, there is a large amount of material pertaining to this one story. In my exploration of the Transfiguration, I concentrate on a few pertinent early Christian texts, where Peter appears as a major witness of Jesus' transfiguration, in order to demonstrate how the Transfiguration story functioned to provide first and second century Christian believers with meaningful solutions for various Christological, ecclesiological, anthropological, apologetic and eschatological issues. The early believers did not simply re-present the story in the same traditional form in which they received it, but re-interpreted and re-wrote it in order to meet their particular needs. In this process, the Transfiguration story continued to grow, acquiring new elements and emphases in its new contexts, especially having to do with the apostle Peter. In this conclusion, I recapitulate four different topics which are the result of my research: (1) Jesus and his transfiguration, (2) Peter, (3) the believers' transformation and the Parousia, and (4) scriptures, traditions, and culture.

7.1 Jesus and His Transfiguration

In the Markan Transfiguration account, Jesus appears not only as a human or human messiah, but also as a divine being in human disguise. According to Mark's theological scheme, Jesus not only fulfills Israelite messianic concepts such as the Son of Man, the Son of God and the Suffering Servant, but also stands as God's Son in the heavenly council with God and angels. Clothed in luminous, white clothes, the transfigured Jesus reinforces the fact of his heavenly belonging, and God's voice issuing from a cloud confirms Jesus' divine Sonship.

Probing into the past of the Markan Transfiguration story, I compare it with Paul's transformation account in 2 Cor 3. I demonstrate how Paul and Mark share similar ideas, including: (1) the use of the rare Greek verb μεταμορφόομαι, (2) the strong δόξα (glory) motif found in Jesus, (3) its legitimating function, (4) the paradoxical character of glorious transformation, i.e. transformation only after suffering, (5) the transformative and apocalyptic quality of the glory, and (6) Jesus as the divine carrier of the glory and the author of believers' transformation. Since it is unlikely that Mark is dependent upon Paul on the literary level or vice versa, I argue that it is reasonable to conclude that behind their accounts lies an early Jesus tradition where Jesus is glorified after his suffering and death and goes beyond Moses as God's Son as well as the carrier of the divine glory. In its first chapters, Hebrews witnesses to this Jesus tradition independently from Mark and Paul, confirming that before the Transfiguration, there is an early Christian description of Jesus in glory in comparison with or in contrast to Moses in glory.

Matthew and Luke, the first readers of Mark, share with Mark the conviction that Jesus as God's Son goes beyond Moses and Elijah. While keeping intact the basic storyline of the Markan Transfiguration, Matthew and Luke strengthen the marvel of Jesus' transfiguration by introducing the new elements of Jesus' brilliant face and his glory. In Matthew's account, Jesus' face shines like the sun, and in Luke's account, the glory becomes Jesus' permanent possession rather than exclusively that of his Father. Matthew and Luke both reinforce the motif of Jesus' divine Sonship at the Transfiguration by relating it to Jesus' birth story where God and the angels are actively involved. For Matthew, Jesus is now Immanuel, and for Luke, Jesus' entire life is divinely orchestrated by God from its beginning to its end. It is no wonder that later Christian readers begin to read the Transfiguration story in connection with Jesus' incarnation (e.g. APt 20).

In APt, Jesus appears as the Christian God who is worthy of being worshipped by the Romans. When Simon Magus ridicules Peter's belief in Jesus as the Christian God, Jesus performs miracles through Peter, appears to believers in the form of Peter, and shows himself in his divine form of

light and then in three human forms. Both the Transfiguration and the polymorphy reveal Jesus' benevolent mercy toward the believers. For APt,
the Transfiguration and the incarnation are not two different stories, but
two different aspects of the one unified story of Jesus. APt claims that at
the incarnation, Jesus appeared on earth in his human form in order to save
humanity from destruction; at the Transfiguration Jesus revealed his divine
form of the light. Furthermore, for APt Jesus continues to appear on earth
in multiple forms (polymorphy) and with multiple names (polyonymy),
because he is willing to intervene in the salvation history for the welfare of
his believers.

7.2 Peter

It is of interest that the Transfiguration is remembered in conjunction with
Peter the apostle, as if he is the guarantor of the story. In Mark, however,
Peter appears spiritually blind, ignorant of Jesus' identity and mission.
When he rejects Jesus' teaching about suffering and death, Jesus calls him
"Satan." In their accounts, and for different reasons, Matthew and Luke
attempt to mitigate the negative tone of the Markan description of Peter.
Luke omits Peter's ignorance of Jesus' teaching because he wants to har-
monize the ministry of the Twelve, which Peter represents, with that of the
Hellenists. Matthew portrays Peter as one who received the revelation of
Jesus' divine Sonship from God. Because of his confession of Jesus as
God's Son, Jesus in Matthew promises that he will build the church upon
the rock, Peter. In this way, Matthew provides a foundational story legiti-
mizing his community's origin.

2 Peter continues to develop this tendency toward the Petrine importance in the Church's remembrance of the Transfiguration story. In 2 Peter,
Peter the apostle appears as the main human character, not because he is
the apostle *par excellence*, but because the church has remembered the story with his special role as the spokesperson of the disciples. When the author of 2 Peter needs someone who can buttress his truth claim for the certainty of the Parousia on the basis of the Transfiguration, he finds Peter the
best candidate. The author makes a word play on the term "tent" and
creates a pseudepigraphic setting of Peter's farewell speech at his death.

Also in ApoPt, Peter's spiritual blindness is forgotten and his importance in relation to the Transfiguration is heightened. Especially in the
Rainer fragment, Peter's death in Rome ("a city ruling over the west") is
understood to be a part of the spiritual Eucharist – Peter must drink the cup
which Jesus promised (R 14:4). Moreover, Peter's martyrdom is the first
eschatological sign of Jesus' judgment. This is true of APt's portrayal of
Peter as well. Similarly to ApoPt and 2 Peter, APt shows the apologetic

tendency of not mentioning Peter's failure in understanding Jesus' mission and identity. Instead, Peter in APt appears as a powerful miracle worker like Jesus and heroically confronts his martyrdom even with his head downwards.

It is interesting that all three of these second century texts remember Peter's death along with the Transfiguration, but with different implications. While in 2 Peter, Peter's death functions as a pseudepigraphic setting of his farewell speech, both ApoPt and APt emphasize his death as martyrdom. For ApoPt, Peter's martyrdom was a spiritual Eucharist and the beginning of the eschatological judgment; for APt, it reveals how the world turned upside down after Adam's fall and how Jesus restored it to right order through his Crucifixion.

Peter is remembered along with the Transfiguration story as its major eyewitness and as the genuine transmitter of the Transfiguration story. He plays an integral role while being invested with new functions that were lacking in the synoptic versions.

7.3 The Believers' Transformation and the Parousia

In the Caesarea-Philippi context, the Markan Transfiguration validates Jesus' teaching about suffering, death, and resurrection as vindication. God's own command, "listen to him" (Mk 9:7), draws the disciples' attention to Jesus' teaching immediately before the Transfiguration. In his teaching, Jesus not only announces his and his disciples' destiny of suffering, death, and resurrection, but he also speaks of his coming as the Son of Man at the Parousia. On his second coming, Jesus, who is now the eschatological Son of Man, will vindicate believers who follow him along the same path. As a part of their vindication, believers are promised that they, too, will experience a transformation in glory similar to Jesus' transfiguration. The appearance of Moses and Elijah strengthens this promise, since for Mark, these two represent the righteous believers in heaven.

Paul shows ideas similar to Mark's in the description of the believers' transformation. In particular, the glorious transformation comes only after persecution and suffering (2 Cor 4:10; Rom 8:17; Phil 3:10). Paul confesses that he is willing to follow Jesus along the path of suffering and death so that the life of Jesus may abound in his mortal body and he may acquire the eternal weight of glory (2 Cor 4:11, 17). For Paul, the glorious risen Lord is the crucified Jesus and suffering with Christ is one of the most crucial aspects of being a believer. For Paul, however, the believers' transformation is not an event in the future, but an ongoing present reality, although it awaits its final climax at the end of time. The believers who have been in the process of glorious transformation, says Paul, will appear before the judgment seat of Christ (2 Cor 5:10) and will receive the eternal glory on the Day of the Lord (2 Cor 5:5; 1 Cor 1:14).

Matthew and Luke make the theme of believers' transformation, which is implicit in Mark, more explicit in their rewritings of Mark. In his description of Jesus' transfiguration, Matthew introduces a new element: Jesus' face, as brilliant as the sun. This idea recalls Matthew's prediction that believers' future existence will be like the sun. Luke introduces the term *glory* not only in his description of Jesus, but also in his description of Moses and Elijah at the Transfiguration. In the Lukan account, the glorious bodies of Moses and Elijah align themselves with other angelic beings. Furthermore, the transformation of Stephen's face into that of an angel informs the readers that the believers in heaven at the end will be like the glorious Moses, Elijah, Stephen and the angels.

The ideas of the believers' transformation and the Parousia continue to grow in the second century CE. 2 Peter's understanding of the believers' transformation is similar to that of Paul for many reasons. For 2 Peter, Jesus' glory and honor at the Transfiguration functions as the evidence of his second coming at the Parousia. However, since there is uncertainty about the exact timing of the Parousia, 2 Peter acknowledges that the delay of the Parousia is an opportunity for both believers and non-believers. For non-believers, the delay is an expression of God's mercy toward sinners, offering them an opportunity for repentance. For believers, it is now in their current lives that they should be partakers of the divine nature, that is, of Jesus' majesty, power, honor and glory. Similarly to the glory of the Lord for Paul, Jesus' divine nature for 2 Peter is not only the motivating power of the believers' present transformation, but also the very goal of their destiny.

For ApoPt, on the other hand, the Parousia is imminent. Since the Parousia will come true very soon, ApoPt does not draw its readers' attention to their present ethical lifestyle or present transformation. Instead, ApoPt urges believers to hope for their glorious existence in paradise. ApoPt presents the glorious bodies of Moses and Elijah at the Transfiguration as the luminous bodies of the believers in the paradisiac garden.

7.4 Scriptures, Traditions and Culture

Because Mark and Paul consider the Hebrew Bible to be the authoritative scriptures, they interpret Jesus' life and ministry in light of the scriptures. For Jesus' Transfiguration and the believers' transformation, respectively, the scriptural story of Moses' transformation in Exodus provides Mark and Paul with their basic storyline. However, their use of the scriptures is not such that the scriptures exclusively dominate their view on Jesus. Early

Christian believers before Mark and Paul actively reinterpreted the scriptures through the new lens of the Jesus event. Furthermore, the scriptures reach the hands of Mark and Paul along with their rich interpretive traditions. We have seen that behind the transformation accounts of Paul and Mark lies an early Jesus tradition with the motifs of glory, the comparison with Moses and the Suffering Servant. Furthermore, Paul and Mark do not exist in isolation from their surrounding culture, but live in relationship to it. Mark finds the general phenomenon of metamorphosis with epiphany useful for his description of Jesus; Paul makes use of a similar idea to a mystery religion – human beings experience transformation by observing their religious hero.

In their retelling of the Transfiguration story, the second century writers not only depend upon the scriptural stories of the Transfiguration, the synoptic version in particular, but also take advantage of extra-canonical traditions and cultural norms of religious expression. Both 2 Peter and ApoPt supplement the synoptic story with the aid of Jewish pseudepigraphic writings, especially the Enochic materials. ApoPt, in its rewriting of the two synoptic stories, the Transfiguration and the Olivet discourse, uses the Enochic traditions and makes two extensive additions of the tour of hell and the paradisiac garden.

In its retelling of the Transfiguration as a polymorphy, APt offers an interesting example of the dynamic relationship between the Scriptures, their interpretive traditions and the existing culture of the time. The community of APt venerates the scriptures in their worship and believes that they contain the divine will. In addition, however, the community claims that it is their interpretive traditions that reveal deeper aspects of the divine will hidden behind the written texts. According to APt's interpretive traditions of the Transfiguration, the Transfiguration is a part of the entire story of Jesus on earth, with its beginning at the incarnation. Both the incarnation and the Transfiguration reveal Jesus' divine mercy toward the believers, expressed, in particular, in his polymorphy and polyonymy. The polymorphy results from the early believers' interpretation of the Transfiguration in light of the Christian incarnation idea and of the Greco-Roman mythology about polymorphism. By putting their interpretive traditions of the Transfiguration story in the mouth of Peter, they make these traditions as genuine and old as the apostle. APt's retelling of the Transfiguration story indicates that the scriptures exist not in a vacuum, but alongside ongoing interpretations by the believers, believers who are necessarily in dialogue with their culture, challenging or accommodating cultural expectations or norms.

Bibliography

Achtemeier, Paul J. "Jesus and the Disciples as Miracle Workers in the Apocryphal New Testament." In *Aspects of Religious Propaganda in Judaism and Early Christianity*, edited by Elisabeth Schüssler Fiorenza, 149–87. Notre Dame: University of Notre Dame Press, 1976.

Adamik, T. "The Description of Paradise in the Apocalypse of Peter." In *The Apocalypse of Peter*, edited by Jan N. Bremer and Istvan Czachesz, 78–90. Leuven: Peeters, 2003.

Alexander, P.S. "Retelling the Old Testament." In *It Is Written. Scripture Citing Scripture.*, edited by D.A. Carson and H.G.M. Williamson, 99–121. Cambridge: Cambridge Press, 1988.

Allison, Dale C. *Matthew: A Shorter Commentary*. London; New York: T & T Clark International, 2004.

— *The New Moses. A Matthean Typology*. Minneapolis: Fortress, 1993.

Andreopoulos, Andreas. *Metamorphosis: the Transfiguration in Byzantine Theology and Iconography*. Crestwood, New York: St Vladimir's Seminary Press, 2005.

Auerbach, E. *Moses*. Detroit: Wayne, 1975.

Bacon, B.W. *Studies in Matthew*. New York: H. Holt and Company, 1930.

Baldwin, Matthew C. *Whose Acts of Peter? WUNT 196*. Tübingen, Germany: Mohr Siebeck, 2005.

Barnett, Paul. *The Second Epistle to the Corinthians*. Grand Rapids, Michigan: William B. Eerdmans Publishing Co., 1997.

Barr, James. "Theophany and Anthropomorphism in the Old Testament." *Vetus Testamentum* 7 (1959): 31–38.

Barrett, C. K. "Stephen and the Son of Man." In *Apophoreta: Festschrift für Ernst Haenchen zu Seinem Siebzigsten Geburtstag*, 32–38. Berlin: Töpelmann, 1964.

Barton, Stephen C. "The Transfiguration of Christ according to Mark and Matthew: Christology and Anthropology." In *Auferstehung – Resurrection*, edited by F. Avemarie and H. Lichtenberger, 231–46. Tübingen: Mohr Siebeck, 1999.

Bauckham, Richard J. "2 Peter and the Apocalypse of Peter." In *The Fate of the Dead*, 290–303. Leiden; Boston: Brill, 1998.

— Apocalypse de Pierre. Introduction." In *Écrits apocryphes chrétiens*, edited by François Bovon and P. Geoltrain, 747–49. Paris: Gallimard, 1997.

— "The Apocalypse of Peter: A Jewish Christian Apocalypse from the Time of Bar Kokhba." *Apocrypha* 5 (1994): 7–111.

— *The Fate of the Dead: Studies on the Jewish and Christian Apocalypses*. Leiden; Boston: Brill, 1998.

— "Jews and Jewish Christians in the Land of Israel at the Time of Bar Kochba War, with Special Reference to the Apocalypse of Peter." In *Tolerance and Intolerance in Early Judaism and Christianity*, edited by Graham N. Stanton and Guy G. Stroumsa, 228–38. Cambridge: University Press, 1998.

— *Jude, 2 Peter. Word Biblical Commentary*. Waco, Texas: Word Books, 1983.

— "Pseudo-Apostolic Letters." *JBL* 107 (1988): 469–494.

— "A Quotation from 4Q Second Ezekiel in the Apocalypse of Peter." *RQ* 15 (1991–92): 437–64.

— "The Two Fig Tree Parables in the Apocalypse of Peter." *JBL* 104 (1985): 269–87.

Behm, J. "μορφή." In *TDNT*, edited by G. Kittel, vol. 4: 743–59, 1967.

Beker, J. Christiaan. *Paul the Apostle: The Triumph of God in Life and Thought*. Philadelphia: Fortress Press, 1984.

Belleville, Linda L. *Reflections of Glory*. JSNTSup 52; Sheffield: JSOT Press, 1991.

— "Tradition or Creation? Paul's Use of the Exodus 34 Tradition in 2 Corinthians 3.7–18." In *Paul and the Scriptures of Israel*, edited by Craig A. Evans and James A. Sanders, 165–86. Sheffield: JSOT Press, 1993.

Betz, Hans D. *Galatians*. Philadelphia: Fortress Press, 1979.

— "Jesus as Divine Man." In *Jesus and the Historian*, edited by F.T. Trotter, 114–33. Philadelphia: Westminster Press, 1968.

Blackburn, Barry. *Theios Aner and the Markan Miracle Traditions*, WUNT. Tübingen: Mohr, 1991.

Bolyki, J. "False Prophets in the Apocalypse of Peter." In *The Apocalypse of Peter*, edited by Jan N. Bremmer and Istvan Czachesz, 52–62. Leuven: Peeters, 2003.

— "'Head Downward': The Cross of Peter in the Lights of the Apocryphal Acts, of the New Testament and of the Society-transforming Claim of Early Christianity." In *The Apocryphal Acts of Peter*, edited by Jan N. Bremmer, 111–22. Leuven: Peeters, 1998.

Bonz, Marianne Palmer. *The Past As Legacy: Luke–Acts and Ancient Epic*. Minneapolis: Fortress Press, 2000.

Boobyer, G. H. *St. Mark and the Transfiguration Story*. Edinburgh: T&T Clark, 1942.

Boring, M. Eugene. "Gospel and Church in 2 Peter." *Mid-Stream* 35 (1996): 399–406.

Bornkamm, Günther. *Die Vorgeschichte des sogenannten Zweiten Korintherbriefe*. Heidelberg: Carl Winter, 1965.

Bousset, Wilhelm. *Kyrios Christos: Geschichte des Christusglaubens von den Anfängen des Christentums bis Irenaeus*. Göttingen: Vandenhoeck & Ruprecht, 1935.

Bovon, François. "Apostolic Memories in Early Christianity." In *Studies in Early Christianity*, 1–16. Tübingen: Mohr Siebeck, 2003.

— "The Dossier on Stephen, the First Martyr." *HTR* 96 (2003): 279–315.

— *Luke*. Vol. 1. Minneapolis: Fortress Press, 2002.

— "Names and Numbers in Early Christianity." *NTS* 47 (2001): 267–88

— *Luke the Theologian*. 2nd ed. Waco, TX: Baylor University Press, 2006.

— "The Effect of Realism and Prophetic Ambiguity in the Works of Luke." In *New Testament Traditions and Apocryphal Narratives*, 97–104. Allison Park, PA: Pickwick Publications, 1995.

Bovon, François and Bertrand Bouvier. "Un fragment grec inédit des Actes de Pierre?" *Apocrypha* 17 (2006): 9–54.

Boyarin, Daniel. *Intertextuality and the Reading of Midrash*. Bloomington & Indianapolis: Indiana University Press, 1990.

Bremmer, Jan N. "The Apocalypse of Peter: Greek or Jewish?" In *The Apocalypse of Peter*, edited by Jan N. Bremmer, 1–14. Leuven: Peeters, 2003.

— *The Apocryphal Acts of Peter*. Leuven: Peeters, 1998.

— "Bibliography of the Apocalypse of Peter." In *The Apocalypse of Peter*, edited by Jan N. Bremmer and Istvan Czachesz, 200–203. Leuven: Peeters, 2003.

Bright, J. *A History of Israel*. London: SCM Press, 1980.

Buchholz, Dennis D. *Your Eyes Will Be Opened: A Study of the Greek (Ethiopic) Apocalypse of Peter*. Atlanta, Ga: Scholars Press, 1988.

Bultmann, Rudolf. *History of the Synoptic Tradition*. New York: Harper and Row, 1976.

Burkert, Walter. *Greek Religion*. Translated by John Raffan. Cambridge: Harvard University Press, 1985.

Burkill, T. A. *Mysterious Revelation: An Examination of the Philosophy of St. Mark's Gospel.* Ithaca, N.Y.: Cornell University, 1963.

Byrne, Brendan. "Jesus as Messiah in the Gospel of Luke: Discerning a Pattern of Correction." *CBQ* 65 (2003): 80–95.

Caragounis, Chrys C. *The Son of Man: Vision and Interpretation.* WUNT 1/38; Tübingen: Mohr–Siebeck, 1986.

Carlson, R.A. "Elie à l'Horeb." *VT* 19 (1969): 416–39.

Carlston, C.E. "Transfiguration and Resurrection." *JBL* 80 (1961): 233–40.

Cartlidge, David R. "Transfiguration of Metamorphosis Traditions in the *Acts of John, Thomas,* and *Peter.*" *Semeia* 38 (1986): 53–66.

Chester, Andrew. "Resurrection and Transformation." In *Auferstehung – Resurrection,* edited by F. Avemarie and H. Lichtenberger, 47–77. Tübingen: Mohr Siebeck, 1999.

Chilton, B. C. *God in Strength: Jesus' Announcement of the Kingdom.* Freistadt: Plöchl, 1979.

Clifford, R.J. *The Cosmic Mountain in Canaan and the Old Testament.* Cambridge: Harvard University Press, 1972.

Coats, G. W. *Moses: Heroic Man, Man of God.* Sheffield: JSOT Press, 1988.

Collange, Jean-François. *Énigmes de la deuxième épître de Paul aux Corinthiens; étude exégétique de 2 Cor. 2:14–7:4.* Cambridge: University Press, 1972.

Collins, Adela Yarbro. "Mark and His Readers: The Son of God among Jews." *HTR* 92 (1999): 393–408.

— "Rulers, Divine Men, and Walking on the Water." In *Religious Propaganda and Missionary Competition in the New Testament World,* edited by L. Bormann, K. del Tredici and A. Standhartinger, 207–27. Leiden/New York: Brill, 1994.

Collins, John. "The Heavenly Representative: the 'Son of Man' in the Similitude of Enoch." In *Ideal Figures in Ancient Judaism,* edited by John J. Collins and George E. W. Nickelsburg. Chico, Calif.: Scholars Press, 1980.

Collins, John J. *Scepter and the Star.* New York: Doubleday, 1995.

Crump, David Michael. *Jesus the Intercessor: Prayer and Christology in Luke–Acts.* Tübingen: J.C.B. Mohr, 1992.

Czachesz, Istvan. "The Grotesque Body in the Apocalypse of Peter." In *The Apocalypse of Peter,* edited by Jan N. Bremer and Istvan Czachesz, 108–126. Leuven: Peeters, 2003.

Danker, F. W. *Benefactor.* St. Louis: Clayton Publishing House, 1982.

Davies, Stevan L. *The Revolt of the Widows: the Social World of the Apocryphal Acts.* Carbondale: Southern Illinois University Press, 1980.

Dawsey, James M. *The Lukan Voice: Confusion and Irony in the Gospel of Luke.* Macon, GA: Mercer University Press, 1986.

Deutsch, Celia. "The Transfiguration: Vision and Social Setting in Matthew's Gospel (Matthew 17:1–9)." In *Putting Body & Soul Together: Essays in Honor of Robin Scroggs,* edited by Virginia Wiles, Alexandra Brown and Graydon F. Snyder, 125–37. Valley Forge, PA: Trinity Press International, 1997.

Dietrich, B. C. "Divine Epiphanies in Homer." *Numen* 30 (2004): 53–79.

Dodd, C. H. *According to the Scriptures: The Sub-culture of New Testament Theology.* New York: Scribner, 1953.

— "The Appearances of the Risen Christ: An Essay in Form-Criticism of the Gospels." In *Studies in the Gospels,* edited by C. H. Dodd. Oxford: Blackwell, 1955.

Donaldson, Terence L. *Jesus on the Mountain.* JSNT Supp. 8; Sheffield: JSOT Press, 1985.

Duling, Dennis C., and Norman Perrin. *The New Testament: Proclamation and Parenesis, Myth and History*. 3rd ed. Fort Worth: Harcourt Brace College Publishers, 1994.

Dunn, James D. G. "2 Corinthians 3.17 – 'the Lord is the Spirit'." *JTS* 21 (1970): 309–20.

— *Christology in the Making*. London: SCM Press, 1989.

— *The Theology of Paul the Apostle*. Grand Rapids: Eerdmans, 1998.

Elliot, J. K. *The Apocryphal New Testament*. Oxford: Clarendon Press, 1993.

Farkasfalvy, Denis. "The Ecclesial Setting of Pseudepigraphy in Second Peter." *The Second Century* 5 (1985/1986): 3–29.

Fee, Gordon D. *God's Empowering Presence*. Peabody: Hendrickson, 1994.

Fitzmyer, Joseph A. "The Composition of Luke, Chapter 9." In *Perspectives on Luke–Acts*, 139–52. Danville, VA: Association of Baptist Professors of Religion, 1978.

— "Glory Reflected on the Face of Christ (2 Cor 3.7–4.6) and a Palestine Jewish Motif." *Theological Studies* 42 (1981): 630–44.

— *The Gospel According to Luke*. Vol. 1. Garden City, NY: Doubleday, 1981.

Fletcher-Louis, C.H.T. "The Revelation of the Sacral Son of Man. The Genre, History of Religions Context and the Meaning of the Transfiguration." In *Auferstehung – Resurrection*, edited by F. Avemarie and H. Lichtenberger, 247–98. Tübingen: Mohr Siebeck, 2001.

Flusser, D. *Jesus*. Translated by R. Walls. New York: Herder & Herder, 1969.

Fornberg, Tord. *An Early Church in a Pluralistic Society*. Uppsala: Gleerup, 1977.

Fossum, Jarl E. *The Image of the Invisible God*. Göttingen: Vandenhoeck and Ruprecht, 1995.

Fox, Robin Lane. *Pagans and Christians*. New York: Alfred A. Knopf, Inc., 1987.

France, R. T. *The Gospel of Matthew*. Grand Rapids, Mich.: William B. Eerdmans, 2007.

Freyne, Sean. *Galilee, Jesus and the Gospel*. Dublin: Gill & Macmillan, 1988.

— "The Geography of Restoration: Galilee–Jerusalem Relations in Early Jewish and Christian Experience." *NTS* 47 (2001): 289–311.

Furnish, Victor P. *2 Corinthians, The Anchor Bible*. Garden City, NY: Doubleday & Company, Inc., 1984.

Gager, John. *Moses in Greco-Roman Paganism*. Nashiville: Abingdon Press, 1972.

Gamble, Harry Y. *Books and Readers in the Early Church*. New Haven: Yale University Press, 1995.

Garcia, Hughes. "La polymorphie du Christ. Remarques sur quelques definitions et sur de multiples enjeux." *Apocrypha* 10 (1999): 16–55.

Gathercole, Simon. *The Preexistent Son: Recovering the Christologies of Matthew, Mark, and Luke*. Grand Rapids, Mich.: W.B. Eerdmans, 2006.

Georgi, Dieter. *Die Gegner des Paulus im 2 Korintherbrief*. Neukirchen–Vluyn: Neukirchen Verlag, 1964.

Gieschen, Charles A. *Angelomorphic Christology*. New York: Brill, 1998.

Gilmour, Michael J. *The Significance of Parallels between 2 Peter and Other Early Christian Literature*. Atlanta: Society of Biblical Literature, 2002.

— *The Significance of Parallels between 2 Peter and Other Early Christian Literature*. Leiden; Boston: Brill, 2002.

Gleason, Randall C. "Paul's Covenantal Contrasts in 2 Corinthians 3.1–11." *Bibliotheca Sacra* 154 (1997): 61–79.

Goguel, Maurice. *La Foi en la Résurrection de Jésus dans le christianisme primitif*. Paris: Ernest Leroux, 1933.

— "A propos du texte nouveau de l'Apocalypse de Pierre." *Revue de l'histoire des religions* 89 (1924): 191–209.

Goldin, Judah. *The Song at the Sea; Being a Commentary on a Commentary in Two Parts.* New Haven: Yale University Press, 1971.

Goodenough, Erwin R. *By Light, Light: The Mystic Gospel of Hellenistic Judaism.* New Haven: Yale University Press, 1935.

— "The Political philosophy of Hellenistic Kingship." In *Yale Classical Studies,* edited by Austin M. Harmon, 55–102. New Haven: Yale University Press, 1928.

Grébaut, Sylvain. "Littérature Éthiopienne pseudo-clémentne." *Revue de l'Orient chrétien* 15 (1910): 198–214, 307–323, 425–439.

Green, Joel B. *The Gospel of Luke.* Grand Rapids, MI: William B. Eerdmans, 1997.

Greenwood, David. "The Lord is the Spirit: Some Considerations of 2 Cor 3:17." *CBQ* 34 (1972): 464–72.

Grindheim, Sigurd. "The Law Kills but the Gospel Gives Life." *JSNT* 84 (2001): 97–115.

Grundmann, W. *Der Brief des Judas und der zweite Brief des Petrus.* Berlin: Evangelische Berlagsanstalt, 1974.

Gundry, Robert. *Mark: A Commentary on His Apology for the Cross.* Grand Rapids, Mich.: Eerdmans, 1993.

Gunther, J. J. *St. Paul's Opponents and Their Background: A Study of Apocalyptic and Jewish Sectarian Teachings.* Vol. 35, *NovTSup.* Leiden: Brill, 1973.

Hafemann, Scott J. *Paul, Moses, and the History of Israel.* Tübingen: Mohr, 1995.

Hahn, Ferdinand. *The Titles of Jesus in Christology.* Cambridge: James Clarke & Co., 2002.

Hanson, A. T. *Studies in Paul's Technique and Theology.* London: SPCK, 1974.

Harrington, Daniel J. *The Gospel of Matthew. Sacra Pagina Series.* Collegeville, MN: The Liturgical Press, 1991.

— *Jude and 2 Peter. Sacra Pagina Series.* Collegeville, Minnesota: A Michael Clazier Book?

Harris, Murray. *The Second Epistle to the Corinthians, The New International Greek Testament Commentary.* Grand Rapids, Michigan: William B. Eerdmans Publishing Co., 2005.

Hasitschka, Martin. "'Diener eines neuen Bundes'. Skizze zum Selbstverständnis des Paulus in 2 Kor." *ZKT* 121 (1999): 291–99.

Heil, John P. *The Transfiguration of Jesus.* Rome: Editrice Pontificio Instituto Biblico, 2000.

Hengel, Martin. *Judaism and Hellenism: Studies in Their Encounter in Palestine during the Early Hellenistic Period.* 2 vols. Philadelphia: Fortress, 1974.

Hermann, Ingo. *Kyrios und Pneuma; Studien zur Christologie der paulinischen Hauptbriefe.* München: Kösel–Verlag, 1961.

Hilhorst, A. "The Text of the *Actus Vercellenses.*" In *The Apocryphal Acts of Peter,* edited by Jan N. Bremer, 148–60. Leuven: Peeters, 1998.

Hill, Craig C. *Hellenists and Hebrews: Reappraising Division within the Earliest Church.* Minneapolis: Fortress Press, 1992.

Hills, Julian V. "Parables, Pretenders, and Prophecies: Translation and Interpretation in the *Apocalypse of Peter* 2." *RB* (1991): 560–573.

Holladay, C. R. *Theios Aner in Hellenistc Judaism.* Missoula: Scholars Press, 1977.

Hooker, Morna Dorothy. *A Commentary on the Gospel according to St. Mark.* London: A & C Black, 1991.

Hurtado, Larry W. *One God, One Lord: Early Christian Devotion and Ancient Jewish Monotheism.* New York: Continuum, 1998.

Isaac, E. "1 Enoch." In *The Old Testament Pseudepigrapha,* edited by James H. Charlesworth, 5–89. New York; London; Toronto; Sydney; Auckland: Doubleday, 1983.

Jacoby, A. "Altheidnisch-Aegyptishes im Christentum." *Sfinx* (1903): 107–17.

James, M.R. "A New Text of the Apocalypse of Peter I–III." *JTS* 12 (1911): 36–54, 362–83, 573–83.

— "The Rainer Fragment of the Apocalypse of Peter." *JTS* (1931): 270–79.

Jaubert, Annie. *La notion d'alliance dans le judaisme aux abords de l'ère chrétienne.* Paris: Éditions du Seuil, 1963.

Jeremias, J. "Moses." In *TDNT*, 4:848–873, 1967.

Jones, F Stanley. "Principal Orientations on the Relations between the Apocryphal Acts (Acts of Paul and *Acts of John*; Acts of Peter and *Acts of John*)." In *Society of Biblical Literature Seminar Papers*, 485–505, 1993.

Junod, Eric. "Polymorphie du Dieu Sauveur." In *Gnosticisme et monde hellénistique*, edited by J. Ries, 38–46: Publications de l'institut orientaliste de Louvain 27; Louvain–La–Neuve: Université catholique de Louvain, 1982.

Junod, Eric, and Jean-Daniel Kaestli. *Acta Iohannis.* 2 vols, *Corpus Christianorum* 1–2. Turnhout: Brepols, 1983.

Kahana, Menahem. "The Editions of the *Mekilta de-Rabbi Ishmael* on Exodus in the Light of Geniza Fragments." *Tarbiz* 45 (1986): 515–20.

Käsemann, E. "An Apologia for Primitive Christian Eshatology." In *Essays on New Testament Themes*, 169–95. London: SCM, 1964.

— "Der Glaube Abrahams." In *Paulinische Perspektiven*, edited by E. Käsemann, 140–77. Tübingen: Mohr, 1969.

Kee, H.C. "The Transfiguration in Mark: Epiphany or Apocalyptic Vision?" In *Understanding the Sacred Texts*, edited by J. Reumann, 135–52. Valley Forge, Pa: Judson Press, 1972.

Keel, O. *The Symbolism of the Biblical World: Ancient Near Eastern Iconography and the Book of Psalms.* New York: Seabury Press, 1978.

Keener, Craig S. *A Commentary on the Gospel of Matthew.* Grand Rapids, MI: William B. Eeerdmans, 1999.

Kelber, W. H. *The Kingdom in Mark. A New Place and a New Time.* Philadelphia: Fortress Press, 1974.

Kenny, A. "The Transfiguration and the Agony in the Garden." *CBQ* XIX (1957): 444–52.

Kertelge, Karl. "Buchstabe und Geist nach 2 Kor 3." In *Paul and the Mosaic Law*, edited by James D. G. Dunn, 117–30. Tübingen: J.C.B. Mohr, 1996.

Kim, Seyoon. *Paul and the New Perspective.* Tübingen: Mohr Siebeck, 2002.

King, Karen. *The Secret Revelation of John.* Cambridge, Ma: Harvard University Press, 2006.

— *What is Gnosticism?* Cambridge, Ma: Harvard University Press, 2003.

Kingsbury, J. D. "The 'Divine Man' as the Key to Mark's Christology – The End of an Era?" *Interpretation* 35 (1981): 243–57.

— *Matthew. Structure, Christology, Kingdom.* Philadelphia: Fortress, 1975.

Kittel, G. "δόξα." In *TDNT*, II:233–55.

Klein, H. "Zur Auslegung von Psalm 2: Ein Beitrag zum Thema: Gewalt und Gewaltlosigkeit." *TBei* 10 (1979): 63–71.

Klinger, Jerzy. "The Second Epistle of Peter: An Essay in Understanding." *St. Vladimir's Theological Quarterly* 17 (1973): 152–69.

Knight, Jonathan. *Disciples of the Beloved One.* Sheffield: Sheffield Press, 1996.

Knox, W. L. "The 'Divine Hero' Christology in the New Testament." *HTR* (1948): 229–49.

Koester, Helmut. *History and Literature of Early Christianity*. 2 vols. Philadelphia: Fortress, 1982.

Kraus, H.J. *Die Königsherrschaft Gotes im Alten Testament*. Tübingen: J. C. B. Mohr, 1951.

Kuntz, John Kenneth. *The Self-Revelation of God*. Philadelphia: Westminster Press, 1967.

Künzi, M. *Das Naherwartungslogion Markus 9.1 par. Geschichte seiner Auslegung*. Tübingen: Mohr, 1977.

Kuschnerus, Bernd. "You Yourselves are Our Letter." In *Metaphor, Canon and Community*, edited by Ralph Bisschops and James Francis, 93–111. New York: Peter Lang, 1999.

Lalleman, Pieter J. *The Acts of John: A Two-stage Initiation Into Johannine Gnosticism*. Leuven: Belgium, 1998.

— "Polymorphy of Christ." In *The Apocryphal Acts of John*, edited by Jan N. Bremmer, 97–118. Kampen, The Netherlands: Kok Pharos, 1995.

— "The Relation between *the Acts of John* and *the Acts of Peter*." In *The Apocryphal Acts of Peter*, edited by Jan N. Bremmer, 161–68. Leuven: Peeters, 1998.

Lambrecht, J. "Paul and Suffering." In *God and Human Suffering*, edited by J. Lambrecht and Raymond F. Collins, 47–67. Louvain [Belgium]: Peeters Press, 1990.

— "Structure and Line of Thought in 2 Cor 2.14–4.6." *Biblica* 64 (1983): 344–80.

Lanzillotta, L. Roig. "Does Punishment Reward the Righteous? The Justice Pattern Underlying the Apocalypse of Peter." In *The Apocalypse of Peter*, edited by Jan N. Bremer and Istvan Czachesz, 127–157. Leuven: Peeters, 2003.

Leaney, A.R.C. *The Christ of the Synoptic Gospels*. Auckland: Pelorous Press, 1966.

Liefeld, Walter L. "Theological Motifs at the Transfiguration Narrative." In *New Dimensions in New Testament Study*, edited by Richard N. Longenecker and Merrill C. Tenney, 162–79. Grand Rapids: Zondervan Pub. House, 1974.

Lietaert Peerbolte, L.J. *The Antecedents of Antichrist: a Traditio-Historical Study of the Earliest Christian Views on Eschatological Opponents*. Leiden; New York; Köln: E.J. Brill, 1996.

Longenecker, Bruce W. "Contours of Covenant Theology in the Post-Conversion Paul." In *The Road from Damascus*, edited by Richard N. Longenecker, 125–146. Grand Rapids, Michigan: William B. Eerdmans, 1997.

Loymeyer, E. *Das Ebangelium des Markus*. Gottingen: Vandenhoeck & Ruprecht, 1967.

Luz, Ulrich. *Matthew*. Translated by James E. Crouch. Edited by Helmut Koester. 3 vols. Vol. 2, *Hermeneia*. Minneapolis: Fortress Press, 2001.

— *Studies in Matthew*. Translated by Rosemary Selle. Grand Rapids, MI: W.B. Eerdmans Pub. Co., 2005.

MacDonald, Dennis R. "The Acts of Paul and the Acts of Peter: Which Came First?" *Society of Biblical Literature Seminar Papers* 31 (1992): 214–24.

— *Christianizing Homer: The Odyssey, Plato, and the Acts of Andrew*. New York: Oxford University Press, 1994.

— *The Homeric Epics and the Gospel of Mark*. New Haven & London: Yale University Press, 2000.

— "Which Came First? Intertextual Relationships Among the Apocryphal Acts of the Apostles." *Semeia* 80 (1997): 11–41.

Mánek, Jindrich. "The New Exodus in the Books of Luke." *Novum Testamentum* 2 (1958): 8–23.

Marcus, Joel. *Mark*. Vol. 1. New York: Doubleday, 2000.

— *The Mystery of the Kingdom of God*. Atlanta: Scholars Press, 1986.

— *The Way of the Lord*. Louisville, Kentucky: John Knox Press, 1992.

Marrassini, P. "Note sur le texte éthiopien." In *Écrits apocryphes chrétiens*, edited by François Bovon and P. Geoltrain, 750–52. Paris: Gallimard, 1997.

Marshall, I. H. *The Gospel of Luke*. Grand Rapids: Eerdmans, 1978.

— *Luke: Historian and Theologian*. Exeter: Paternoster P., 1970.

Martin, Ralph P. *Carmen Christi*. Cambridge: Cambridge University Press, 1967.

— *Reconciliation: A Study of Paul's Theology*. Atlanta: John Knox, 1980.

Martin, Thomas W. "What Makes Glory Glorious? Reading Luke's Account of the Transfiguration over against Triumphalism." *JSNT* (2006): 3–26.

Matthews, Christopher R. "The *Acts of Peter* and Luke's Intertextual Heritage." *Semeia* 80 (1997): 207–222.

McGuckin, John A. *The Transfiguration of Christ in Scripture and Tradition*. New York: Edwin Mellen Press, 1986.

McNamara, M. *Targum and Testament*. Grand Rapids, MI: Eerdmans, 1972.

Meeks, Wayne A. *The Prophet King*. Leiden: Brill, 1967.

Ménard, Jacques E. "Transfiguration et polymorphie chez Origène." In Epektasis, edited by Jacques Fontaine and Charles Kannanengiesser, 367–72. Paris: Beauchesne, 1972.

Metzger, Bruce M. *A Textual Commentary on the Greek New Testament*. 2nd ed. Stuttgart: Deutsche Bibelgesellschaft; United Bible Societies, 1994.

Miller, Robert J. "Historicizing the Trans-historical: the Transfiguration Narrative." *Foundations & Facets Forum* 10 (1994): 219–48.

— "Is There Independent Attestation for the Transfiguration in 2 Peter?" *New Test. Stud.* 42 (1996): 620–25.

Moessner, David P. "Luke 9:1–50: Luke's Preview of the Journey of the Prophet like Moses of Deuteronomy." *JBL* 102 (1983): 575–605.

Moingt, Joseph. "Polymorphisme du corps du Christ." *Le temps de la réflexion* 7 (1986): 47–62.

Moses, A.D.A. *Matthew's Transfiguration Story and Jewish-Christian Controversy, Journal for the Study of the New Testament Supplement Series 122*. Sheffield: Sheffield Academic Press, 1996.

Moss, Candida R. "The Transfiguration: An Exercise in Markan Accommodation." *Biblical Interpretation* 12 (2004): 69–89.

Müller, C.D.G. "Apocalypse of Peter." In *The New Testament Apocrypha*, edited by Wilhelm Schneemelcher, 620–36. Westminster: John Knox Press, 1991–1992.

Nardonni, E. "A Redactional Interpretation of Mark 9:1." *CBQ* 43 (1981): 365–84.

Neirynck, F. "Minor Agreements – Matthew–Luke in the Transfiguration Story." In *Orientierung an Jesus; Zur Theologie der Synoptiker. Für Josef Schmid*, edited by Paul Hoffmann, 253–66. Freiburg: Herder, 1973.

Newman, Carey C. *Paul's Glory-Christology: Tradition and Rhetoric*. NTSup 69; Leiden: E.J. Brill, 1992.

Neyrey, J. *The Passion According to Luke: A Redaction Study of Luke's Soteriology*. New York: Paulist Press, 1984.

Neyrey, J. H. "The Symbolic Universe of Luke–Acts: "They Turn the World Upside Down"." In *The Social World of Luke–Acts*, edited by J. H. Neyrey, 271–303. Peabody, MA: Hendrickson, 1991.

Ngayihembako, Samuel. *Les temps de la fin: approche exégetique de l'eschatologie du Nouveau Testament*. Genève: Labor et Fides, 1994.

Neyrey, Jerome H. *2 Peter, Jude, The Anchor Bible*. New York: The Anchor Bible, 1993.

— "The Apologetic Use of the Transfiguration in 2nd Peter 1:16–21." *CBQ* 42 (1980): 504–19.

— "The Form and Background of the Polemic in 2 Peter." *JBL* 99 (1980): 407–32.

Nickelsburg, George E. W. *1 Enoch: A Commentary on the Book of 1 Enoch*. Minneapolis: Fortress, 2001.

— "Enoch, Levi, and Peter: Recipients of Revelation in Upper Galilee." *JBL* 100 (1981): 575–600.

— "Son of Man." In *Anchor Bible Dictionary*, VI:137–150.

Nolland, John. *The Gospel of Matthew*. Grand Rapids, MI: William B. Eerdmans, 2005.

O'Leary, Anne M. *Matthew's Judaization of Mark: Examined in the Context of the Use of Sources in Graeco-Roman Antiquity*. London; New York: T & T Clark, 2006.

O'Toole, Robert F. "The Parallels between Jesus and Moses." *Biblical Theology Bulletin* 20 (1990): 22–29.

— *The Unity of Luke's Theology*. Wilmington, DE: Michael Glazier, Inc., 1984.

Pao, David W. "Physical and Spiritual Restoration: The Role of Healing Miracles in the *Acts of Andrew*." In *The Apocryphal Acts of the Apostles*, edited by François Bovon, Ann Graham Brock, and Christopher R. Matthews, 259–80. Cambridge: Harvard University Press, 1999.

Perkins, Judith B. "The Acts of Peter as Intertext: Response to Dennis MacDonald." In *Society of Biblical Literature Seminar Papers no. 32*, 627–33, 1993.

— "This World or Another? The Intertextuality of the Greek Romances, the Apocryphal Acts and Apuleius' *Metamorphoses*." *Semeia* 80 (1997): 247–260.

Perkins, Pheme. *Peter: Apostle for the Whole Church*. Columbia, S.C.: University of South Carolina Press, 1994.

Pervo, Richard I. "Egging on the Chickens: A Cowardly Response to Dennis MacDonald and then Some." *Semeia* 80 (1997): 43–56.

Pesthy, Monika. "Cross and Death in the Apocryphal Acts of the Apostles." In *The Apocryphal Acts of Peter*, edited by Jan N. Bremmer, 123–33. Leuven: Peeters, 1998.

— "Thy Mercy, O Lord, is in the Heavens; and Thy Righteousness Reacheth unto the Clouds." In *The Apocalypse of Peter*, edited by Jan N. Bremmer, 40–51. Leuven: Peeters, 2003.

Peterson, Eric. *Frühkirche, Judentum und Gnosis*. Rome; Fribourg; Vienne, 1959.

Radl, Walter. *Paulus und Jesus im lukanischen Doppelwerk*. Bern: Herbert Lang, 1975.

Ravens, D.A.S. "Luke 9.7–62 and the Prophetic Role of Jesus." *NTS* 36 (1990): 119–29.

Reid, Barbara E. *The Transfiguration: A Source– and Redaction– Critical Study of Luke 9:28–36*. Paris: J. Gabalda et Cie, 1993.

Reitzenstein, Richard. *Hellenistic Mystery-religions: Their Basic Ideas and Significance*. Translated by John E. Steely. Pittsburgh: Pickwick Press, 1978.

Renwick, David. *Paul, the Temple, and the Presence of God*. Atlanta, GA: Scholars Press, 1991.

Richard, E. "Polemics, Old Testament and Theology. A Study of II Cor. III, 1–IV, 6." *RB* 88 (1981): 340–67.

Riches, John K. *Conflicting Mythologies: Identity Formation in the Gospels of Mark and Matthew*. Edinburgh: T & T Clark, 2000.

Riesenfeld, Harald. *Jésus transfiguré, l'arriére-plan du récit évangélique de la transfiguration de Notre-Seigneur*. Kobenhavn: E. Munksgaard, 1947.

Ringe, Sharon H. "Luke 9:28–36: the Beginning of an Exodus." *Semeia* 28 (1983): 83–99.

Robinson, Henry S. *Corinth: A Brief History of the City and a Guide to the Excavations*. Athens: American School of Classical Studies, 1964.

Robinson, J. A., and M.R. James. *The Gospel according to Peter and the Revelation of Peter*. London: C.J. Clay, 1892.

Robinson, J.M. "On the Gattung of Mark (and John)." *Perspective* 11 (1970): 99–129.

Robinson, James M. and Helmut Koester. *Trajectories through Early Christianities.* Philadelphia: Fortress Press, 1971.

Roehrs, W.R. "God's Tabernacles among Men: A Study of the Transfiguration." *CTM* 35 (1964): 18–25.

Rordorf, Willy. "The Relation between the *Acts of Peter* and the *Acts of Paul*: State of the Question." In *The Apocryphal Acts of Peter*, edited by Jan N. Bremmer, 178–91. Leuven: Peeters, 1998.

Russell, D. S. *The Method and Message of Jewish Apocalyptic 200 B.C. – 100 A.D.* Philadelphia: Westminster, 1964.

Schäfer, P. *Der Bar-Kokhba-Aufstand.* Tübingen: Mohr Siebeck, 1981.

Schlier, Heinrich. "παρρησία." In TDNT vol. 5, 871–86.

Schmidt, David Henry. "The Peter Writings: Their Redactors and Their Relationships." Ph.D book, Northwestern University, 1972.

Schneemelcher, Wilhelm. *The New Testament Apocrypha.* Translated by R. McL. Wilson. Rev ed. 2 vols. Louisville: Westminster/John Knox, 1991–1992.

Schneider, Paul G. *The Mystery of the Acts of John.* San Francisco: Mellen Research University Press, 1991.

Schramm, Tim. *Der Markus-Stoff bei Lukas: Eine Literarkritische und Redaktionsgeschichtliche Untersuchung.* Cambridge [Eng.]: University Press, 1971.

Schulz, Siegfried. "Die Decke des Moses : Untersuchungen zu einer vorpaulinischen Überlieferung in 2 Cor 3:7–18." ZNW 49 (1958), 1–30.

Schürmann, Heinz. *Das Lukasevangelium.* Freiburg: Herder, 1969.

Schweizer, E. *The Good News According to Mark.* Atlanta: John Knox Press, 1970.

Smith, Terence V. *Petrine Controversies in Early Christianity: Attitudes Towards Peter in Christian Writings of the First Two Centuries.* Tübingen: Mohr, 1985.

Smith, Warren. "The Disguises of the Gods in the *Iliad*." *Numen* 35 (2004): 161–78.

Spicq, C. *Les épîtres de saint Pierre.* Paris: Gabalda, 1966.

Spitta, Friedrich. "Die evangelische Geschichte von der Verklärung Jesu." *Zeitschrift für Wissenscaftliche Theologie* 54 (1911): 97–167.

Stanton, Graham N. *A Gospel for a New People: Studies in Matthew.* Louisville, KY: Westminster/John Knox Press, 1993.

Starr, James M. *Sharers in Divine Nature: 2 Peter 1:4 in Its Hellenistic Context.* Stockholm, Sweden: Almqvist & Wiksell International, 2000.

Stegner, William Richard. "The Use of Scripture in Two Narratives of Early Jewish Christianity (Matthew 4.1–11; Mark 9:2–8)." In *Early Christian Interpretation of the Scripture of Israel*, edited by Craig A. Evans and James A. Sanders, 121–40. Sheffield: Sheffield Academic Press, 1997.

Steichele, Hans-Jörg. *Der Leidende Sohn Gottes*: Münchener Universitäts-Schriften; Regensburg: Pustet, 1980.

Stein, Robert H. "Is the Transfiguration (Mark 9:2–8) a Misplaced Resurrection–Account?" *JBL* 95 (1976): 79–96.

Stendahl, Krister. *Paul Among Jews and Gentiles and Other Essays.* Philadelphia: Fortress, 1976.

Stockhausen, C. K. *Moses'Veil and the Glory of the New Covenant: The Exegetical Substructure of 2 Cor 3.1–4.6.* AnBib 116. Rome: Pontifical Biblical Institute, 1989.

Stoops, Robert F. "The *Acts of Peter* in Intertextual Context." *Semeia* 80 (1997): 57–86.

— "The *Acts of Peter* in Intertextual Context." *Semeia* 80 1997 (1997): 57–86.

— "Christ as Patron in the *Acts of Peter*." *Semeia* 56 (1992): 143–57.

— "Patronage in the Acts of Peter." *Semeia* 38 (1986): 91–100.

— "Peter, Paul, and Priority in the Apocryphal Acts." *Society of Biblical Literature Seminar Papers* 31 (1992): 225–33.

Strauss, Mark L. *The Davidic Messiah in Luke–Acts: the Promise and Its Fulfillment in Lukan Christology*. Sheffield: Sheffield Academic, 1995.

Stroumsa, Gedaliahu G. "Form(s) of God: Some Notes on Metatron and Christ." *HTR* 76 (1983): 269–88.

— "Polymorphie divine et transformations d'un mythologème: l'apocryphon de Jean et ses sources." *Vigiliae Christianae* 35 (1981): 412–34.

Stuckenbruck, Loren T. *Angel Veneration and Christology: A Study in Early Judaism and in the Christology of the Apocalypse of John*. Tübingen: J.C.B. Mohr, 1995.

Talbert, Charles H. "2 Peter and the Delay of the Parousia." *Vigiliae Christianae* 20 (1966): 137–45.

Tannehill, Robert C. *The Narrative Unity of Luke–Acts: A Literary Interpretation*. 2 vols. Philadelphia: Fortress Press, 1994.

Theissen, Gerd. *The Social Setting of Pauline Christianity: Essays on Corinth*. Philadelphia: Fortress, 1982.

— *Social Reality and the Early Christians: Theology, Ethics, and the World of the New Testament*. Trans. Margaret Kohl. Minneapolis: Fortress, 1992.

Theobald, M. *Die überströmende Gnade. Studien zu einem paulinischen Motivfeld*. Würzburg: Echter, 1972.

Thomas, Christine M. "Canon and Antitype: the Relationship between the *Acts of Peter* and the New Testament." *Semeia* 80 (1997): 185–205.

— "Word and Deed: the *Acts of Peter* and Orality." *Apocrypha* 3 (1992): 125–64.

Thrall, Margaret E. *The Second Epistle to the Corinthians*. 2 vols, *A Critical and Exegetical Commentary*. Edinburgh: T&T Clark, 1994.

— "Super-Apostles, Servants of Christ, and Servants of Satan." *JSNT* 6 (1980): 42–57.

Thuren, Lauri. "Style Never Goes out of Fashion: 2 Peter Re-Evaluated." In *Rhetoric, Scripture and Theology: Essays from the 1994 Pretoria Conference*, edited by Stanley Porter and Thomas Olbright, 329–47. Sheffield: Sheffield Academic Press, 1996.

Tigchelaar, Eibert. "Is the Liar Bar Kokhba? Considering the Date and Provenance of the Greek (Ethiopic) *Apocalypse of Peter*." In *The Apocalypse of Peter*, edited by Jan N. Bremer and Istvan Czachesz, 63–77. Leuven: Peeters, 2003.

Tolbert, M. A. *Sowing the Gospel: Mark's World in Literary-Rhetorical Perspectives*. Minneapolis: Fortress, 1989.

Toorn, Karel van der. "The Public Image of the Widow in Ancient Israel." In *Between Poverty and the Pyre: Moments in the History of Widowhood*, edited by Jan N. Bremmer and Lourens van den Bosch, 19–30. New York: Routledge, 1995.

Trites, Allison A. "The Prayer Motif in Luke–Acts." In *Perspectives on Luke–Acts*, edited by Charles H. Talbert, 168–86. Danville, VA: Association of Baptist Professors of Religion, 1978.

— "The Transfiguration in the Theology of Luke: Some Redactional Links." In *The glory of Christ in the New Testament*, edited by L.D. Hurst and N. T. Wright, 71–81. Oxford: Clarendon Press, 1987.

Trobisch, David. *The First Edition of the New Testament*. Oxford; New York: Oxford University Press, 2000.

Urbach, Efraim Elimelech. *The Sages: Their Concepts and Beliefs*. 2nd ed. Jerusalem: Magnes Press, 1987.

Van Minnen, Peter. "The Greek Apocalypse of Peter." In *The Apocalypse of Peter*, edited by Jan N. Bremmer and Istvan Czachesz, 15–39. Leuven: Peeters, 2003.

Van Ruiten, Jacques. "The Old Testament Quotations in the Apocalypse of Peter." In *The Apocalypse of Peter*, edited by Jan N. Bremmer and Istvan Czachesz, 158–73. Leuven: Peeters, 2003.

— *Primaeval History Interpreted: the Rewriting of Genesis 1–11 in the Book of Jubilees.* Leiden: Brill, 2000.

Van Unnik, W. C. "'With Unveiled Face', An Exegesis of 2 Cor 3:12–18." *NovTest* 6 (1963): 153–69.

Vermes, G. *Post-Biblical Jewish Studies*. Leiden: Brill, 1975.

Vernant, Jean-Pierre. *Mortals and Immortals: Collected Essays*. Edited by Froma I. Zeitlin. Princeton, N.J.: Princeton University Press, 1991.

von den Osten-Sacken, P. *Rabbi Akiva*. Berlin: Institut Kirche und Judentum, 1987.

Wagner, G. "Alliance de la lettre, alliance de l'esprit. Essai d'analyse de 2 Corinthiens 2/14 à 3/18." *ETR* 60 (1985): 55–68.

Weeden, T. J. *Mark – Traditions in Conflict*. Philadelphia: Fortress Press, 1971.

Weigandt, Peter. *Der Doketismus im Urchristentum und in der theologischen Entwicklung des zweiten Jahrhunderts*. Doctoral Book; Heidelberg, 1961.

Weiss, Johannes. *Earliest Christianity. A History of the Period A.D. 30–150*. Translated by Frederick C. Grant. 2 vols. New York: Harper, 1959.

Wenham, David. *Paul: Follower of Jesus or Founder of Christianity?* Grand Rapids; Cambridge: William B. Eerdmans, 1995.

Wenham, David, and A.D.A. Moses. "'There are Some Standing Here...': Did They Become the 'Reputed Pillars' of the Jerusalem church? Some Reflections on Mark 9:1, Galatians 2:9 and the Transfiguration." *Novum Testamentum* 36 (1994): 146–63.

Windisch, Hans. *Der Zweite Korintherbrief*. 9 ed. Göttingen: Vandenhoeck und Ruprecht, 1970.

Witherington, Ben. "A Petrine Source in Second Peter." In *Society of Biblical Literature 1985 Seminar Papers*, edited by Kent Harold Richards, 187–92. Atlanta, Georgia: Scholars Press, 1985.

Wrede, William. *The Messianic Secret*. Translated by J.C.G. Greig. Cambridge, England: J. Clarke, 1971.

Wright, N. T. *The Climax of the Covenant: Christ and the Law in Pauline Theology*. Minneapolis: Fortress Press, 1993.

Wünsch, Hans-Michael. *Der paulinische Brief 2 Kor 1–9 als kommunikative Handlung: eine rhetorisch-literaturwissenschaftliche Untersuchung*. Münster: Lit Verlag, 1996.

Zeller, Dieter. "The ΘΕΙΑ ΦΥΣΙΣ of Hippocrates and of Other Divine Men." In *Early Christianity and Classical Culture*, edited by John T. Fitzgerald, 46–69. Leiden; Boston: Brill, 2003.

— "New Testament Christology in its Hellenistic Reception." *NewTestStud* 46 (2001): 312–33.

Ziesler, J.A. "The Transfiguration Story and the Markan Soteriology." *ExpTimes* 81 (1969–70): 263–68.

Index of Ancient Sources

2. Pseudepigrapha and DSS

3. New Testament

4. NT Apocrypha

5. Church Fathers and Other Greek/Latin Sources

Index of Modern Authors

Index of Subjects and Key Terms

Wissenschaftliche Untersuchungen zum Neuen Testament

Alphabetical Index of the First and Second Series

Bergmeier, Roland: Das Gesetz im Römerbrief und andere Studien zum Neuen Testament. 2000. *Vol. 121.*

Bernett, Monika: Der Kaiserkult in Judäa unter den Herodiern und Römern. 2007. *Vol. 203.*

Betz, Otto: Jesus, der Messias Israels. 1987. *Vol. 42.*

– Jesus, der Herr der Kirche. 1990. *Vol. 52.*

Beyschlag, Karlmann: Simon Magus und die christliche Gnosis. 1974. *Vol. 16.*

Bieringer, Reimund: see *Koester, Craig.*

Bittner, Wolfgang J.: Jesu Zeichen im Johannesevangelium. 1987. *Vol. II/26.*

Bjerkelund, Carl J.: Tauta Egeneto. 1987. *Vol. 40.*

Blackburn, Barry Lee: Theios Aner and the Markan Miracle Traditions. 1991. *Vol. II/40.*

Blanton IV, Thomas R.: Constructing a New Covenant. 2007. *Vol. II/233.*

Bock, Darrell L.: Blasphemy and Exaltation in Judaism and the Final Examination of Jesus. 1998. *Vol. II/106.*

Bockmuehl, Markus N.A.: Revelation and Mystery in Ancient Judaism and Pauline Christianity. 1990. *Vol. II/36.*

Bøe, Sverre: Gog and Magog. 2001. *Vol. II/135.*

Böhlig, Alexander: Gnosis und Synkretismus. Vol. 1 1989. *Vol. 47* – Vol. 2 1989. *Vol. 48.*

Böhm, Martina: Samarien und die Samaritai bei Lukas. 1999. *Vol. II/111.*

Böttrich, Christfried: Weltweisheit – Menschheitsethik – Urkult. 1992. *Vol. II/50.*

– and *Herzer, Jens* (Ed.): Josephus und das Neue Testament. 2007. *Vol. 209.*

Bolyki, János: Jesu Tischgemeinschaften. 1997. *Vol. II/96.*

Bosman, Philip: Conscience in Philo and Paul. 2003. *Vol. II/166.*

Bovon, François: New Testament and Christian Apocrypha. 2009. *Vol. 237.*

– Studies in Early Christianity. 2003. *Vol. 161.*

Brändl, Martin: Der Agon bei Paulus. 2006. *Vol. II/222.*

Breytenbach, Cilliers: see *Frey, Jörg.*

Brocke, Christoph vom: Thessaloniki – Stadt des Kassander und Gemeinde des Paulus. 2001. *Vol. II/125.*

Brunson, Andrew: Psalm 118 in the Gospel of John. 2003. *Vol. II/158.*

Büchli, Jörg: Der Poimandres – ein paganisiertes Evangelium. 1987. *Vol. II/27.*

Bühner, Jan A.: Der Gesandte und sein Weg im 4. Evangelium. 1977. *Vol. II/2.*

Burchard, Christoph: Untersuchungen zu Joseph und Aseneth. 1965. *Vol. 8.*

– Studien zur Theologie, Sprache und Umwelt des Neuen Testaments. Ed. by D. Sänger. 1998. *Vol. 107.*

Burnett, Richard: Karl Barth's Theological Exegesis. 2001. *Vol. II/145.*

Byron, John: Slavery Metaphors in Early Judaism and Pauline Christianity. 2003. *Vol. II/162.*

Byrskog, Samuel: Story as History – History as Story. 2000. *Vol. 123.*

Cancik, Hubert (Ed.): Markus-Philologie. 1984. *Vol. 33.*

Capes, David B.: Old Testament Yaweh Texts in Paul's Christology. 1992. *Vol. II/47.*

Caragounis, Chrys C.: The Development of Greek and the New Testament. 2004. *Vol. 167.*

– The Son of Man. 1986. *Vol. 38.*

– see *Fridrichsen, Anton.*

Carleton Paget, James: The Epistle of Barnabas. 1994. *Vol. II/64.*

Carson, D.A., O'Brien, Peter T. and *Mark Seifrid* (Ed.): Justification and Variegated Nomism.
Vol. 1: The Complexities of Second Temple Judaism. 2001. *Vol. II/140.*
Vol. 2: The Paradoxes of Paul. 2004. *Vol. II/181.*

Chae, Young Sam: Jesus as the Eschatological Davidic Shepherd. 2006. *Vol. II/216.*

Chapman, David W.: Ancient Jewish and Christian Perceptions of Crucifixion. 2008. *Vol. II/244.*

Chester, Andrew: Messiah and Exaltation. 2007. *Vol. 207.*

Chibici-Revneanu, Nicole: Die Herrlichkeit des Verherrlichten. 2007. *Vol. II/231.*

Ciampa, Roy E.: The Presence and Function of Scripture in Galatians 1 and 2. 1998. *Vol. II/102.*

Classen, Carl Joachim: Rhetorical Criticsm of the New Testament. 2000. *Vol. 128.*

Colpe, Carsten: Griechen – Byzantiner – Semiten – Muslime. 2008. *Vol. 221.*

– Iranier – Aramäer – Hebräer – Hellenen. 2003. *Vol. 154.*

Coppins, Wayne: The Interpretation of Freedom in the Letters of Paul. 2009. *Vol. II/261.*

Crump, David: Jesus the Intercessor. 1992. *Vol. II/49.*

Dahl, Nils Alstrup: Studies in Ephesians. 2000. *Vol. 131.*

Daise, Michael A.: Feasts in John. 2007. *Vol. II/229.*

Deines, Roland: Die Gerechtigkeit der Tora im Reich des Messias. 2004. *Vol. 177.*

– Jüdische Steingefäße und pharisäische Frömmigkeit. 1993. *Vol. II/52.*

– Die Pharisäer. 1997. *Vol. 101.*

Deines, Roland and *Karl-Wilhelm Niebuhr* (Ed.): Philo und das Neue Testament. 2004. *Vol. 172.*

Dennis, John A.: Jesus' Death and the Gathering of True Israel. 2006. *Vol. 217.*

Dettwiler, Andreas and *Jean Zumstein* (Ed.): Kreuzestheologie im Neuen Testament. 2002. *Vol. 151.*

Dickson, John P.: Mission-Commitment in Ancient Judaism and in the Pauline Communities. 2003. *Vol. II/159.*

Dietzfelbinger, Christian: Der Abschied des Kommenden. 1997. *Vol. 95.*

Dimitrov, Ivan Z., James D.G. Dunn, Ulrich Luz and *Karl-Wilhelm Niebuhr* (Ed.): Das Alte Testament als christliche Bibel in orthodoxer und westlicher Sicht. 2004. *Vol. 174.*

Dobbeler, Axel von: Glaube als Teilhabe. 1987. *Vol. II/22.*

Docherty, Susan E.: The Use of the Old Testament in Hebrews. 2009. *Vol. II/260.*

Downs, David J.: The Offering of the Gentiles. 2008. *Vol. II/248.*

Dryden, J. de Waal: Theology and Ethics in 1 Peter. 2006. *Vol. II/209.*

Dübbers, Michael: Christologie und Existenz im Kolosserbrief. 2005. *Vol. II/191.*

Dunn, James D.G.: The New Perspective on Paul. 2005. *Vol. 185.*

Dunn , James D.G. (Ed.): Jews and Christians. 1992. *Vol. 66.*

– Paul and the Mosaic Law. 1996. *Vol. 89.*

– see *Dimitrov, Ivan Z.*

–, *Hans Klein, Ulrich Luz,* and *Vasile Mihoc* (Ed.): Auslegung der Bibel in orthodoxer und westlicher Perspektive. 2000. *Vol. 130.*

Ebel, Eva: Die Attraktivität früher christlicher Gemeinden. 2004. *Vol. II/178.*

Ebertz, Michael N.: Das Charisma des Gekreuzigten. 1987. *Vol. 45.*

Eckstein, Hans-Joachim: Der Begriff Syneidesis bei Paulus. 1983. *Vol. II/10.*

– Verheißung und Gesetz. 1996. *Vol. 86.*

Ego, Beate: Im Himmel wie auf Erden. 1989. *Vol. II/34.*

Ego, Beate, Armin Lange and *Peter Pilhofer* (Ed.): Gemeinde ohne Tempel – Community without Temple. 1999. *Vol. 118.*

– and *Helmut Merkel* (Ed.): Religiöses Lernen in der biblischen, frühjüdischen und frühchristlichen Überlieferung. 2005. *Vol. 180.*

Eisen, Ute E.: see *Paulsen, Henning.*

Elledge, C.D.: Life after Death in Early Judaism. 2006. *Vol. II/208.*

Ellis, E. Earle: Prophecy and Hermeneutic in Early Christianity. 1978. *Vol. 18.*

– The Old Testament in Early Christianity. 1991. *Vol. 54.*

Elmer, Ian J.: Paul, Jerusalem and the Judaisers. 2009. *Vol. II/258.*

Endo, Masanobu: Creation and Christology. 2002. *Vol. 149.*

Ennulat, Andreas: Die 'Minor Agreements'. 1994. *Vol. II/62.*

Ensor, Peter W.: Jesus and His 'Works'. 1996. *Vol. II/85.*

Eskola, Timo: Messiah and the Throne. 2001. *Vol. II/142.*

– Theodicy and Predestination in Pauline Soteriology. 1998. *Vol. II/100.*

Fatehi, Mehrdad: The Spirit's Relation to the Risen Lord in Paul. 2000. *Vol. II/128.*

Feldmeier, Reinhard: Die Krisis des Gottessohnes. 1987. *Vol. II/21.*

– Die Christen als Fremde. 1992. *Vol. 64.*

Feldmeier, Reinhard and *Ulrich Heckel* (Ed.): Die Heiden. 1994. *Vol. 70.*

Fletcher-Louis, Crispin H.T.: Luke-Acts: Angels, Christology and Soteriology. 1997. *Vol. II/94.*

Förster, Niclas: Marcus Magus. 1999. *Vol. 114.*

Forbes, Christopher Brian: Prophecy and Inspired Speech in Early Christianity and its Hellenistic Environment. 1995. *Vol. II/75.*

Fornberg, Tord: see *Fridrichsen, Anton.*

Fossum, Jarl E.: The Name of God and the Angel of the Lord. 1985. *Vol. 36.*

Foster, Paul: Community, Law and Mission in Matthew's Gospel. *Vol. II/177.*

Fotopoulos, John: Food Offered to Idols in Roman Corinth. 2003. *Vol. II/151.*

Frenschkowski, Marco: Offenbarung und Epiphanie. Vol. 1 1995. *Vol. II/79* – Vol. 2 1997. *Vol. II/80.*

Frey, Jörg: Eugen Drewermann und die biblische Exegese. 1995. *Vol. II/71.*

– Die johanneische Eschatologie. Vol. I. 1997. *Vol. 96.* – Vol. II. 1998. *Vol. 110.* – Vol. III. 2000. *Vol. 117.*

Frey, Jörg and *Cilliers Breytenbach* (Ed.): Aufgabe und Durchführung einer Theologie des Neuen Testaments. 2007. *Vol. 205.*

– and *Udo Schnelle (Ed.):* Kontexte des Johannesevangeliums. 2004. *Vol. 175.*

– and *Jens Schröter* (Ed.): Deutungen des Todes Jesu im Neuen Testament. 2005. *Vol. 181.*

–, *Jan G. van der Watt,* and *Ruben Zimmermann* (Ed.): Imagery in the Gospel of John. 2006. *Vol. 200.*

Freyne, Sean: Galilee and Gospel. 2000. *Vol. 125.*

Fridrichsen, Anton: Exegetical Writings. Edited by C.C. Caragounis and T. Fornberg. 1994. *Vol. 76.*

Gäbel, Georg: Die Kulttheologie des Hebräerbriefes. 2006. *Vol. II/212.*

Gäckle, Volker: Die Starken und die Schwachen in Korinth und in Rom. 2005. *Vol. 200.*

Garlington, Don B.: 'The Obedience of Faith'. 1991. *Vol. II/38.*

– Faith, Obedience, and Perseverance. 1994. *Vol. 79.*

Garnet, Paul: Salvation and Atonement in the Qumran Scrolls. 1977. *Vol. II/3.*

Gemünden, Petra von (Ed.): see *Weissenrieder, Annette.*

Gese, Michael: Das Vermächtnis des Apostels. 1997. *Vol. II/99.*

Gheorghita, Radu: The Role of the Septuagint in Hebrews. 2003. *Vol. II/160.*

Gordley, Matthew E.: The Colossian Hymn in Context. 2007. *Vol. II/228.*

Gräbe, Petrus J.: The Power of God in Paul's Letters. 2000, ²2008. *Vol. II/123.*

Gräßer, Erich: Der Alte Bund im Neuen. 1985. *Vol. 35.*

– Forschungen zur Apostelgeschichte. 2001. *Vol. 137.*

Grappe, Christian (Ed.): Le Repas de Dieu / Das Mahl Gottes. 2004. *Vol. 169.*

Gray, Timothy C.: The Temple in the Gospel of Mark. 2008. *Vol. II/242.*

Green, Joel B.: The Death of Jesus. 1988. *Vol. II/33.*

Gregg, Brian Han: The Historical Jesus and the Final Judgment Sayings in Q. 2005. *Vol. II/207.*

Gregory, Andrew: The Reception of Luke and Acts in the Period before Irenaeus. 2003. *Vol. II/169.*

Grindheim, Sigurd: The Crux of Election. 2005. *Vol. II/202.*

Gundry, Robert H.: The Old is Better. 2005. *Vol. 178.*

Gundry Volf, Judith M.: Paul and Perseverance. 1990. *Vol. II/37.*

Häußer, Detlef: Christusbekenntnis und Jesusüberlieferung bei Paulus. 2006. *Vol. 210.*

Hafemann, Scott J.: Suffering and the Spirit. 1986. *Vol. II/19.*

– Paul, Moses, and the History of Israel. 1995. *Vol. 81.*

Hahn, Ferdinand: Studien zum Neuen Testament.

Vol. I: Grundsatzfragen, Jesusforschung, Evangelien. 2006. *Vol. 191.*

Vol. II: Bekenntnisbildung und Theologie in urchristlicher Zeit. 2006. *Vol. 192.*

Hahn, Johannes (Ed.): Zerstörungen des Jerusalemer Tempels. 2002. *Vol. 147.*

Hamid-Khani, Saeed: Relevation and Concealment of Christ. 2000. *Vol. II/120.*

Hannah, Darrel D.: Michael and Christ. 1999. *Vol. II/109.*

Hardin, Justin K.: Galatians and the Imperial Cult? 2007. *Vol. II /237.*

Harrison; James R.: Paul's Language of Grace in Its Graeco-Roman Context. 2003. *Vol. II/172.*

Hartman, Lars: Text-Centered New Testament Studies. Ed. von D. Hellholm. 1997. *Vol. 102.*

Hartog, Paul: Polycarp and the New Testament. 2001. *Vol. II/134.*

Heckel, Theo K.: Der Innere Mensch. 1993. *Vol. II/53.*

– Vom Evangelium des Markus zum viergestaltigen Evangelium. 1999. *Vol. 120.*

Heckel, Ulrich: Kraft in Schwachheit. 1993. *Vol. II/56.*

– Der Segen im Neuen Testament. 2002. *Vol. 150.*

– see *Feldmeier, Reinhard.*

– see *Hengel, Martin.*

Heiligenthal, Roman: Werke als Zeichen. 1983. *Vol. II/9.*

Heliso, Desta: Pistis and the Righteous One. 2007. *Vol. II/235.*

Hellholm, D.: see *Hartman, Lars.*

Hemer, Colin J.: The Book of Acts in the Setting of Hellenistic History. 1989. *Vol. 49.*

Hengel, Martin: Jesus und die Evangelien. Kleine Schriften V. 2007. *Vol. 211.*

– Die johanneische Frage. 1993. *Vol. 67.*

– Judaica et Hellenistica. Kleine Schriften I. 1996. *Vol. 90.*

– Judaica, Hellenistica et Christiana. Kleine Schriften II. 1999. *Vol. 109.*

– Judentum und Hellenismus. 1969, ³1988. *Vol. 10.*

– Paulus und Jakobus. Kleine Schriften III. 2002. *Vol. 141.*

– Studien zur Christologie. Kleine Schriften IV. 2006. *Vol. 201.*

– Studien zum Urchristentum. Kleine Schriften VI. 2008. *Vol. 234.*

– and *Anna Maria Schwemer:* Paulus zwischen Damaskus und Antiochien. 1998. *Vol. 108.*

– Der messianische Anspruch Jesu und die Anfänge der Christologie. 2001. *Vol. 138.*

– Die vier Evangelien und das eine Evangelium von Jesus Christus. 2008. *Vol. 224.*

Hengel, Martin and *Ulrich Heckel* (Ed.): Paulus und das antike Judentum. 1991. *Vol. 58.*

– and *Hermut Löhr* (Ed.): Schriftauslegung im antiken Judentum und im Urchristentum. 1994. *Vol. 73.*

– and *Anna Maria Schwemer* (Ed.): Königsherrschaft Gottes und himmlischer Kult. 1991. *Vol. 55.*

– Die Septuaginta. 1994. *Vol. 72.*

–, *Siegfried Mittmann* and *Anna Maria Schwemer* (Ed.): La Cité de Dieu / Die Stadt Gottes. 2000. *Vol. 129.*

Hentschel, Anni: Diakonia im Neuen Testament. 2007. *Vol. 226.*

Hernández Jr., Juan: Scribal Habits and Theological Influence in the Apocalypse. 2006. *Vol. II/218.*

Herrenbrück, Fritz: Jesus und die Zöllner. 1990. *Vol. II/41.*

Herzer, Jens: Paulus oder Petrus? 1998. *Vol. 103.*

– see *Böttrich, Christfried.*

Hill, Charles E.: From the Lost Teaching of Polycarp. 2005. *Vol. 186.*

Hoegen-Rohls, Christina: Der nachösterliche Johannes. 1996. *Vol. II/84.*

Hoffmann, Matthias Reinhard: The Destroyer and the Lamb. 2005. *Vol. II/203.*

Hofius, Otfried: Katapausis. 1970. *Vol. 11.*

– Der Vorhang vor dem Thron Gottes. 1972. *Vol. 14.*

– Der Christushymnus Philipper 2,6–11. 1976, ²1991. *Vol. 17.*

– Paulusstudien. 1989, ²1994. *Vol. 51.*

– Neutestamentliche Studien. 2000. *Vol. 132.*

– Paulusstudien II. 2002. *Vol. 143.*

– Exegetische Studien. 2008. *Vol. 223.*

– and *Hans-Christian Kammler:* Johannesstudien. 1996. *Vol. 88.*

Holmberg, Bengt (Ed.): Exploring Early Christian Identity. 2008. *Vol. 226.*

– and *Mikael Winninge* (Ed.): Identity Formation in the New Testament. 2008. *Vol. 227.*

Holtz, Traugott: Geschichte und Theologie des Urchristentums. 1991. *Vol. 57.*

Hommel, Hildebrecht: Sebasmata.
Vol. 1 1983. *Vol. 31.*
Vol. 2 1984. *Vol. 32.*

Horbury, William: Herodian Judaism and New Testament Study. 2006. *Vol. 193.*

Horn, Friedrich Wilhelm and *Ruben Zimmermann* (Ed.): Jenseits von Indikativ und Imperativ.
Vol. 1. 2009. *Vol. 238.*

Horst, Pieter W. van der: Jews and Christians in Their Graeco-Roman Context. 2006. *Vol. 196.*

Hvalvik, Reidar: The Struggle for Scripture and Covenant. 1996. *Vol. II/82.*

Jauhiainen, Marko: The Use of Zechariah in Revelation. 2005. *Vol. II/199.*

Jensen, Morten H.: Herod Antipas in Galilee. 2006. *Vol. II/215.*

Johns, Loren L.: The Lamb Christology of the Apocalypse of John. 2003. *Vol. II/167.*

Jossa, Giorgio: Jews or Christians? 2006. *Vol. 202.*

Joubert, Stephan: Paul as Benefactor. 2000. *Vol. II/124.*

Judge, E. A.: The First Christians in the Roman World. 2008. *Vol. 229.*

Jungbauer, Harry: „Ehre Vater und Mutter". 2002. *Vol. II/146.*

Kähler, Christoph: Jesu Gleichnisse als Poesie und Therapie. 1995. *Vol. 78.*

Kamlah, Ehrhard: Die Form der katalogischen Paränese im Neuen Testament. 1964. *Vol. 7.*

Kammler, Hans-Christian: Christologie und Eschatologie. 2000. *Vol. 126.*

– Kreuz und Weisheit. 2003. *Vol. 159.*

– see *Hofius, Otfried.*

Karakolis, Christos: see *Alexeev, Anatoly A.*

Karrer, Martin und *Wolfgang Kraus* (Ed.): Die Septuaginta – Texte, Kontexte, Lebenswelten. 2008. *Vol. 219.*

Kelhoffer, James A.: The Diet of John the Baptist. 2005. *Vol. 176.*

– Miracle and Mission. 1999. *Vol. II/112.*

Kelley, Nicole: Knowledge and Religious Authority in the Pseudo-Clementines. 2006. *Vol. II/213.*

Kennedy, Joel: The Recapitulation of Israel. 2008. *Vol. II/257.*

Kieffer, René and *Jan Bergman* (Ed.): La Main de Dieu / Die Hand Gottes. 1997. *Vol. 94.*

Kierspel, Lars: The Jews and the World in the Fourth Gospel. 2006. *Vol. 220.*

Kim, Seyoon: The Origin of Paul's Gospel. 1981, ²1984. *Vol. II/4.*

– Paul and the New Perspective. 2002. *Vol. 140.*

– "The 'Son of Man'" as the Son of God. 1983. *Vol. 30.*

Klauck, Hans-Josef: Religion und Gesellschaft im frühen Christentum. 2003. *Vol. 152.*

Klein, Hans: see *Dunn, James D.G.*

Kleinknecht, Karl Th.: Der leidende Gerechtfertigte. 1984, ²1988. *Vol. II/13.*

Klinghardt, Matthias: Gesetz und Volk Gottes. 1988. *Vol. II/32.*

Kloppenborg, John S.: The Tenants in the Vineyard. 2006. *Vol. 195.*

Koch, Michael: Drachenkampf und Sonnenfrau. 2004. *Vol. II/184.*

Koch, Stefan: Rechtliche Regelung von Konflikten im frühen Christentum. 2004. *Vol. II/174.*

McDonough, Sean M.: YHWH at Patmos: Rev. 1:4 in its Hellenistic and Early Jewish Setting. 1999. *Vol. II/107.*

McDowell, Markus: Prayers of Jewish Women. 2006. *Vol. II/211.*

McGlynn, Moyna: Divine Judgement and Divine Benevolence in the Book of Wisdom. 2001. *Vol. II/139.*

Meade, David G.: Pseudonymity and Canon. 1986. *Vol. 39.*

Meadors, Edward P.: Jesus the Messianic Herald of Salvation. 1995. *Vol. II/72.*

Meißner, Stefan: Die Heimholung des Ketzers. 1996. *Vol. II/87.*

Mell, Ulrich: Die „anderen" Winzer. 1994. *Vol. 77.*

– see *Sänger, Dieter.*

Mengel, Berthold: Studien zum Philipperbrief. 1982. *Vol. II/8.*

Merkel, Helmut: Die Widersprüche zwischen den Evangelien. 1971. *Vol. 13.*

– see *Ego, Beate.*

Merklein, Helmut: Studien zu Jesus und Paulus. Vol. 1 1987. *Vol. 43.* – Vol. 2 1998. *Vol. 105.*

Metzdorf, Christina: Die Tempelaktion Jesu. 2003. *Vol. II/168.*

Metzler, Karin: Der griechische Begriff des Verzeihens. 1991. *Vol. II/44.*

Metzner, Rainer: Die Rezeption des Matthäusevangeliums im 1. Petrusbrief. 1995. *Vol. II/74.*

– Das Verständnis der Sünde im Johannesevangelium. 2000. *Vol. 122.*

Mihoc, Vasile: see *Dunn, James D.G..*

Mineshige, Kiyoshi: Besitzverzicht und Almosen bei Lukas. 2003. *Vol. II/163.*

Mittmann, Siegfried: see *Hengel, Martin.*

Mittmann-Richert, Ulrike: Magnifikat und Benediktus. *1996. Vol. II/90.*

– Der Sühnetod des Gottesknechts. 2008. *Vol. 220.*

Miura, Yuzuru: David in Luke-Acts. 2007. *Vol. II/232.*

Mournet, Terence C.: Oral Tradition and Literary Dependency. 2005. *Vol. II/195.*

Mußner, Franz: Jesus von Nazareth im Umfeld Israels und der Urkirche. Ed. von M. Theobald. 1998. *Vol. 111.*

Mutschler, Bernhard: Das Corpus Johanneum bei Irenäus von Lyon. 2005. *Vol. 189.*

Nguyen, V. Henry T.: Christian Identity in Corinth. 2008. *Vol. II/243.*

Niebuhr, Karl-Wilhelm: Gesetz und Paränese. 1987. *Vol. II/28.*

– Heidenapostel aus Israel. 1992. *Vol. 62.*

– see *Deines, Roland*

– see *Dimitrov, Ivan Z.*

– see *Kraus, Wolfgang*

Nielsen, Anders E.: "Until it is Fullfilled". 2000. *Vol. II/126.*

Nielsen, Jesper Tang: Die kognitive Dimension des Kreuzes. 2009. *Vol. II/263.*

Nissen, Andreas: Gott und der Nächste im antiken Judentum. 1974. *Vol. 15.*

Noack, Christian: Gottesbewußtsein. 2000. *Vol. II/116.*

Noormann, Rolf: Irenäus als Paulusinterpret. 1994. *Vol. II/66.*

Novakovic, Lidija: Messiah, the Healer of the Sick. 2003. *Vol. II/170.*

Obermann, Andreas: Die christologische Erfüllung der Schrift im Johannesevangelium. 1996. *Vol. II/83.*

Öhler, Markus: Barnabas. 2003. *Vol. 156.*

– see *Becker, Michael.*

Okure, Teresa: The Johannine Approach to Mission. 1988. *Vol. II/31.*

Onuki, Takashi: Heil und Erlösung. 2004. *Vol. 165.*

Oropeza, B. J.: Paul and Apostasy. 2000. *Vol. II/115.*

Ostmeyer, Karl-Heinrich: Kommunikation mit Gott und Christus. 2006. *Vol. 197.*

– Taufe und Typos. 2000. *Vol. II/118.*

Paulsen, Henning: Studien zur Literatur und Geschichte des frühen Christentums. Ed. von Ute E. Eisen. 1997. *Vol. 99.*

Pao, David W.: Acts and the Isaianic New Exodus. 2000. *Vol. II/130.*

Park, Eung Chun: The Mission Discourse in Matthew's Interpretation. 1995. *Vol. II/81.*

Park, Joseph S.: Conceptions of Afterlife in Jewish Insriptions. 2000. *Vol. II/121.*

Pate, C. Marvin: The Reverse of the Curse. 2000. *Vol. II/114.*

Pearce, Sarah J.K.: The Land of the Body. 2007. *Vol. 208.*

Peres, Imre: Griechische Grabinschriften und neutestamentliche Eschatologie. 2003. *Vol. 157.*

Philip, Finny: The Origins of Pauline Pneumatology. 2005. *Vol. II/194.*

Philonenko, Marc (Ed.): Le Trône de Dieu. 1993. *Vol. 69.*

Pilhofer, Peter: Presbyteron Kreitton. 1990. *Vol. II/39.*

– Philippi. Vol. 1 1995. *Vol. 87.* – Vol. 2 2000. *Vol. 119.*

– Die frühen Christen und ihre Welt. 2002. *Vol. 145.*

– see *Becker, Eve-Marie.*

– see *Ego, Beate.*

Pitre, Brant: Jesus, the Tribulation, and the End of the Exile. 2005. *Vol. II/204.*

Plümacher, Eckhard: Geschichte und Geschichten. 2004. *Vol. 170.*

Pöhlmann, Wolfgang: Der Verlorene Sohn und das Haus. 1993. *Vol. 68.*

Pokorný, Petr and *Josef B. Souček:* Bibelauslegung als Theologie. 1997. *Vol. 100.*

– and *Jan Roskovec* (Ed.): Philosophical Hermeneutics and Biblical Exegesis. 2002. *Vol. 153.*

Popkes, Enno Edzard: Das Menschenbild des Thomasevangeliums. 2007. *Vol. 206.*

– Die Theologie der Liebe Gottes in den johanneischen Schriften. 2005. *Vol. II/197.*

Porter, Stanley E.: The Paul of Acts. 1999. *Vol. 115.*

Prieur, Alexander: Die Verkündigung der Gottesherrschaft. 1996. *Vol. II/89.*

Probst, Hermann: Paulus und der Brief. 1991. *Vol. II/45.*

Räisänen, Heikki: Paul and the Law. 1983, ²1987. *Vol. 29.*

Rehkopf, Friedrich: Die lukanische Sonderquelle. 1959. *Vol. 5.*

Rein, Matthias: Die Heilung des Blindgeborenen (Joh 9). 1995. *Vol. II/73.*

Reinmuth, Eckart: Pseudo-Philo und Lukas. 1994. *Vol. 74.*

Reiser, Marius: Bibelkritik und Auslegung der Heiligen Schrift. 2007. *Vol. 217.*

– Syntax und Stil des Markusevangeliums. 1984. *Vol. II/11.*

Reynolds, Benjamin E.: The Apocalyptic Son of Man in the Gospel of John. 2008. *Vol. II/249.*

Rhodes, James N.: The Epistle of Barnabas and the Deuteronomic Tradition. 2004. *Vol. II/188.*

Richards, E. Randolph: The Secretary in the Letters of Paul. 1991. *Vol. II/42.*

Riesner, Rainer: Jesus als Lehrer. 1981, ³1988. *Vol. II/7.*

– Die Frühzeit des Apostels Paulus. 1994. *Vol. 71.*

Rissi, Mathias: Die Theologie des Hebräerbriefs. 1987. *Vol. 41.*

Röcker, Fritz W.: Belial und Katechon. 2009. *Vol. II/262.*

Röhser, Günter: Metaphorik und Personifikation der Sünde. 1987. *Vol. II/25.*

Rose, Christian: Theologie als Erzählung im Markusevangelium. 2007. *Vol. II/236.*

– Die Wolke der Zeugen. 1994. *Vol. II/60.*

Roskovec, Jan: see *Pokorný, Petr.*

Rothschild, Clare K.: Baptist Traditions and Q. 2005. *Vol. 190.*

– Hebrews as Pseudepigraphon. 2009. *Vol. 235.*

– Luke Acts and the Rhetoric of History. 2004. *Vol. II/175.*

Rüegger, Hans-Ulrich: Verstehen, was Markus erzählt. 2002. *Vol. II/155.*

Rüger, Hans Peter: Die Weisheitsschrift aus der Kairoer Geniza. 1991. *Vol. 53.*

Sänger, Dieter: Antikes Judentum und die Mysterien. 1980. *Vol. II/5.*

– Die Verkündigung des Gekreuzigten und Israel. 1994. *Vol. 75.*

– see *Burchard, Christoph*

– and *Ulrich Mell* (Ed.): Paulus und Johannes. 2006. *Vol. 198.*

Salier, Willis Hedley: The Rhetorical Impact of the Semeia in the Gospel of John. 2004. *Vol. II/186.*

Salzmann, Jorg Christian: Lehren und Ermahnen. 1994. *Vol. II/59.*

Sandnes, Karl Olav: Paul – One of the Prophets? 1991. *Vol. II/43.*

Sato, Migaku: Q und Prophetie. 1988. *Vol. II/29.*

Schäfer, Ruth: Paulus bis zum Apostelkonzil. 2004. *Vol. II/179.*

Schaper, Joachim: Eschatology in the Greek Psalter. 1995. *Vol. II/76.*

Schimanowski, Gottfried: Die himmlische Liturgie in der Apokalypse des Johannes. 2002. *Vol. II/154.*

– Weisheit und Messias. 1985. *Vol. II/17.*

Schlichting, Günter: Ein jüdisches Leben Jesu. 1982. *Vol. 24.*

Schließer, Benjamin: Abraham's Faith in Romans 4. 2007. *Vol. II/224.*

Schnabel, Eckhard J.: Law and Wisdom from Ben Sira to Paul. 1985. *Vol. II/16.*

Schnelle, Udo: see *Frey, Jörg.*

Schröter, Jens: Von Jesus zum Neuen Testament. 2007. *Vol. 204.*

– see *Frey, Jörg.*

Schutter, William L.: Hermeneutic and Composition in I Peter. 1989. *Vol. II/30.*

Schwartz, Daniel R.: Studies in the Jewish Background of Christianity. 1992. *Vol. 60.*

Schwemer, Anna Maria: see *Hengel, Martin*

Scott, Ian W.: Implicit Epistemology in the Letters of Paul. 2005. *Vol. II/205.*

Scott, James M.: Adoption as Sons of God. 1992. *Vol. II/48.*

– Paul and the Nations. 1995. *Vol. 84.*

Shi, Wenhua: Paul's Message of the Cross as Body Language. 2008. *Vol. II/254.*

Shum, Shiu-Lun: Paul's Use of Isaiah in Romans. 2002. *Vol. II/156.*

Siegert, Folker: Drei hellenistisch-jüdische Predigten. Teil I 1980. *Vol. 20* – Teil II 1992. *Vol. 61.*

– Nag-Hammadi-Register. 1982. *Vol. 26.*

– Argumentation bei Paulus. 1985. *Vol. 34.*

– Philon von Alexandrien. 1988. *Vol. 46.*

Simon, Marcel: Le christianisme antique et son contexte religieux I/II. 1981. *Vol. 23.*

Smit, Peter-Ben: Fellowship and Food in the Kingdom. 2008. *Vol. II/234.*

Snodgrass, Klyne: The Parable of the Wicked Tenants. 1983. *Vol. 27.*

Söding, Thomas: Das Wort vom Kreuz. 1997. *Vol. 93.*

– see *Thüsing, Wilhelm.*

Sommer, Urs: Die Passionsgeschichte des Markusevangeliums. 1993. *Vol. II/58.*

Sorensen, Eric: Possession and Exorcism in the New Testament and Early Christianity. 2002. *Vol. II/157.*

Souček, Josef B.: see *Pokorný, Petr.*

Southall, David J.: Rediscovering Righteousness in Romans. 2008. *Vol. 240.*

Spangenberg, Volker: Herrlichkeit des Neuen Bundes. 1993. *Vol. II/55.*

Spanje, T.E. van: Inconsistency in Paul? 1999. *Vol. II/110.*

Speyer, Wolfgang: Frühes Christentum im antiken Strahlungsfeld. Vol. I: 1989. *Vol. 50.*

– Vol. II: 1999. *Vol. 116.*

– Vol. III: 2007. *Vol. 213.*

Spittler, Janet E.: Animals in the Apocryphal Acts of the Apostles. 2008. *Vol. II/247.*

Sprinkle, Preston: Law and Life. 2008. *Vol. II/241.*

Stadelmann, Helge: Ben Sira als Schriftgelehrter. 1980. *Vol. II/6.*

Stein, Hans Joachim: Frühchristliche Mahlfeiern. 2008. *Vol. II/255.*

Stenschke, Christoph W.: Luke's Portrait of Gentiles Prior to Their Coming to Faith. *Vol. II/108.*

Sterck-Degueldre, Jean-Pierre: Eine Frau namens Lydia. 2004. *Vol. II/176.*

Stettler, Christian: Der Kolosserhymnus. 2000. *Vol. II/131.*

Stettler, Hanna: Die Christologie der Pastoralbriefe. 1998. *Vol. II/105.*

Stökl Ben Ezra, Daniel: The Impact of Yom Kippur on Early Christianity. 2003. *Vol. 163.*

Strobel, August: Die Stunde der Wahrheit. 1980. *Vol. 21.*

Stroumsa, Guy G.: Barbarian Philosophy. 1999. *Vol. 112.*

Stuckenbruck, Loren T.: Angel Veneration and Christology. 1995. *Vol. II/70.*

–, *Stephen C. Barton* and *Benjamin G. Wold* (Ed.): Memory in the Bible and Antiquity. 2007. *Vol. 212.*

Stuhlmacher, Peter (Ed.): Das Evangelium und die Evangelien. 1983. *Vol. 28.*

– Biblische Theologie und Evangelium. 2002. *Vol. 146.*

Sung, Chong-Hyon: Vergebung der Sünden. 1993. *Vol. II/57.*

Tajra, Harry W.: The Trial of St. Paul. 1989. *Vol. II/35.*

– The Martyrdom of St.Paul. 1994. *Vol. II/67.*

Theißen, Gerd: Studien zur Soziologie des Urchristentums. 1979, ³1989. *Vol. 19.*

Theobald, Michael: Studien zum Römerbrief. 2001. *Vol. 136.*

Theobald, Michael: see *Mußner, Franz.*

Thornton, Claus-Jürgen: Der Zeuge des Zeugen. 1991. *Vol. 56.*

Thüsing, Wilhelm: Studien zur neutestamentlichen Theologie. Ed. von Thomas Söding. 1995. *Vol. 82.*

Thurén, Lauri: Derhethorizing Paul. 2000. *Vol. 124.*

Thyen, Hartwig: Studien zum Corpus Iohanneum. 2007. *Vol. 214.*

Tibbs, Clint: Religious Experience of the Pneuma. 2007. *Vol. II/230.*

Toit, David S. du: Theios Anthropos. 1997. *Vol. II/91.*

Tolmie, D. Francois: Persuading the Galatians. 2005. *Vol. II/190.*

Tomson, Peter J. and *Doris Lambers-Petry* (Ed.): The Image of the Judaeo-Christians in Ancient Jewish and Christian Literature. 2003. *Vol. 158.*

Toney, Carl N.: Paul's Inclusive Ethic. 2008. *Vol. II/252.*

Trebilco, Paul: The Early Christians in Ephesus from Paul to Ignatius. 2004. *Vol. 166.*

Treloar, Geoffrey R.: Lightfoot the Historian. 1998. *Vol. II/103.*

Tsuji, Manabu: Glaube zwischen Vollkommenheit und Verweltlichung. 1997. *Vol. II/93.*

Twelftree, Graham H.: Jesus the Exorcist. 1993. *Vol. II/54.*

Ulrichs, Karl Friedrich: Christusglaube. 2007. *Vol. II/227.*

Urban, Christina: Das Menschenbild nach dem Johannesevangelium. 2001. *Vol. II/137.*

Vahrenhorst, Martin: Kultische Sprache in den Paulusbriefen. 2008. *Vol. 230.*

Vegge, Ivar: 2 Corinthians – a Letter about Reconciliation. 2008. *Vol. II/239.*

Visotzky, Burton L.: Fathers of the World. 1995. *Vol. 80.*

Vollenweider, Samuel: Horizonte neutestamentlicher Christologie. 2002. *Vol. 144.*

Vos, Johan S.: Die Kunst der Argumentation bei Paulus. 2002. *Vol. 149.*

Waaler, Erik: The *Shema* and The First Commandment in First Corinthians. 2008. *Vol. II/253.*

Wagener, Ulrike: Die Ordnung des „Hauses Gottes". 1994. *Vol. II/65.*

Wahlen, Clinton: Jesus and the Impurity of Spirits in the Synoptic Gospels. 2004. *Vol. II/185.*

Walker, Donald D.: Paul's Offer of Leniency (2 Cor 10:1). 2002. *Vol. II/152.*

Walter, Nikolaus: Praeparatio Evangelica. Ed. von Wolfgang Kraus und Florian Wilk. 1997. *Vol. 98.*

Wander, Bernd: Gottesfürchtige und Sympathisanten. 1998. *Vol. 104.*

Wasserman, Emma: The Death of the Soul in Romans 7. 2008. *Vol. 256.*

Waters, Guy: The End of Deuteronomy in the Epistles of Paul. 2006. *Vol. 221.*

Watt, Jan G. van der: see *Frey, Jörg*

Watts, Rikki: Isaiah's New Exodus and Mark. 1997. *Vol. II/88.*

Wedderburn, A.J.M.: Baptism and Resurrection. 1987. *Vol. 44.*

Wegner, Uwe: Der Hauptmann von Kafarnaum. 1985. *Vol. II/14.*

Weiß, Hans-Friedrich: Frühes Christentum und Gnosis. 2008. *Vol. 225.*

Weissenrieder, Annette: Images of Illness in the Gospel of Luke. 2003. Vol. II/164.

–, *Friederike Wendt* and *Petra von Gemünden* (Ed.): Picturing the New Testament. 2005. *Vol. II/193.*

Welck, Christian: Erzählte ‚Zeichen‘. 1994. *Vol. II/69.*

Wendt, Friederike (Ed.): see *Weissenrieder, Annette.*

Wiarda, Timothy: Peter in the Gospels. 2000. *Vol. II/127.*

Wifstrand, Albert: Epochs and Styles. 2005. *Vol. 179.*

Wilk, Florian: see *Walter, Nikolaus.*

Williams, Catrin H.: I am He. 2000. *Vol. II/113.*

Wilson, Todd A.: The Curse of the Law and the Crisis in Galatia. 2007. *Vol. II/225.*

Wilson, Walter T.: Love without Pretense. 1991. *Vol. II/46.*

Winn, Adam: The Purpose of Mark's Gospel. 2008. *Vol. II/245.*

Winninge, Mikael: see *Holmberg, Bengt.*

Wischmeyer, Oda: Von Ben Sira zu Paulus. 2004. *Vol. 173.*

Wisdom, Jeffrey: Blessing for the Nations and the Curse of the Law. 2001. *Vol. II/133.*

Witmer, Stephen E.: Divine Instruction in Early Christianity. 2008. *Vol. II/246.*

Wold, Benjamin G.: Women, Men, and Angels. 2005. *Vol. II/2001.*

Wolter, Michael: Theologie und Ethos im frühen Christentum. 2009. *Vol. 236.*

– see *Stuckenbruck, Loren T.*

Wright, Archie T.: The Origin of Evil Spirits. 2005. *Vol. II/198.*

Wucherpfennig, Ansgar: Heracleon Philologus. 2002. *Vol. 142.*

Yates, John W.: The Spirit and Creation in Paul. 2008. *Vol. II/251.*

Yeung, Maureen: Faith in Jesus and Paul. 2002. *Vol. II/147.*

Zangenberg, Jürgen, Harold W. Attridge and *Dale B. Martin* (Ed.): Religion, Ethnicity and Identity in Ancient Galilee. 2007. *Vol. 210.*

Zimmermann, Alfred E.: Die urchristlichen Lehrer. 1984, ²1988. *Vol. II/12.*

Zimmermann, Johannes: Messianische Texte aus Qumran. 1998. *Vol. II/104.*

Zimmermann, Ruben: Christologie der Bilder im Johannesevangelium. 2004. *Vol. 171.*

– Geschlechtermetaphorik und Gottesverhältnis. 2001. *Vol. II/122.*

– (Ed.): Hermeneutik der Gleichnisse Jesu. 2008. *Vol. 231.*

– see *Frey, Jörg.*

– see *Horn, Friedrich Wilhelm.*

Zugmann, Michael: „Hellenisten" in der Apostelgeschichte. 2009. *Vol. II/264.*

Zumstein, Jean: see *Dettwiler, Andreas*

Zwiep, Arie W.: Judas and the Choice of Matthias. 2004. *Vol. II/187.*

For a complete catalogue please write to the publisher
Mohr Siebeck • P.O. Box 2030 • D–72010 Tübingen/Germany
Up-to-date information on the internet at www.mohr.de